Athens, Attica and the Megarid

Figure 1 Map of Attica.

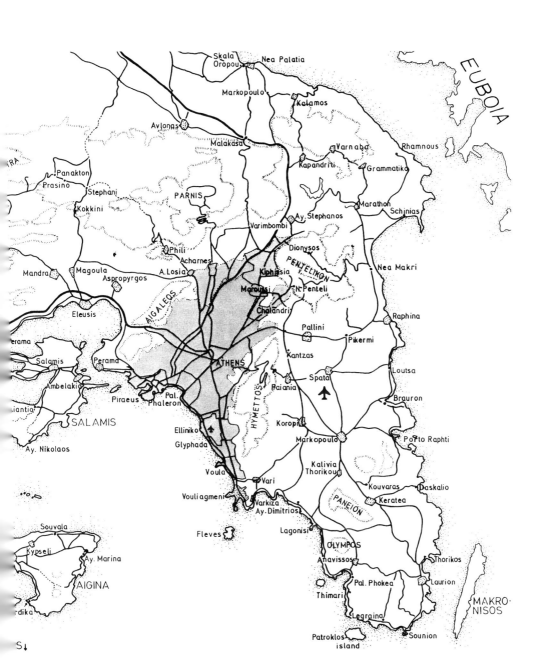

EUBOIA

Skala Oropou
Nea Palatia

Markopoulo
Kalamos

Avlonas

Malakasa

Varnaba
Rhamnous

Panakton
Kapandriti
Grammatika

Prasino

Stephani
PARNIS
Marathon
Schinias

Kokkini
Ay. Stephanos

Varimbombi

Phili
Dionysos
PENTELIKON

Mandra
Magoula
Acharnes
Kiphisia
Nea Makri

Aspropyrgos
A. Losia

Maroussi
N. Penteli

AIGALEOS
Chalandri

Raphina

Eleusis
Pallini
Pikermi

Perama
Kantzas

Salamis
Spata
Loutsa

Perama
Paiania

Ambelakio
ATHENS
Braveron

siantio
HYMETTOS

Piraeus
Pal.
Phaleron
Koropi

SALAMIS
Elliniko
Markopoulo
Porto Raphti

Ay. Nikolaos
Glyphada
Kalivia
Thorikou

Voula
Kouvaras
Daskalio

Vari
Keratea

Souvala
Vouliagmeni
Varkiza
Ay. Dimitrios
PANEION

Kypseli
Ay. Marina
Fleves
Lagonisi
OLYMPOS

AIGINA
Anavissos
Thorikos

rdika
Pal. Phokea
Laurion

Thimari
MAKRO-
NISOS

Legraina

Patroklos
island
Sounion

S↓

Athens, Attica and the Megarid

An archaeological guide

Hans Rupprecht Goette

London and New York

First edition (German language) published
1993 by Böhlau-Verlag, Cologne, Germany
© 1993 by Böhlau-Verlag

Revised and updated English edition published 2001 by Routledge
11 New Fetter Lane, London EC4P 4EE

Simultaneously published in the USA and Canada
by Routledge
29 West 35th Street, New York, NY 10001

Routledge is an imprint of the Taylor & Francis Group

© 2001 Hans Rupprecht Goette

Typeset in Times New Roman and Helvetica by
Florence Production Ltd, Stoodleigh, Devon
Printed and bound in Great Britain by
Biddles Ltd, Guildford and King's Lynn

British Library Cataloguing in Publication Data
A catalogue record for this book is available from the
British Library.

Library of Congress Cataloging in Publication Data
Goette, Hans Rupprecht.
  [Athens, Attika, Megaris. English]
  Athens, Attica, and the Megarid: an archaeological guide/
Hans Rupprecht Goette.
    p. cm.
  Includes bibliographical references and index.
  1. Athens (Greece)—Antiquities—Guidebooks. 2. Attika
(Greece)—Antiquities—Guidebooks. 3. Megara (Greece)—
Antiquities—Guidebooks. I. Title.
  DF275.G5413 2001
  914.95′120493—dc21   00-062811

ISBN 0–415–24370–X

Contents

Illustrations

All illustrations are copyright of the author unless otherwise indicated

Figures

Plates

Foreword

The idea for this guidebook arose from a sojourn of several years in Greece. During this period it became clear from visits to many sites that, in spite of the large number of tourist guides dealing with Greece (especially with Athens, Attica and the Megarid), there was no guide which really filled the need for reliable academic information, and which gave accurate information on routes and detailed descriptions of less well-known sites. The present book attempts to fill this gap.

While working on this guidebook I was able to make use of the library and photographic archive of the German Archaeological Institute in Athens. The guidebook has greatly profited from this and from lively discussions with colleagues in the Institute and with O. Palagia who read the manuscript and the proofs and proposed many corrections – an inestimable help. I thank P.A. Mountjoy for some information on the prehistoric sites; she translated the German manuscript.

I could not have written this guidebook without the unfailing support and active help of my wife in the many stages of its preparation. I dedicate it to her as a souvenir of our excursions over the years.

Information for the reader

This guidebook deals with the heartland of Greece describing its cultural sights in their historical context. The description of each site is arranged to provide a series of practical tours. Many sites are most easily and comfortably reached by car; the visitor who decides not to use a car will find that the public transport system is limited and time-consuming and that he must often plan for lengthy excursions. The latter method of travel will offer a better impression of Greece and closer contact with its people, but, if the visitor is short of time, his itinerary of sites must be carefully planned. Whichever form of travel he chooses, the guidebook should inform him about the art and monuments and help him with his choice of route and with finding his way around the country. The general sections on the history and development of individual sites are best read beforehand at home; in contrast the descriptions, which generally follow a planned walk, are to be read at the site.

Numbers in bold refer to the plans and figures in the text. The visitor who wishes to concentrate on monuments of a particular period or on particular categories of art can choose them from the chronological list (pp. 372–5) and find the entry in the guidebook from the Index of sites (pp. 376–86). Since 1998 road signs have been put up throughout Greece (in yellow and white on a brown background) to facilitate visiting archaeological sites, museums and churches.

Superscript numbers within the text refer to items in the Bibliography (pp. 387–403)[1].

1 Athens and Piraeus

1 Athens: a historical overview

The modern visitor sees Athens as an impenetrable expanse of monotonous concrete buildings which fills the entire basin lying between the mountain ranges of Aigaleo in the west, Parnes and Pentelikon in the north, Hymettos in the east and the sea in the south. In fact Athens consists of many municipalities, each one with its own name, which have only grown together in the last decades to turn it into a large city. By the name 'Athens' the Greeks themselves understand only the quarter around the Acropolis, especially the area north of the ancient citadel.

The reasons for the growth of this huge concrete desert are easily described. Athens was a small town until 1834, when it became the capital of the Kingdom of Greece (Plates 1, 2, 5, 18). Then it grew in several stages into a city of millions. After the influx of 1922, when many Greeks had to leave their cities on the west coast of Asia Minor, there were already about half a million inhabitants. Since World War II, especially since the early 1960s, the populace has left the countryside in ever-growing numbers and come into the cities from the villages and the islands. Farming areas are desolate and only elderly people remain in the villages; in contrast the huge cities are facing lack of accommodation, structural chaos and air and sea pollution, as well as a shortage of water. This is particularly true of the largest Greek city, the Greater Athens area, which is inhabited by about four million people today, about 40 per cent of the population of the entire country.

A 'concrete desert'? This is certainly not what the visitor to Athens expects, and it is indeed only a first impression. For the rugged hill of the Acropolis, visible for miles, rises out of the amorphous mass of the modern capital and immediately conjures up the ruins of antiquity; these can be seen in many different forms on this citadel and around it; their presence illustrates the importance of Athens for the history of the art and culture of Europe and the Western civilisations. Moreover, the visitor can find much of interest on his walk amidst all the modern city buildings, which in some areas have recently been turned into welcome pedestrian zones: charming Byzantine churches (Plate 11) or

Neoclassical houses and villas of architectural interest (Plate 28) and also the old town, Plaka, with its narrow alleys and noisy businesses and craftshops (Plate 22). The topography of the capital is also impressive with its mountain ranges and isolated hills from which the visitor can obtain a good view over the sea of buildings to the edge of the basin of Greater Athens and over the Saronic Gulf with its islands of Aigina and Salamis.

It was the geographical advantages which drew the first prehistoric settlers here, such as the favourable trading locality near the sea, the fertile plain and the hills which offered safe refuges. This type of landscape has given rise to settlement centres all round the Mediterranean; it can be seen constantly in Greek settlements, whether in Greece itself or in Greek colonies elsewhere, such as Nice and Marseilles.

On the rock of the Acropolis, the steepest hill on the plain, there are traces of a settlement dating back to Neolithic times, that is 4000–3000 BC. The first datable building remains belong to the Mycenaean period, when the citadel was enclosed by a massive fortification wall and sheltered the king's palace. From the eleventh to the eighth century BC the entire social structure of Greece was disrupted by the arrival of pastoral tribes from the north; during this time – the so-called Dark Ages – Attica, like the rest of Greece, was a victim of these disturbances (there seems to have been no continuity of culture in Athens). A new social order did not arise until the eighth century. Thereafter, noble families ruled the city-state and the citadel became a cult centre gradually losing its status as the seat of the ruler. Thanks to ancient historiography the most important developments of Greek history can be closely followed from now on. They are described briefly below with particular reference to Athens and to her role as the leader in Attica.

At the end of the seventh century law and order was established by the rigid law code of Drakon (624 BC), which was reformed by Solon (594 BC) and transformed into a first constitution. The result was the division of the populace into classes according to the land they possessed. Between 560 and 510 BC the Peisistratids, a noble family from Brauron, ruled in Athens as 'Tyrants' (= single ruler, not pejorative) and the city blossomed culturally. After the expulsion of the last son of Peisistratos, Kleisthenes reformed the constitution of Solon in 508/507 BC and thereby paved the way for the first democracy. Attica was divided into three units (Trittys) from which groups of three geographically separate units formed a tribe (Phyle). There were ten tribes, each being composed of many boroughs (Demes). Each tribe chose a leader (Strategos) and fifty councillors (Bouleutes). The chairman of the council which ruled Attica changed ten times a year. Ostracism was established – perhaps under Kleisthenes or a bit later – to counter the threat of a single politician seizing absolute power; a person with too much power could be banished for ten years on the vote of the Assembly of the people. The voting slips were sherds from broken pots (ostraka) on which the name of the candidate for banishment was scratched.

The following decades were dominated by the Persian Wars. In 490 BC the Athenians and the Plataians defeated the Persian army at the Battle of Marathon;

ten years later in 480 BC a Greek fleet composed of swift, manoeuvrable triremes defeated the Persians in the naval Battle of Salamis. Shortly beforehand, the Spartans under King Leonidas had tried in vain to hold the Persian forces at the Battle of Thermopylae; a year later at the Battle of Plataia the Greeks finally defeated the Persians. Athens, the real victor of the Persian wars, founded the naval Confederacy of Delos (the Delian League) in 477 BC as a defensive alliance against the Persians; at first the members had to supply ships, but later this was commuted to paying tribute to the treasury, which was moved to Athens in 454 BC from the Sanctuary of Apollo on Delos. The profits from this and from the silver mines at Laurion provided the financial foundation for the golden age of Athens after 460 BC under the leadership of Perikles (*c.* 500–427 BC). During this golden age the famous temples on the Acropolis and in Attica were built and 'Classical' art was born, as manifested in sculpture and painting (the latter known almost only from its reflection in vase painting). Athens with its democracy set itself politically even more strongly against the aristocratically-ruled city-states led by Sparta. The conflict for the supremacy of Greece peaked in the Peloponnesian War 431–404 BC from which Sparta emerged as the victor. It set up the 'Thirty Tyrants' as rulers in Athens. At the end of the fifth century BC the Tyrants tried but failed to destroy the democracy in Athens together with its supporters. In the fourth century BC the rivalry between Sparta, Thebes and Athens determined the course of history; the country was shaken by many conflicts with shifting alliances between the Greek city-states. Philip II of Macedon recognised the weaknesses of the city-states and won supreme rule in Greece at the Battle of Chaeronea in 338 BC. After his murder in 336 BC, his son Alexander the Great ruled until 323 BC and extended his empire by warfare into the east as far as India and into the south as far as Egypt. However, after his death his empire collapsed; his successors (Diadochs) divided it into many kingdoms which were in a state of constant conflict. During the Hellenistic Age 323–146 BC until the time of the Roman Empire, large numbers of new political and cultural centres evolved in the eastern Mediterranean in addition to Athens. Athens survived on its past glory under different rulers; the city was adorned with generous gifts from the Hellenistic kings as a tribute to the 'Classical Ideal'. In spite of Greek resistance to the new might of Rome, Greece became the Roman province of Macedonia and Achaia in 146 BC. The new rulers were much influenced by Greek culture, which, especially under the Roman emperors, spread over the whole of the Mediterranean. Athens was especially friendly to Rome until it abruptly changed sides in 88 BC and was sacked therefore by Sulla in 86; Piraeus was burned and never really recovered until the twentieth century. Numerous Roman politicians studied at the famous schools of philosophy and rhetoric in Athens and some of the Caesars also had contacts with Greece, especially with Athens; in the arts Greek ideas, decorative schemes and other ornamental elements were taken over and reproduced in a Roman style. Roman rulers, especially Pompey, Caesar, Augustus, Nero, Hadrian and Marcus Aurelius showed their respect to Athens by gifts of buildings and monuments, as well as by visits, during which they could see themselves as successors to the great men of Greek history. Wealthy private citizens,

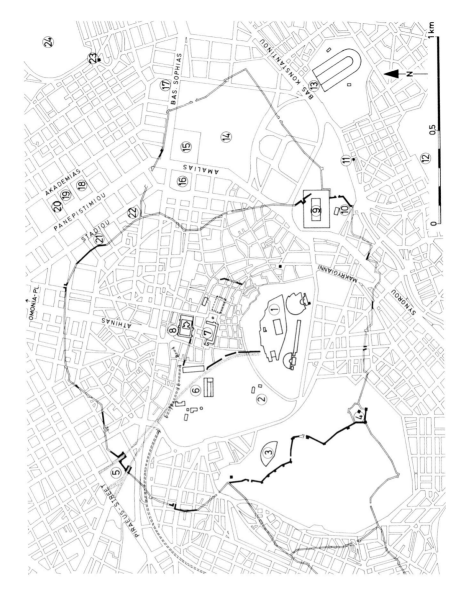

Figure 2 Map of the historical centre of Athens with the important ancient monuments.

1: Acropolis; 2: Areopagos; 3: Pnyx; 4: mausoleum of Philopappos; 5: Kerameikos; 6: Agora; 7: Roman market; 8: library of Hadrian; 9: Olympieion; 10: Ilissos area; 11: Temple by the Ilissos; 12: First Cemetery; 13: stadium of Herodes Atticus; 14: National Garden; 15: Palace (Parliament); 16: Syntagma (Constitution) Square; 17: Benaki Museum; 18: Akademy; 19: University; 20: National Library; 21: Ay. Theodoroi; 22: Old Parliament; 23: Hadrianic water reservoir; 24: Lykabettos.

such as Herodes Atticus (second century AD), followed their example. The beginning of the collapse of the Roman Empire undermined the influence of Athens as an intellectual centre, and the invasion of the German tribe of the Herulians in the mid-third century AD played a decisive role in the decline of the city. From this time on defensive constructions are almost the only things of interest; these were, however, built from earlier ruined or collapsed buildings. Under Constantine the Great, Christianity was proclaimed as the state religion in 312 AD and the capital of the Roman Empire moved to Constantinople. The heathen schools of philosophy and the temples were closed under Theodosius (379–395 AD) and Justinian (527–565 AD). New excavations south of the Acropolis provide some information about building activity during the seventh century AD, but the city then sank into an obscurity which lasted for centuries.

Greece became the stamping ground of foreign powers. In the thirteenth century the Frankish crusaders divided the country. In 1456 Athens was taken over by the Turks, who allowed the land to go to waste in the following centuries during their continual struggles with the Venetians. Their rule was finally broken during the War of Independence (1821–1830) with the help of the great powers, France, Great Britain and Russia. According to a decision of the powers in London, with which the National Assembly of Greece agreed, Wittelsbach Prince Otto, son of Ludwig I of Bavaria, became King Otto I of Greece. Athens, which at that time comprised about 300 households, became the capital in 1834. In 1830 the first systematic investigation of the ancient monuments began and a new city (Figure **2**) was designed by Bavarian and Prussian architects (Klenze, Schinkel, Ziller, the Danish brothers Hansen amongst others) and carried out following Neoclassical models (Plates 2, 28). In the 1912–13 Balkan Wars Greece gained Epirus, parts of Macedonia, Crete and Samos as part of its territory. In 1922 after a Greek invasion against Turkey about 1.6 million Greeks had to abandon Asia Minor and flee to Greece. In World War II the country was occupied by the Italians and the Germans, but gained the Dodecanese at Liberation. In 1967 a military junta abolished the constitutional monarchy under King Constantine II and in 1973 it proclaimed a republic. On 25 November 1973 the dictator, George Papadopoulos, was removed. In 1974–75 democracy was re-established under President K. Karamanlis and the constitution of the junta was abolished, though Greece remained a republic. In 1981 Greece entered the European Union; the socialists under A. Papandreou ruled until 1989, followed by a Conservative government under K. Mitsotakis, which was replaced in its turn in 1993 by another socialist government (A. Papandreou, K. Simitis).

2 The Acropolis (Figure 5.6)

A t the time of the earliest settlement in Attica the hill of the Acropolis did not look as it does today; without the high retaining walls on its south, east and north sides, it did not appear nearly so precipitous in

Figure 3 The Acropolis from the south-west (Nointel and d'Ortières 1674/1678).

Photo DAI Athens (Akr 436)

spite of its steep slopes. The area on the top of the rock was smaller and not so level, since the citadel had not yet been planed and filling and terracing had not yet taken place. The rock probably still had a layer of earth covered with scrub amongst which were placed the simple huts of the Neolithic inhabitants. Pot sherds found in crevices in the rock provide evidence for this phase of the settlement.[2]

The first real architecture, of which remains can be seen even today, dates from the Mycenaean period.[3] At this time the Acropolis was the site of a palace which, according to mythology, belonged to the Kings Erechtheus and Aigeus. Scant remains of this building consisting of traces of terrace retaining walls have been found in the area of the later Erechtheion and the Old Temple of Athena. At that time, similarly to other Mycenaean palaces, the citadel was surrounded by a massive fortification wall (Figure 5.5) constructed from skilfully arranged stone blocks; a well-preserved fragment of this fortification wall is visible today south of the Propylaea; it separates the temenos of the Temple of Athena Nike from the south wing of the Classical entrance building to the Acropolis (Figure 6). Parts of the wall can also be seen in two excavations on the south side of the Parthenon. A bastion[4] belonging to it stood on the site of the later Temple of Nike. Their mythical past was so important to the Classical Athenians that they intentionally left a polygonal opening in the northern revetment of the substructure of the Nike Temple (bastion) so that the

Figure 4 Explosion on the Acropolis, 27 September, 1687: view from the north-east.
(F. Fanelli, Atene – Attica 1707, 64)

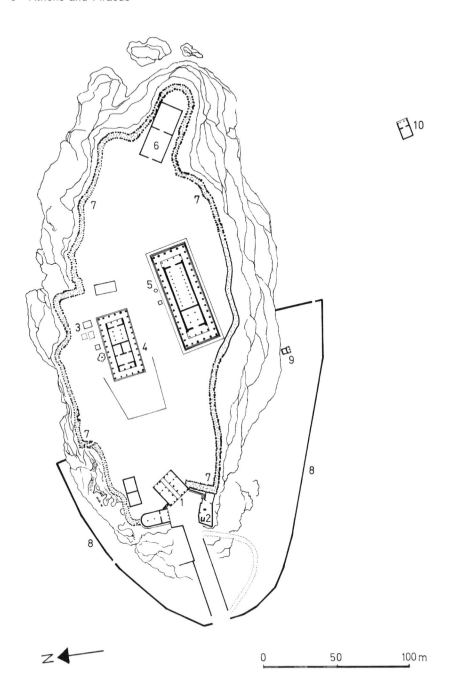

Figure 5 The Acropolis of Athens shortly before 480 BC.

1: Propylaea; 2: Sanctuary of Athena Nike; 3: Temple of Athena Polias and Kekropion; 4: Old Athena
Temple; 5: Old Parthenon with the Sanctuary of Athena (Ergane?); 6: precinct of Pandion;
7: Mycenaean wall; 8: Pelargikon; 9: fountain house; 10: Temple of Dionysos.

remains of the Mycenaean bastion could be seen. Water was supplied by a spring in the rock on the north slope accessible through a hidden stairway. Nearby there was a simple, narrow exit below the later Erechtheion (Figure **6**.33); a second exit on the south slope is indicated by some steps hewn out of the rock, which begin above the Theatre of Dionysos and lead up to the south-east corner of the Acropolis.

By the Archaic period (sixth century BC)[5] at the latest the citadel had changed from being the seat of the ruler to the cult centre of the city. The core of the cult centre was the Temple of Athena Polias which stood in the area of the later Erechtheion, and a second temple, the Hecatompedon, which was subsequently built over by the Parthenon. In the east beyond the two temples there was a large altar which served both (Figure **5**.3). The earliest pair of temples belong to the Geometric period. While the small temple in the area of the Erechtheion continued in use, the first peripteral temple (the Hecatompedon) was built as early as 580 BC in the area of the later Parthenon. During the second half of the sixth century the Peisistratids commissioned a second large temple of Athena and embellished it with a marble pediment (Plate 3). This 'Old Temple of Athena' (or the Dörpfeld Temple, after its excavator) was built between the two earlier cult centres west of the altar; the area was still free as it had been used by those taking part in sacrifices. Finds from levelling layers and from the foundations of the Classical buildings furnish evidence of other buildings; it seems there were many small Archaic treasuries on the citadel, some of which were richly ornamented and which contained gifts of wealthy donors.[6] Larger pedimental fragments, such as Herakles wrestling with the Triton (see p. 42), have been assigned to the Archaic Temple of Athena (Hecatompedon); only a few fragments of the architectural superstructure of this building are preserved.

Under the leadership of the Peisistratids (561–510 BC) the appearance of the Acropolis was much changed. The Peisistratids were a noble family and were the last rulers to have their seat on the Acropolis for a time in the Mycenaean tradition. They carried out a proper building policy. As well as constructing the Old Athena Temple (Figure **5**.4), they transferred to the Acropolis the cult of Artemis from their native town of Brauron in east Attica and built a Brauronion (Figure **6**.8) directly east of the western ascent to the citadel. Building activity also took place on the citadel wall and at the entrance of the Acropolis (Figure **5**.1). In the south-west corner of the citadel an altar and a shrine were built for Athena Nike (Figure **5**.2), perhaps in connection with the founding of the Panathenaic Festival in 566 BC.

In addition to these buildings the appearance of the Acropolis was enriched by many dedications. There seems to have been much competition over the adornment of the citadel amongst the noble families who influenced Athenian politics. Later on, towards the end of the sixth century, the common people also began to give gifts to Athena. These consisted not only of modest clay offerings and of costly bronze cauldrons and weapons, but also of gaily painted marble sculptures, such as reliefs and statues depicting horses, dogs and young women or riders;[7] their bright colours enhanced their cheerful appearance.

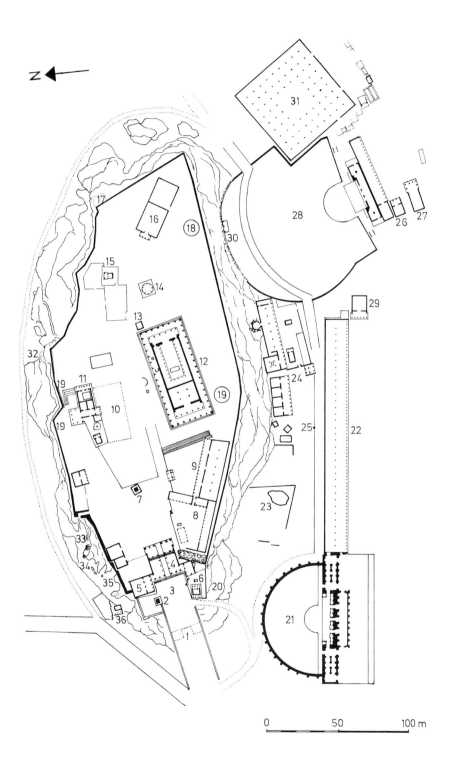

N

0   50   100 m

In order to achieve a realistic picture of the Archaic Acropolis the visitor must imagine the open areas between the buildings and the steps of the temples as densely strewn with these offerings (Plate 16).

After the expulsion of the Tyrants and after the military and constitutional reforms of Kleisthenes, the city-state of Athens was shaken by the first Persian invasion (in 490 BC). The new democratic government or the victory at Marathon, which has gone down in history as the particular achievement of the Athenians, lies behind an ambitious building project, which Athens generated in order to glorify herself. It began with the construction of a large Propylaea and a huge temple, which would serve as monuments to the victory. The huge peripteral temple, the Old Parthenon, was to be built next to the Old Athena Temple on its own specially made platform with immense retaining walls on the south side; it incorporated Ionic elements in the Doric architecture and was to be made entirely of Pentelic marble; it was to replace the Hecatompedon and take over its function as the seat of cult, but at the same time it was to have a secular function, as a victory monument and a treasury (Plate 3). This enormous building, to which there was no parallel in Greece, was never completed because all the public money and then the entire might of Athens was needed to fight off the second Persian invasion. In 480 BC, under the leadership of Themistocles, the city was abandoned to the enemy, who ransacked the citadel, burning down the monuments. However, the Greeks managed to repel the Persian hordes a second time, first at the naval battle of Salamis, then on land at Plataia and finally in another naval battle off Mykale opposite Samos. The danger had passed for the moment; the fleet of the Delian League would provide a safe defence against further possible Persian attacks.

After the complete destruction of Athens and the Acropolis, the temples were largely left in ruins as a memorial of Persian impiety. The entrance and the most important cult buildings were repaired, but attention was really concentrated on the fortification of the city and its harbour, Piraeus. It was not until thirty years later that a comprehensive clearance took place on the Acropolis. The whole area was levelled and expanded by means of retaining walls. The remains of the Archaic buildings and their sculptures were buried under masses of earth so that they would be preserved for the patron deity of the Acropolis. This produced an archaeological layer rich in monuments, the so-called Persian destruction fill (Plate 3). This layer has helped to preserve the colour on marble

---

Figure 6 The Acropolis of Athens and the slopes *c.* AD 180.

1: Beulé Gate; 2: Agrippa monument; 3: ramp; 4: Propylaea; 5: north wing with Pinakotheke; 6: south wing with Temple of Athena Nike; 7: location of Athena Promachos; 8: Sanctuary of Artemis Brauronia; 9: Chalkotheke; 10: Old Athena temple; 11: Erechtheion; 12: Parthenon; 13: pillar monument 14: Temple of Roma and Augustus; 15: Sanctuary of Zeus Polieus; 16: Sanctuary of Pandion; 17: Belvedere; 18: museum; 19: north wall with spolia of the Old Athena Temple and with column drums of the Old Parthenon; 20: Temple of Aphrodite; 21: Odeion of Herodes Atticus; 22: stoa of Eumenes; 23: metal foundry; 24: Asklepieion; 25: Horos inscription of the fountain house; 26: Archaic Temple of Dionysos; 27: Classical Temple of Dionysos; 28: theatre of Dionysos; 29: choregic monument of Nikias; 30: choregic monument of Thrasyllos and Thrasykles; 31: Odeion of Perikles; 32: Sanctuary of Eros and Aphrodite; 33: staircase; 34: Sanctuary of Pan; 35: Sanctuary of Apollo Hypoakraios and Zeus; 36: Klepsydra.

sculptures thus making it possible for the first time to study the paint on Archaic monuments. Even today the richly painted decoration of the sculptures and of the architectural elements in the museum is impressive; it has been better preserved in the earth than the painting on the later buildings and sculptures, which has been eroded over the centuries.

It was also decided that the Persian destruction of the city should remain before the eyes of the Athenians in perpetuity, so Archaic architectural fragments were incorporated as a memorial into the north wall of the citadel facing the city (Figures **6**.19; **11**); from the Plaka one can see, next to a row of column fragments from the Old Parthenon, pieces from the architrave, metopes and triglyphs and parts of the cornice of the Old Athena Temple set in the same position as they were on the Peisistratid building. Architectural fragments from the Hecatompedon are built into the south and south-east walls of the Acropolis above the Theatre of Dionysos, but they are harder to see.

After the area had been levelled, a building programme was begun in 448 BC, which, although interrupted many times during the Peloponnesian War, resulted, in the course of only fifty years, in the famous temples and buildings of the Acropolis (Plate 4) and Attica (Plates 46, 51, 61) known to us today as Classical art. The Parthenon (Figure **6**.12; Plates 9, 11) with its entire sculptural decoration (Plates 13–15) was built in 448–432 BC on the site of the earlier Hecatompedon and Old Parthenon, the functions of which, temple, treasury and victory monument, it took over. The new Propylaea (Figure **6**.3–5; Plate 5) was under construction from 438 until the beginning of the war in 432; the Athena Nike Temple (Plate 6) was begun at the same time, but was not finished until 410 with the erection of a parapet with relief sculptures (Figure **6**.6). The Erechtheion (Figure **6**.11; Plates 7–8), which was built between 438 and 406 BC, united under one roof cults which had formerly been housed in separate small shrines, including the shrine of Athena Polias. Alongside these temples another cult area, surrounded by a wall, dedicated to Pandion (Figure **6**.16), a mythical Attic hero, lay where the modern museum now stands. The older Temple of Zeus, which lay north-east of the Parthenon (Figure **6**.15), must also have been renovated. The Peisistratid Sanctuary of Artemis Brauronia gained two projecting wings, which made up a triangular courtyard (Figure **6**.8). The bronze statue of the Trojan horse, mentioned by Pausanias, was exhibited here; its marble pedestal has been found. The area between the Temple of Artemis and the rocky slope west of the Parthenon was already in use in the Classical period; an oblong hall, the Chalkotheke (Bronze storehouse), contained countless bronze offerings: an inventory for the year 353/2 BC lists weapons, vases and other objects (Figure **6**.9).

Building skills thus developed which led to differing architectural forms, but all the different types of building and sculpture were soon seen as a unified style, the ideal of the Classical period; even today they invite admiration. The stunning artistic achievement of this era in Attica (the contemporary building projects in Attic rural communities must also be borne in mind) was only possible because of unlimited financial support, which was derived in particular from the treasury of the Delian League and from the south Attic silver mines, and because of the democracy, which had the confidence to set up a monument to itself and its politics. The design of these buildings was the result of countless negotiations and decisions by the citizens; they closely supervised the projects and checked that the money was properly spent. Since the accounts were written on stone and displayed to the public (today in the Epigraphical Museum of Athens), we have information not only about the cost and the chronology of the buildings, but also about the wages of the workers and of the existence of monuments which are lost.

After the High Classical period, that is after the city-state of Athens lost the war against Sparta, no more buildings were constructed on the citadel as a result of the collective efforts of the citizens. As in crises in any age, the interest of the citizen turned to his private affairs. The only monuments erected were those dedicated to single persons, such as statues of well-known politicians and generals. On the whole, people were satisfied with the embellishment and restoration of the large buildings already in existence.

In the second half of the fourth century BC, as part of the restoration programme of the Athenian politician Lykourgos, the large, round stone theatre of Dionysos (Figure 6.28) was finished in the Sanctuary of Dionysos on the south slope of the Acropolis in the neighbourhood of the Periclean Odeion, a roofed building with many columns (Figure 6.31). The old plays of the Classical period were staged in the theatre, out of nostalgia for a bygone age, although they were written for the much smaller Classical theatre of the old oblong type. A little earlier, a new shrine (Figure 6.27) for the god Dionysos had been built, which replaced the earlier temple (Figures 5.10; 6.26). In conjunction with the annual dramatic festival for the god, a new group of monuments was also created, which honoured particular people; the sponsors (choregoi) of certain plays (dithyramboi) were allowed to set up monuments with their name engraved on them, known as choregic dedications, if the performance of the play they had sponsored won the victor's prize of a bronze tripod (Figures 6.29–30; 17; 30).

It was also in the fourth century BC that the temple of Asklepios, the god of healing, which had been founded in 419 BC, was converted into marble (Figure 6.24). It was situated on the south slope of the Acropolis west of the theatre of Dionysos and was built around a spring (Figure 5.9), which had been in use from the Archaic period; it was furnished with stoas and also contained shrines to other healing divinities.

During the Hellenistic and Roman periods construction work took place on and around the Acropolis. In the second century BC the Pergamene royal family was prominent in Athens as a result of its numerous gifts of buildings and statues. Two high statue bases were erected on the Acropolis, each carrying a four-horse chariot (quadriga) with a statue of the donor. One of these monuments, which is almost completely preserved, was rededicated in the time of the Early Roman Empire to the general Agrippa, the son-in-law of Augustus, and can be seen at the entrance to the Acropolis (Figure 6.2). A second, which was similarly constructed, but a little larger and more richly adorned, stood on the north-east corner of the Parthenon; it has been broken in the course of time into its separate components. This was later also rededicated to a Roman Emperor, perhaps to Claudius (Figure **6**.13). Another large architectural dedication from Pergamon is the stoa of Eumenes (Figure **6**.22), a long two-storeyed stoa on the south slope of the Acropolis, which retains and protects the crumbling slopes. There is little left today of this gift of King Eumenes II (197–159 BC), but the back retaining wall with its vaulted construction is impressive. An idea of its appearance can be gained from the reconstructed stoa of Attalos in the Athenian Agora, donated to the city of Athens by Attalos II, the successor of Eumenes on the Pergamene throne (Figure **21**.19; Plate 21).

Construction on the Acropolis itself began again during the Roman Empire. Under Augustus (27 BC–14 AD),[8] who made much use of Classical art in his skilled and highly intellectual cultural policies, the damage to the temples and the Propylaea was repaired. This interest in the Classical Age is also apparent in a new building, the circular Temple of Roma and Augustus east of the Parthenon, in which Augustus was worshipped together with Roma, the city goddess of the new world power of Rome (Figure **6**.14). The individual elements of decoration on this building were exact copies of those on the Erechtheion. This was a characteristic of Augustan art policy; there are copies not only of these decorative elements, but also, for example, of the Caryatids of the Erechtheion, on building projects of Augustus and of other rulers throughout the Roman Empire. Similarly, during the first two centuries AD earlier Greek sculpture was much copied and used everywhere as decoration in public and private buildings, further proof of the influence of the Classical art of the Acropolis.

The construction of a large, roofed theatre, the Odeion of Herodes Atticus (Figure **6**.21), was an impressive building project below the Acropolis. This wealthy private citizen,[9] who had contacts with the philhellene Emperor Hadrian and with the Emperor family of the Antonines, left both public bequests throughout Greece, Asia Minor and Italy and the private villas in which he had lived at different times of the year. The Odeion next to the Hellenistic Stoa of Eumenes on the south slope of the Acropolis must have been built between AD 160 and 170; it accommodated about 5,000 spectators (Plate 4).

In the third century AD Athens lost more and more of its former glory.[10] The decline of the once cultured state is reflected in a final building project on the Acropolis. A fortification wall largely composed of spolia, that is reused material from demolished or ruined buildings, was put round the entire city and another round the Acropolis for protection from the incoming barbarian hordes. In this way not only are almost all the blocks from the late fourth century BC choregic monument of Nikias preserved in the west entrance to the Acropolis, the Beulé Gate (Figure **6**.1), but also other building components can in the meantime be assigned to their original monuments, thereby providing information on the history of these monuments in the Late Roman period. With the prohibition of heathen cults and the closure of the temples in Greece in the reign of Theodosius the ancient history of the buildings on the Acropolis came to an end.

In the following centuries are attested structural alterations to the monuments. First, Christian churches were built in the Erechtheion and in the Parthenon; the church in the latter was converted by the Turks into a mosque. When the Venetians led by Morosini besieged Athens, the buildings on the Acropolis, in which the Turkish garrison was entrenched, were much damaged. On 27 September 1687 a ball from a cannon placed on the Hill of Philopappos hit the Turkish gunpowder magazine in the Parthenon. The terrible explosion destroyed most of the building, which had been preserved almost intact until that moment (Figures **3**; **4**). Later the Turks built a small mosque in the inner room of the Parthenon which was now open to the sky (Figure **16**). A village had long since grown up around this monument. Sometimes the ancient temples were converted into churches and sometimes the blocks from their walls were reused to build houses, thereby often being moved far from their original location. The Propylaea had already been turned into a fortress by the Franks in the thirteenth century AD and walled up (Figure **7**). The stones from the Temple of Athena Nike, for example, were reused in an outwork in front of a defensive tower on the south-west corner of the Classical entrance building. In the late eighteenth century Europeans on the Grand Tour, antiquarians or ambassadors, such as Lord Elgin, travelled through Greece and, in addition to investigating ancient art and architecture, they began to acquire sculptures and architectural fragments from the Acropolis. Lord Elgin obtained large parts of the Parthenon frieze, the pedimental sculptures and the metopes, as well as a Caryatid from the Erechtheion and a column from its east porch, and slabs from the south and west friezes of the Nike temple.

After the end of Turkish rule a programme for the restoration of the ancient buildings was initiated in 1834. Later additions and changes to the buildings were removed in order to regain as much as possible of their original appearance (Plates 5, 8, 11). From the end of the nineteenth century until 1940 building after building was restored under the leadership of the Greek architect Balanos and researched as far as the state of knowledge at that time allowed. This undertaking resulted in far-reaching changes to the ruinous state of the buildings and has given rise to the appearance of the Acropolis as we see it today. The changes are apparent when illustrations of the monuments before and after the work of Balanos are compared. In 1977 a new restoration programme was undertaken aimed not only at correcting the mistakes of earlier conservators (for example, by the removal of rusty iron dowels), but primarily at investigating scientifically all the surviving fragments, both architectural elements and sculptures, and then integrating them wherever possible into their original building contexts; they should thus be effectively protected from further destruction, especially from pollution. Moreover, it is not planned just to restore the Acropolis to its original Classical appearance, but the changing history of the monuments is also to be documented and appropriately displayed to the visitor. In 1988 the restoration work on the Erechtheion was finished and it is possible for the visitor to check the results. The work was carried out with great resourcefulness and devotion by a team of Greek architects and technicians under the careful supervision of a committee, which regularly sought

Figure 7 Athens, Acropolis: Propylaea from the south, *c.* 1820. (W. Kinnard).
Photo DAI Athens (Akr 435)

advice and opinions from international scholars. Most importantly, all the measures undertaken in the present restorations can be reversed, should this be necessary later on.

A tour of the Acropolis (Figures **5**; **6**; Plate 4). The entrance to the Acropolis is on the west side (reached either by the Hill of the Areopagus or from Dionysiou-Areopagitou Street); the entrance ticket is obtained outside the fenced area after which the visitor enters from above the Odeion of Herodes Atticus.

Before visiting the site the visitor must realise that many buildings are covered in scaffolding because of the urgent restoration and research work necessary as a result of their deterioration. Although this impedes the view of the buildings, it does offer the opportunity of obtaining an insight into the methods of restoration. The visitor must also remember that future generations will wish to visit and learn about these masterpieces of the European cultural heritage and this would soon not be possible without the present restoration works. The following description of the buildings[11] includes the results of recent research arising from the present restoration campaign.

The main entrance, the **Beulé Gate** (Figure **6**.1), which was built almost entirely from older reused blocks (spolia) in the late third century AD, is framed by two towers. The Gate is named after the French archaeologist Ernest Beulé, who discovered and investigated it in 1852/3. Spolia of special interest include marble blocks belonging to an architrave, a Doric frieze and a cornice (geison) which have been incorporated over the entrance. The choregic monument from which they come, in the form of a temple with six columns on the front, originally stood on the south slope of the Acropolis west of the theatre of Dionysos. It was dedicated by Nikias,[12] who sponsored a theatrical performance in 320/19 BC (Figure **6**.29). The name, Nikias, and his office are listed on the architrave. More spolia are to be found inside the entrance. They include a fine statue base with olive wreaths in relief, which denote a state decree in honour of a citizen. Nearby are marble sculptures of dogs dating to the fourth century BC, which once adorned tombs at a distance from the Acropolis.

The **Agrippa monument** (Figures **6**.2; **8**.2). The impressive façade of the Acropolis entrance with the mighty six-columned portal of the Propylaea in the centre framed by two almost symmetrical wings lies inside the Beulé Gate. To the right set on a high tower is the charming Ionic temple of Athena Nike, while on the left below the north wing a tall pillar base can be seen. This pedestal, made of bluish-grey white-veined Hymettian marble, was erected in the mid-second century BC and carried the four-horse chariot of a Pergamene king;[13] the latter was replaced by a likeness of the Roman general Agrippa, the son-in-law and comrade of Augustus. At the time of the replacement (27–12 BC) the inscription naming the Pergamene king was almost entirely erased and replaced by the name Marcus Vipsanius Agrippa; it can be read on the west side, two-thirds up the pillar, if the light from the side is favourable.[14]

Ascent and Ramp (Figures **6**.3; **8**.1). Today a zigzag path leads up to the west façade of the Propylaea, but this does not reflect the ancient ascent. Standing inside the Beulé Gate roughly on the axis of the Propylaea it is possible to see a retaining wall of irregular stones, each accurately adjusted to fit its neighbour. This fine polygonal wall, built of Acropolis limestone, supported an Archaic ramp leading to the ascent, either to the early Propylaea or to the Peisistratid entrance. The foundations for the Classical ramp can be clearly differentiated: below the Agrippa monument there are still some regular ashlar blocks of poros stone which show the inclination of the ascent. From this it is possible to deduce that in the Classical period a long ramp led up to the monumental entrance building, rising exactly on the axis of and extending to the full width of the Propylaea façade; the sides of the ramp were exactly on a line with the sides of the north and south wings and can be seen in the rock cutting next to the modern steps. The revetment of the substructure of the Athena Nike Temple also takes account of the edge of the ramp.

The **Propylaea** and its wings (Figures **6**.4–5; **8**). The entrance to the central temple of Athens is designed as a monumental edifice with façades which give

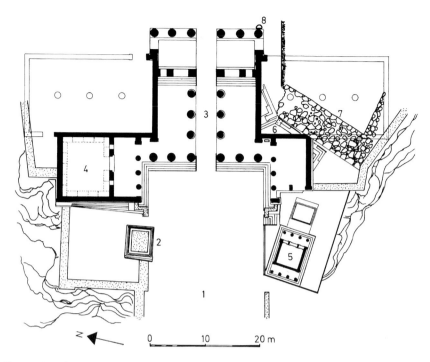

Figure 8 Athens, Acropolis: Propylaea.

1: ramp; 2: Agrippa monument; 3: Propylaea; 4: Pinakotheke; 5: Temple of Athena Nike; 6: courtyard in front of the Archaic Propylaea; 7: Mycenaean wall; 8: statue base of Athena Hygieia.

the impression of a temple lying between two lateral projecting wings. The Propylaea (literally: entrances) is bordered at entrance and exit (that is on the west and east sides) by a six-columned portico in the Doric style with a pediment (Plate 5). These porticoes had to be constructed on different levels due to the rising ground of the Acropolis with the result that a complicated roofing system was needed. In addition to the two pediments on the east and west façades, a step in the roof and a third pediment had to be constructed roughly in the middle of the entrance building. Then a further problem arose: the height in the interior of the building was so great that Doric columns could not be used to support the marble roof because, according to Classical proportions, their diameter would have been too large; as a result, Mnesikles, the architect in charge, chose tall, slender Ionic columns for the interior. These stand on the lower west level with a few steps leading up from them to the five doors and the higher eastern level.[15]

The architecture of the Propylaea was planned to impress the visitor, an obvious concept to us today, but an entirely new one then. Religious and political considerations are also responsible for some of the peculiarities of the building. For example, the extended ramp, which perhaps had grooves across the middle, was built with the Panathenaic Festival in mind. Numerous cattle and other animals were brought up to the Acropolis for sacrifice at this festival, so the ascent had to be suitable for them. Mnesikles also had to accommodate the width of the entrance to the Panathenaic procession. For this reason the doors have different sizes varying from very wide in the middle to much smaller at the sides. This in turn affected the architecture of the façade of the Propylaea. Whereas in Doric architecture one triglyph was put over each column and only one more in the middle between the columns (intercolumniation), this principle had to be broken in this case; because of the wider central entrance two triglyphs with three metopes were placed over the middle of the façade in the intercolumniation and the distance between the central columns was widened from 3.62 m to 5.44 m. This unusual solution, which involved breaking an architectural principle, had far-reaching consequences. Once conceived it led to an ever-increasing disintegration of the Doric order so that finally in the Hellenistic and Roman periods a large number of metopes and triglyphs could appear over an intercolumniation; the original derivation of this system from actual wooden structures (the triglyphs covered the ends of the beams of the roof framework, the metopes the spaces in between) was finally forgotten and the components were treated as purely decorative elements.

The entrance façade of the Propylaea is framed by two wings which look almost symmetrical from a distance, but which in fact are not so, because the original plan was changed.[16] In the north-west wing (Figure **8**.4) a three-columned portico and a vestibule lead to an almost square room entered via an off-centre door with a window on either side of it. Since it is known from an observation of Pausanias that paintings by famous Greek artists were exhibited in this room, the north wing of the Propylaea is known as the 'Pinakotheke'. However, it was not only used as a picture gallery but also as a reception room for pilgrims to rest before they entered the precinct; it is highly probable that seventeen couches (klinai) lined its walls. Opposite the Pinakotheke a symmetrically-shaped building was probably planned, for which there was finally no room due to the simultaneous construction of the Athena Nike Temple. For this reason the south-west wing was radically cut down from Mnesikles' original plan and shortened; behind the three-columned Doric portico there was only one room, which was open on its west side to the Temple of Nike and so could be used as an entrance to that precinct. The side wall was shortened to one pillar, while a further pillar carried the entablature of the west side up to the south back wall.

The new restorations carried out since 1990 have provided the opportunity for examining numerous details. It has thus been ascertained that the ceiling of the Propylaea was repaired during the days of the Early Roman Empire. The roof, a particularly exposed part of the building, had to be continuously maintained. This was especially so in the case of the Propylaea, since, for example, the roof beams with the ceiling coffers, which are in a very bad state today, had an enormous span for marble blocks; as a special precaution for their safety the ancient architect had inserted thin bronze bands into the tops of the marble beams which they thought would support the coffered roof.[17] An architectural detail which gave an unusual optical impression was the addition of a black course to the structure;

layers of Eleusinian dark grey limestone were added into the marble wall, both below the windows in the inner room of the Pinakotheke and in the side walls and thresholds of the middle area between the east and west façades, and thus the architecture was obviously articulated. In later Hellenistic and Roman buildings the combination of different coloured marbles was very popular; the Propylaea furnishes an important precedent for this luxurious building technique.

A further peculiarity of the building, which, curiously enough, provided a precedent for later architecture, is its unfinished state. On the walls, especially on the outer south side of the Propylaea, and on the floors and steps one can still see the lifting bosses for moving the blocks during construction (Figure **13**) or the unfinished protective surfaces. During the final polishing, which was carried out from top to bottom, the bosses and the mantle ought to have been removed. This indeed occurred in the upper part of the Propylaea, and the painted decoration, consisting of stars on the ceiling coffers, was added; after the removal of the necessary scaffolding a final finishing was not carried out, probably because of the outbreak of the Peloponnesian War. Some scholars have suggested that this final finishing was deliberately not carried out and that the charming optical effect of unfinished masonry was discovered at this time.[18] It is certainly true that masonry was left unfinished in later times; rustication used as decorative features is common in the Hellenistic period; however, in the case of the Propylaea the political situation seems most likely to have been responsible for the break in the work. Indeed, a comparison with the inferred plan makes it clear that the construction of the entire complex was interrupted before completion; in some areas building components exist (for example, an anta below the west wall of the Pinakotheke and another on the east side of the central building, as well as preparations for a ceiling in the south-east wing) which can only be explained if they were to be part of further rooms or wings; as a result of the outbreak of war these were not even begun. Further evidence for this assumption is the fact that the building accounts are also unfinished.

As mentioned above, the Classical Propylaea which we see today had an Archaic predecessor, the Old Propylaea,[19] which was begun either by the new democracy or after the Battle of Marathon at the latest and destroyed by the Persians in 480 BC (Figure **5**.1). There are only a few remnants of this building and these are not accessible to tourists. Beneath the middle entrance, which has been protected from the ravages of hordes of visitors by a wooden platform, and in two gaps in the pavement on each side of the middle entrance, where the paving stones are missing, the rock cutting for the foundations of the walls of the previous entrance has been found. In addition, on the south side of the Classical Propylaea architectural remains (part of a vestibule of which the revetment of the back wall, the Mycenaean fortification wall, was composed of metopes belonging to the Hecatompedon), and even the base of a bronze tripod, have been preserved; together with other remains they suggest that the Archaic Propylaea was constructed at an angle to the Classical one. It is clear from these remnants that its position was much better adapted to the topography of the Acropolis, whereas the Perikleian building ignored the natural landscape and dominated the hill with its monumental architecture. However, the Classical Propylaea has been the prototype for numerous monumental gateways throughout the European history of architecture. Repairs were carried out in many places on the Old Propylaea after the Persian destruction, when the Acropolis was refortified by repairing the entrances and rebuilding the side walls. During the construction of the Classical Propylaea of Mnesikles the Old Propylaea was mostly removed and replaced by the new buildings.

After Antiquity the entrance to the Acropolis was changed many times.[20] In the thirteenth century AD the Franks turned it into a fortification by constructing walls between the porticoes (Figure **7**). A second storey was built inside; the sockets for the joists can still be seen in the marble walls today. A tower was built above the south wing to rise high over the ancient building, and the architectural members of the Temple of Nike were used for a bastion built between its substructure and the Agrippa monument. The appearance of the Acropolis at that time is illustrated by some engravings and drawings which are also of interest to modern scholars. After the War of Independence architects from Germany and Denmark removed the post-Antique buildings.[21] In 1835 wide-ranging restoration was begun which also led to the rebuilding of the Temple of Nike, the original foundation of which was found in front of the Propylaea on a high bastion. It was put together between 1835 and 1844, but had to be taken down and rebuilt from 1935–39 because the foundations were sinking. Even this restoration will not be the last; in the next few years the building will be taken apart and reconstructed to remove its rusting iron dowels and to protect the ancient frieze, which was removed from the building in 1999. Now to the temple itself:

The **Temple of Athena Nike** (Figures 6.6; **9**). This temple, which was probably designed by the architect Kallikrates in 437 BC (inscriptions only say that Kallikrates designed an entrance to the temenos) and constructed in the following years,[22] was built over an earlier temple. It is probable that a temple for Athena was established here as early as the time of the Peisistratids (561–510 BC). There are Archaic remains belonging to it preserved in the Classical bastion (Figure **5**.2); under the Temple of Nike two altars were found (one with a dedication of a certain Patrokles to Athena Nike) and the foundations of a small shrine in which stood a cult image of Athena (of wood plugged into a stone base). After the destruction of the Acropolis by the Persians in 480 BC (the cult figure was taken to Salamis for safety) a new shrine with a larger altar of Aiginetan limestone was built and the ancient cult figure was set up in it again. The building was not enlarged until the time of Perikles, when the cult was made one of the city cults of Athens through the appointment of a priestess elected from the people.

The architects disagreed on the proposed building plans of the Propylaea and the Nike Temple. A compromise was reached between the two architectural plans and a tower-like substructure, the Nike Bastion, was set up for the Nike Temple, which had an opening in its revetment in which a stone from the earlier Mycenaean Cylopean wall can be seen. On one side the Nike Bastion was flanked by the ramp of the Propylaea, while on the other side it followed the orientation of the Archaic temple, as also did the Nike Temple. Superficial cuttings on the

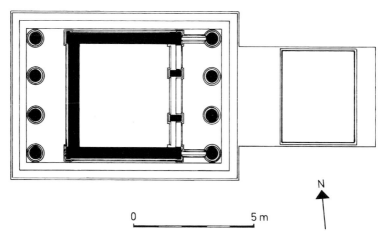

0 _____ 5 m

N

Figure 9 Athens, Acropolis: Temple of Athena Nike with altar.

stretchers suggest the revetment wall of ashlar blocks was built with alternating courses of headers and stretchers, but this is not the case. Later on, perhaps in the Roman period, the limestone blocks were covered with thin slabs of marble, as can be seen from dowel holes set at a regular distance from each other.

The Temple of Athena Nike (Plate 6) forms a great contrast to the monumental Propylaea both as an entity and in its details. Four graceful Ionic columns with fine volute capitals adorn the front and back side of the small temple (amphiprostyle). The cella itself is extremely small, as it had to be shortened in a change of design because of the lack of space on the bastion, so the vestibule (pronaos) and cella are combined. The east side was open, apart from screens between the columns, and consisted of only two piers framing a central entrance and the two screened side openings. The original appearance of the temple, probably also designed by Kallikrates, can be reconstructed from that of the Ilissos Temple (see p. 101). The design of the building was obviously regarded as a success in Antiquity since five more copies are known, one on top of the neighbouring Areopagos and the rest in Attica.[23]

The ornamental elements of the column bases, the capitals and the entablature together with the sculptured frieze, all made of fine Pentelic marble, give the impression of a jewel box; the sculptured figures on the pediments – of Parian marble – are now almost completely lost, as well as the acroteria above the corners of the pediments.[24] The themes of the frieze (now to be found in the museum) consist of an assembly of the gods, depicted on the east frieze, and, on the other sides, battles, partly between Greeks and mounted orientals, and partly Greeks against Greeks.[25] The mythical or historical events represented have probably been intentionally left vague: Athenians defeat Persians and other Greek city-states. Finally the Archaic wooden cult image of Athena stood inside the Temple of Nike, holding in her hands, according to Harpokration, her helmet and a pomegranate, symbols of might and fertility.

In front of the temple there was an altar where acts of cult could be carried out. Presumably a sacred enclosure existed beyond the altar, dedicated to the Graces;[26] the area was limited by the earlier Mycenaean polygonal wall lying against the south part of the Propylaea and the higher-lying Brauronion (Figures **5**.7; **8**.7).

Towards the end of the fifth century BC a c. 1.50 m-high marble parapet was added on to the top of the substructure of the temple, the Nike Bastion, with bronze grilles on top of it; there were reliefs on the exterior of the parapet (in the Acropolis Museum).[27] These show Nikai preparing a sacrifice and erecting trophies; one is adjusting her sandals; Athena appears once on each of the three sides. The figures are in relief with deep folds, the bodies modelled by the clinging garments. The message of the frieze is clear: Athens is victorious and will remain so.

The **Area between the Propylaea, Parthenon and Erechtheion**. When the visitor enters through the Propylaea today, the large expanse of the Acropolis opens up with the ruins of the Erechtheion on the left and of the Parthenon on the right as well as a few marble blocks scattered on the rock. In Antiquity the visitor got a completely different, diverse and colourful impression. Numerous votive offerings and statues depicting gods and humans, with representations of myths and historical events were seen. Shining marble buildings rose behind them, consisting not only of the two temples, but also of covered porticoes and smaller shrines; the porticoes also partly concealed the Parthenon which dominates the view today. The pilgrim of Antiquity saw history and myth everywhere in the form of both honorary decrees and religious monuments. A guide of that time would have had numerous myths to recount relating to the individual monuments (Pausanias repeats many of them), as, for example, that of Prokne and Itys (see p. 46).

The numerous representations of Athena, the city goddess, predominated. The colossal c. 9 m-high bronze statue of Athena Promachos, the 'Champion', sculpted by Pheidias,[28] was placed exactly opposite the east façade of the Propylaea (Figure **6**.7); it was placed on a large square pedestal, of which a few (Roman repair) blocks with a huge egg-and-dart moulding[29] remain near the original rock cutting. Since she was made soon after the Persian Wars, she personified the military strength of Athens and was, therefore, shown armed and with a spear. The bronze statue was taken to Constantinople, probably in the reign of Justinian, where it was destroyed in 1204 AD. Other statues of Athena are known from Roman copies, including a Classical statue by Pheidias depicting the goddess who has removed her helmet and is looking at it thoughtfully. A small marble relief of Athena looking down at a pillar or a stele is a related piece of similar character (see p. 45).

Other divinities were also worshipped on the Acropolis.[30] In front of the south-east column of the Propylaea there is a marble base, still in its original position, on which, according to the inscription, a bronze figure of Athena in her capacity as Hygieia, the goddess of health, was set up (Figure **8**.8). A few steps further east, on the right of the path is the semicircular rock cutting in which the many-stepped base of a group of figures stood; it is only one example of numerous statues of historical personalities of Greek and Roman history (from Perikles to the Roman emperors). A second similar exedra base with figures of the two politicians, Konon and Timotheos, father and son (early or mid-fourth century BC),[31] was placed north of the Parthenon, approximately in the middle of the long side. The cutting for it in the rock, a few pieces of marble, on which the names are carved, and the Eleusinian limestone base can be seen. They lie near a rock-cut dedication to Gaia, the earth goddess, for whom, in the Roman period, an inscription was cut in the rock and a figure of the goddess was placed in front of it; it is mentioned by Pausanias together with the statues of Konon and Timotheos. Today the inscription and cutting for the statue of Gaia are surrounded by a small fence. The path over the Acropolis is bordered by many oblong slots in the rock in which marble slabs – stelai with votive or document reliefs or only inscriptions – were once set. We can reconstruct the ancient pilgrim's path from their orientation; the modern cement path follows it. Because the rock was being worn down and becoming dangerously slippery as a result of the thousands of tourists walking over it and important archaeological information was on the point of disappearing for ever, it was decided to construct the cement path and to rope off the ancient rock.

South of the main path there were two building complexes. First next to the semicircular exedra base there is a stair to the Sanctuary of **Artemis Brauronia** (Figure **6**.8), whose cult was probably brought to Athens by the Peisistratids as part of a programme to centralise religion and cults.[32] The horizontal cuttings for the foundations of porticoes and two oblong side rooms can be seen in the surface of the rock. They frame (on the plans, the one on the west is recon-structed to the design of that on the east) an almost square area, in which, according to Pausanias, the bronze statue of the Trojan horse stood (the blocks of the marble base lie in the area to the west of it). There must also have been a small temple which contained the cult statue of Artemis, a work of Praxiteles according to Pausanias; it has just recently been possible to identify the head of this colossal statue.[33]

A further portico lay next to this temple in the east; its back wall ran along the retaining wall of the Acropolis (Figure **6**.9). It was used for the storage of bronze ritual gifts and so was called the **Chalkotheke** (chalkos = bronze).[34] The north-east corner of a colonnade built in front of this stoa in the fourth century BC cut into the steps hewn from the rock which led up to the Parthenon; they were also used for the display of votive stelai. These steps were cut out of the rock in such a way that they had a slight curve to take into consider-ation the optical foreshortening which occurs when the visitor looks at the west façade of the Parthenon from the Propylaea. The steps must, therefore, have been planned and constructed together with the Parthenon. In the south, where the outcropping rock was not sufficient, blocks were used from the lime-stone stylobate of the Old Athena Temple to construct the steps. (The area of the Chalkotheke is used at the moment as a depot – not open to the public – for important inscriptions and statue bases, until there is enough museum space for them.)

The **Old Temple of Athena** (Figures **5**.4; **6**.10). The limestone foundations of this temple, which can be seen between the Erechtheion and the Parthenon, are the only visible architectural remains today belonging to the temples of the Archaic period on the Acropolis.[35] There are only decorative elements, such as pediment and cornice decoration, surviving from the other cult buildings dating to before the Persian destruction. The interpretation of the surviving foundations is difficult and there is still disagreement, but it is clear that the building was completed under the Peisistratids between 520 and 515 BC. There seems not to have been an earlier temple on this spot, but only an altar with a forecourt. Nothing here can be assigned to the Mycenaean palace mentioned by Homer; moreover, the column bases of a small Geometric temple, which can be seen between the large foundations, are not in their original places. The Old Athena Temple consisted of a cella divided into many rooms (a typical ground plan for the Acropolis cult buildings) with a colonnade round it of 6 columns on the fronts and 12 on the sides (6 by 12). The remains of the foundations for the walls as well as for the columns are made of different types of limestone, which allow the arrangement of the columns in the front and back porches and in the cella to be reconstructed; at first it was thought that the different foundation materials belonged to two building phases; but the similar stone-working techniques showed that this was not the case. The building itself (Plates 3, 7) was of poros limestone. The architectural members of this temple are scattered around the Acropolis: its big yellow-brown Doric capitals, their colour changed by burning, can be seen in the Chalkotheke and on the north-east corner, while parts of the entablature are built into the north wall of the Acropolis, easily seen from the Plaka (Figures **6**.19; **11**). The metopes, pediment and cornices with pseudo-water-spouts in the form of ram heads stand out from the limestone, which was once decorated with stucco and painted, as they are made of marble. One ram head, which remained built into the fountain of the monastery at Kaisariani for hundreds of years (see p. 155) has been replaced by an excellent copy and is now in the Acropolis Museum. The east pediment depicted the battle of the gods and giants, a very old Greek mythological theme, and the west probably a combat of animals.

The Old Temple of Athena, which perhaps housed the cult figure of Athena Polias under the Peisistratids, was destroyed by the Persians in 480 BC; some of its building components were put into the north wall of the Acropolis as a memorial of the Persian destruction (Figure **11**.4b); blocks from the stylobate were used on the south-west side of the Parthenon to complete the steps. Most of the remaining pieces vanished into the Persian destruction fill in the Classical period. Since the porch of the Caryatids on the neighbouring Erechtheion rests on the foundations of the earlier temple, there was nothing more to see of the Old Athena Temple after the fifth century BC at the latest, until the German architect, Wilhelm Dörpfeld, excavated its foundations at the end of the nineteenth century.

The **Erechtheion** (Figures **6**.10; **10**). This temple, which is completely irregular in plan, was called the 'Erechtheion' only in two ancient sources; its official name is the 'Temple on the Acropolis with the old statue', that is the wooden cult

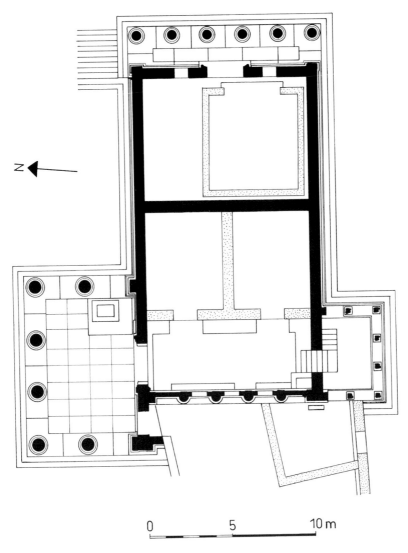

0   5   10 m

Figure 10 Athens, Acropolis: Erechtheion.

figure of Athena, which was adorned with a new garment during the Panathenaic Festival. Although there are many sources for this building, since, in addition to descriptions by Pausanias, a large number of building accounts and documents concerning its construction are extant (Epigraphical Museum),[36] yet the exact interpretation of its different components and the location of the different cults within the temple is uncertain,[37] as a result of its conversion into a Christian church in the seventh century AD. As its real name says, it was above all a cult building for the city goddess Athena (Polias). In addition, it housed the cults of the ancient Attic kings, Erechtheus and Kekrops, as well as those of Poseidon,

Boutes and Hephaistos. This complicated cultic situation gave rise to a particularly unusual type of building, in which each of the four sides has a completely different appearance.

On the east side the temple had the usual appearance: the façade with six Ionic columns stands in front of an almost square cella, which is interpreted as the cult place of Athena. In the interior, however, this main area of the temple is surprising; behind the cella façade, which had two windows and the door, the visitor had to step down to a special shrine which functioned as the Athena Polias Temple.[38] It was already standing in the Archaic period and must have been repaired for the protection of the wooden cult statue immediately after the Persian Wars. Architectural details in the interior as well as the building accounts verify this unusual arrangement. Thus the cult centre for the city goddess was not on the same level as the east façade or the shallow porch built onto the south side, the entablature of which was supported by six maidens (Caryatids)[39] on a podium. This Porch of the Caryatids (Plate 7), which was connected by a stairway to the descending interior of the Erechtheion on the west, must have been used as a cult place for the mythical early kings; the Caryatids, who were carved with old-fashioned dress and hair, seem to have also had a ritual function since they have libation phialai in their hands, and were either servants of a cult or guards at the grave of the early kings.[40] That the grave of Kekrops was really thought to lie beneath the south-west corner of the Erechtheion is suggested by the bedrock foundations of a huge Ionic column, set up as a votive monument right next to the foundations of the Old Athena Temple, which have, therefore, been a little incurved;[41] in addition it is noteworthy that the south-west corner of the Erechtheion does not rest on the rock, but the weight of the building is distributed on the three surrounding sides by means of enormous marble blocks, so that the ancient cult area of Kekrops below remained untouched. Since the grave was bounded by a square temenos in the Classical period the final polishing of the outer wall of the Erechtheion on the south-west side was omitted. The peribolos of Kekrops could be entered by a door next to the porch of the Caryatids. A parapet was attached to the porch on its west side; north of it the Ionic ornamentation has not been finished.

The inner room of the temple lies, as stated, at a level three metres below the east and south sides. On the north a lofty, richly decorated porch was erected; it served as an entrance to a vestibule (prostoon) and two rooms in the western half of the Erechtheion. The north porch was also a cult place. In the coffered ceiling a square opening is left under which was a rectangular reservoir, which was turned into a cistern in the Middle Ages. These two ancient features refer to the mythical contest between Athena and Poseidon for the land of Attica. Poseidon struck the Acropolis rock with his trident, causing a salt spring to gush out, whereupon Athena made an olive tree sprout, which could be seen in the neighbouring sanctuary of Pandrosos to the west and which has been replanted in modern times. The reservoir under the north porch was connected to the inner cella by a small entrance. The lintel above this opening in the foundation of the north wall of the Erechtheion consists of two big marble blocks which had originally been used as a door-frame.[42] They are of particular interest because they belonged to the Late Archaic Old Propylaea (Plate 3), which was taken down in 438 BC. Since much marble was needed in these years for all the building projects on the Acropolis and since old blocks were reused everywhere, the two architectural projects must be chronologically connected: the foundations of the Erechtheion cannot have been begun much later than 438 BC, which means that the Erechtheion is a Perikleian temple both in its plan and in its foundation. The fact that only Mnesikles could know when the two Old Propylaea blocks would be free for placing in the Erechtheion, the fact that in both the Propylaea and the Erechtheion there are so many unusual innovations in the architecture and that in both buildings the problems of architecturally uniting many earlier cult areas on totally different levels have been successfully resolved – all give rise to the suggestion that Mnesikles was also the architect of the Erechtheion, although this is nowhere stated. If the building was begun in the time of Perikles and not, as has been thought, during the Peace of Nikias, we could more easily explain why, according to the first building documents, when construction was resumed towards the end of the Peloponnesian War (409/8 BC), the Erechtheion was almost finished up to the roof; most of the work mentioned in the building accounts of 409 BC involves the completion of the decoration, the fluting of the columns, the polishing of the walls and the carving of the figures of the frieze; the building itself was almost completely finished and the Caryatids were already in place supporting the Ionic entablature, on which, according to the inscription of 409/8 BC, the rosettes still had to be carved; this in fact never took place; probably rosette motives were just painted onto the round discs on the architrave.

East of the north porch there is a yard with rectangular steps, which could be used as seats by those taking part in the cult ceremonies.

If the three sections just described were an unusual architectural combination, the west side of the Erechtheion (Plate 8) must have appeared almost revolutionary to the Athenians of that time. It was in complete contrast to the east side. Above the door at the west end was a façade composed of half-columns in the Ionic order with intercolumnar walls and – higher up – five windows with grilles; until the construction of this façade columns were carved fully in the round and stood on the ground on a stylobate. The west portico gives the impression of a flat façade rather than of a fully three-dimensional entity. It is the first example of such a concept in the history of European architecture.

In addition to its unusual ground plan and elevation the Erechtheion was correspondingly decorated with a most sumptuous ornamentation, which went far beyond that of the Temple of Nike. The bases of the Ionic columns of the north porch are carved with a guilloche of two designs, in which bright glass beads were set. The Ionic capitals have a necking decorated with lotus and palmettes; a similar band is carried round the entire temple at the top of the walls.[43] The Ionic capitals had leaf gold in the eyes of the volutes, while the mouldings of bead-and-reel, egg-and-dart and Lesbian cyma, were outlined in colour. These decorative forms soon became so 'Classical' that they were much imitated, not only in Roman times but right down into European Classicising art. The frame of the north door, which is richly ornamented, can be taken as a pattern book of architectural decoration. To understand the impression this building ornamentation made on the ancient visitor one must remember that the decorative bands were all painted and that, in addition, glass insets and gold leaf added to the sumptuous effect.[44] The impression was completed by a figured frieze above the fascias on the architrave consisting of white marble relief figures (in the museum),[45] which were separately clamped onto blocks of dark Eleusinian limestone. Here the contrast of the different materials was intentional (see Propylaea).

The Restoration of the Erechtheion.[46] Between 1977 and 1988 the Erechtheion was restored and reinvestigated. The building, which had already been removed once almost to its foundations, was completely taken down again. The rusty iron dowels, which were splitting the marble, were removed and the sculptured decoration, including the Caryatids, was replaced with casts of silaceous sand (ground quartz). This has also made the restoration of the ancient supports of the south porch possible, so that the Caryatids alone support the entablature instead of the steel girders put between them before 1977. During the reconstruction of the walls, the gaps, whether they consisted of complete blocks or just broken pieces, were filled with Pentelic marble. Titanium was used for the dowels and clamps; it was put into the ancient holes and sealed with lead. All the replacements have the date of the restoration engraved on them, so that it will be possible to tell them apart from the original pieces later on when the colour of the new parts has blended into the old surface. Finally, all the walls were covered with lead sheets to prevent water penetration. The north corner column in the east porch has been restored (the original is in the British Museum with one of the Caryatids) so that the east façade has regained its original appearance. In the interior the choir screen of the Christian church has been set up to illustrate the later history of the building. There are no traces today of the harem which was quartered in the Erechtheion in the Ottoman period. A path encircles the whole building so that all sides of the temple can be inspected. Some column drums from the Old Parthenon can also be seen in the Acropolis wall from the north side of the Erechtheion.

The **Hecatompedon**, the **Old Parthenon** and the **Parthenon** (Figures **5**.5; **6**.12; **10–16**).[47] The Hecatompedon (Temple of a Hundred Feet), attested by numerous architectural and sculptured fragments, must have stood on the site of the Parthenon in the early sixth century BC; no other site on the Acropolis can be assigned to this building. The fact that its limestone architrave was built into the south wall of the Acropolis suggests its original position should have been on the south side of the Acropolis in the area of the later Parthenon which is nearby; in addition an earlier building phase could be recognised in the foundations of the Late Archaic Old Parthenon. Doric capital fragments with flat echinus appear in three different sizes (perhaps from the exterior, the vestibule and the interior) and there are parts of at least thirteen different big capitals of the surrounding colonnade (peristasis). This proves that the Hecatompedon must have been a peripteros. Metopes of Hymettian marble, some with relief figures (leopards, lions, horses) clamped on and some plain, can also be assigned to it together with roof gutters (sima) of the same stone with fine floral ornament. The pediments

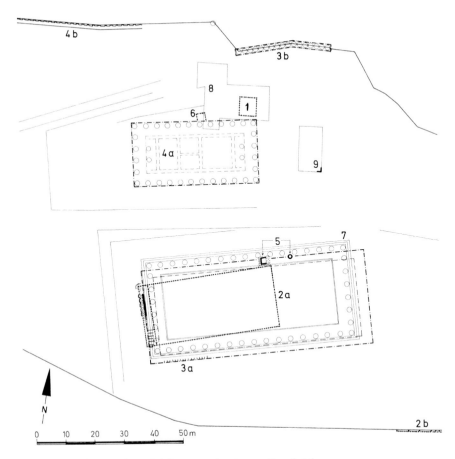

Figure 11 The temples of Athena on the Acropolis of Athens.

1: Temple of Athena Polias; 2a: Hecatompedon; 2b: architectural members of the Hecatompedon built into the south wall; 3a: Old Parthenon; 3b: column drums of the Old Parthenon built into the north wall; 4a: Old Athena Temple; 4b: entablature of the Old Athena Temple built into the north wall; 5: temple and altar (of Athena Ergane?); 6: Kekropion; 7: Parthenon; 8: Erechtheion; 9: altar of all Athena temples.

were decorated with painted limestone figures (supposedly Herakles and Triton, groups of fighting animals; see Museum). When the peristasis of this building was removed and the construction of the Old Parthenon began around the untouched cella containing the cult statue (the Athena which is painted on Panathenaic prize amphorae?), the plain marble metopes were reused to cover the Mycenaean fortification wall outside the Old Propylaea, while the famous Hecatompedon inscriptions (486/5 BC), the rules for seemly behaviour on the Acropolis, were inscribed on two other plain metopes.

Even before 480 BC, perhaps at the time of the new democratic constitution or perhaps only after the Battle of Marathon (490 BC), a large marble temple, the Old Parthenon,[48] was begun (Plate 3) to replace the old-fashioned

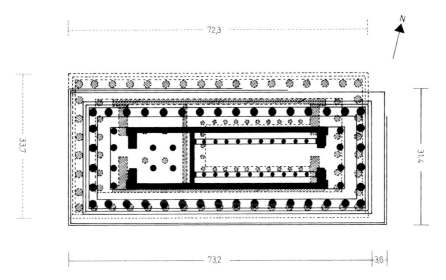

Figure 12 Athens, Acropolis: Old Parthenon (black) and Parthenon (hatched).

Hecatompedon; however, it was burnt down during the second Persian invasion before it could be completed (Figure **12**). Large parts of its very long foundation were reused for a new building, the Parthenon, which was in the High Classical style. The substructure of the Old Parthenon can be seen clearly on the south side (Plate 10) as well as on the east, where it is cut into the rock a few metres in front of the Parthenon steps and then comes to a dead end; there are also clear traces on the west side in the northern area of the high substructure as a result of the widening of the foundations for the Parthenon, which is shorter and wider. Parts of the marble structure, especially column drums left blocked out (Figure **13**), were built into the north wall of the Acropolis (Figure **6**.19), together with architectural fragments from the Old Temple of Athena; others are lying in different places on the Acropolis. On the south side of the Parthenon, to the west next to the restoration workshops, parts of the cella wall have been restored from fragments: the lowest courses of the temple wall (orthostates) were built on a stylobate with a slight upward curvature; these architectural blocks are unfinished and retain their protective surfaces. Traces of burning on the blocks, which have been built into the foundations of the Parthenon, show that the Old Parthenon was destroyed when the Persians ransacked Athens, so it must have been built before 480 BC. Recent research[49] has shown that the inner part of the cella of the Old Parthenon, like the later Parthenon, the Erechtheion and the Old Temple of Athena, must have been divided into two rooms. This confirms what we know from later inventories of the treasures of the Parthenon, i.e. that the temple had four different chambers: the pronaos, the opisthodomos, the Parthenon and the Hecatompedon. The name of the Early Archaic building lives on in the last name, the Hecatompedon, which refers to the actual cella with the cult image; it also appears on the inscriptions with the rules for seemly

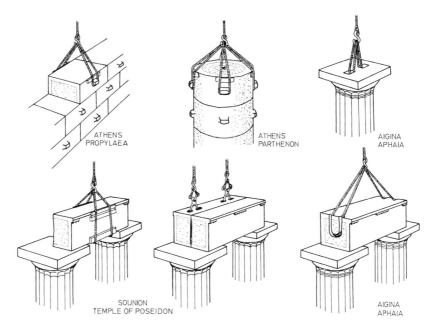

Figure 13 Methods of lifting architectural members during construction work.

behaviour on the Acropolis. The term Parthenon actually refers to the west chamber, which opens into the opisthodomos.

The huge building of the Parthenon[50] has dominated the Acropolis since the Classical period (Figure **14**; Plates 4, 9, 11). Some scholars think that it was never a temple in the real sense of the word but that, in contrast to its appearance, it had only a secular function, that of a treasury and a victory monument.[51] It is concluded from hints in some written sources and from the lack of an altar on the east side that no cult ever took place inside it or in front of it. There are, however, important counter arguments to this theory: the building plan with a second chamber is surely designed with cult in mind; Athena Parthenos was worshipped on the citadel from 500 BC at the latest; statues of wood, gold and ivory, like the Parthenos, were always cult figures in other temples; and, above all, on the site of the Parthenon there was already (Figure **11**) an Early Archaic temple (the Hecatompedon), while Geometric roof tiles suggest the existence of an even earlier temple. The rock of the Acropolis had been a cult place for centuries, so a change to secular use is unthinkable. Moreover, a few years ago, in the north colonnade of the Parthenon the existence of a small separate cult place – of Athena Ergane? – was ascertained, which goes back to the Archaic period when it stood next to the Old Parthenon (and its predecessor; Figure **11**) on the surface of the rock a few metres below it.[52] It had no connection with the Parthenon itself, but was incorporated into its colonnade, because the Classical building was wider than its predecessor. It is noteworthy that the east front of this small shrine, which is perhaps that mentioned by Pausanias

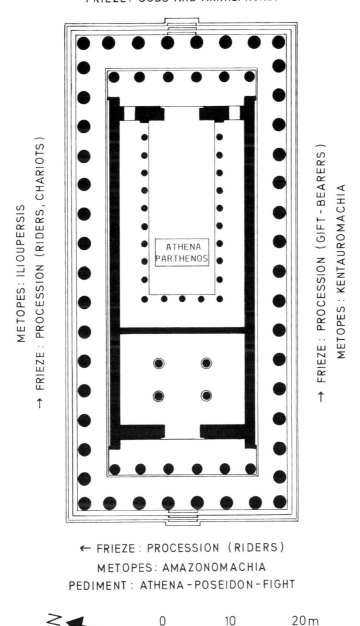

PEDIMENT: BIRTH OF ATHENA
METOPES: GIGANTOMACHIA
FRIEZE: GODS AND ARRHEPHORIA

METOPES: ILIOUPERSIS
→ FRIEZE: PROCESSION (RIDERS, CHARIOTS)

ATHENA
PARTHENOS

FRIEZE: PROCESSION (GIFT-BEARERS)
→ METOPES: KENTAUROMACHIA

← FRIEZE: PROCESSION (RIDERS)
METOPES: AMAZONOMACHIA
PEDIMENT: ATHENA-POSEIDON-FIGHT

N

0   10   20 m

Figure 14 Athens, Acropolis: Parthenon, plan and distribution of sculptural programme.

as dedicated to Athena Ergane, is aligned with the façade of the Old Temple of Athena and the cella façade of the Erechtheion (which indeed takes an earlier shrine into account) giving rise to the suggestion that the Hecatompedon also had its façade on this line, and thus should have lain below the present Parthenon.

The harmonious appearance of the Parthenon embodies the epitomy of Classical architecture; it also illustrates the peak of architecture in the Western world in the perfection of its smallest details; at the same time it encapsulates the situation at the high point of Attic democracy through its subtle portrayal of political ideals and programmes; we can allude to it only briefly in what follows.

The Architectural Design.[53] The temple was built in the few years from 448–432 BC on the foundations of the Old Parthenon (31.39 m × 76.81 m), which was a little longer and narrower than the Classical building. The architecture itself must have been almost finished in time for the Panathenaic Festival of 438 BC, since the gold and ivory statue of the Athena Parthenos by Pheidias was dedicated in that year. The remaining years of construction must have been used particularly for the finishing, the colouring and the ornamental sculpture. 'The most wonderful aspect was its speed; it was built for eternity in such a short time', thus Plutarch (second century AD) praised the Perikleian building policy and also mentioned its economic aspects: 'many technicians were employed for a long while' (Plutarch, *Life of Perikles*: 12–13). The leading artists and architects were Pheidias, Iktinos and Kallikrates, who obviously worked closely together. The entire project was carried out under the continuous observation of the Athenian Assembly, at whose decision it was taking place.

The architectural design can be described from interior to exterior, since the temple was planned around the colossal statue of the Athena Parthenos, or it can be described the other way round. It is clear that from its inception the plan took both aspects into account, that is the effective display of the huge statue and the harmonious impression of the exterior of the building, which was the result of its simple plan and elevation.

A pteron of 8 × 17 Doric columns on a three-stepped substructure (26.19 m × 69.61 m) encircles the cella (Figure **14**) with six more columns on the front and back ends (amphiprostyle with peristasis). On the east end a wide door gave entrance to the long cella, behind which, in the western third of the building, a separate chamber was divided off by a crosswall. In the eastern main room the interior had two superimposed tiers of columns forming a gallery, enclosing on three sides the statue of Athena Parthenos; in contrast in the back part of the cella, which could only be entered from the west end and which was called just 'the Parthenon', four large Ionic columns reached to the ceiling. The interior of the east cella was lit from the door and from two recently discovered windows, which were situated on the axis between the walls and the row of inner columns high up in the wall of the pronaos; light from them fell indirectly onto the colossal statue. On the inside of this wall a stairway led up to the roof beams, which had to be regularly maintained.

Architectural details. The ground plan, which appears so simple, did not come about by chance, but was the result of difficult decisions. Thus, all the building components and the entire plan and elevation are constructed in particular scales, and in ratios independent of exact measurements. The ratio of 4:9 is common, corresponding roughly to the ratio of the height of the temple to its width and of its length to its width; this is also the ratio of the span of the columns or capitals (distance from the centre of one column to the centre of the next) to their height. Other proportions are equally simply chosen, as, for example, the relation of the lower column diameter to the height as 1:5. These proportions were fixed, because a module, which was available to every building worker, was made for all the measurements, in the form of a string or a wooden measuring rod (they did not count in centimetres, but in 'feet' or 'fingers'; for the Parthenon the module was 28.627 cm). The simple proportions both made accurate construction easy and contributed greatly to the impressive appearance. In addition there are some important architectural details which add to the harmonious picture.

Each Doric column is a 'living' entity, which supports the burden of the upper part of the building. This can be seen in the slight convex curve on the column (called 'entasis') which gives rise to the greatest diameter about a third of the way up. In addition each column leans slightly inwards, while the corner columns slant diagonally towards the interior, as they are a combination of front and side supports. Also, the entire building is not built on a level platform, but on a platform curving slightly upwards. If bearings are taken along the steps, the curvature, which on the long sides has a 10 cm difference in height, is very clear; it continues up to the roof. This building detail meant that for the stone-masons no square was really right-angled, but was always slightly trapezoidal, and that no column drum had a regular side, top or bottom; a consideration only of these minimal differences shows that the Parthenon is an unbelievable piece of work. (For the modern scholar the slight shifts of proportion, in conjunction with, for example, surface weathering, offer the possibility of locating the exact position of an isolated architectural member.) The overall impression of this living structure, which must be likened to a sculptured body, is governed by the harmony of the whole; for example, the substructure would not look optically correct without the upward curvature and the temple would thus lose much of its attraction (compare the 1:1 copy in Nashville, USA, which does not have these optical refinements).

Another detail is also important. There is a basic problem with Doric architecture in that the triglyphs, which are normally set over the middle of each column, cannot lie over the angle columns on the corner of the temple, since they should finish off the frieze at the corner (the so-called corner triglyph problem, which does not exist in the continuous Ionic frieze). Therefore, either the outside metope was widened on the older buildings or the angle column was set closer in order to close the gap; the outside triglyph was then on the corner of the entablature. However, even when combined, both solutions were immediately apparent and disturbed the overall impression. The builders of the Parthenon had a new solution, which can only be observed by the practised eye if the viewer is aware of it: the angle columns are closer together, thus creating a narrower intercolumniation; an additional correction is the contraction of the corner metopes over the outer intercolumniation which however become wider towards the centre.

The degree to which a Classical building project, even one as clever as this, can alter during construction is shown by a recently observed change of design. On the east side of the pronaos, the lower column drums, which had already been set into their places, were taken down again relatively early in the construction, moved a few centimetres to the west and put closer together; and the steps of the pronaos were cut back some 5 cm. Probably the cause of this was the design of the frieze, which would later be carved *in situ*, but for which the depth of the reliefs and the projection of the figures as well as the projecting cyma above the frieze had to be calculated at this point. The fact that strips (regulae) are present under the frieze, which actually belong to a Doric metope and triglyph frieze, not to an Ionic relief frieze, had long since given rise to the idea that the building plan had been changed here. The modifications now known in the stylobate and in the columns of the pronaos verify these alterations, the cause of which, the inclusion of the frieze, was so important to the builders, that they did not shrink from laborious changes.

The Architectural Sculpture (Figure **14**). In addition to the usual painted decoration found on all ancient temples the rich adornment of this building contributed to its impressive appearance. Four different types of sculpture make the building stand out: the pedimental figures and the relief metopes on the outside and the continuous frieze round the top of the cella and the huge gold and ivory statue of Athena Parthenos inside. The complete ornamentation presents a closely woven tapestry of political messages in mythical dress, the majority of which were unique in their time. Most of the sculptures are no longer on the building today, but in different European museums, especially in London. However, there is still a lot to see in Athens itself. Some pieces which are being replaced by silaceous sand casts, are stored in the Acropolis museum. The Makriyanni Museum south of the Acropolis, opposite the Theatre of Dionysos, houses plaster casts of the sculptures scattered all over the world and reconstructions of the originals. (There are also many models of the Acropolis in its different historical phases here, as well as documentation of the restorations.)

The Pedimental Sculptures (Figure **15**).[54] The visitor to the Acropolis saw the west pediment first (Plate 9), but in fact the east pediment on the entrance side of the Parthenon was more important. The birth of Athena springing fully armed from the head of Zeus is depicted here. Both gods are shown larger than life-size in the middle of the pediment, while on either side of them, reaching to the corners, the other gods attend the event. The entire scene is framed by two chariots, that of the sun god and that of the moon goddess, symbolising a day in the life of the world. The representation is easy to interpret: Athena (and Athens with her) is widely acclaimed, both as the daughter of Zeus and because of her intellectual ability ('born from the head'). The west pediment depicts another myth, that of the contest between Athena and Poseidon for the land of Attica. The two divinities embody the important foundations on which the might of Athens was based, namely trade (olive oil) and mastery of the sea. Their dramatic conflict emphasises the particular importance of Attica; everybody knew that both divinities were united on the Acropolis in the Erechtheion.

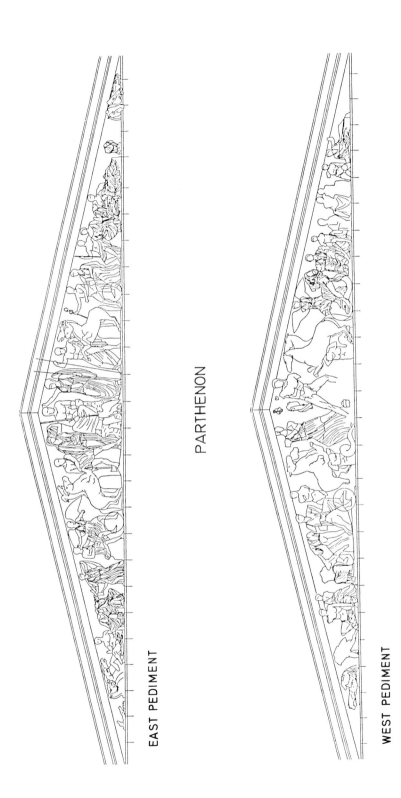

EAST PEDIMENT

PARTHENON

WEST PEDIMENT

Figure 15 Athens, Acropolis: Parthenon, the pedimental sculptures (after Berger).

The Metopes.[55] Whereas the pediments had religious themes, the metopes, of which there were ninety-two, depicted in mythical garb the heroic acts of the Athenians during the Persian Wars. On the east side the mythical war of the gods against the giants was depicted; on the other sides Greeks fight barbarians (Amazons and Trojans) and Centaurs. In summary, one could say everything non-Greek was rough and uncivilised and justified its defeat by the excellence of Greek heroism, as illustrated in the mythical past and in recent history.

The Frieze.[56] This building component breaks up the Doric order of the temple; it really belongs to the Ionic order and was put in as an extra element (after a change of building plan). The regulae and guttae, which should really only be put under the triglyphs of the Doric order (see Figure **108**), appear below it (Plate 13). Their presence makes it clear that metopes were planned for the short sides of the cella, as in the Temple of Zeus at Olympia. In the original c. 160 m-long continuous frieze, the Panathenaic Festival was depicted in an ideal form. Many details of the procession can be imagined: the sacrificial animals, the votive offerings and the stewards; there are, however, also many timeless, non-individual motifs; the nakedness of the youths depicts the general conception of Athenian youth; state organisations are embodied, such as the Tribes (Phylai), and the assembly of gods on the east pediment must also be seen in this connection. The theme was not only that of the most important festival of democratic Athens, that is the procession through the city to the Acropolis in honour of Athena and the handing over of the newly woven vestment (peplos) for the ancient statue of the city goddess, but other religious festivities were also represented. The Hydria-carriers, for example, refer to the payment of tribute (aparche) by the members of the Delian League, which took place during the Festival of Dionysos, and the picture on the east frieze in which girls carry covered objects on trays should refer to the arrhephoroi. The horse racing and chariot races, which take up more than half the length of the frieze, add an aristocratic, and, therefore, an old un-democratic trait, to the pictorial theme. In spite of the disunity of the themes the composition offers a unified picture. It was in two parts: two processions, consisting of riders (Plate 14), chariots, gift-bearers and other personnel, set out from the south-west corner in opposite directions (the part on the west side was still on the building a few years ago and is very much damaged today) until they met in the centre of the east end where the gods, relaxing on their stools and thrones, frame the highpoint of the festival (the arrhephoria and the giving of the peplos). The event is portrayed as timeless and as an eternal ritual and thus embodies the attempt of Athens to win primacy and leadership. (New evidence – a Lesbian cyma at the top of the wall – was found to show that there was an interior frieze in the pronaos above the door and the windows which is lost today.)

The Athena Parthenos.[57] The 12 m-high statue of Athena Parthenos, clothed in a richly decorated garment of pale ivory and shining gold, stood in the interior of the building, emphasised by clever lighting and architectural framing (Plate 15; small Roman copies in the National Museum, Room 20, see p. 120). Pausanias tells us that there were sphinxes, winged horses and griffins on her helmet and a huge shield on her left side, which had reliefs of the Battle of the Amazons on the outside and a painting of the Gigantomachy on the inside; there were even reliefs on the soles of her shoes: a battle of Greeks and Centaurs, repeating once more the theme of the metopes. The assembly of the gods on the east frieze appears yet again on the base of the figure, on which the myth of Pandora is portrayed. The peaceful statue of Athena Parthenos stretches out her right hand on which a Nike hovers symbolising victorious Athens. A further function of the statue incorporated the political programme of that time: her gold sheeting was part of the city treasure; other valuable articles were also stored in the inner sanctuary (known from inventory inscriptions), which thus, like all ancient temples, became a kind of bank (treasury).

When admiring the Parthenon the visitor must have two things in mind, that is first the harmonious beauty of the architecture and sculpture, which had never been achieved before, and second the political programme embodied in the entire work of art. The visitor can see the ruins as just a marble relic of times gone by, or can admire a successful combination of art and politics.

The Later History of the Parthenon.[58] In the period immediately after the completion of the Parthenon no extensive alterations were undertaken. After the Battle of Granikos (334 BC) Alexander the Great gave a gift of shields to Athens, of which a selection was clamped onto the east architrave with a dedicatory inscription; as the conqueror of the Persians, he saw himself as the successor of the Classical Athenians, whose legacy he had taken over. Other Hellenistic rulers erected larger monuments, for example, the Pergamenes gave a pillar with a chariot on it, which was put up in front of the north-east corner of the Parthenon, in the most prominent place (Figure **6**.13);[59] after its destruction its components were scattered around the Acropolis; the cutting for it in the rock can still be seen today. In AD 61/62 the Emperor Nero had a three-line inscription added to the east architrave,[60] made of individual bronze letters and pinned on in alternation with the shields of Alexander. This inscription took account of the pillar base of the Pergamenes, which was still standing and which, under the Roman emperors, carried the statue of a Roman leader of the Julio-Claudian family (Augustus?). The Parthenon first underwent extensive alterations in late Antiquity. The inner row of columns was replaced after a fire by columns taken from a Hellenistic building (once in the Plaka area), and the main room was turned into a three-aisled basilica. Towards the end of the sixth century AD, when pagan cults had long since been forbidden, the Parthenon became a Christian church. The pronaos with the church apse, as well as the peristasis, were still almost intact until the Venetian destruction of 1687. After this the Turks built a small mosque in it (Figure **16**). At the beginning of the nineteenth century the Scottish Lord Elgin obtained a large portion of the Classical sculptures, had them torn down from the building and took them to London (of some sculptures which then were in a much better condition than today – for example the west frieze – he took casts: Plate 14). Cleaning began in the building after 1834; during this all the Turkish remains were removed. It was not until the beginning of the twentieth century that restoration was started with partial rebuilding, which is being corrected and continued at present.

Figure 16 Athens, Acropolis: the Parthenon with the mosque and the Turkish village, *c.* 1750 (after Stuart and Revett).

Photo DAI Athens (Akr 435)

The Restoration.[61] As is the case of all the Acropolis buildings, so too with the Parthenon, the removal of the rusty clamps and dowels and of the sculptures, which had been eroded by pollution, was an urgent necessity, even though it had already been restored and partly rebuilt between 1898 and 1933 (Plate 11). An exact inventory of all the blocks scattered over the Acropolis has enabled the restoration of the architecture, which had long disappeared, with the original material. In the 1980s and 1990s the east and west sides and the cella walls were the focus of a huge restoration project (Plate 12). The east metopes were removed in 1990 and replaced with silaceous sand casts. Much care has been lavished on the restoration of the pronaos: large parts of the six columns destroyed in 1687 and the entablature above them have been found and can now be rebuilt, and a cast of the frieze be put in its original place. Thus the east façade would lose its ruined aspect and appear again as a unity, close to its original appearance. However, even the post-Classical alterations will not entirely disappear; it is planned to indicate the chancel of the Christian basilica with some blocks and to put up some columns in the interior of the cella. Since the work is being carried out conscientiously and responsibly, its completion will take many years.

The **Acropolis east of the Parthenon**. East of the Parthenon and aligned with its central axis there is a rectangular foundation and two curved entablature blocks, of which one bears the dedicatory inscription for a **temple of Roma and**

Augustus (Figure **6**.14).[62] Together with other building components they suggest the reconstruction of a round temple with no cella, only with nine columns standing on a platform, which replicate those of the Erechtheion. The distance between the columns was widened on one side to allow an unobstructed view of the statues of the city goddess of Rome and the first Roman emperor, which must be imagined inside the monopteros which looked like a baldachin. Since the Classical Parthenon was in the background, the two claimants to political leadership thus met in architectural form: the visitor saw the personification of Rome and Augustus in front of Athena Parthenos, who was visible through the open cella doors.

Further east and north the whole surface of the Acropolis rock is cut and prepared for foundation beddings. The **Temple of Zeus Polieus** (Figure **6**.15),[63] the leader of the Olympian gods in his role of protector of the city, and the **Heroon of Pandion**, the mythical Attic hero (Figure **6**.16), were situated here.[64] Both basically consisted of open areas surrounded by walls in which perhaps simple altars or, if need be, small shrines formed the centres of these ancient cults.

Panorama. On the east end of the Acropolis a modern platform, the Belvedere, has been built (Figure **6**.17) from which a rewarding view of Athens can be obtained. At the foot of the rock the Lysikrates Monument can be seen while the Arch of Hadrian and the Olympieion lie on the axis of this monument and Lysikrates Street. Further south-east the marble stadium of Herodes Atticus shines amongst the pines and opposite it lies the National Garden with the Zappeion, a building for state receptions and exhibitions, while, beyond, the view extends over the modern city to Mt. Hymettos. A walk round the Acropolis walls to see the view from all sides gives a very good sense of orientation. In the north the tiled roofs of the Plaka and the excavation area of the Roman Agora with the Tower of the Winds and the Library of Hadrian can be seen (Plate 22); further west the Athenian Agora lies behind the reconstructed Stoa of Attalos. In the background the modern city seems to stretch without limit; it engulfs Lykabettos Hill and Tourkovounia and stretches to the foothills of Mts Parnes and Pentelikon. On the south side of the Parthenon a good impression of the Theatre of Dionysos and the Asklepieion can be obtained; the ground plan of this area is easy to make out from the heights of the Acropolis. Further west the Odeion of Herodes Atticus is cut into the rock. Finally, from the steps of the Propylaea there is a wonderful view of Mouseion Hill to the west with the Philopappos Monument and the Pnyx (Meeting Place of the Assembly), of the Hill of the Nymphs with the old Observatory and of the Areopagos right at the foot of the Acropolis. In the distance Piraeus can be seen and the mountains of Salamis, further south Aegina and, in clear weather, the east coast of the Peloponnese.

The **Temple of Aphrodite** (Figure **6**.20).[65] On entering or leaving the Acropolis a plateau in the rock with a few marble blocks, upon which a small temple once stood, can be seen to the south below the Temple of Nike. A few entablature blocks have been assigned to this building; they lie near the Beulé Gate at the ascent to the Propylaea and show a frieze of doves, Aphrodite's sacred birds. The inscription on the flat architrave announces that the Late Classical temple was erected to Aphrodite Pandemos. The temple was conflated by the written sources of late Antiquity with the sanctuary of Aphrodite on the north slope of the Acropolis; this has led to lengthy discussions over the position of the Archaic Agora (see pp. 69–70).

The **Acropolis Museum**. The museum is built in a hollow in the south-east corner of the Acropolis, where there must have been a small entrance in the Mycenaean period. It mostly contains finds from the Acropolis and is arranged chronologically according to the development of Greek art.[66] A new museum is planned below the Acropolis because the storerooms are overfull. A visit to the Makriyanni Museum is recommended as an interesting supplement to the Acropolis Museum, which is one of the most important in Greece. At the Makriyanni Museum there is much information concerning the Parthenon and its sculptures from models and casts, as well as changing exhibitions. The following tour round the Acropolis Museum describes only the most important objects; the numbers refer to the inventory numbers on the exhibits. The entrance ticket to the Acropolis includes entry to the museum.

Beyond the vestibule (see p. 46) Room I contains monuments belonging to the early sixth century BC. Of importance is a painted limestone relief, which belonged to the Old Athena Temple, depicting a lioness devouring a calf; a second lion must have been opposite (4). The figure of a gorgon with a snake belt (701) probably once crowned the roof (akroterion) of the Hecatompedon, while relief fragments of panthers, a lion's head and a four-horse chariot adorned its metopes. The pedimental relief belonging to an unknown small building depicts Herakles fighting the nine-headed Hydra (1). In the entrance to the next room are a snake (41) and a small owl, the symbolic animals of the city of Athens and of Athena (56); both were probably once parts of pedimental decoration.

Room II. The pedimental reliefs and statues from three unknown buildings are the most important pieces after the Calf-bearer (Moschophoros). On the left, next to the entrance, the introduction of Herakles to Olympos by Hermes is shown with Zeus enthroned in the centre with his wife Hera (9, 55). On the long wall on the left Herakles fights Triton (35); opposite is a limestone pediment with a monster with three bodies, on which the original colour can still be seen, as well as the expressive faces of the old men (2). Scholars have combined both pedimental groups with the lioness and calf in Room III, so that, symmetrically doubled, it filled the middle of the tympanon and the two mythical images filled the corners. An unproven theory suggests that it is the decoration of the pediment of the Hecatompedon. In the middle of the room is the marble statue of the Calf-bearer (624), an old man with long curly hair and beard clad in a thin cloak, who carries a male sacrificial calf on his shoulders. This Archaic statue (c. 570/560 BC) is a standard type: the Archaic smile, the frontal stance and the left foot placed forward are typical of this type, which is found on all male Archaic figures ('kouroi'). Although the inscription on the base names the dedicator as Rhombos and the statue is supposed to portray him, yet the representation is entirely conventional. The individual parts and the limbs of the body do not form a unified whole, as they do in the Late Archaic and Classical periods. The social rank of the donor is rarely known, but in the Early and Middle Archaic period only aristocratic families had enough wealth for such gifts. Dedications from less wealthy people, such as craftsmen, are not known (see below) until around 500 BC.

Room III. On the left wall are the remains of a group depicting a lion attacking a bull, which perhaps belonged to the Hecatompedon. On the right are maidens from sculpture workshops in the Cyclades (619, 677) and statues of seated females, perhaps Athena (618, 620).

Room IV. In this room, which is divided into three parts, the masterpieces, which were part of the statuary decoration of the Acropolis before the Persian Wars, can be seen. They illustrate both the rich variety and the development of Archaic art, as a few examples will show, and answer some socio-historical questions. To begin with there are three typically Attic sculptures: the Peplos Kore, the Rampin Rider and a crouching dog. The nobles were the riders and owners of horses in the Archaic period (more examples on the left) and so this type of gift, as well as the sculpture of the dog (143), which portrays the aristocracy at its leisure-time pursuit of hunting, were typical dedications of the Attic upper classes to the goddesses Athena and Artemis. The same applies to the korai (maidens). In the victory odes, which were sung in the homes of the nobles, women were often compared to thoroughbred horses and their beauty praised, as if they were ornaments. The votive statues of korai also indicate the high standard of living of the upper class, not only in Attica, but also in other regions and islands of Greece. The Rampin Rider (590; c. 550 BC), named after a French excavator, who took the head to the Louvre in Paris (that in Athens is a copy), wears an oak leaf crown on the head suggesting a human victor in horse racing; recently more Archaic riders have been restored from fragments on the Acropolis, one of them with painted Persian clothes, worn by Athenian riders as well. The Peplos Kore (679; c. 540 BC; Plate 16) is a typical representation of the austere Archaic Attic maiden in marble sculpture. Recent research (beaming colour-activated UV light onto the statue) has shown that the sculpture was richly painted, with figuratively decorated friezes, which softened the simple appearance we see today. (Surprisingly it has been proposed that the original garment was not the severe Doric peplos, but that originally the painting depicted three garments worn one above the other and that the Peplos Kore should be interpreted as Athena.) The painting of the almond-shaped eyes and the long curls of hair hanging on the shoulders give the statue a life-like appearance. In contrast to the sober sculpting of this figure the Athenian maiden statues developed a luxurious multiplicity of forms and motifs under the influence of Ionic and pre-Ionic art. The undergarments are more richly folded; the cloaks often hang diagonally across the upper body and are occasionally drawn towards the side with the left hand; thus a charming contrast develops between the sharp vertical folds of the undergarments and the fan-shaped effect with zigzag borders arising where the cloak is gathered to the side. In addition the Ionic garment appears softer and thinner and moulds itself more closely on the bodies of the maidens in contrast to the peploi almost without folds worn by maidens sculpted in the pure Attic style. The fact that the marble was painted added to the highly ornamental appearance of the statues; this was more apparent in antiquity. A large number of both types of maiden statue are collected at the back of Room IV: two statues of differing sizes by a Chian artist dating to c. 520 BC (small 675, large 682); Attic maidens with obvious Ionic influence, but with more restrained garments and faces (670, 685, 674; all c. 500 BC); in the middle of the semicircle is a seated Athena (625; c. 530 BC) wearing a chiton with an aegis over it, a characteristic part of the 'clothing' of this goddess, which is decorated in the middle with a hideous gorgon; this headless and much worn statue could be the Athena of Endoios mentioned by Pausanias and would then be one of the few statues which was set up again after the Persian destruction, probably because it was a cult image. On the right side of the room there are some seated statuettes of scribes (the most interesting one is 629; the head has recently been recognised from a fragment in the Louvre – plaster copy here – and from a fragment in the Acropolis storeroom and united with the body), on which the influence of Egyptian sculpture is particularly apparent in the frontal position and the stance. Some Archaic votive reliefs which depict gods are also worth mentioning (in the entry to Room IV: 581, a family offering gifts to Athena; in the doorway to Room V: 121, Athena Promachos; 1342/3, two fragments of a frieze with Hermes, recognisable from his broad-brimmed hat, together with a charioteer and a four-horse chariot).

Room V. The most important sculptures in this room are the pediment figures with the Gigantomachy from the east side of the Old Temple of Athena (631; c. 515 BC): Athena and Zeus facing outwards from the middle of the pediment fight against two giants lying on the ground. The giants embody ancient monsters against which the intellectually superior Olympian gods have successfully fought; the theme is repeatedly portrayed as an act of war in Greek art. The Antenor Kore (681; c. 520 BC) is very similar to the pedimental figures in marble technique and style; she stands out on account of her size and her rich garments with deep undercut and drilled folds; indeed in her formal severity she appears almost monumental. The base at her side, which probably belongs to her, carries an inscription naming the Attic sculptor Antenor as her creator commissioned by a certain Nearchos. It is interesting that a potter of this name is known from that time, so that it can perhaps be concluded that potter and donor were the same person and that the offering is, therefore, that of an Attic craftsman; furthermore, it suggests that the simple citizen now had the means and the self-confidence to give offerings as costly as those of the nobles. Apparently the same sculptor could work for people of different social class, for according to the sources Antenor also worked for the noble family of the Alcmaeonids; he further carried out a commission from the state, carving the first portrait group of the Tyrannicides, Harmodios and Aristogeiton, which was removed by the Persians in 480 BC. In the small side-room of Room V the frieze of the Temple of Nike has been on show since autumn 1998: reliefs with the depiction of battles of Greeks against enemies and an assembly of the Olympian gods (of the east side of the temple).

Room VI. The best sculptures dating to the transition from the Archaic to the Classical period can be seen here. A relief fragment shows a potter in a richly folded garment sitting on a stool (1332; *c.* 500 BC); he holds two drinking cups in his hand as a sign of his trade; the representation, which indicates the growing self-confidence of the simple citizen of Athens in the Late Archaic period, unites the old elements of form (the garment) with the new ones (the short hair). The Euthydikos Kore, named after the dedicatory inscription on her base (686, 609; *c.* 490 BC), wears a garment sculpted in the Archaic fashion, but she no longer has Archaic features. In the Kritios Boy (698), a statue of a youth which was made around the time of the Persian destruction in 480 BC, the new style of Greek sculpture can be seen. The limbs are not carved as separate components, as in the case of the Early Archaic figures, but have been carved as a physical entity; the frontal stance of the figure and the former rigid position of the feet have been slightly eased; the head bends slightly downwards and to the side and the weight is distributed between the supporting leg and the relaxed leg. In sense of form the Blond Boy (689; shortly before 480 BC) combines old and new elements. At first glance the long Archaic curls seem to have given way to a modern haircut, for the face is framed only by short strands of hair pulled forward. However, from the sides and from behind the long plaits, relics of a long-gone age, can be seen curving artistically round the head to form a knot. The small stele of the 'mourning' Athena is a masterpiece dating to the early phase of Classical art, the Severe Style. She stands, wearing a girded peplos and a helmet on her head, with her right hand resting on a lance, before a pillar, the meaning of which is unclear; it might be a boundary stone, a casualty list or a votive stele. The calm, severe stance and the simple form are typical of this type of art, which appears in monumental form in the pediments of the Temple of Zeus at Olympia. The winged Nike (on the other side of the door) was set up on the Acropolis just after the Battle of Marathon (490 BC) commemorating the Greek leader (polemarchos) Kallimachos who promised this votive gift before the battle; it must have been set up by some other persons since Kallimachos died at Marathon. The base, an Ionic column with the dedicatory inscription (Epigraphical Museum), was heavily damaged and hacked into many pieces by the Persians as an act of revenge during the sack of Athens in 480 BC.

Room VII. This small room contains reconstructed models of the Parthenon pediments (13) and some ornamental sculptures from it (see p. 36). They include the torso of Poseidon from the west pediment (1885), some smaller fragments of metopes and a complete slab depicting a Centaur attacking a Lapith woman.

Room VIII. The Parthenon frieze from the north side of the cella is represented by slabs with figures of riders, of young men who jump on and off chariots at full speed (Apobates), of officials, kithara players and bearers of gifts as well as men with sacrificial animals, which include two beautifully carved cows (the picture tries to suggest that one is running directly towards the sacrifice, for the agreement of the animal was necessary for its sacrifice). Slabs from the south frieze again show riders, but are not so well preserved. Some of the reliefs from the east frieze with the assembly of the gods are noteworthy. The bearded

Poseidon can be recognised in conversation with the young Apollo, as well as Artemis and Aphrodite with the young Eros nestling up to her (extensively restored after an old cast). Part of the room is closed for the restoration of the west frieze (Plates 13–14). For this reason the sculptures of the Erechtheion frieze are temporarily not on view (see p. 29). The white marble figures used to be displayed against a modern dark background as they were on the temple; their clothes show the same Rich Style as the parapet reliefs from the Nike bastion, which adorned the three sides of the high substructure of the temple (at the end of the room on the right). On these reliefs the flowing, mobile bodies in their draperies, in which the contrast between the sharp ridges of the folds and the material clinging closely to the body is emphasised, are rightly famous as master-pieces of Classical art. The sculpture here has reached an artistic peak in a completely different way from the Parthenon reliefs. On the Parthenon the content of the pictures corresponds to the festive rhythm and the quiet Classical forms, whereas the light, elegant art form here is in complete contrast to the forceful and bloody activity of the representation, the sacrifice of the bull (temporarily not on view).

Room IX. Four of the Caryatids which supported the roof of the south porch of the Erechtheion are displayed in this air-conditioned room behind a glass screen; a fifth is in London and the sixth is being treated in the restoration work-shop in an attempt to stop the damage to the marble. The figures wear the heavy peplos with overfall and belt; their heads support the echinus of the capi-tals decorated with bead-and-reel and egg-and-dart. The overall proportions, the shape of the body, which can be seen clearly under the garments, and the flowing folds were an innovation at that time; in contrast, the long hair and the plaits round the head (compare the Blond Boy, Room VI) as well as the frontal stance of the figures appear old-fashioned. On the wall opposite there is the fragment of a well-known relief with part of the depiction of a trireme (triere).

Vestibule. Next to two bases with relief scenes, a pyrrhic dance with a chorus of singers (1338; 323 BC) and the Apobates (leaping on and off a speeding chariot), a group is displayed which is one of the few original Classical votive statues remaining on the Acropolis. Most Greek sculptures were made of bronze and were victims of metal robbing in later ages; we know of them today only from Roman marble copies. The fragmentary group of Prokne and Itys (1358; c. 420 BC) is an exception. It is based on a gruesome myth: Prokne, the daughter of the Attic King Pandion, was married to Tereus, King of the Thracians, by whom she had a son, Itys. Tereus committed adultery with his wife's sister, Philomele; he raped her and then cut her tongue out so that she could not tell her fate. However, Philomele wove the story into a garment and thus informed Prokne, who punished her husband by killing their son Itys and serving him up to Tereus as a meal. The group depicts, with typical Classical restraint, the moment in which Prokne decides on the murder, while her son leans against her legs in ignorance of his fate; it is not the gory deed which is shown but rather the dramatic psychological moment of decision. The myth then describes how Tereus pursued both sisters and how all were turned into birds; Tereus into a hoopoe, Prokne into a nightingale and Philomele into a swallow. In the Classical period statuary groups on the Acropolis certainly had other functions beyond depicting myths. At a time when Athens was turning against foreign immigrants and making war on insubordinate allies, the statues should also be understood as a political warning: the Athenian Prokne takes violent revenge on a barbaric foreigner. A portrait of Alexander the Great (1331; c. 330 BC or a late Hellenistic invention of the first century BC, to the left of Prokne) is also a fine piece of work; opposite is the head of the cult statue of Artemis Brauronia, an original work of Praxiteles (mid-fourth century BC), and at the side wall a Roman portrait head of a bearded philosopher (fourth/fifth century AD).

3   The slopes of the Acropolis and the Peripatos (Figures **5**.8–10; **6**.20–36)

I n Antiquity a path ran round the Acropolis about halfway up. This **Peripatos** (ring road) was bordered by numerous sanctuaries which were built on the slopes of the Acropolis from very early on and continued to be founded in the Classical period. There were sanctuaries of Dionysos and Asklepios on the south side and of Aphrodite, Pan, Apollo and Zeus on the north slope. In addition to these sanctuaries with their temples there are also secular buildings: the Odeion of Perikles, the Stoa of Eumenes and the Odeion of Herodes Atticus are impressive buildings on the south slope, while on the north slope a fountain house supplied water to the city.

At the present time the Peripatos is being restored and it is not possible to go round the Citadel along its complete length. The protection of the rock face, which has suffered as much as the ancient buildings from modern pollution, is of particular importance. In the last few years an important basis for the preservation of the monuments on and below the Acropolis has been set up by injecting sealing fluid into the numerous cracks and by reinforcing larger boulders. In addition, a long-term research project on the precinct of Dionysos on the south slope of the Acropolis has been started together with the restoration of its adjacent sanctuaries, which will be continued over the next years.

Walk round the Acropolis (Plate 4). The entrance to the precinct of Dionysos is on Dionysiou Areopagitou Street. (The visitor can leave the south slope below the Temple of Nike and above the Odeion of Herodes Atticus and visit the Temple of Aphrodite Pandemos at the foot of the Nike Bastion (see pp. 41–2).

The **Odeion of Herodes Atticus** (Figure **6**.21). On the south-west side of the Acropolis a large semicircle of marble seats is built onto the rock, a gift of the rich Athenian Herodes Atticus between AD 160 and 170 in memory of his wife Regilla.[67] The layout of the Odeion differs in two important points from that of a Greek theatre. First, the front has a 28 m-high three-storey stage façade of limestone blocks and masonry with a core of rubble, which cuts the auditorium exactly on the half circle. In contrast, the auditorium of a Greek theatre is usually almost a three-quarter circle. Moreover, Greek theatres were open to the sky, but that of Herodes Atticus was roofed, making it an Odeion. This roof was a technical masterpiece of its time and remains so today. Extra-long cedars from Lebanon had to be imported for the roof timbers to cover the huge span of the area (38 m radius). On the interior the floor mosaics, the walls panelled with different coloured marble, the decoration of the columns on the stage and the statues displayed in niches were all most impressive; none exist today. After excavation had taken place the marble seats were restored in the 1950s so that in summer the theatre, now open to the sky, can be used for performances: concerts, plays by ancient Greek and modern authors and ballet are all on the programme; it is particularly relaxing to sit below the floodlit buildings of the Acropolis in the mild night air in a 'Classical' surrounding and recover from the heat of the day.

Older houses dating back to the Classical period had to be torn down for the construction of the Odeion. The remains of some such houses can be seen below it; there was also a sanctuary of the nymphs here, to which an inscribed boundary stone bears witness.

The **Stoa of Eumenes** (Figure **6**.22). On the level of the Odeion vestibule a 163 m-long two-storey portico extends eastwards, the interior of which is divided into two aisles by a row of columns.[68] Today little remains of this huge building, which was donated by the Pergamene King Eumenes II (197–159 BC) to protect visitors to the Theatre of Dionysos from the weather. The terrace for the stoa with the foundations for the middle row of columns and the massive retaining wall with its series of arches, built against the hillside which had been partly dug out for the building, can all be recognised. However, the 64 outer columns are missing as well as all the supports for the interior and for the upper floor and the two staircases on the sides. In Antiquity the stoa looked very similar to the Stoa of Attalos in the Greek Agora (apart from the absence of the back rooms), which was perhaps designed by the same architect. It is astonishing that the marble components (capitals, cornices, etc.) were transported from distant Pergamon in Asia Minor; only the blocks of the back wall were made of blue-grey Hymettian marble. The old Peripatos ran right above the stoa, but care was taken to preserve it when the stoa was built; in contrast in the area of the Odeion to the north it was relocated to lead round the back of the Odeion and a stairway was built at the junction of the stoa and the Odeion to give access to it.

Metal Foundry (Figure **6**.23). In the north-east above the Odeion of Herodes Atticus there is a huge oval pit surrounded by a modern wall. Bronze remains found here indicate that it was a foundry in which votive statues for the Acropolis were probably made. The pit was the centre of a workshop onto which two stoas were joined as wings.

The Asklepieion lies east of this bronze foundry; it was founded in 419 BC and expanded over the years; other divinities were also worshipped here, such as Hygieia and Isis. At the end of the area in the west are the foundations of two smaller shrines (probably Roman, one is supposed to be a temple to Isis, and south of these lies a huge barrel-vaulted Byzantine cistern.

Asklepieion (Figure **6**.24). The Asklepieion[69] is bordered in the east and above the Stoa of Eumenes by the Peripatos. It consists of two large buildings with stoas, with a spring at the centre of each. These springs, which were probably in use from prehistoric times, were most likely the reason for the establishment of the healing cult here. To the west on the rock behind a small diagonally placed temple there was an **Archaic spring basin** (Figure **5**.9), the walls of which are constructed of well-made polygonal masonry. This Archaic spring basin was bordered by a small shrine with a three-columned Doric façade. An inscription in the precinct wall on the south side refers to the spring house with the words 'boundary of the spring (Horos Krenes)' (Figure **6**.25). To the east adjoining the spring house was a building consisting of four square rooms containing beds with a stoa in front. The pilgrims underwent the healing sleep here (Incubation Stoa = enkoimeterion) and participated at the symposia (banquets) during the religious festivals. Between this and the second more easterly building of the Asklepieion a gate from the Peripatos gave entry to the entire area. The remaining buildings date to a later period, but were probably modelled on the Classical (wooden?) predecessors. The east part of the sanctuary consisted of a court-yard with a small prostyle temple and the Altar of Asklepios together with a small stoa on the south and a larger one on the north side. The limestone rock of the Acropolis was cut back to a great height to accommodate the latter. This stoa was divided into two aisles by an interior supporting wall and had an upper storey reached by a stairway at the east end. The second spring house of the Asklepieion could be reached from this stoa; it was a circular room cut out of the rock, which was originally a cave that had been widened; there was prob-ably cult activity at this place before 419 BC. The sacred tradition of the place has continued right up to today, with the foundation of a small chapel in the cave in the Byzantine period. There was a separate open square building with a deep round shaft in its centre to the west of the stoa on a higher terrace. It was covered by a baldachin supported on four columns. It is a Bothros, a pit into which dedications were thrown to the earth (chthonic) deities. The Asklepieion was apparently much used immediately after its foundation and in the following centuries. Numerous votive gifts, including many reliefs (representations of the gods Asklepios and Hygieia with worshippers as well as depictions of medical apparatus, today in the National Museum), bear witness to this, as well as 'daughter' shrines at other Greek sites (known, for example, at Sounion from an inscription). The building was destroyed in the third century AD but quickly rebuilt. In the sixth century the ancient building was torn down and a three-aisled basilica for the Ay. Anargyroi (the Holy Doctors) built on the terrace; its walls contained numerous building components and pieces of broken sculpture. Today nothing is left of this church except a few marble blocks with a cross on them.

The Asklepieion was founded in 420/419 BC by a man called Telemachos who brought the cult from Epidauros to the Acropolis via the Athenian Eleusinion. The festival of Asklepios was, therefore, closely connected to the Eleusinian one both in its content and in its placing on the Attic festival calendar. The endowment is known from a fragmentary votive relief with an inscription below it (there is a reconstruction of all fragments in the Makrygianni Museum); this is a strange document which raises many questions: how could a private citizen in those particular years found a temple in such a prominent place? On what state and religious support was he relying? Had the foundation anything to do with the dreadful plague of 429 BC and with the Peloponnesian War which began in 431 BC? Is Asklepios, whose cult quickly spread in Attica (see the Temple of Amphiaraos at Oropos, which is almost contemporary), a god of 'crisis' who would protect people from future similar disasters? The foundation of the Asklepieion falls in the time of the peace of Nikias, but the citizens could not have known how short that would be. The votive relief, which shows parts of the temple, also raises topographic and architectural questions, such as the position of the entrance building illustrated (the propylon of the temple or another entrance?) and the meaning of the stork-like bird (the symbol of the ancient Pelargikon (pelargos = stork), which surrounded the Acropolis in Mycenaean times).

The **Sanctuary of Dionysos**. The Peripatos rises a few steps from the Asklepieion to the **Theatre of Dionysos** (Figure **6**.28), which it crosses on an aisle which runs through the theatre round the seats. The theatre (Plate 17) is the most impressive part of the sanctuary today, but it was not the focal point and in its present form does not belong to the oldest buildings of the precinct. The cultic centre of the god of wine was his temple on the south side in front of the later stage building.[70] The small temple (Figures **5**.10; **6**.26) lay at the west end of a long Doric stoa first built in the fourth century BC. The temple faced east and had two columns in antis; only the stones in the north-west corner are left from its building components; parts of the Doric poros architecture, a piece of a pedimental relief and fragments of marble sculptures from the tympanon have also been found.[71] It must have been built in the second half of the sixth century, c. 530 BC, and then rebuilt c. 480 BC; it contained the old wooden cult figure of Dionysos Eleuthereus. In the late fifth century, Alkamenes, a pupil of Pheidias, produced a new chryselephantine cult figure. It is not known where this statue was kept initially; in the middle of the fourth century it was placed in a new Temple of Dionysos (Figure **6**.27), which stood on the south side next to the old one on breccia foundations, while the superstructure was of fine limestone blocks, now almost completely gone. The new temple was larger and its façade was emphasised with a deep colonnaded forecourt, as was fitting for the famous cult statue of Alkamenes. Different altars, on which acts of sacrifice could be carried out, stood in a precinct surrounded by a wall with a propylon on the east side. A round altar dating to c. 100 BC (to be found today under a protective roof to the east of the area) is carved with thick garlands of leaves above theatre masks.

There was a wooden theatre[72] facing the opposite direction from this cult centre, three metres higher up the south slope, in the late sixth and fifth century BC, the form of which is unknown; it probably had an almost rectangular plan, similar to that known from some other early theatres (see Trachones p. 186); this is suggested by some of its stone blocks, marked by their inscriptions as seats for dignitaries of the late fifth century BC; they have no curvature, but form a straight line (they were reused as a drain cover and are put inside the stage building today). In the sixth and early fifth century plays were probably performed in a make-shift wooden building (ikria) here on the south slope of the Acropolis and in the Agora. The monumental marble Theatre of Dionysos (Figure **6**.28), still extant today, was completed under the Athenian orator and conservative politician Lykourgos (c. 390–324 BC), but had already been begun around 360 BC. Lykourgos had the ideal of Classical Athens in mind as he revived the city cults and decorated the city with new buildings. So, for example, he had statues of the three great dramatists of the fifth century, Aischylos, Sophocles and Euripides, set up in the theatre and had their plays officially published. The renovation of the theatre (although certainly begun earlier) dates to this time; marble seats were put up for the Athenian priesthood and dignitaries in a round orchestra which probably had an altar of Dionysos in the centre; the throne of the priest of Dionysos in the middle is ornamented with reliefs (Plate 18); behind are rows of limestone seats on the slope of the Acropolis, which seated about 17,000 people; on the upper edge of the auditorium the rock is cut back to make more room. Only a fraction of the seats remain today. The spectator could enter the theatre through two passages running between the side retaining walls for the seats and the stage (parodoi), or from the Peripatos above, which divided the auditorium into two circles. In the Hellenistic period the stage was elevated, as was then fashionable. The round orchestra, which was now only used by the chorus, was bounded on the south side by a building with two side projections; it had a stage façade in the middle with columns carved fully in the round standing in front of the walls. In the Hellenistic period the players acted with the upper stage façade (of wood?) on the first floor of the stage building as a backdrop. This new arrangement allowed the display of statues and thrones, which were later, under the Roman emperors, placed at a higher level and integrated into the spectators' seats. The building history of the theatre is very complicated in its details and has not yet been finally clarified; it is however certain that the building underwent many changes in the following centuries; the relief frieze and the figures of cowering Satyrs of the mid-second century AD belong to these alterations. The frieze[73] honours Dionysos, who is portrayed in the company of other gods; a careful examination of the dowel holes of the frieze, which is built into the border for the orchestra on the south side, has shown that it was reused; the position and building context of its primary use is unknown. The orchestra was also changed under the Roman emperors; it received a marble floor made of different coloured lozenges (recent investigations, not proven by excavation, have already suggested a Hellenistic date for this sectile floor); the slabs of the parapet were thickly sealed with water tight plaster so that under the emperors aquatic games (sea battles) could take place in the resulting basin. In late Antiquity a Christian church was built in the east entrance and the orchestra was used as a yard with a small spring. However, even these buildings disappeared over the centuries and finally only a small chapel was left in the orchestra, which was moved by the excavators to the east next to the theatre. The archaeological investigation of the area began in 1838 and is still not finished today. The sculpture from the theatre is displayed under a protective roof on the south-east corner of the precinct as part of the recent investigations; it includes huge statues of Satyrs and Poseidon (once standing on bases within the parodoi) as well as statues of seated playwrights; the original of the seated figure of the famous comedy writer Menander (342/1–293 BC) can be restored from the many Roman copies of the lost original; it stood on an oblong pedestal with the inscription 'Menandros' and the names of the sculptors, Kephisodotos and Timarchos, the sons of Praxiteles.[74]

The Theatre of Dionysos dating to the time of Lykourgos is the place in which the great Greek tragedies and comedies were enacted from the fourth century BC onwards. The performances took place at the chief festival of Dionysos, the Great Dionysia, in March, during which the tribute (aparche) was shown to the assembled people and children orphaned during wars were presented. On the three following days, after the performance of dithyrambic songs a tetralogy was enacted consisting of one comedy and three tragedies; performances of satyr-plays were added on. The playwright who wanted to present his work proposed a chorus and a producer (choregos) to the first official of the city, the archon, and the city supplied the actors. The plays were produced in competition; a jury of ten people judged them on their quality, but the spectators also took a lively part in the theatrical proceedings and in judging the works. The victorious choregos received a bronze tripod from the state for financing the dithyrambic production.

Choregic Monuments in the Sanctuary of Dionysos (Figure **6**.29–30). From the fourth century BC the performance of the festival plays was financed by Athenians prominent in public life, the choregoi (literally leader of the chorus). The choregos was allowed to set up his state victory prize of a tripod next to the theatre itself or along the Street of the Tripods, which led from the Sanctuary of Dionysos first east and then north round the Acropolis to the Agora. The choregos inscribed the contest in question (chorus of boys or adult males), his name and the year of his victory on the stone pedestal under the tripod. He had to pay for the erection of the pedestal himself. There was competition amongst the rich and famous politicians as to who could produce the most striking and ornate pedestal for the tripod; these could even take the form of small temples or circular buildings on high bases.[75] One such is a building which lay west of the theatre right next to the east end of the Stoa of Eumenes (Figure **6**.29). Its foundations can still be seen today, but almost all the parts of the temple-like Doric marble building are to be found in the late Antique bastion at the entrance to the Acropolis, the Beulé Gate (Figure **6**.1; see p. 17). The building was set up by the choregos Nikias in 320/319 BC. In the same year the Athenian, Thrasyllos,[76] constructed a Doric façade on the smooth rocky wall (katatome) in front of a cave above the Theatre of Dionysos and set up his tripod on it (Figure **6**.30). This monument, of which a few remains can be seen today framing the entrance to the chapel of the Panayia Spilaiotissa, was not destroyed until 1827; its original appearance is known from early engravings (Figure **17**). Thrasykles, the son of Thrasyllos, also added a large statue of

Figure 17 Athens, Acropolis: south slope with the choregic monument of
Thrasyllos, *c.* 1750 (after Stuart and Revett).
Photo DAI Athens (Hege 2536)

Dionysos on top of the façade in 271/270 BC when he, too, was victorious as
choregos (then called agonothetes). The statue is in the British Museum today.
The two columns above the Thrasyllos Monument (the cutting for a third can be
seen in the rock) are later dedications from other choregoi;[77] these extremely high
pedestals, each set on a separate base, also each carried a bronze tripod. The
Street of the Tripods[78] began east of the Theatre of Dionysos; it had countless
tripods along its left side. The foundations of other buildings which displayed victory prizes can be seen right next to the theatre.[79] The best-known tripod base,
however, lies a few hundred metres further east in the Plaka, the Lysikrates
Monument dating to 335 BC (see pp. 97–8; Figure **30**).

The **Odeion of Perikles** (Figure **6**.31). 'The Odeion was to be a copy and an
imitation of the tent of the Persian King. Inside it had a large number of seats
and many columns, while the roof, descending from a single peak (like a pyramid),
sloped down all the way round. Perikles was also responsible for this building.'
In addition to this note from Plutarch we know from Pausanias and Vitruvius that
the large, roofed multi-purpose building for concerts and musical contests lay in
the neighbourhood of the Theatre of Dionysos. The Odeion of Perikles can thus
be identified with the large squarish building to the east of the theatre; the
supporting wall of the latter makes a sharp angle to take the earlier Periclean

Odeion into account. The roofed concert hall itself is only partly excavated; its numerous interior supports, recalling the Telesterion at Eleusis, are still buried in a massive layer of earth. The Odeion, which probably was constructed by Themistokles,[80] was destroyed in 86 BC when Sulla sacked Athens, but was restored to its original appearance about 25 years later by a donation from the Cappadocian King Ariobarzanes II.

The **Sanctuaries on the East and North Slopes** (mostly not open to the public). If one follows the Acropolis round its short eastern side on the Peripatos, one arrives at the north slope with its many sanctuaries, in caves and overhangs, which can only be reached from this path. On the east side the visitor first reaches a large natural cave. A few years ago an inscription[81] was found in its entrance announcing that it was the **Aglaurion**, a shrine for Aglauros, daughter of Kekrops, which had earlier been thought to be on the north side of the Acropolis. Important new information on the Archaic topography of Athens was thus obtained from the discovery of this inscription. It is known from ancient sources that the Archaic Agora lay near the Aglaurion and that means on the east side of the Acropolis; the Prytaneion should be placed near it; in addition, the information that the city lay on the south side of the Acropolis in the time of Theseus is now plausible.[82] It is also now clear that the Greek Agora with its state administrative buildings known from the American excavations (see pp. 69–86) resulted from a replanning of the city, which was probably connected to the reforms of Kleisthenes 508/7 BC or even some years later.

On the north-east corner of the Acropolis there is a large rock right over the pathway on the front of which is an inscription describing the circular path as the Peripatos and giving its length in feet (unfortunately incompletely preserved). Next to this in a niche in the rock below the projecting rock near the Erechtheion is the **Sanctuary of Eros and Aphrodite** (Figure **6**.32). There are rectangular cuttings in the surface of the steep rock in which ancient votive reliefs were placed.[83] Inscriptions were found between these cuttings which describe the area as the Sanctuary of Aphrodite, an identification which is supported by dedications found during the excavation, such as reliefs with representations of genitals, similar to those found in the Shrine of Aphrodite at Daphni (see p. 151). Further west a **stair** (Figure **6**.33) cut in the rock leads up in the direction of the Erechtheion to a small back entrance to the Acropolis. This ascent was closely connected to the cult in the Erechtheion and was used by the girls (arrhephoroi), who carried the secret cult equipment of a fertility rite in baskets up to the Acropolis (arrhephoria, see p. 38). At the foot of this stair is a niche in the rock and a small cave in which the **Shrine of Pan** (Figure **6**.34) was situated. The niche later contained the shrine of Ay. Ioannis Chrysostomos, from which a few fresco fragments and a poros sarcophagus are preserved. Cuttings in the rock can be seen on all sides of the shrine for receiving votive offerings and niches for votive reliefs. The cult figure of the god in the form of a ram was probably on display in the cave; it is perhaps partly preserved in a fine Classical marble head (in Cleveland).[84] The shrine, like all Pan shrines, was established after the victory of the Athenians at Marathon (490 BC), as a thank-offering for the help of the god who had caused the Persians to be 'panic-stricken'. A few metres further west and on the same level above the Peripatos are the **sanctuaries of Apollo Hypoakraios** ('Apollo under the heights') **and of Zeus** (Figure 6.35). These two cults[85] were housed in two roomy caves in the rock; only cuttings for relief slabs in the sides of the caves are preserved today. There is a wide panorama from here to the north over the city to Mt Parnes. Still further west was another niche with some rock-hewn seats in front of it. Below this was a fountain, the so-called **Klepsydra** (Figure 6.36). A little above it a spring in the rock was connected to the top of the Acropolis by a stair in the Mycenaean period; today a domed room with brick walls can be seen with a well; it is a third century AD construction, put up after the old spring house had been destroyed by rock falls. Below this room lay the fifth century BC Klepsydra spring house, a simple building with a rectangular basin behind a marble balustrade. Next to this spring house and a little further east, a large paved court was constructed in the Classical period, probably to catch the rainwater which ran down from the Acropolis. It can be seen today right next to the Peripatos. On the north-west corner of the Acropolis the Peripatos meets the processional Panathenaic Way, which ran from the Sacred Gate in the Kerameikos across the Agora to the Citadel. A large inscription cut into the wall high up on the north side of the Acropolis, which supports the Pinakotheke, refers to it.

4   The Areopagos, the Hill of the Nymphs, the Mouseion Hill with the Pnyx, the Philopappos Monument and the Kerameikos (Figures 2; 18; 19)

The hills to the west, which group themselves in a gentle curve round the Acropolis (Figures 2.3–4; 18), offer a good walk, if it is not possible to visit anything else in the city or if, in the late afternoon, the sinking sun is bathing the ancient centre of Athens in a warm golden light. While the visitor wanders round these Athenian hills covered with trees and undergrowth, many good views of the Acropolis can be obtained with its shining marble buildings which make an imposing picture from this distance. All the hills, including the south-west slope of the Acropolis, were built over, foundations being partly cut into the limestone; portions of walls, steps, small rooms with benches and yards were also partly hewn out of the rock (for this reason the term 'rock-cut Athens' is used for this quarter). The visitor with a trained eye can make out the house plans and can mentally reconstruct individual houses. The houses[86] generally had at least two storeys, the rooms being grouped round a small yard, part of which was roofed while the rest was paved; occasionally there was a cistern beneath the yard in which rainwater from the roofs could be collected. A wooden stair led to the upper floor and the living rooms, while below it business and social life was carried out. The walls were made of plastered rubble or mudbrick set on firm foundations. There were only small window apertures on the outside, the rooms generally opening onto the inner yard. The houses were reached by wide roads rutted with cart tracks,

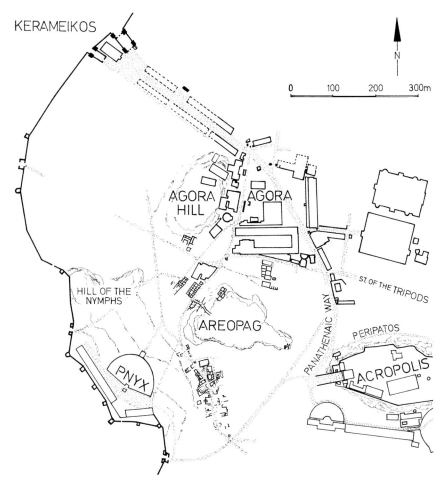

Figure 18 Athens, the ancient city and its hills.

artificially sunk so that the cart could not slip off, and with pavements grooved against slipping; they ran alongside the houses without any regular plan, often lined with small shops. Small narrow alleys with steps led up from the street between the separate houseblocks. The intensive cleaning which has been carried out since 1998 has enabled all these details to be appreciated much more clearly than before.

As well as dwelling houses there were also important public buildings on the hills. The court house was on the **Areopagos**, the 'Hill of Ares' just north-west below the Acropolis; the Supreme Court of Greece today is named after this rock. The myths on which the tragedies, 'Electra' of Sophocles and Euripides and 'The Eumenides' of Aischylos were based, took place here and the Apostle St Paul spoke to the Athenians here, when he stopped in Athens (*Apostles* 17.19). On the east peak of the hill, where there is a good view of the Acropolis, the foundations of a temple have only recently been made out, because the cuttings for it in the rock have been worn smooth; it must have had a similar plan to the Temple of Nike;[87] a stair hewn out of the limestone leads up to it from the south.

West of a valley, in which there is a Roman house with mosaics as well as Classical houses, there are two low hills, the Mouseion Hill and the Hill of the Nymphs. The **Hill of the Nymphs** has an observatory on its top built in 1842 (Plate 5). On the rock to the west in front of this building there is a Classical votive inscription to the Demos, the embodiment of the people of Attica, and to the Nymphs, which has given its name to this whole area of the hill.[88] Houses stretch around to the east below the Church of Ay. Marina, the protector of marriage and birth; their foundations are easy to see now that the rock has been cleaned. Among the houses at the side of a path halfway up the hill there are two boundary inscriptions, which frame a depression in the rock. The name of Zeus on the inscriptions suggests that the crack could have been struck by lightning – in the Early Classical period judging from the form of the letters. A valley south of the Observatory between the Hill of the Nymphs and the Pnyx, the exact position of which is unknown, was the place of execution for those condemned to death from Antiquity up until the Turkish period.

The largest hill west of the Acropolis is the **Mouseion Hill**. Its most important public structure was the **Pnyx**[89] which was surrounded by many houses. The assembly of the people (Ekklesia) took place here from the late sixth century BC (Kleisthenes) to the Early Hellenistic period. Its present form is the result of two rebuildings. Initially the male Athenian full citizens (only they had the right to vote) gathered in a semicircle which was orientated northwards towards the speaker's platform (Bema), following the natural slope of the hill. In the late fifth century the auditorium was reversed and placed to the north of the Bema so that the citizens no longer had an unimpeded view of the city and the Attic plain with their distractions, and every voter could concentrate better on the speaker. Two sloping retaining walls belong to the second building phase (they can be seen in the excavation trenches, within the semi-circle of the third phase), as well as two stairs hewn from the rock in front of the high north retaining wall.[90] As a result of the building policy of Lykourgos the theatre-like construction was much enlarged; a large amount of earthfill was brought in and retained by a monumental curving wall[91] in the north (Plate 5, on the left). A 12 m-wide freestanding stair on the axis offered an entrance through the retaining wall (the position of this stair can be seen on the upper course of the monumental wall). In the south the assembly area was greatly enlarged by cutting back the limestone for quite a distance; only a large stepped block was left for the speaker's platform. Above the area of the Bema two long stoas were planned to give protection from bad weather, but were never finished. They were to border an area in which stood altars, a famous sundial and also, probably, the entrance to the entire Pnyx. According to some scholars the Altar of Zeus Agoraios perhaps stood in a cutting in the rock just south of the Bema (see p. 78); it was moved from an unknown place, probably this one, to the Agora. Behind the stoas defensive works were erected in the Early Hellenistic period to protect the city at this point. These walls continued further south to the hill with the Philopappos Monument; they were connected to a transverse wall (Diateichisma), which had already been built in the late fifth century BC, with the result that part of the Pnyx was cut off from the city and the houses there had to be abandoned.

The Pnyx is one of the most important places for the development and practice of Attic democracy. All the decisions which defined Classical politics as well as the building policies of the Acropolis were taken here, and all the political disputes which influenced the history of the city were carried out here. Taking part in the assembly was initially considered a particular honour, but soon, under the influence of the radical democrats with their continual meetings, it became so boring and time consuming, that Perikles introduced a remuneration (the diaita) for the participants in a vote.

Today the visitor can enjoy the *son et lumière* from the Pnyx. The buildings on the Acropolis are floodlit to a soundtrack of readings from ancient texts; the impressive view of the area provides a good evening's entertainment.

If the visitor goes southwards from the Pnyx (Figures **2**.3; **18**), he passes numerous cuttings in the rock for Classical houses. Chambers cut into the rock and a small area hewn out of the limestone with seven seats are noteworthy. Stone surfaces, from which huge blocks have been cut, can be seen; a practised eye will perhaps find some of the countless rock inscriptions which were cut into the rock surface by skilled or unskilled hands in almost all ages. A wide paved path winds to the top of the Mouseion Hill on which stands the **mausoleum of Philopappos** (Plate 2), which is visible far and wide. Gaius Iulius Antiochus Philopappos was the last descendant of the King of Commagene (in east Turkey). He was exiled to Athens by the Romans and distinguished himself as an Attic citizen, Roman consul suffect and a benefactor of the city. His richly decorated grave monument[92] was erected on the Mouseion Hill in AD 114–116; it consisted of a large, almost square mausoleum (the stones from it were reused in the staircase of the minaret of the mosque in the Parthenon) with a two-storey marble façade facing the city. The façade has a frieze on its lower storey and statues of the deceased and two of his ancestors in niches on the upper storey. The frieze depicts Philopappos as a Roman magistrate (consul) in a four-horse chariot surrounded by numerous civil servants (lictors and charioteers); the missing third of the façade on the right, together with the back portion of the frieze and the third statue in its niche on the upper storey, was standing until the late fifteenth century, after which it was destroyed. In the Hellenistic period the summit of the hill was surrounded by a **Macedonian fortification** of Demetrios Poliorketes (built in 294 BC); part of this wall can be seen today in the north on the slope below the monument as well as on the path leading up to it.

The small church of **Ay**. **Demetrios Loumbardiaris** dating to the Turkish period stands on the wide paved ascent to the Philopappos Monument; ancient spolia and sherds are built into its walls; to the west of the chapel lies a huge, unfinished column drum. The church is a modern restoration but goes back to a ninth century predecessor. An old oral tradition says that the Turks wanted to shoot at it from the Acropolis on 26 October 1656 during the liturgy, but this plan was foiled by lightning striking the Propylaea which then exploded.

T he **Kerameikos** (Figure **19**). North of the Temple of Hephaistos in the excavation area of the Greek Agora the Street of Paul the Apostle, which runs through the valley between the Areopagos and the Hills of the Muses and Nymphs, crosses the underground railway line. The railway line cuts through the antiquities between the Agora and the Kerameikos, the area of the ancient city gate, from which the most important street, the Panathenaic Way, led into the city centre (Figure **18**).

The church of **Ay. Asomatoi** is located in the adjoining square, deep beneath the present street level. It dates to the fourteenth century and has well-constructed Byzantine walls. The dome is supported by ancient columns of Euboean marble. Leaving the square, the visitor goes west to Hermes Street (Ermou) from which the site of the Kerameikos can be reached about 250 m down the road on the right.

The Kerameikos[93] takes its name from the city quarter (deme) of Kerameis, and this in turn derives from the hero of the potters called Keramos, from which we have the word 'ceramic'. The name Kerameikos can, therefore, be translated as 'Potters' Quarter'. The deme extended from the Agora *c.* 1.5 kilometres to the north-west to Plato's Academy. It thus included a very large area, both inside and outside the city. The Kerameikos cannot, therefore, just be called the 'Cemetery of Athens', as it often is today, since only the area outside the Classical city wall was a cemetery; inside the wall with its two entrances lay houses, workshops and public buildings.

The excavated area of the Kerameikos covers only a small portion of the ancient deme. This area, which lies at the lowest point of ancient Athens in the valley of the River Eridanos, is divided by the city wall into the two areas of the city and the cemetery. The Kerameikos today belongs to one of the prettiest ancient quarters of Athens. The monuments, which are partly reconstructed and partly original, are set in a garden modelled on the flora of Antiquity, with the stream of the Eridanos, a home to frogs and densely growing lilies, flowing through it; they offer an unforgettable picture, in which the teaming city around is almost forgotten (during recent years the flora and fauna have become endangered because of the lack of water, which is pumped off in the area of the Athenian Agora).

The impression gained today of a divided area was not the original one; the division took place with the construction of the Themistokleian city wall after the Persian Wars in 478 BC. Before this there was only a small wall, the Peribolos, which lay further in towards the city. This wall, too, was only constructed in historical times. The area of the Eridanos marsh was used as a cemetery from the end of the third millennium, at first for single burials and then as an organised cemetery from about 1200 BC. Numerous cist graves, in which burial offerings of pots and weapons were placed, give evidence for this.

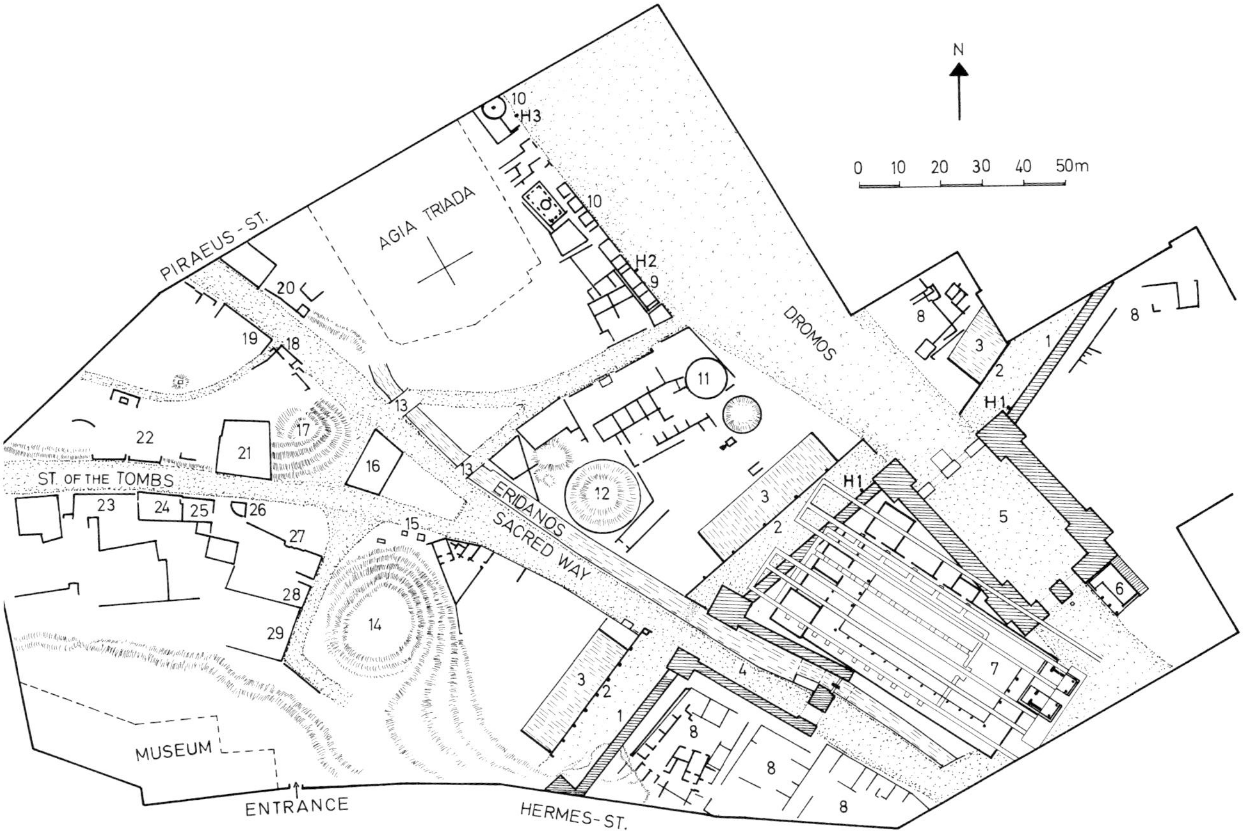

Figure 19 Athens, Kerameikos.

1: city wall; 2: Proteichisma; 3: protective ditch; 4: Sacred Gate; 5: Dipylon; 6: fountain house; 7: Pompeion; 8: dwelling houses; 9: tomb of the Lakedaimonians; 10: tombs; 11: bath; 12: burial mound; 13: bridges over Eridanos; 14: South Hill (burial mound); 15: Ambassador Graves; 16: precinct of the Tritopatres; 17: burial mound; 18: grave plot of Ampharete; 19: grave plot of Aristomache; 20: grave plot with small grave relief; 21: mudbrick grave plot; 22: grave plot of Koroibos with the stele of Hegeso; 23: grave plot of Lysimachides; 24: grave plot of Dionysios of Kollytos; 25: grave plot of the brothers from Herakleia; 26: grave plot of the family of Lysanias of Thorikos with the stele of Dexileos; 27: terrace with five grave plots; 28: grave plot of Demetria and Pamphile; 29: grave plot of Philoxenos of Messene; H 1–3: boundary stones.

The hollow was too damp for settlement at that time; the houses lay on the hills to the south. In the Geometric period (*c.* 900–700 BC) the population became richer and so correspondingly did the offerings in the Kerameikos graves. Geometric ornaments and maeanders cover the clay vases together with representations of biers, mourning and funeral games. A well-known example which is characteristic is the huge Dipylon Amphora in the National Museum, which stands almost as high as a man; it was a monument on a mid-eighth century BC grave in the area of the Dipylon (see p. 113).

In the Archaic period the graves were concentrated on the south bank of the Eridanos along the Sacred Way to Eleusis. Grave mounds of ever-increasing size (Figure **19**.12, 14, 17) were put up, which covered numerous shaft graves containing the ashes of the dead. Offering channels, in which the mourners could put grave offerings, such as pots and statuettes, were set on the surface of the grave mounds. Small stucco grave buildings or stone monuments stood on the grave mound; occasionally it was crowned with pots. An increase in the size of the monuments at the end of the seventh century BC required a corresponding increase in the size of the grave ornament; this resulted in the huge statue of a youth, the Dipylon Kouros (see p. 114). A few decades later the Kerameikos was full of marble grave monuments, such as relief stelai, depicting warriors and youths, and statues, some with bases decorated with friezes. During the excavation no sculpture was found in its original position. After the Persian destruction of 480 BC, all the Archaic sculpture was built into the city wall in 478 BC on the decision of the Assembly following a proposal of Themistokles. Two grave mounds, which cover graves of that time, are still visible: in the fork between the Sacred Way and the Street of the Tombs was a tumulus (Figure **19**.17) which must have belonged to a noble family, while the South Hill (Figure **19**.14) was a state grave for ambassadors of the Peisistratid era (second half of the sixth century BC).

The Kerameikos gained a totally different appearance with the building of the new city wall, which was moved further out all the way round (Figure **19**.1). Parts of the former cemetery were removed and its monuments put in the foundations of the wall; the dead thus lost their grave cult. At the same time two large city gates were erected in the Kerameikos, which dictate the topography of the area even today. The Processional Way ran through the Sacred Gate (Figure **19**.4) to Eleusis, while further north the double gate, the Dipylon Gate (Figure **19**.5), connected the city to the area of the Academy. A wide road, the Dromos, on which torch races took place during the Panathenaic Festival, passed through this gate. The Panathenaic Procession went on this road from the Kerameikos to the Agora and from there up to the Acropolis (Figures **2**; **18**). In front of the Dipylon Gate on each side lay the state graves (of which only a very small portion have been found: Plates 29–30), such as, for example, that of the Athenians who fell in the Peloponnesian War and those of Perikles and Kleisthenes. Three stelai with inscriptions, which give the boundary of the Kerameikos (ΟΡΟΣ ΚΕΡΑΜΕΙΚΟΥ), have been found on this road (Figure 19.H1–3); since the boundary stones stand on both sides of the road (there is a copy of one on the north side of the Dipylon Gate; a fifth one was found at the north-west corner of the Athenian Agora) they appear to separate the street from the area of the Kerameikos. The streets south of the Eridanos, the Street of the Tombs and the Sacred Way, were lined with sepulchral monuments belonging to the families of rich private citizens; placed above high terrace walls they make an impressive setting for the cemetery today with their reliefs, shrines and other monuments. They all date to before the late fourth century BC. Then a law against the increasing luxury of grave monuments, proposed by Demetrios of Phaleron in 317 BC, ended the Attic art of decorating grave stones. From then on only small columns or square marble blocks bearing the name of the dead were allowed as grave stones. The rich gifts of the Classical period, such as vases, jewellery, toys, etc., are completely absent later; only grey unguentaria were given to the dead in the following centuries. Large grave monuments were not built again until the Roman period; then they took the form of buildings. However, little is left of them today; new excavations on the Dromos have produced foundations of these mausolea. A large marble sarcophagus in the form of a couch comes from one such grave monument dating to the late second century AD, which once stood here (Figure **19**, near 9).

After the grave monuments the city walls of Athens, of which a long stretch has been dug in the area of the Kerameikos (Figure **19**.1), make the deepest impression. Outside the wall a street ran all round the city. The street was bounded on the outside by an outer wall, the Proteichisma (Figure **19**.2), in front of which a ditch (Figure **19**.3) made difficulties for any attackers. The wall itself consisted of a *c.* 1 m-high stone socle, carrying a *c.* 8 m-high plastered wall of mudbrick. It was crowned by a crenellated parapet. The socle of the city wall was raised many times because of the rise in the ground level in the whole area of the Kerameikos; but the structure stayed more or less the same throughout all the renovations, whether they were due to the effects of war or to natural catastrophes. The expert can recognise five different phases of repairs from the building technique of the wall socle. Blocks in the upper courses of the wall in the south of the area, for example with relief decorations of wreaths, are obviously reused material; they date to the last building phase of the Roman Empire. A few metres to the north a small part of the upper wall of mudbrick can still be seen (under a protective concrete roof).

The *c.* 200 m length of the city wall is broken here by two huge entrance buildings. To the south is the Sacred Gate (Figure **19**.4). A deep courtyard, lying between two side walls with protruding corner towers with the bed of the Eridanos on its north side, led to the gate. The stream was drained, vaulted over and (in a last brick building phase) closed with a grating at this point and also inside the city. Its present appearance dates to a Roman imperial renovation of the gate, which was repaired many times throughout its history.

To the north of the excavated area lie the remains of the Dipylon (or Thriasian Gate as it is aligned towards the Thriasian plain around Eleusis; Figure **19**.5), the largest and most splendid of the city gates of ancient Athens. Today there is little left of this once mighty structure because of the softness of the stone. The topography of the area is also obscured by a modern concrete canal which cuts through it. The Dipylon was originally a deep courtyard, which, as in the case of the Sacred Gate, made it possible for the defenders to shoot from the sides at enemies storming the gate. On the inside of the gate a large fountain house (Figure **19**.6) on the north side of the street offered fresh water to arriving travellers. In the Late Hellenistic period the Dipylon was turned into a fort and a double entrance was also made on the west side at the height of the corner towers. In the second century AD a pedestal base of old building material with a bench was erected in front of its middle pillar; the once high base probably supported the statue of an emperor.

Inside the walls in the area between the two gates lies an important public building, the Pompeion (Figure **19**.7), where the procession (Greek: pompe) in honour of Athena formed for the Panathenaic Festival (Plate 19). In the Classical period the Pompeion consisted of a large courtyard surrounded by columns and some banquet rooms in which the sacrificial meat for the festival was eaten by the nobility of Athens. The courtyard was adorned with statues, for example of Socrates, and paintings, for example of Menander, and the banquet rooms with pebble mosaics. The people, who also profited from a hekatomb, a sacrifice of 100 cows, and according to a literary source, received the meat in the Kerameikos, possibly ate in the Dipylon courtyard; heaps of bones found during excavations in front of the city wall support this idea. The area south of the Sacred Gate and north of the Dipylon was used for housing from the Classical period. There were buildings with small inner courtyards, which were converted, levelled after disturbances and repeatedly rebuilt over the centuries. In late Antiquity potters settled behind the Sacred Gate and built many kilns in the old ruins.

In 86 BC the Kerameikos suffered greatly during the sacking of Athens by the troops of Sulla; they breached the south wall of the Sacred Gate and pulled it down. The Pompeion and the buildings south and east of the Sacred Gate were destroyed. The accompanying plunder and murder is described by the historian Plutarch and characterised as a blood bath with the words: 'The slaughter in the Agora alone overflowed the area up to the Dipylon with blood, and much blood flowed through the gates into the outer city'.

A two-storeyed storehouse with three aisles was constructed in the area of the Pompeion (Figure **19**.7; Plate 19) in the second century AD; it was destroyed by the attack of the Heruli about 100 years later in AD 267. Potters settled in its ruins and built their kilns until *c.* AD 500, when two parallel colonnades with shops were erected on either side of the street. In the west they ran over the old city wall, while in the east a Festival Gate with three entrances led into the city. When hordes of Slavs descended on Attica at the end of the sixth century, the area of the Kerameikos with its gates, streets and the Eridanos disappeared under the earth. Not until April 1863, when a Greek worker, digging for sand in the area, dug up an upright stele, was the world again aware of the Kerameikos. Excavations began in 1870 under the auspices of the Greek Archaeological Society and continued from 1913 until today under the German Archaeological Institute.

Outside to the west of the fenced-off excavation area the necropolis continued along the arterial roads. Graves have always been known in the area of the Botanical Gardens on the Sacred Way (Iera Odos). During the construction of a new underground station a huge grave mound has recently been investigated in which many of the Athenians, who died of the plague in 429 BC, were buried.[94] Further burials have been found in building plots along Academy Street, which follows the Dromos, as well as a necropolis which is interpreted by the Greek excavators as a part of the Demosion Sema, the state cemetery.

Tour of the Kerameikos Excavations. The following description confines itself to the most important monuments and is not meant to be exhaustive. There is a good general view from Ermou Street. A **plan** of the excavations is located on the South Hill (Figure **19**.14) opposite the entrance; a guidebook with detailed information can be obtained from the ticket booth.

The **city wall** is only a few metres to the right of the entrance (Figure **19**.1); at this point, south of the Sacred Gate, the different building phases are easy to recognise. The two bottom layers belong to the first building phase (478 BC); above them lies the wall socle for renovations during the Peloponnesian War (c. 420 BC, after a big earthquake), while the large blocks of the fourth layer belong to the time after this war (394 BC; current research at the Sacred Gate may alter the accepted chronology). The two courses of rectangular blocks lying above belong to the end of the fourth century BC and the layers above them to late Antiquity, either to before the attack of the Heruli (AD 267) or to the mid-sixth century AD; the decoration of wreaths and the slots for stelai show that the stones are reused material put up in a hurry. Above the wall socles of each layer the fortification wall was of mudbrick, which is partly preserved at this point.

The road once ran through the **Sacred Gate** (Figure **19**.4) from Athens to Eleusis following the course of the Eridanos. The closure of the stream, by setting gratings in its bed, dates in its present form to late Antiquity. South of the Sacred Gate three large houses (Figure **19**.8) have been excavated, which were renovated many times from the fifth century BC right up to the time of the Roman Empire. They consisted of a central inner courtyard around which rooms, sometimes large, were grouped; the central house seems not to have been used as living quarters but for banquets. The preservation of these buildings is very poor; the different building phases cut into each other and lie directly above each other with no interim habitation deposit and even the foundation stones were stolen (the best view of this area can be obtained from Ermou Street). The only things easy to recognise are some well preserved kilns; they are small domed constructions with a central support and a serving-entrance.

The visitor can now walk along beside the socle of the city wall (Figure **19**.1) on his tour. The foundations of the Pompeion and the late Antique colonnaded street extend to the right (east) (Figure **19**.7). On the left, below the path, the outer wall (**Proteichisma** Figure **19**.2) protrudes, in front of which was the protective ditch (Figure **19**.3). One of the Kerameikos **boundary stones**, with the vertical inscription ΟΡΟΣ ΚΕΡΑΜΕΙΚΟΥ, is still standing next to the wall in front of the corner tower (Figure **19**.H1); a corresponding stone was situated on the opposite side of the Dipylon behind the north corner tower (a cast today). In the north of the excavated area the visitor reaches a modern concrete canal, on which he can wander along the **Dipylon** (Figure **19**.5). The outer double gate was set up between the Classical corner towers in the Hellenistic period; in front of its middle column is a large statue base, probably once a pillar, with a bench on its façade; it is made from old reused blocks and probably supported a statue of a second century AD emperor. The deep Dipylon courtyard is closed in the east by the original double entrance, behind which stands a small round altar, which was dedicated to the gods Zeus (as bestowing protection) and Hermes (the guide of travellers and traders) and to the tribe hero Akamas (inscription). North of the gate in the corner made by the east wall with the former ascent to the tower are the remains of a large **fountain house** (Figure **19**.6), which dates, in its present form, to the late fourth century BC, but which had a predecessor on the same spot. The traveller could get water to refresh himself from the fountain basin behind the columned façade. The water running down the sides of the basin has left deep gulleys in the marble floor of the vestibule.

To the south lies the area of the **Pompeion** (Figure **19**.7), with its large gate with three entrances and its colonnaded courtyard with attached banquet rooms (Plate 19); the latter sometimes have pebble floors and one room even has a mosaic of pebbles depicting groups of fighting animals (museum). The Pompeion was destroyed in Sulla's pillage of the city. The walls of masonry with a rubble core cutting across the area today belong to a second century AD storehouse and to two colonnaded buildings (*c.* AD 500), which stood on each side of a street.

North of the Dipylon are the storerooms and workrooms of the German excavations. A few house remains have been found in this area (Figure **19**.8).

Leaving the ancient city again through the Dipylon and following the course of the **Dromos** (to the south, lying below the modern surface), the visitor finds the first state tombs on his left, to which further west – still not yet found – the graves of the Athenians fallen in war and of famous politicians, such as Kleisthenes and Perikles, can be added. The **Tomb of the Lakedaimonians** (opposite a second century AD Roman marble sarcophagus), which could be identified from an inscription (cast on the west corner), is visible (Figure **19**.9). Thirteen Spartans, who were killed during an Athenian rebellion against the oppressive Spartan tyranny after the Peloponnesian War (Xenophon, *Hellenica* II 4.28–33), are buried in this grave. The grave inscription mentions the names of the Spartan leaders, in Spartan custom from right to left and in the Spartan alphabet; they are also mentioned by Xenophon. Inside the grave there were thirteen skeletons; the wounds could still be seen on the bones. In front of the grave stands a third Kerameikos boundary stone (Figure **19**.H2). Adjoining this are more, unidentified, graves (Figure **19**.10) and finally below the retaining wall of Piraeus Street another boundary stone (Figure **19**.H3). These boundary stones (horoi) were probably renewed over the ages; some of their inscriptions have letter forms which are later than their position suggests (for example, the Tomb of the Lakedaimonians, where the base of the stone lay below the façade of the grave);

also, they seem to have been prepared beforehand, since on the backsides, not visible in their present position, the surface has been finely picked and the area for the inscription smoothed. The large **grave near the third boundary stone** (Figure **19**.H3) had a circular interior set in a rectangular building, on the top of which was a marble Panathenaic amphora; this suggests the grave was a special one, perhaps for the family of a victor in the Panathenaic Games around 400 BC.

The area east of the Church of Ay. Triada up to the Eridanos contains a **bath house** (Figure **19**.11), many rectangular grave plots and two tumuli. The large **tumulus** next to the Eridanos (Figure **19**.12) contained burials dating to the seventh–fifth century BC. In the fourth century BC the tumulus was partly enclosed by a wall on its south side. The long sequence of burials in it suggests it belonged to an important noble family, perhaps, according to Pausanias (I 36.3), the Kerykes of Eleusis, who were heralds at the Mysteries.

Two **bridges** (Figure **19**.13) crossed the Eridanos in Antiquity; a road crossing the bridges connected the Dromos with the Sacred Way. On the latter, west of the walls, there is a high grave mound, the **South Hill** (Figure **19**.14), which is used today as a viewing platform. It contained two sixth century BC burials, the grave offerings of which suggest they were foreign dignitaries from Asia Minor. In the late sixth century BC the tumulus was used for the graves of citizens, while during the High Classical period state graves, the **Ambassador Graves** (Figure **19**.15), were placed on its north slope. The stelai of these graves, simple smooth slabs with no relief ornament, have been standing in place since the fifth century BC; their inscriptions give information about the fate of the dead men. One ambassador (right-hand stele) called Pythagoras, came to Athens from Selymbria on the Black Sea and died here; he may have brought the news of the entry of his native city into the Delian League (451 BC) and for this received a state burial. Next is the gabled stele of the ambassadors Thersandros and Simylos from Kerkyra (Corfu), who probably came to Athens in 433 BC to join a league against the Peloponnesians. During their stay they died and received a state grave, which was destroyed in 375 BC, but later restored.

In the middle of the Sacred Way is an unfenced area where the road forks. The main branch, the Sacred Way, continues towards Eleusis, while the other is a side street, the Street of Tombs. The area where the roads fork (Figure **19**.16) was the **sacred precinct of Tritopatres**, possibly the advocate of the souls of the ancestors; several inscriptions identify the area, such as one saying: 'Boundary of the Temenos of Tritopatres. Entrance forbidden.' and another on a stone about 30 m east, which is worn by chariot wheels. The temenos, which already existed in the sixth century BC (inscription on a natural rock set into the south wall), probably belonged to the large tumulus of a contemporary noble family, which lay west of it on the edge of a big cemetery.

If the visitor follows the **Sacred Way** (the right-hand fork) away from the city he will see more burial plots on its south side, which are divided into two groups by a passage running through the middle. In the east group he can see the rise in the street level, which is apparent from the different levels of the socles of the terrace walls, arising from the custom of spreading a layer of earth over

previous burials and erecting new stelai on top; this increase in level was particularly rapid at the end of the fourth century BC and in the third century; as a
result of this the walls of the Late Classical plots disappeared almost completely
under the earth. On the corner of this eastern area near the passage is the **grave
plot of Ampharete** (Figure **19**.18); a fine grave relief was found here (in the
entrance of the Kerameikos Museum; late fifth century BC) depicting a seated
woman with a baby in her arms. The inscription on the architrave of the stele
lets Ampharete speak for herself: 'I am holding the child of my daughter, my
love, which I held on my lap, while we looked at the light of the sun when we
were alive; now I am holding the dead child being dead myself.' The west group
of grave plots, which lie each side of a passage to the graves in the south, is
made up of four parts, which were all founded shortly after 338 BC. In the north
corner a marble lekythos on a round base with a relief picture of Aristomache
(Figure **19**.19) saying goodbye to her husband can be seen. Next to its stuccoed façade is another plain façade, a narrow passage, a plot with a fine polygonal wall and two more stuccoed façades, all dating to the Early Hellenistic
period. Excavation, however, has produced proof (sarcophagus graves, older
foundations of terrace walls, etc.) that the area was used for burials and monuments as early as the fifth century.

Opposite on the north side of the Sacred Way are two grave plots: that to
the west, now grown over, dates to the Early Classical period, when reliefs did
not decorate graves. Next to it (Figure **19**.20) is a late fourth century BC terrace
on which a relief stele (cast), which shows a woman, a boy with a leaping dog
and a servant, is placed.

Visitors going round the tumulus (Figure **19**.17) near the Tritopatreion, reach
the **Street of the Tombs**, one of the highlights of the Kerameikos cemetery with
its reliefs on high terrace walls. The large mudbrick building next to the tumulus
(Figure **19**.21), in which perhaps the family of Alkibiades was buried from the
end of the fifth century BC, is no longer recognisable in its original form. Rich
grave offerings, including remains of silk, show that this was an important grave.
To the west next to the mudbrick building are three late fourth century BC grave
monuments which belong together and then the important **burial plot of
Koroibos** (Figure **19**.22). Almost nothing remains of its rich façade, but excavation has revealed its grave stelai. In the middle of them is the high, early fourth
century BC stele of Koroibos himself, crowned with an anthemion, on which his
name and those of his sons and grandson are engraved below two rosettes, as
well as the name of someone called Sosikles from a different family. On the right
is a stele with the relief of a loutrophoros, which is the symbol that the dead
person was young and unmarried, in this case a Kleidemos from the family of
Koroibos. The earliest monument of the stele group is the relief of Hegeso (original in the National Museum), which was placed in a secondary usage next to
the stele of Koroibos. It dates to the late fifth century BC and is one of the best
of the Attic grave reliefs. Hegeso sits on an elegant chair, deep in thought, and
holds in her right hand a jewel, once painted, which she has taken from a box
held by her servant; but she is not looking at the object; rather her gaze seems
to go beyond it. Her garments, a mantle pulled over her head and a chiton

buttoned down her arm, emphasise the curves of her body. Her hair is loosely confined by a band. All the grave stelai were defaced after the Battle of Chaironeia (338 BC) and their bases and façade stones reused to rebuild the city wall. Later, however, the grave plot of Koroibos was restored.

An impressive row of grave terraces lies on the south side of the Street of the Tombs (Plate 20). The terrace walls are partly of polygonal masonry, with the monuments on top. Opposite the grave of Koroibos the **plot of Lysimachides** is almost completely preserved (Figure **19**.23); it was founded after 339 BC, when he was archon in Athens, and before the end of Attic grave relief art (317 BC). On the corners were two Molossian hounds (only one is preserved, cast), while in the middle is an impressive relief (cast): two bearded old men flanked by women recline eating; there are many cakes lying on the table in front of them; in the foreground is a barbaric looking bearded man in a ship, an indication that the owner of the impressive grave monument had gained his wealth from sea trade with the northern corn-producing areas. Behind the façade over thirty sarcophagi were found in which the members of the family of Lysimachides were buried.

The eastern adjoining **plot of Dionysios of Kollytos** (Figure **19**.24) with its high base and large naiskos-stele, crowned by a marble bull on a pillar, is particularly impressive. It dates between 345 BC (in this year Dionysios was elected treasurer in the Samian Heraion) and 338 BC, when the grave plot was robbed of its façade. Two opposing figures were painted in the naiskos; it had no marble decoration; however, its base and architrave have epigrams inscribed on them which praise Dionysios as a prudent and respected man in Athens and on Samos. He died before his mother, unmarried, and is buried in a marble sarcophagus behind the bull pillar.

To the east is the **grave plot of two brothers from Herakleia on the Black Sea** (Figure **19**.25). The high anthemion-crowned stele with the names of the two brothers was the reason for the discovery of the Kerameikos in 1863, when a sand digger chanced on it. The grave plot, which was founded before 338 BC, also contained a stele (once with a painted picture), a grave relief and a marble lekythos with the relief of a farewell scene.

On the other side of a small gap, in which two grave plots are set back a little, is the impressive **monument of the family of Lysanias of Thorikos** (Figure **19**.26). It is crowned by the slightly curving grave relief of Dexileos (cast; original in Kerameikos Museum), on the base of which a long inscription gives information about the fate of the dead man; he was born in 414/13 BC and fell in battle at Corinth against the Corinthians in 394/3 aged 20 (Plate 31). His bones were not put in this private grave but in the state grave, the Demosion Sema, which lay on the Dromos; on that stele, preserved by chance, next to the list of those fallen at Corinth, among them Dexileos, is a list of the Athenians killed in the same year at Koroneia in Boeotia (see p. 120; Plates 29–30). Thus, Dexileos' grave never received his body, but was erected by his family as a cenotaph in honour of their son. He is portrayed as a victorious rider trampling over his opponent; with its curved substructure and its setting diagonal on the grave plot (Plate 20) it must have made a striking impression on passers by. Other more simple stelai for the brothers and sisters of Dexileos were erected next to his securely-dated monument.

Beside the plot of the family from Thorikos is a **long terrace** (Figure **19**.27) with partly preserved polygonal walling on which the few remains of five grave plots were found. Some grave reliefs from here are in the National Museum; other monuments are set up again at the back of the plot (lekythos, bases). In the east this corner terrace ends at a path running south flanked by two grave plots. The more impressive is that of **Demetria and Pamphile** (Figure **19**.28) dating to the late fourth century BC. The grave relief, set up again in its original place, which was produced shortly before the decree against grave luxury (317 BC), shows the dead Pamphile sitting on a throne with her sister in front of her. Demetria must have already died at the time of the relief. She is on a second grave relief (in the National Museum) represented as sitting holding the hand of her sister, Pamphile. This second stele stood on the north side of the plot. South of this is the **grave plot of Philoxenos of Messene** (Figure **19**.29), extending over a large area with more than seventy burials. In the plot are some block-shaped marble bases, a grave relief of a seated woman and three small marble stelai, which all reached their present place after the destruction of the plot in 338 BC; they show, along with many other examples, that the destruction of the cemetery was not accepted and that the monuments were set up again later.

In the **Kerameikos Museum** some stelai from the Archaic and Classical cemetery are placed in the vestibule. The monuments, which were made before 480 BC (statues, stelai and relief decorated statue bases), were built into the Themistokleian city-wall (478 BC) and were found during excavations. The most important reliefs from the Classical cemetery have already been described on the tour. The remaining rooms of the museum, which are arranged in chronological order, contain above all vases and other burial offerings. Of special interest are some of more than 9,000 ostraka found in a pit on which are inscribed the names of some important politicians of the early fifth century BC.

5   The Greek Agora, the Roman Market, the Library of Hadrian and Monastiraki

The Agora was the political and business centre of the city, as was usual in ancient Greece, while the Acropolis was the cult centre. Most of the public administrative buildings stood in the Agora, festivals were celebrated there and business was carried out. The Agora of Athens[95] was not only of particular importance for the whole ancient world as the place of influential political decisions, but, together with the Pnyx, it is also seen today as the historic centre of European democracy.

The Agora, which lies below the Acropolis to the north and has been known since the American excavations began in 1931, was not by any means the first market place of ancient Athens. In the Archaic period the administrative centre must have lain to the east below the citadel. Ancient sources testify to this, placing it directly in the neighbourhood of the Aglaurion (see p. 54), and they are supported by the find of an inscription in a cave on the east slope of the Acropolis, although it is true that up until now no archaeological remains of the Archaic agora have been found. The partial removal of the Agora to the flat area north of the Acropolis may be connected with the beginning of Attic democracy under Kleisthenes;[96] perhaps the Agora used earlier by the Peisistratids – the use as a burial place ended 100 years earlier – was integrated into the administrative centre of the new constitution (see p. 54). However, some important functions did remain in the Archaic Agora: the Prytaneion continued to be there and the young ephebes were also sworn in there until late Antiquity, and the list of their names was exhibited there engraved on marble stelai.

Unfortunately, the buildings in the Agora which mirrored the political change in ancient Athens are in poor condition; until the beginning of the excavation (1931) a modern living quarter stood here with countless small houses. The visitor must first walk around to familiarise himself with the complicated archaeological landscape in order to understand the development of the area from a marshy plain to a wide square with buildings round it to a collection of closely packed large civic buildings (Plate 21).

The area of the Agora is accessible from three entrances. One lies on the north side in Adrianou Street approached via a bridge over the railway line; a second is in the south-east corner on the path which leads up to the Acropolis; a third is on the west side leading to a terrace next to the Hephaisteion from which the visitor can get a good overview. A plan of the American excavations is on show close to this last entrance (Figure **21**.P).

As in the case of the Kerameikos, the area of the ancient Agora was used as a cemetery in prehistoric times. Numerous graves were found in the excavations, especially on the slopes of the Areopagos and on the hill of Kolonos Agoraios (Figure **18**), both family graves in chambers with a corridor in front and small cremation burials. The offerings of pottery and jewellery allow conclusions to be drawn as to the social status of the dead and the standard of living over the centuries. The population apparently settled on the surrounding hills in the centuries before the Geometric period (before 900 BC), while the dead were buried on the plain. 'The city consisted of only the present Acropolis and the area on its south slope', wrote Thucydides in his description of the prehistoric period in which the Athenian hero Theseus is said to have reigned. This observation is supported by the recent localisation of the Aglaurion and some houses in the area of the Makrygianni Museum.

From the late sixth century BC the Agora developed as the centre of the city of Athens; the area was marked off with boundary stones ('I am the boundary of the Agora' is inscribed on them) from the public streets surrounding it, and the first civic buildings were put up for the administration of the city-state; they lay on the west side at the foot of the hill of Kolonos Agoraios. In the south-west was a house with a large courtyard, perhaps the Prytanikon, the assembly place of the High Council (prytaneis) (Figure **20**, under the tholos);

next door is the building in which the Council of 400, the Boule, met. Recent research by the American excavators suggests that the large house with a court-yard was the house of the Peisistratids, which was then deliberately built over as part of the political programme of the newly appointed Council of the new democracy. Next to this meeting house were three temples, one being for the Mother of the Gods with the state archive. On the north-west corner of the area next to the wide Panathenaic Way, which led from the Dipylon diag-onally across the Agora to the Acropolis, stood the small Stoa Basileios, in which the administrative offices of the Archon Basileus were housed, the second highest official in the hierarchy (the first official was the Eponymous Archon, after whom the civic year was named). In the open area itself there were two more sacred precincts, which lay close together in the north next to the Panathenaic Way. They consisted of an open yard for the altar of the Twelve Gods and a bothros in a small enclosure. In the south were two more public buildings, comprising a large courtyard, which was perhaps the most impor-tant Athenian lawcourt, the Heliaia (but this has also been placed on the north-east corner of the Agora under the later Stoa of Attalos, see n. 109), and a fountain house dating to 530–520 BC, which provided water for the populace. It has been suggested that the Peisistratids wanted to raise their image with the people by means of this installation and make certain of their leadership in the contest with other noble families. This has given rise to the suggestion that the area of the later Agora was first used by the Tyrants.

The area was used at that time, and also in the fifth and fourth century BC, as a place for performances, whether for plays or sportive events, such as eques-trian contests. Temporary wooden stands (ikria) were erected for the specta-tors to watch these. When such performances were not taking place, the Agora was a lively place in which traders offered their wares on simple stalls, craftsmen worked and everyone discussed the latest happenings.

The newly erected buildings of the Agora were destroyed in 480 BC when the Persians sacked Athens. However, the most important administrative build-ings and the cult places were quickly repaired. A circular building, the Tholos, the administrative office of the prytaneis, was constructed on the west side (Figure **20**) below the Kolonos Agoraios above the Archaic house with a court-yard (of the Peisistratids?) (Plate 21). Next the Metroon was rebuilt and much widened, as well as a new Bouleuterion for the Council of 500. In the east opposite these buildings there was a long statue base surrounded by a fence on which stood the figures of the eponymous heroes, symbols of the political tribes (Phylai) of Attica. It was moved here from an earlier unknown location (? the Pnyx). The base was used to advertise official announcements, such as meetings of the Assembly, court sittings, etc.

Beyond several rows of seats (the Synedrion = meeting place), in front of which the Temple of Apollo Patroos was constructed in the fourth century BC, a large stoa, the Stoa of Zeus, was built in 429 BC. It was dedicated to Zeus Eleutherios, the 'Freer', had a large altar in front of the façade and contained numerous paintings in which the mythical and historical exploits of Athens and personifications, such as Demokratia, were depicted. The place was one of the

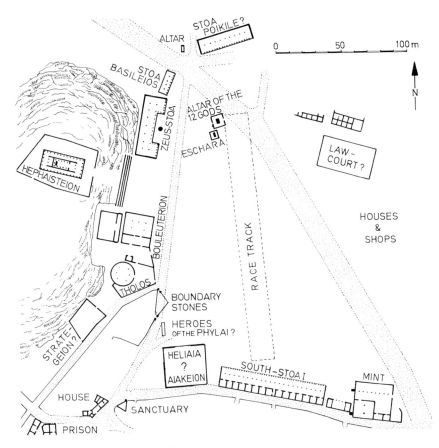

Figure 20 Athens, Agora, *c.* 400 BC.

popular meeting points for Athenians, including Socrates and his friends and disciples.

Next to this large, imposing marble stoa the small Stoa Basileios must have almost disappeared. It was rebuilt in its old position after the destruction of 480 BC and the Archaic building material was incorporated into the founda-tions. Two small side wings, added on later, were used to display law tablets. A female statue was placed on a square pedestal in front of the façade (perhaps Themis, the Goddess of Law).

In the fifth and fourth century BC some functions of the Agora were moved to other areas, for example theatrical performances went to the new Theatre of Dionysos, and, as well as renovations, new buildings were also erected in the Agora. The area thus achieved a stronger architectural unity. In the north next to the altar of Aphrodite a large stoa was built, while the south side was bordered by the old law court, a stoa, the fountain house and the mint. The north stoa, the Stoa Poikile, is especially well known from references by ancient authors. The works of famous Athenian painters, such as the Battle of Marathon,

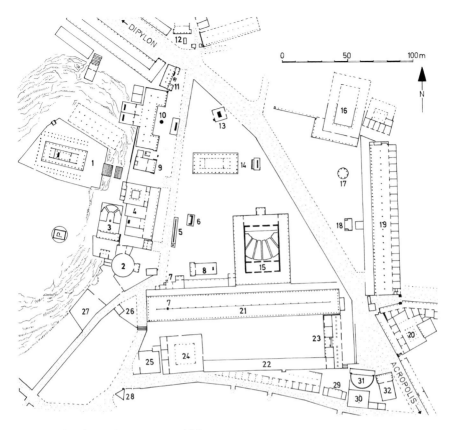

Figure 21 Athens, Agora, *c.* AD 180.

1: Hephaisteion; 2: Tholos (Prytanikon); 3: Bouleuterion; 4: Metroon; 5: Eponymous Heroes; 6: altar;
7: boundary stones; 8: South-west Temple; 9: Temple of Apollo Patroos; 10: stoa of Zeus
Eleutherios; 11: stoa Basileios; 12: altar of Aphrodite Ourania; 13 Peribolos of the Twelve Gods; 14:
Temple of Ares; 15: Odeion of Agrippa; 16: Basilica; 17: Rotunda; 18: Bema; 19: stoa of Attalos; 20:
Library of Pantainos; 21: Middle stoa; 22: South stoa; 23: offices of the Metronomoi; 24: Heliaia (or
Aiakeion); 25: South-west fountain house; 26: cobbler's workshop; 27: Strategeion (?); 28: Triangular
sanctuary; 29: South-east fountain house; 30: mint; 31: Nymphaion; 32: South-east Temple; P:
Panorama.

were hung here and war trophies were displayed. The stoa was used as a
place for lawcourt sittings and as a meeting place for those people who wanted
to be introduced to the Eleusinian Mysteries. Around 300 BC the philosopher
Zeno collected his disciples here, so the members of his newly founded school
of philosophy were called 'Stoics'. Next to this stoa was the Stoa of the Herms
named after the large number of statues of Hermes (herms) displayed there.
Opposite the South Stoa there was an administrative or office building in
which city officials, such as the controllers of weights and measurements
(metronomoi), met and had their dining room. The Athenian mint was on the
south-east corner of the Agora; in this workshop bronze coins, not the beautiful Athenian silver coins, were minted in many forges. The money could

come quickly into circulation in the business area which was right in the neighbourhood. The south-west corner contained an administrative building which was probably used by the generals (Strategoi); it was partly built into the side of the hill, which has been cut back, and is very badly preserved.

In the Classical period some private houses and workshops were located outside the area of the Agora to the south, behind the south buildings, belonging, for example, to marble and bronze workers and to potters. There was a small cobbler's shop directly by the boundary stone of the Agora, and it seems very likely that it was in this small house that Socrates taught the Athenian children. The city prison was further to the south-west, a building complex, closed on the outside, with single cells grouped round a courtyard.

On the way to the prison there is a small shrine dating to the mid-fifth century BC at a crossroads; it is a triangular enclosure with fine walling with an inscribed marble boundary stone at the north-east corner.

In the mid-fifth century BC, at about the same time as the Parthenon was built, the large Temple of Hephaistos, the so-called Theseion, was constructed (Figures **20**; **21**.1; **111**) overlooking the Agora on the hill of Kolonos Agoraios; since it was converted *c.* AD 450 into the Church of St George (Figure **22**), it is one of the best preserved Greek temples today. Hephaistos, the god of crafts, and Athena were worshipped in the quarter of the metalworkers in the Agora and in the area of the Kerameikos; statues of both divinities stood on a base in the cella.

In the Hellenistic period the appearance of the Agora changed again (Figure **21**). The impressive trade network and the political might of Athens were lost, but large donations from Hellenistic kings allowed the construction of new

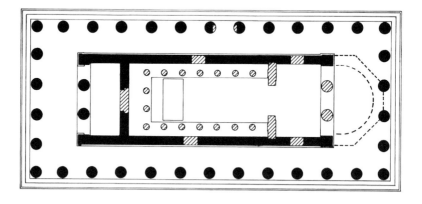

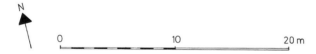

Figure 22 Athens, Hephaisteion, reconstructed plan and the church of Ay. Georgios.

buildings, which gave the Agora a unified architectural frame. The Stoa of Attalos is the best known of these buildings. It was constructed in the second half of the second century BC and consists of a long two-storeyed colonnade with numerous shops on the back side and a terrace in front of the façade (Figure **21**.19). It was built over a large square courtyard which had been used as a lawcourt. The American archaeologists have reconstructed the stoa (Plate 21) to house the Agora Museum and their excavation offices. In the interior the visitor gets a good impression of an ancient stoa; it gives protection from wind and rain in the winter and it is cool and shady in summer.

The Agora also gained a new building on the south side, in addition to the new constructions bordering it in the east. A second South Stoa (Figure **21**.22) was built onto the Heliaia over the earlier South Stoa; it framed a separate business area together with a building in the east set at a right angle to it (Figure **21**.23) and another business hall with two aisles, the Middle Stoa (Figure **21**.21). Only the foundations of these buildings remain today. The money changers probably had their tables in the east building, right next to the mint, while the real business was carried out in the small rectangular area between the Middle and second South Stoas, which was now separated from the Agora.

To unify the line of buildings on the west side a colonnade was constructed in front of the Metroon-Bouleuterion complex (Figure **21**.3–4), which concealed the irregular buildings behind it, and a Propylon common to both buildings was erected. Together with these buildings the colonnade of the Apollo Patroos Temple, the Stoa of Zeus and the Stoa Basileios (Figure **21**.9–11) beyond them now gave the west side of the Agora a unified appearance.

After this Hellenistic unification of the area the changes of the following years, that is during the time of the Roman Empire, could only destroy the clarity. The construction of a large stoa, the Basilica, in the north-east (Figure **21**.16), did fit into the Hellenistic system of framing the Agora. However, the erection of a large roofed concert hall, the Odeion (Figure **21**.15), disturbed the traditional use of the area as a meeting place; the Odeion was donated by Agrippa, general and son-in-law of the Emperor Augustus, in the years between 27 and 12 BC and renovated again in the mid-second century AD.

Other buildings seem to belong to a cult programme aimed at centralising the Attic cults in Athens. Temples or parts of cult buildings from different places in Attica were moved to the Agora. They include the Classical Temple of Ares (Figure **21**.14), which was carefully moved from Pallene (on the road to Marathon) and rebuilt in the open area north of the Odeion. Building material from two south Attic sites, consisting of Doric architectural fragments from Thorikos and Ionic columns from the Temple of Athena at Sounion, was incorporated into two other temples, one in the south-west corner of the area (Figure **21**.8) and one on the Panathenaic Way in the far south-east (Figure **21**.32).

Amongst the additions to the old buildings during the Roman period two changes are especially worth mentioning: the old Tholos (Figure **21**.2) acquired an imposing entrance façade with a columned porch on its east side, and a two-room extension was put onto the back of the Stoa of Zeus (Figure **21**.10), in which perhaps the Roman emperor was worshipped.

Apart from the Odeion of Agrippa two other new buildings were erected in the Agora in the early second century AD. The first was a library (Figure **21**.20), donated by a rich Athenian private citizen, Titus Flavius Pantainos, which lies south of the Stoa of Attalos. It has the Panathenaic Way on one side and a colonnaded street, which ran eastwards to the Roman Agora, on the other side. The second building was a Nymphaion (Figure **21**.31), which was built over the mint and bore witness to the aid of the Roman emperors in providing water for the city.

The late Antique phase of the Agora saw many changes to the earlier build-ings. The removal of many, sometimes ruined, buildings, especially temples and stoas, after the raid of the Heruli on Athens (AD 267) was particularly disastrous; their building components were used for the fortification wall of Valerian, which was built along the Panathenaic Way and across the shops of the ruined Stoa of Attalos (some scholars think that the building was torn down shortly before the attack of the Heruli as a last, useless protection against the barbarians). The spolia wall, of which a large part still exists today running along the Panathenaic Way, enclosed only a small part of the Classical city, which had to be protected against further attacks of barbarian hordes. As a result of this the old centre of Athens, the Agora, was now outside the city wall. A large gymnasium and two courtyards with a bathhouse and galleries were built over the Odeion and the stoas bordering it in the south; the entrance to this complex was adorned by the high bases with figures of giants and tritons, which had originally belonged to the renovation of the Odeion in the second century.

Some villas on the slope of the Areopagos bear witness to the fact that the former business area of the Agora was now a residential area; they were deco-rated with earlier sculptures and marble panels and thus achieved some splen-dour. As well as functioning as dwelling houses they were also used for the schools of philosophy. Any signs of life here were finally eradicated when the Slavs invaded Athens in AD 582 and destroyed the remains of the city archi-tecture; the buildings were abandoned. One of the few building operations was the conversion of the Hephaisteion into the Church of Ay. Georgios (Figure **22**). The inner columns and pronaos wall were torn out and an apse put into the eastern part; the cella walls in the west and south were closed with doors.

Tour of the Agora Excavations (Figure **21**). Coming from the Pnyx or the Kerameikos the visitor enters the Agora from the west entrance and finds a plan for orientation on the hill of Kolonos Agoraios. Before going down into the area a visit should first be made to the Hephaisteion on the hill itself.

The Hephaisteion (Figures **21**.1; **22**; **111**). The Temple of Hephaistos and Athena is a model of Doric Classical cult architecture (built *c.* 450–440 BC). The temple, consisting of a cella with a pronaos and opisthodomos, is surrounded by a peristyle of 34 columns (forming a rectangle of 6 columns by 13). The pronaos at the east end has the antae in line with the axes of the third columns of the peristyle. Originally, there may have been internal columns in the cella along the wall and behind the cult statues of Hephaistos and Athena (foundations for them show at least that they were planned by the architect); the walls, which stood on an Ionic moulded base, were probably painted inside, because the surface has been picked in preparation for a wall painting. There are some unusual details of construction which connect the Hephaisteion architecturally with the Temple of Poseidon at Sounion; the vestibule (front pteroma) has been widened for half the interaxial space and made into a separate room by a figured frieze which extends over the front of the pronaos up to the north and south peristyles; in contrast the frieze over the opisthodomos covers only the width of the cella. The east façade of the temple is thus emphasised, and this impression is strengthened as there are sculptured metopes only on the outer eastern side and over the first two interaxial spaces on the north and south sides at the east end, while the remaining metopes were left blank. The decorative themes of the sculpture[97] are the heroic deeds of Herakles (front) and Theseus (long sides) and a battle of Greeks watched by a god (pronaos frieze) and a battle of Greeks and Centaurs (opisthodomos frieze); the few remains of the pedimental decoration cannot be deciphered; the figure from the apex of the pediment, a hurrying female with wind-blown robes, is in the Agora Museum. There is almost nothing left of the Church of Ay. Georgios inside the temple; only the barrel-vault of the cella roof and the doors in the side and opisthodomos walls survive from this conversion. An interesting detail of the temple was the artistically planned garden around it; huge clay pots have been found which were put into the earth on three sides of the temple for shrubs and bushes; this find shows that attention was given to the landscape and that the temple had plenty of water. The present selection of plants emulates the ancient one. A problem for the interpretation of this temple remains: there is no place for an altar within the temenos, but we know of religious festivals for Hephaistos (Hephaisteia) with sacrifices and contests; it seems possible that there was elsewere in Athens a second sanctuary for this god where these events took place.

Prytanikon (Figure **21**.2). Below the hill of Kolonos Agoraios the circular area of the Tholos can be seen, the meeting place for the administrative officers, who directed the city business. There was a house here in the Archaic period with many rooms and a courtyard, perhaps the dwelling of the Peisistratids, which was replaced in the Classical period by the circular building. In the Roman period the Tholos was given an entrance with columns (there is a blue-grey marble inscription plaque reused in the foundations of the vestibule).

Bouleuterion and Metroon (Figure **21**.3, 4). Individual buildings can hardly be recognised in the ruined area on the north side. The Bouleuterion (Council House;[98] Figure **21**.3) must have stood in the background; it can be restored with a U-shaped seating plan by comparison with examples in other Greek cities. Before the Persian invasion (480 BC) the council may have met in the eastern building lying in front (Figure **21**.4); later the temple of the Mother of the Gods (Metroon) and the state archive occupied the newly constructed eastern building.

This heterogeneous group of rooms gained a common eastern façade in the Hellenistic period, next to which a Propylon gave entry to the Bouleuterion.

Monument of the Eponymous Heroes (Figure **21**.5). To the east opposite the Metroon complex was a long base surrounded by a fence of stone posts and crossbars; the construction of the fence suggests there was a wooden original which was later replaced in stone and renovated many times (suggested by the differing types of stone used for the posts and by different mortice and tenon joints). The personification of the ten Attic tribes, the eponymous heroes,[99] stood on it between two tripods. The base itself was used as a 'notice board' for public announcements, such as calling up the soldiers who were registered in their phylai. Excavation has revealed that the present monument was put here c. 330 BC, having been brought from elsewhere and rebuilt, since a monument for the eponymous heroes is known from ancient sources from at least 420 BC. The monument was widened during the course of history, whenever a famous leader (in the Hellenistic and Roman periods, for example, Hadrian) was honoured by being taken into the row of phyle heroes. The Hadrianic widening can be clearly seen at the south end of the monument, next to one of the cornice-shaped tripod bases which framed the hero figures.

The **Altar of Zeus Agoraios** (Figure **21**.6). Next to the Eponymous Heroes is a large marble altar with fine ornamentation. It is possibly the altar of Zeus Agoraios (others think of Peace or of Compassion), which may once have stood on the Pnyx (or in the Archaic Agora) and was brought here later (incised letters have facilitated the second arrangement of the blocks and date the removal of the altar to the Early Roman Empire). The eponymous archon, the highest civil servant in the city, who gave his name to the civil year, took his oath at this altar. The fact that two steps have been cut from one large marble block, instead of being assembled from two separate blocks, is of architectural interest; this system gives more weight to each stone and means much marble from the quarried blocks was wasted.

Boundary Stone (Figure **21**.7). In the south-west corner of the Agora, east of the Tholos and at a lower level today, one of the Archaic boundary stones has been excavated (c. 500 BC). It has a rough picked centre and a smooth outer edge on which is engraved, as though the stone itself speaks: 'I am the boundary of the Agora' (ΗΟΡΟΣ ΕΙΜΙ ΤΕΣ ΑΓΟΡΑΣ). This, and a second similar stone under the Middle Stoa (Figure **21**.21), separated the Agora from a public road which ran along the Great Drain; as in the case of the Dromos in the Kerameikos area (see pp. 61–2), here too a street was cut off from the Agora by boundary stones. Just south-west of this stone the American excavators found the workshop of the cobbler Simon (Figure **21**.26), in which Socrates taught his young disciples.

The **South-west Temple** (Figure **21**.8). This very badly preserved temple east of the boundary stone had a Doric portico (four or six columns); the building material came from Thorikos (see p. 218; Plate 51). It was first constructed under the

Roman Empire (probably in the first century AD), when the whole Agora was covered with buildings and some Attic temples were brought to Athens from the countryside.

The **Temple of Apollo Patroos** (Figure **21**.9) was built about the mid-fourth century BC in front of a row of seats of poros blocks. In the mid-sixth century BC there was a bronze foundry here, in which fragments of a terracotta mould of a kouros statuette were found; the foundry was fenced off on the slope by a curved wall, which initially gave rise to the idea that an earlier temple existed here. The oblong Classical building had six columns on the façade, similar to the east façade of the Erechtheion,[100] and housed two statues of Apollo (by Leochares and Kalamis, probably in the vestibule) and the famous colossal statue by the sculptor Euphranor, which was found nearby during excavations (today inside in front of the south wall of the Stoa of Attalos). To the north next to and in front of a side-room of the Apollo Temple the foundations of a small shrine can be seen, which was built onto the larger temple. Scholars think it belonged to Zeus Phratrios and Athena Phratria, because of the religious connection of the phratries to Apollo Patroos, and have, therefore, erected an altar with a dedicatory inscription to both these gods in front of the building, although the stone was found far away and its inscription is probably not contemporary with the carving of the altar but a Roman imperial 'archaising' copy. A sacrificial pit (bothros), which was still in use c. 400 BC, was abandoned and built over to make way for the shrine.

Stoa of Zeus Eleutherios (Figure **21**.10). This large stoa dates to c. 420 BC. In the Roman period two rooms were built on to its back side, perhaps as a place for emperor worship. The building was of Pentelic marble and had Doric columns outside and Ionic ones inside; the roof was crowned with statues of Nike. The two protruding wings are noteworthy in that the Doric frieze, unusually, must have had to meet in an internal angle (see also Brauron p. 223). The name of the stoa derives from Pausanias who speaks of a statue of Zeus Eleutherios and then mentions the stoa, although he does not explicitly say that it was a cult building of the god; but the presence of a big altar in front of the building supports this idea. Pausanias notes that paintings were hung in it (the Twelve Gods, Demokratia, Demos and Theseus, battle scenes, etc).

The **Stoa Basileios** (Figure **21**.11). Today the Agora is cut off from the following monuments by the railway line and Adrianou Street. However, an impression of the stoa and also of the area to the north can be gained from the street.[101] The small 'Royal Stoa' was the place where the Archon Basileus carried out his business, which was mostly connected to cult and religious matters. It is a stoa open to the east with an inner row of columns onto which two wings were built in the Late Classical period. Inscriptions of law decrees were displayed and the lawcourt was held here. A huge statue of Themis, the Goddess of Law, or Agathe Tyche, the Goddess of Good Fortune, is reconstructed on a base in front of the building (see p. 83). On the entrance steps, placed on one step and backed against the next, is a large natural stone (perhaps once the lintel of a Mycenaean grave), on which the Archon Basileus took his oath. The stoa, which is mentioned by Pausanias during his tour, is identified from dedications as the Stoa Basileios: three marble bases can still be seen with sockets for herms, on the front of which different Archons Basileis are named as dedicators.

The **Altar of Aphrodite Ourania** and the **Stoa Poikile** (Figure **21**.12). The American excavations have continued to the north on the other side of Adrianou Street in recent years. A small rectangular altar dating from *c.* 500 BC, which was dedicated to Aphrodite (perhaps with the epithet Ourania = heavenly; others think that it was for Hermes Agoraios),[102] has been found here. It is made of slabs of marble from the Cyclades; the top is flat with a pediment above each narrow end. Bones were found inside belonging to animals sacrificed to the goddess.

North of the altar the excavation came upon part of a foundation which might be the (later) temple to which the altar was attached. Next to it on the east the lowest steps of the west end of a stoa can be seen. A description by Pausanias suggests it may be the Stoa Poikile (Painted Portico; but it could be the Stoa of the Herms, too), named after the large number of paintings of mythical and historical events which it housed.[103] It was built between 475 and 450 BC and was used as a lawcourt, for informal encounters and as the meeting place for those who wished to take part in the Eleusinian Mysteries. Many Classical herms were found near this stoa, some of which were mended in Antiquity (in the museum in the Stoa of Attalos); it is likely that they were defaced in the mutilation episode instigated by Alcibiades and described by Thucydides: 'In a single night the faces of most of the herms were mutilated. There seemed to be a conspiracy behind the deed aimed at a revolution and the overthrow of the democracy'. Next to the stoa the excavators have restored an arch on two existing bases (on which, rather unconvincingly, a rider placed in side view to the arch is said to have stood); since the bases are not aligned with each other, they should be interpreted as pedestals of separate (statue) monuments.

The **Peribolos of the Twelve Gods** (Figure **21**.13). Directly against the wall which separates the railway from the Agora excavations the corner of the marble foundation of a roughly square enclosure is preserved; it contained an altar to the twelve Olympian gods.[104] The sacred temenos is identified from an inscribed statue base found next to the west entrance ('Leagros has dedicated this to the Twelve Gods'). The site was considered as the starting point for the calculation of all distances from Athens. The enclosure had two building phases (only the later is visible); the earlier, of poros stone, was built over by a later one of marble. Since the Leagros base, which had a bronze statue clamped onto it, lies on the level of the later enclosure dating to the late fifth century BC, the statue must have been erected after the Persian Wars (not before 480 BC, as has been thought). Leagros is generally identified with a youth described as 'beautiful' (kalos) on late sixth century BC vase paintings; he fell in battle against the Thracians in 465/4 BC, as joint leader of an Athenian cleruchy expedition; his statue base has unconvincingly been used by scholars as evidence that the altar of the twelve gods was dedicated by him. Both the poros and the marble architecture imitate a fence made of wood which thus can be reconstructed as a first, late Archaic construction of this sanctuary which was destroyed by the Persians.

The **Temple and Altar of Ares** (Figure **21**.14). In the Early Roman period a Classical marble temple was transported from Pallene to the Agora,[105] as the excavation of its foundations has now proved (see pp. 236–7). The building first was dedicated to Athena Pallenis and is similar to the Hephaisteion; when it was taken down every block was marked with mason's marks to facilitate reconstruction. These marks can be clearly seen on the few building components which are still extant today. The site is indicated by a gravel fill. The altar belonging to the building is situated in front of it on the east side. A statue of Ares, God of War, made by Alkamenes, a pupil of Pheidias, stood in the shrine, as well as a statue of Athena, to whom the temple originally belonged. There is a ritual connection between Athena Pallenis and Ares in that the cult in Pallene was supervised by an association,[106] which was composed not only of citizens from the neighbouring communities, but also of those from the Deme of Acharnai (lying far away on the south foothills of Mt Parnes), and in Acharnai there was a prominent sanctuary of Ares and Athena Areia. The peripteros might have become a Temple of Ares under the Early Roman Empire because Augustus encouraged the worship of the god Mars Ultor, the Latin version of Ares, who was his personal protector. Perhaps this first Roman Emperor, who had studied in Athens as a young man, was responsible for the relocation and rededication of the temple.[107]

The **Odeion of Agrippa** (Figure **21**.15). The concert hall, dedicated by Marcus Vipsanius Agrippa, the son-in-law of the Emperor Augustus, occupied the large area in the centre of the Agora.[108] The interior, which was once roofed, housed an auditorium with eighteen rows of seats, a few of which are preserved today, surrounded by foyers. The stage façade was decorated with a row of Classicising herms (in the Stoa of Attalos). The high building was roofed without the aid of inner supports, a noteworthy architectural feat; however, this risky construction collapsed in an earthquake in the second century AD, and the whole building had to be completely rebuilt. The entrance was decorated in this second century AD renovation by pedestals on which stood two Tritons and two Giants; the upper bodies of these giant figures are copies of gods from the west or the east pediment of the Parthenon. In late Antiquity, after the Odeion was destroyed in the sack of the Heruli (AD 267), the foundation of the whole building was used as a large entrance yard for a gymnasium (sports precinct). Earlier statues and other monuments were built into the late Antique walls. Two statues of philosophers (?) in Greek mantles sitting on throne-like chairs can be seen today, behind the façade with the Giants.

Numerous **statues** were displayed in the Agora, which gradually became more and more built over with edifices, such as the Temple of Ares and the Odeion.

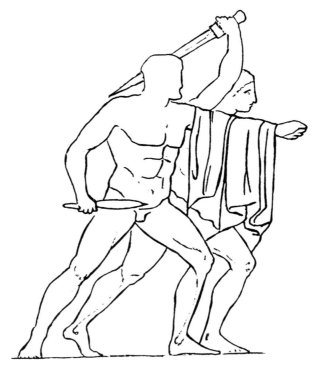

Figure 23 Statue group of the Tyrannicides, Harmodios and Aristogeiton

The most famous statues were the two figures of the Tyrannicides, Harmodios and Aristogeiton (Figure **23**), and the portrait of Demosthenes.

Basilica, Rotunda and Bema (Figure **21**.16–18). A huge basilica was also erected in the Roman period (c. AD 120–130) on the north-east corner of the Agora, where excavation has recently begun. It was built over many small shops which lay on this side of the area earlier on. Many monuments stood in front of the long façade of the Stoa of Attalos, including a round columnar building (Figure **21**.17) and an orator's platform (Figure **21**.18). The Rotunda, or monopteros, consisted of eight columns supporting a brick dome above an entablature; there were no walls inside, so the building, which dates to the mid-second century AD, must have been light and airy (compare with the Temple of Roma and Augustus on the Acropolis; see p. 41). In the middle in front of the Stoa of Attalos the excavators have reconstructed a speaker's platform (bema) on a rectangular conglomerate base. A number of steps probably led up to it so that the orator stood much higher than his public, who gathered on the Panathenaic Way. However, the remains preserved could perhaps be interpreted as a statue monument.

Stoa of Attalos (Figure **21**.19). The Stoa,[109] which was dedicated by the Pergamene King Attalos II (159–138 BC), falls into several components. In front of it is a terrace with a pillar monument in the middle of it; it was similar to the Agrippa Monument in front of the Propylaea and looked exactly the same as the one at the north-east corner of the Parthenon on the Acropolis; it also supported a quadriga, containing a statue of the Pergamene king, Attalos; it was later re-dedicated (together with the inscription) to the Emperor Tiberius. The stoa itself is divided into two aisles by an inner row of columns, behind which were twenty shops (used today as museum rooms); in the south-east corner a stair leads to the upper floor of the two-storey stoa. It has been possible for the American archaeologists to restore the building completely (1953–56), since enough orig-inal building elements had survived to allow an accurate reconstruction (Plate 21). The 116 m-long façade has Doric columns below and Ionic on the floor above; the lower third of the Doric columns is left unfluted; the space between the Ionic half-columns which are connected by pillars are closed by a marble balustrade. In the interior the columns are changed: Ionic columns without flutes are used on the ground floor and columns decorated with Egyptian palm leaf capitals on the upper floor. The building offers the visitor a pleasant impression of an ancient stoa in a southern climate. There is only one small fault in the restoration: the carving of the protruding tongues of the lion head waterspouts on the edge of the roof was forgotten with the result that today the rain water falls onto the steps of the stoa instead of into the water-channel on the terrace.

The **Museum** in the Stoa of Attalos. As well as the restoration rooms, store-rooms and offices of the Agora excavations, the Stoa of Attalos also contains a museum in which a large number of finds from the Agora excavations are exhib-ited. Since all the objects cannot be fully treated here, a general description is given for the visitor to orientate himself.

At the south end of the portico: statue of Apollo Patroos by Euphranor c. 330 BC; at the bottom of the stairs and beside them along the long wall of the stoa: parts of Ionic columns with traces of fine painting, from an unknown building, which was brought to the Agora in the Roman period; two armed female statues from the Library of Pantainos (Figure **21**.20) which personify the Iliad and Odyssey of Homer; stage façade of the Odeion of Agrippa with Classicising herms; statue of a Nereid c. 400 BC; fragments from the Hephaisteion, Athena and Herakles attributed to the east pediment, an acroterion figure and a head from one of the east metopes; reliefs from horse contests: base with the representation of armoured men jumping onto chariots (Apobates) and stele fragment of a victory monument erected by the tribe Leontis (inscription and part of a lion relief on the back side) on the occasion of their victory in a cavalry contest; colossal statue of Themis from the Stoa Basileios (usually dated to c. 330 BC; other the-ories interpret the figure as Demokratia or Agathe Tyche); some Roman portrait heads including Trajan with a laurel crown and a general's bust of Antoninus Pius. On the short north side: statue of a late Antique official in a toga with folds in low relief; acroterion figure of a Nike from the Stoa of Zeus c. 420 BC. Along the inner colonnade: some document reliefs, lawsuit inscriptions (one has to do with the Salaminians, who were settled in the deme of Sounion); lease records from the silver mines in the Lavrion, statue bases and statuettes; a nymph with a water jug from the Nymphaion, second century AD (Figure **21**.31) after a

Classical original; at the south end a tripod base with archaising reliefs of heroes (perhaps Theseus, his father Aigeus and Medea). The exhibition in the back rooms of the museum begins with many showcases of pottery found in graves and wells in the Agora and dating from the prehistoric to the Geometric period. An ivory pyxis (Case 5) decorated in relief from a Mycenaean chamber tomb (c. 1400 BC; see model) is of especial interest; in the third compartment (Case 17) the famous terracotta chest with Geometric decoration and five miniature granaries on its lid is displayed; it perhaps refers to the division of the populace into classes based on their land (a practice not dated with certainty until the time of Solon), which was measured according to the bushels of grain obtained; following this theory the woman in the grave with the chest and many other burial gifts belonged to the rich upper class. The following vases in the Orientalising Style depict human figures and animals; in contrast Geometric patterns are far fewer. In the next compartments, which contain Archaic and Classical finds, there are many objects pertaining both to daily life and to the political administration of the city-state. The objects from private life comprise, for example, a child's potty, terracotta toys in the form of animals and many clay oil lamps. Public life is represented by inscribed slabs with decrees, fragments of the original statue base of the Tyrannicides, Harmodios and Aristogeiton, the base of a monument for those fallen in the Persian Wars, an archon list (probably inscribed in the fourth century BC) which goes back to the early Athenian democracy, library rules carved in marble, official ballots and vase fragments with the names of politicians for ostracism, a machine for the allotment of jury and officials, a waterclock in the form of two clay basins which measured the time allowed for speeches in the lawcourts and standard weights and measures for market control. There are also some dedications with a similar official character, such as a Spartan bronze shield captured at the Battle of Sphakteria (Pylos) (425 BC), which was exhibited in the Stoa Poikile and seen by Pausanias. Other objects on display represent crafts and trade; the terracotta mould of a bronze statue, for example, was used for the production of bronze sculpture, in this case a kouros, which is less than life-size and without attributes which would reveal his identity (from the workshop in the area of the later Temple of Apollo Patroos); other objects come from potters' workshops; bone eyelets, cobbler's nails and a clay cup with a name on the bottom come from the cobbler Simon's shop (Figure **21**.26) in which Socrates taught Athenian children (see the statuette of the philosopher found in the prison). A fine terracotta oil flask in the form of a kneeling youth binding his hair as a victor in an athletic contest stands out (c. 530 BC). At the north end of the museum Roman portrait heads are on display. Similar heads, which served as portraits of important Athenians, are to be found on the upper floor (mostly closed), where models, plans and photos of the monuments of the Agora and other important Athenian monuments are also on display.

The **Library of Pantainos** (Figure **21**.20). South of the Stoa of Attalos, on the other side of a colonnaded street running eastwards to the Roman Market, the Athenian Flavius Pantainos had a public library built. On the lintel above entrance a dedicatory text suggests a date for the building *c.* 98–102 AD. There were shops facing the street, while the actual library comprised a large square room opening through a row of columns to a courtyard on the west side. Two adjacent side rooms were probably for the use of the readers, since the preserved list of rules shows it was a non-lending library, so no text rolls could be lent out ('No book can be removed . . . The library is open from 1 to 6'). The post- (or ante- ?) Herulian city wall, the so-called Valerian wall, built on the ruins of the façade of the Library of Pantainos, runs along the Panathenaic Way up to the Acropolis. Numerous building components from the destroyed buildings in the Agora, such as column drums, marble blocks and inscriptions, can be seen in this wall.

The **Southern Market** with the **Heliaia** (or **Aiakeion**) and the **South-west Fountain House** (Figure **21**.21–25). In the Hellenistic period a small part of the Agora was divided off for use as a real market place for trading. It was framed on the north side by the Middle Stoa (Figure **21**.21) and opposite by the Second South Stoa (Figure **21**.22), which lay over the earlier South Stoa containing the rooms of the market controllers (Metronomoi). On the east the area was bordered by a stoa with a central propylon, in front of which the money changers may have had their tables on the eastern end, as suggested by some paving stones with four clamp holes. Unfortunately all these buildings are very badly preserved; the long colonnade of the Middle Stoa, divided into two aisles by an inner row of columns, can be best made out; on the outside the columns were linked by grilles. The small South Market was bordered on one side by the large court- yard of the Heliaia (Figure **21**.24), the lawcourt founded in the Archaic period (other scholars put it in the north-east of the Agora and locate here the Aiakeion). In front of this lawcourt the remains of a water clock are still visible; it worked like its well preserved contemporary in the Amphiareion at Oropos, which has a similar construction (see pp. 253–4). Further west is a large fountain house which had an L-shaped water basin in an almost square enclosing wall.

Cobbler's Workshop and **Strategeion** (Figure **21**.26–27). To the south outside the area of the ancient Agora directly adjacent to the Agora boundary stone (Figure **21**.7) the American archaeologists found a small house, which they have assigned to a certain Simon from a cup with an inscribed name, and identified as a cobbler's shop from hobnails, bone eyelets and ties. From ancient sources we know that a cobbler called Simon had a workshop next to the Agora in which Socrates taught the Athenian children, who were not yet allowed to enter the Agora area themselves. Five hundred years later when the cobbler's shop had long since disappeared, Plutarch imagined himself in the interesting atmosphere of the cobbler's shop: 'I wish I was a cobbler in ancient Athens, then Socrates could come in and sit by Perikles in my house and converse with him.' Centuries later a latrine was built in this place. To the west on the other side of the road is an area cut into the hill of Kolonos Agoraios which was perhaps the head- quarters of the strategoi, the Athenian general. This is suggested by finds of clay plaques with the names and titles of military officers.

Triangular Sanctuary (Figure **21**.28). In the south-west corner of the Agora excavations is a small area which has several points of interest. It is a triangular
enclosure built of fine, partly polygonal masonry. In Greek cities such triangular
areas are occasionally dedicated to heroes, and indeed it is known from a
boundary stone on the north side of this place in the Agora that there was a
Hieron, a sanctuary, here. Unfortunately, the inscription does not tell us to whom
the temenos was dedicated. South-west of this sanctuary, on the other side of
the road, the state prison probably lay in which Socrates was imprisoned and
forced to drink the lethal hemlock. During the excavation of this building numerous
small bottles were found which perhaps contained the poison, as well as a statuette of the philosopher, which was probably put up as a memorial soon after
his death, when his execution was regretted.

South-east Fountain House, **Mint**, **Nymphaion**, **South-east Temple** and **Church
of the Holy Apostles** (Figure **21**.29–32). In the south-east corner of the Agora
the original ancient buildings are very difficult to recognise, as they were almost
completely covered over by a church. In the Archaic period there was already a
fountain house here (Figure **21**.29) consisting of two draw basins and a central
room, which could be entered; its architecture can be recognised from its yellowish
poros stone; according to Pausanias it could be the Enneakrounos (fountain house
with nine water spouts) dedicated by the Peisistratids. In the Classical period
the mint was built next door for the manufacture of bronze coins (Figure **21**.30).
After the mint went out of use in the Hellenistic period the Nymphaion of Trajan
(Figure **21**.31) and the South-east Temple (Figure **21**.32) were built in its place.
The latter mostly consisted of Ionic building components from an earlier temple,
the Temple of Athena, which had been transferred from Sounion (see p. 204).
Today parts of some Doric columns of south Attic marble have been set up here,
but these belong to the South-west Temple (Figure **21**.8).

On the foundations of the Nymphaion the Church of the Ay. Apostoloi (Holy
Apostles) was built c. AD 1000 (Figure **24**). It is one of the oldest Athenian
churches and its architecture is of particular interest. This much destroyed church
was restored by American scholars in 1954–57, during which later additions
were removed so that the building now has its original Byzantine appearance.
The church is the cross-in-square domed type consisting of a square hall with
a central dome supported by four columns, ancient in this case; each arm of
the cross ends in a conch and there are cross conches over the corner bays.
On the west side the usual small narthex precedes the church combining harmo-
niously with the main building. The lower courses of the walls are composed of
large unworked stones, but above they are made in cloisonné technique with
small squared blocks framed by tiles, which in some places imitate Arabic signs
(Arabic Kufic script). In addition to the marble floor, which is restored from original fragments, some fresco remains are preserved in the interior of the church,
which give an impression of how the church walls were once decorated. In
contrast the frescoes in the narthex come from the Chapel of Ay. Spiridon, which
was built over the Library of Pantainos in the seventeenth century and torn down
in 1939.

N

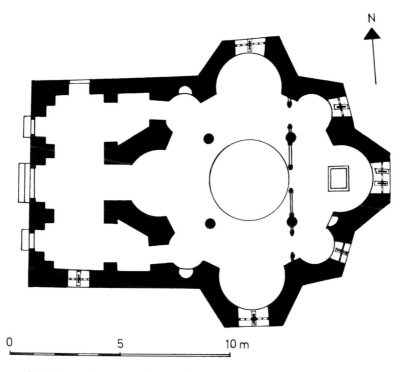

0   5   10 m

Figure 24 Athens, Agora, Ay. Apostoloi.

Eleusinion. In the south outside the fenced area of the excavations there is a sanctuary on the sloping hillside east of the Panathenaic Way, which was dedicated to the Eleusinian goddesses. Only a few architectural remains of the temple foundations and of the enclosure can be seen; a Roman imperial frieze block, which probably comes from this temple, is built into the south side of the Little Metropolis Church (see pp. 95–6). The City Eleusinion was of some religious importance during the preparation for the Eleusinian Mysteries and for the cult of Asklepios whose sanctuary lies on the south slope of the Acropolis. The Street of the Tripods, which began south of the Acropolis near the entrance to the Sanctuary of Dionysos, ended here with two branches, one south and another to the north.

The Roman Market and the Library of Hadrian (Figure 26)

The Roman Market,[110] also called the Market of Caesar and Augustus after the two Caesars who began and finished its construction, lay east of the Greek Agora and was connected to it by a colonnaded street. A large Doric portico on the west side, the Gate of Athena Archegetis (the 'Leader of the Tribe'), with a dedication on the architrave dated to 11–9 BC is still well preserved (Figures **25**; **26**.1; Plate 22). It led into a large area surrounded by

Figure 25 Athens, western gate of Roman Market (Gate of Athena Archegetis),
c. 1750 (after Stuart and Revett).

(Photo DAI Athens (93/38))

stoas; in the east right next to the Tower of the Winds (Figure **26**.4) are the
remains of another gateway. The lower parts of columns and door frames made
of bright Pentelic and Hymettian marbles are preserved, as are the steps of
grey-blue Hymettian marble. The two entrance buildings are not constructed
on the same axis, because they stand above an earlier street, which ran in a
straight line diagonally across the area, going in one direction to the Classical
Agora and in the other, as a Hellenistic colonnaded street, to the Archaic Agora
in the east. Little more than the south half of the site can be seen, as the
north part lies under modern buildings and under the Fetiye Camii (Figure **26**.2),
the victory mosque of the fifteenth century into which numerous ancient
spolia are built; only the lower part of the minaret is extant with the beginning of the spiral staircase. After the sack of the Heruli (AD 267) the administrative centre of ancient Athens was located on this site; a market was held
here in the city centre throughout the Middle Ages up to the nineteenth
century.

East of the Roman Market are the ruins of a **public latrine** (Figure **26**.3)
(the flushing canal round the sides can still be seen), the **arched façade of a
Roman building** (Figure **26**.5), which made up the gate to the Hellenistic
colonnaded street during the Roman period (mid-first century AD), and the
exceptionally well-preserved **Tower of the Winds** (Figure **26**.4; Plate 23). This
octagonal marble construction is a complicated technical building housing a

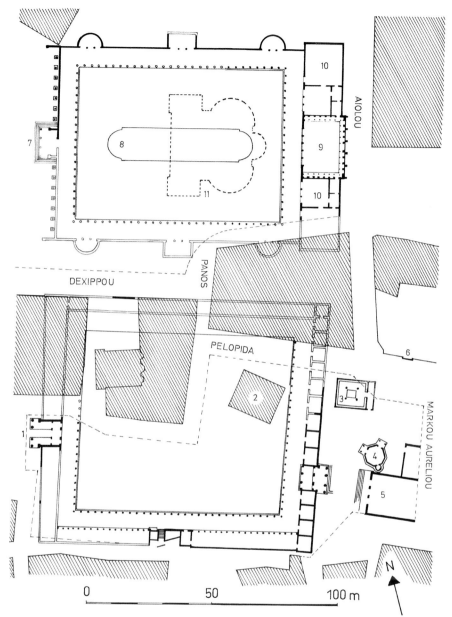

Figure 26 Athens, Roman Market (Agora of Caesar and Augustus) and Library of Hadrian.

1: Gate of Athena Archegetis; 2: Fetiye Camii; 3: latrine; 4: Tower of the Winds; 5: arched entrance of a colonnaded street (so-called Agoranomion); 6: entrance to the Koran Seminary; 7: Propylon of the Library of Hadrian; 8: water basin; 9: library room; 10: lecture rooms; 11: quatrefoil building/ church.

water clock;[111] its exact mechanism has not yet been finally clarified. According to Vitruvius the clock was constructed (finished at least in 34 BC) by Andronikos of Kyrrhos and functioned through a complicated interior system of pipes; the necessary water was kept in a cistern in an almost circular turret attached to the south side of the building; the hours were shown on a 'clockface' and regulated by an even in- and outflow of water through a cylinder in the interior of the building. On the roof was a bronze weathervane in the form of a triton. On the outside below the eaves there are reliefs of the winds, representing these blowing from each direction, portrayed in clothing adapted to the temperature of their weather and with characteristic attributes. In the north, for example, Boreas, the cold north wind, hovers in a long sleeved mantle and high-laced boots, while on the south (Notos) and west (Zephyros) the mild sea winds are only wearing light garments. The names of the winged winds are inscribed above them (Boreas (N), Kaikias (NE), Apeliotes (E), Euros (SE), Notos (S), Lips (SW), Zephyros (W), Skiron (NW)). Below the figures of the winds the hour lines of eight sundials were carved; their dial-hands are missing today. On the north-east and north-west sides of the building there were once small porches with a roof supported by two (Ionic or Corinthian) columns without bases, which framed the entrances to the tower. In the interior of the tower (not open to the public) grooves for the pipes of the waterclock mechanism can be seen in the floor and a wall division into four zones, which were separated from each other by cornices. The wall of the highest zone has small Doric semi-detached columns blended into it. A post-Sullan foundation for the Tower of the Winds, perhaps initiated by Caesar (other scholars believe in a date in the late second century BC), is suggested by the architecture and the style of the reliefs, the style of the lettering of the wind names, the entrance columns without bases, its site between the Archaic and Classical Agoras[112] and directly next to the Roman Market founded and financed by Caesar and the measurements of the sundial, which had a subdivision modelled on Roman Uncae (units of measurement). In the Early Christian period the building was used as a baptistry for a nearby basilica; in the Turkish period it became a room for the dance of the dervishes, an Islamic ritual; for this reason a floor was added at the level of the first cornice; panels with maxims from the Koran, a prayer niche, religious equipment and a chandelier, which hung from the ceiling of the tower, were part of the furnishings of the building at that time.

Opposite the present-day entrance to the Roman Market (by the Tower of the Winds) was a **Koran Seminary** (Medresse; Figure **26**.6); only the entrance remains, but this portal with its Islamic decoration hints at the former splendour of the building. A long dedicatory inscription over the door dates the foundation of the school to 1720/21.

Parallel to the Roman Market, but lying further north a magnificent **library**[113] was erected in the reign of **Hadrian**, as part of his large building programme for beautifying Athens (Plate 22). The site is used today as a storeroom for the Archaeological Service and so is closed to the public, but from outside a good view of the area can be obtained, the most rewarding being that of the north-east corner on Aiolou Street and of the façade on the west side. Further excavations were taking place here recently to clarify the building plan of the area in front of Hadrian's Library. Up until now remains of Late Hellenistic houses[114] have been found built on a slightly different axis, probably orientated onto the large Hellenistic street further north; these houses were removed to make way for the Library.

The complex, which was enclosed by a high wall, was entered from the west through a propylon with a wide ramp (Figure **26**.7). The entrance side, which faced the Greek Agora, was emphasised by an outer courtyard and a costly marble wall with a colonnade, which is being restored at the moment. On the south side of the entrance there was a similar wall (remains found in recent excavations) with columns in front of it (of marble from south Euboia, the so-called Karystos marble or Cipollino). The interior courtyard was framed by colonnades on all sides and had a large central water basin (Figure **26**.8). The main library room (Figure **26**.9) lay along the east side flanked by small side rooms, which could be used as lecture rooms (Figure **26**.10). The whole complex was probably more than a library, a luxurious imperial building for the Athenians to spend their time here, perhaps with a room for the emperors' cult. In late Antiquity[115] a building, quatrefoil in plan (Figure **26**.11), was constructed over the east end of the reservoir; its function is unknown. In the seventh century this open, light building was replaced by a three-aisled basilica. The columns standing here today belong to the successor to the basilica, an eleventh century church. Finally, beside the ancient propylon the cross-domed Church of Ay. Asomatoi was built in 1295; it was torn down in 1842 so that excavation could take place. The remains of frescoes on the walls of Hadrian's Library date to the foundation of the church.

Monastiraki Square (Figure **27**.2) is quickly reached from the Library of Hadrian; the whole neigbouring business quarter is named after it. The centre of Turkish life lay between the Lower Bazar here and the Upper Bazar around the Kapnikarea Church (Figure **27**.16); even today the area has the atmosphere of an oriental town with its many shops, its busy traders and its bustling activity. In the alleys and streets up to Omonia Square (Figure **2**) on both sides of Athinas Street the shops are grouped on the bazar system: one alley for copper implements, another for curtains or spices. Sacks containing herbs, nuts or dried fish stand on the pavement in front of many cellars. Halfway to Omonia Square the fruit and vegetable market is situated on the left of Athinas Street, while in the stoas opposite is the huge meat and fish 'Agora', as the Greeks of today still call the market.

On Monastiraki Square one of the few relics of the Turkish period can be seen: the Mosque (Figure **27**.1), which was built in 1759, is a Museum of Popular Greek Art and has been newly restored. Opposite it is the Pantanassa Church, which belonged to a tenth century monastery (Monastiraki means 'little monastery'). From the outside almost nothing can be seen of the original building material of this three-aisled basilica with elliptical dome.

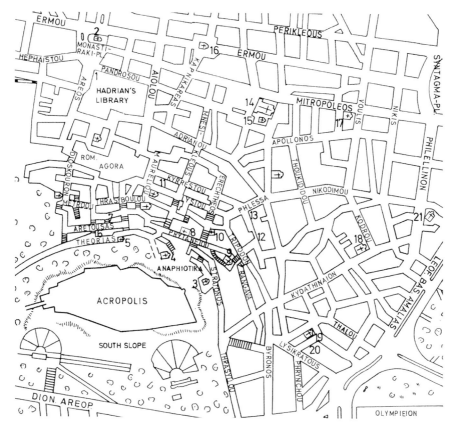

Figure 27 Athens, sketch plan of the Plaka.

A few blocks further north, Athinas (Figure **2**) is crossed by Evripidou Street. Turning into this and going west in the fourth block of houses on the right side a small chapel can be seen dedicated to **Ay. Ioannis 'stin colonna'** (at the column). An ancient Corinthian column rises above the roof of the chapel, which, according to folklore, is supposed to heal malaria.

The **Square of Ethnikis Anastaseos** ('of national regeneration') is located a few steps further north along Athinas Street; it was a large excavation zone. The foundations of a nineteenth century Neoclassical theatre lay in the west part, opposite the town hall of Athens, while in the eastern area, separately fenced, a part of a Classical street bordered by some late Antique plain sarcophagi and a few house remains have been uncovered. In the lower levels graves were found which go back to the Geometric period.[116]

6   Plaka, Olympieion, Ilissos Area, the First Cemetery and the Stadium of Herodes Atticus (Figures 27–32)

Plaka (Figure 27). The Athenian Old Town, which stretches north and east of the Acropolis between Vas. Amalias, Dionysiou Areopagitou and Mitropoleos Streets and the Greek Agora, is called Plaka. The origin of this name, which was first applied in 1862 and was then used for the area around the Lysikrates Monument, is disputed: one explanation is that the expression has come from 'the flat area' in contrast to the high Acropolis rock; another traces the word to Albanian where it means 'old' and says the name was given by Albanian mercenaries in the Turkish army.

Plaka is a quarter full of narrow twisting streets and is mostly a pedestrian zone. Right below the Acropolis rock is the 'Anaphiotika' (reached from Theorias and Stratonos Streets) which calls to mind Cycladic architecture with its steeply rising stepped alleys, small, square, sometimes whitewashed, houses with yards and tiny gardens and colourful flowerpots in front of blue and green shutters. And, indeed, after the War of Independence craftsmen from the Cyclades settled here, brought in to decorate the new capital city of King Otto, such as, for example, highly skilled marble cutters from Tenos. The first houses here were built by two master builders from the island of Anaphe. The quarter received a further influx after 1922, when refugees from Asia Minor arrived.

Besides this island architecture there are interesting Byzantine churches in the Plaka[117] and fine old houses (Plate 22). There is very little left of buildings dating to the Turkish period which, with their inner courtyards, recall ancient houses, or of the magnificent Neoclassical buildings; many are in very bad condition. On the edges of many roofs terracotta decorations can be seen, often palmettes, occasionally also figural representations. Most of these acroteria are modern and modelled on ancient examples; only a few date to the last century.

There are traces of Antiquity everywhere in the Plaka. Antique foundations appear below some of the tumbled down nineteenth-century houses; blocks, capitals and columns from ancient buildings can be seen reused in the walls of old houses and churches or as ornamental pieces in gardens and yards. Plaka today is particularly well known and loved by tourists because of its numerous restaurants, discotheques and souvenir shops. A folklore programme designed for foreign visitors drove out the locals in the last decades. Old houses had to give way to modern buildings or collapse after the departure of their inhabitants. In addition to the restoration programme for the Acropolis, restoration work has also been carried out for Plaka; many of the old buildings have been restored and are in use today, until now mostly by civil services, such as the Archaeological Service or Museums.

Round Tour. Coming from the Theatre of Dionysos before reaching the Ana-phiotika the visitor arrives at the small church of Ay. Georgios tou Vrachou (St George on the Rock; Figure **27**.3) directly below the rock of the Acropolis. The small, simple church with side chapels dates to the thirteenth century; it has been repeatedly whitewashed and is decorated with ancient spolia. Immediately east of the Anaphiotika is the post-Byzantine Church of Ay. Simeon (Figure **27**.4). The pretty Church of Metamorphosis Sotiros (Transfiguration of Christ; Figures **27**.5; **28**) in Theorias Street dates to the fourteenth century and has the typical soaring proportions of that epoch. The masonry of this cross-domed church allows the later additions and alterations to be seen easily from the out-side, for example on the narthex. The altar comprises an ancient capital; a small side chapel is cut into the rock. The Kanellopoulos Museum is located in a renovated house dating to *c.* 1830 (Theorias, corner of Panos; Figure **27**.6). It houses a private collection of antiquities of minor arts (pottery dating from Neolithic to Roman, Greek terracotta statuettes, jewellery, two Roman marble portrait heads dating to *c.* AD 120, remnants of Coptic textiles and, in the court-yard, Classical grave stelai) and Byzantine ecclesiastical objects and icons of the fourteenth to the nineteenth centuries. The pieces on exhibit are of high quality and provide a thorough and interesting overview of minor Greek arts from pre-history until modern times; the peaceful atmosphere of the house (imitations of Pompeian ceiling decorations) at the foot of the Acropolis with its teaming visi-tors may offer a welcome interlude. Other distinguished buildings are found on Arethousa and Panos Streets. After its foundation in 1837, Athens University was first installed in the private house of the Neoclassical architects Kleanthes and

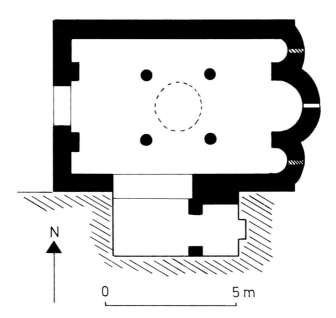

Figure 28 Metamorphosis Sotiros on the north slope of the Acropolis.

Schaubert (Tholou 5; Figure **27**.7). Its first professors included seven Germans amongst whom was the archaeologist Ludwig Ross, the first Director of Greek Antiquities. The building on Prytaneiou (Figure **27**.9) is a further example of successful restoration; today it houses the office of educational programmes, which has a small teaching exhibition on the development of writing. A few steps further along Prytaneiou Street the monastery of Metochi tou Panayiou Taphou (Figure **27**.8) is a dependency of the church of the Holy Sepulchre of Jerusalem. The chapel of the Anargyroi in this monastery was built in the seventeenth century and contains gilded wood carving; the iconostasis is particularly worth seeing. It is pleasant to spend time in the peaceful monastery courtyard which contains many ancient marble fragments. The original building of Ay. Nikolaos Rangavas (Prytaneiou, corner with Epicharmou; Figure **27**.9) dates from the eleventh–twelfth centuries. However, the appearance of the original church, which for a time belonged to the mansion of the noble family of Rangavas, is very unclear because of later additions and plastering. The walls of cloisonné masonry contain ancient spolia (for example from choregic dedications which once bordered the Street of the Tripods). In contrast the small cross-domed church of Ay. Ioannis Theologos dating to the twelfth century has remained unaltered (Erechtheos, corner of Erotokritou; Figure **27**.10). The columns of the church, which is hemmed in on two sides by new concrete buildings, are adorned with ancient capitals; further spolia can be seen in the forecourt. In the 1970s restoration work uncovered some fragments of thirteenth century frescoes. The Turkish Bath (Figure **27**.11) in a building on Kyrrhestou Street is only recognisable from the red crescents in the lattice work of the windows. The house of Sir Richard Church (Philhellene, commander-in-chief of the Greek army and privy councillor to King Otto) is located in a towerlike building in Scholiou 5 (Figure **27**.12). The founding of a German School (Figure **27**.13) in Athens was instigated by the architect and former director of the German Archaeological Institute, W. Dörpfeld. He also designed the first school building, the Demotic School, which is situated at the corner of Scholiou and Phlessa. Plaka is bordered on the north side by Mitropoleos Street. This street is named after the Athenian cathedral, the church of the Metropolitan bishop. The 'Large Metropolis' (Figure **27**.14) is a ponderous building dating to 1840–55; its original plan, which was later much altered, was designed by Schaubert. It was constructed on the site of a monastery, whose tradition goes back to the seventh century; in 1827 most of the monastery buildings were destroyed; only the catholikon was preserved, that is the pretty and interesting 'Little Metropolis' (Figure **27**.15) on the south side of the modern church (Plate 24). It is an cross-in-square domed chapel; in the interior the original columns were replaced by four pillars in 1833. From 1841 the church was used as a library. The real charm of this twelfth century church derives from its masonry, which consists of large marble and limestone blocks, ancient grave reliefs, sculptured friezes, inscription slabs and fragments of sarcophagi. Over 100 building components come from other contexts, mostly ancient or Early Christian. 'Heathen' symbols or representations were 'Christianised' by carving the sign of the cross on them. One big block is carved with triglyphs and metopes decorated with torches, animal skulls and a phiale, which suggest a provenance

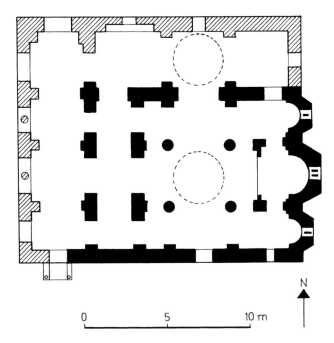

Figure 29 Kapnikarea Church.

from the Eleusinian cult; perhaps the block comes from the Eleusinion above the Greek Agora. The most interesting piece is a frieze in two parts over the entrance façade (first century BC), which depicts the Attic calendar with its religious festivals (zodiac symbols, the Panathenaic procession, harvest, etc.). In contrast the coats of arms belonging to the families of Villhardouin and de la Roche date from the Middle Ages. The 'Little Metropolis' is dedicated to the Panayia Gorgoepikoos (quickly-helping Mother of God) and Ay. Eleutherios (Helper in childbirth). A side street leads north into the parallel street, Ermou. Standing in the middle is a small Byzantine church (Figures 27.16; **29**), the Kapnikarea. It was built in the eleventh century as a cross-domed church and is dedicated to the Virgin. It is named after its dedicator, who introduced the smoking tax (Kapnikaris). In the seventeenth century a side aisle dedicated to Ay. Barbara was built onto the north side and the whole complex provided with a common outer narthex. The masonry of the original building is very characteristic; the lower part is built of large irregular stones, the upper in cloisonné technique. The paintings on the interior date to the nineteenth century. This Byzantine gem almost fell victim to the Neoclassical city plan of Athens; the designers wanted to make long axial avenues up to the palace and had planned to tear down the Kapnikarea. Only the personal intercession of King Ludwig I of Bavaria saved the church, which, in addition to its art historical value, was also of great idealistic importance, as it had been the meeting place of the Greek population during the Turkish period. East of the large metropolitan cathedral on Mitropoleos, between the pillars of a concrete highrise building, the chapel of Ay. Dynamis (Holy Strength) is a striking example of a clash of different cultural epochs (Figure **27**.17); the tiny church dating to the Turkish period is almost crushed by the modern building of the Ministry of Education. Going now southwards again towards the Acropolis via Voulis and Kodrou the visitor reaches Kydathinaion where the Church of Soteira tou Kottaki (Figure **27**.18) is situated on a square with ancient columns. This cross-domed church dating to the twelfth century was later turned into a three-aisled basilica; the original, richly decorated dome supported on four columns is well preserved in the centre of the building. Until 1847 this church was used as the Russian Orthodox church (now moved to the Nikodemos Church; see p. 106). Shelley Street leads from here to Lysikrates Square. The small excavated area, bordered by street cafés, contains some bases belonging to choregic dedications as well as the Lysikrates Monument (Figure **30**; Plate 25), which is almost completely preserved.[118] As choregos (producer) in 335 BC Lysikrates won the prize of a tripod with the dithyramb chorus which he had sponsored. Instead of a simple stone plinth to support his tripod he put up a circular marble building on a high square limestone base, on the roof of which a finial of acanthus leaves supported the tripod. The columns of the monument are crowned with Corinthian capitals, the earliest example in Greek architecture of the use of the Corinthian order externally. The architrave, decorated with fascias, carries the dedicatory

Figure 30 Lysikrates Monument as a library of a Capuchin convent, *c.* 1750 (after Stuart and Revett).

(Photo DAI Athens (93/41)

inscription on the east side; the frieze depicts the transformation of the Tyrrhenian pirates into dolphins by Dionysos. A statue may have stood in Antiquity in the interior of the monument, which in ancient times was not closed on the east side facing the Street of the Tripods (Pausanias describes an unidentified choregic monument as having a satyr by Praxiteles as interior decoration). Between 1669 and the beginning of the nineteenth century the small building was used as a library by the neighbouring Capuchin convent and went by the name of the 'Lantern of Demosthenes' (Figure **30**). As a result of this reuse the choregic monument remained in good condition and needed little restoration. This monument was only one of many similar monuments (see pp. 52–3), standing around the Theatre of Dionysos and along the Street of the Tripods, which ran round the east and north sides of the Acropolis and led to the Eleusinion above the Classical Agora. Today the view of the site of the Lysikrates Monument is spoilt by the brick walls of a late Antique sewage system, which was built partly over the bases of the tripod monuments. In the immediate neighbourhood of this square on the corner of Lysikratous and Vyronos is the church of Ay. Aikaterina (Figure **27**.19) dating from the eleventh to twelfth century. The original cross-domed church has been added on to and restored many times. Only in the apses, the dome and the roof area of the cross arms can the original masonry in the cloisonné technique be recognised. The whole interior is modern. In front of the church, at a deeper level, the remains of two wings of a colonnade[119] have been uncovered, which made up the border of a square in the Roman period. On the south side a modern building of several storeys houses the Museum of Folk Art (Figure **27**.20).

T**he Arch of Hadrian and the Olympieion** (Figures **2**.9; **31**; **32**). From the Lysikrates Monument, Lysikrates Street leads to the two-storeyed Arch of Hadrian (Figure **31**.1). This site was the border between the old Athens of the early King Theseus and the new city of Hadrian, according to the two inscriptions on the inner and outer entablature over the entrance. There were two Corinthian columns on each side of the gate attached by a cornice to the narrow arch;[120] the same Corinthian order was used on the corner pilasters and in the upper storey of the arch. On the upper storey the four Corinthian pilasters enclosed three rectangular bays, of which the middle one was closed in Antiquity by a marble slab. There was no statuary decoration on the arch.

The second century AD Arch of Hadrian played an important role in the Hadrianic building programme (Hadrian's Library [see p. 91] and the Olympieion were other large projects initiated by this emperor [Pausanias I.18.9]). It is not by chance that it lies directly on the Acropolis-Zeus Temple (Olympieion) axis. On this exposed place it marked a fictitious border between old and new Athens; it was planned to link the old cult centre of the city to the new Hadrianic centre, connecting the hero Theseus and the city patron, Hadrian. A body called the Panhellenic Synedrion (Panhellenion)[121] played a leading role in defining the programme, which fostered ancient, traditional ties between Athens and other cities and communities of the Antique world – today

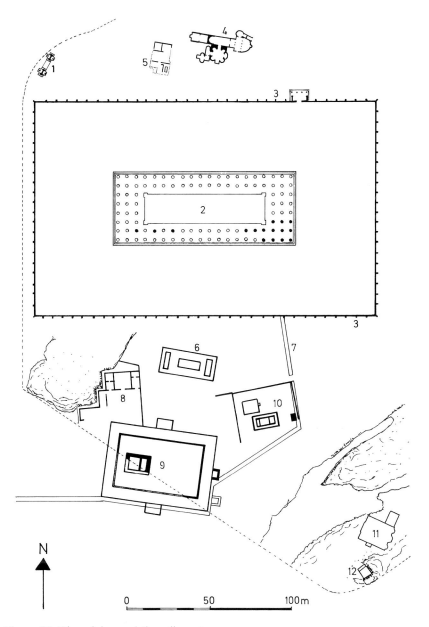

Figure 31 Olympieion and the adjacent area.

1: Arch of Hadrian; 2: Temple of Olympian Zeus; 3: precinct with the propylon; 4: bath; 5: dwelling house; 6: Temple of Apollon Delphinios; 7: Valerian city wall; 8: lawcourt at the Delphinion; 9: courtyard complex (for the emperors' cult ?); 10: Sanctuary of Kronos and Rhea; 11: Ay. Photeini; 12: Sanctuary of Pan.

it would be called city partnership – and made a religious centre for these connections. The Panhellenion was responsible for the emperor cult of Hadrian, which was centred on the Olympieion.

The Temple of Olympian Zeus (Figure **31**.2), the largest marble building in the Corinthian order in Greece, remained as an unfinished building project until the time of Hadrian.[122] It was originally begun in the early Archaic period, enlarged by the Peisistratids and planned as a huge building in the Ionic order, but it did not get much beyond the foundations for the dipteros (temple with a double row of columns round the cella) because the new democracy deliberately stopped the building projects of the Tyrants and concentrated on the new buildings on the Acropolis. Some of the large unfinished column drums of the Archaic Olympieion lie on the north side of the site, where they were built into the Themistokleian city wall; some show deep incisions, where it was planned to cut the blocks into smaller pieces. In the late fourth century BC the Athenian politician Lykourgos restarted the temple building project using the earlier foundations,[123] now building a dipteros in the Corinthian order. This project was then resumed between 175 and 164 BC by the Hellenistic King Antiochos with the Roman architect Cossutius based on the earlier plans. This building, too, was incomplete when Antiochos died. Sulla had some of its columns taken to Rome *c.* 80 BC, where they were built into the Temple of Jupiter on the Capitoline. Although the building must have had gaps in it, it must nevertheless have been quite far advanced. After an interim building phase under Augustus the gaps were finally filled in under Hadrian and the temple was finished at last having been over 600 years in construction. It is most probable that the emperor took part in the dedication ceremony (AD 131/132).

The huge Corinthian temple (Figure **31**.2) was built on a wide plateau on a substructure (Plate 2) measuring *c.* 110 m by 44 m surrounded by a colonnade with 104 columns, of which today 15 are still standing (Plate 26); one collapsed in 1852 as the result of a thunderstorm. On the ends there were three rows of columns and on the long sides two. The oblong cella housed a large chryselephantine cult image of Zeus; curiously enough no altar has been found in front of the temple where remains of a marble pavement are to be seen. This huge temple of Olympian Zeus is surrounded by a long precinct wall of poros blocks (*c.* 209 m by 129 m) which is strengthened with buttresses and reaches quite a height on the south side (Figure **30**.3). On the north side a relatively small marble propylon leads into the precinct which was paved with marble flagstones and which was otherwise closed off from the surrounding area. In the interior statues of the gods and representations of prominent personalities of the time were displayed. Pausanias notes, for example, that every city which was a member of the Panhellenion had dedicated a statue of Hadrian; some of the statue bases can still be seen today in the area of the Olympieion. The whole precinct was dedicated to the worship of Zeus Olympios, but it was also dedicated to Hadrian. The Emperor had taken the Zeus-title of 'Olympios' a few years earlier, and in the dedicatory year AD 131/132 he also took the title of 'Panhellenios'.

During excavations in the twentieth century remains of Roman baths (Figure **31**.4) and dwelling houses were uncovered (Figure **31**.5) north of the surrounding wall of the Olympieion. In the latter a small Roman relief (second century AD; cast on site) was found on which an Eleusinian high priest (hierophant) is portrayed together with the goddesses Demeter and Kore.

The **Ilissos Area** (Figures **31**.6–12; **34**). South of the Olympieion (Plate 2) the ruins of some temples and buildings lie in the area sloping down to the Ilissos river,[124] which is today closed to the public for restoration works. The foundations of a Classical Temple of Apollo can be seen among the bushes (Figure **31**.6); it was dedicated to the Olympian brother and sister, Apollo Delphinios and Artemis Delphinia, and dismantled in the third century AD so that its building components could be used for the city wall of Valerian (Figure **31**.7). The limestone foundation, which supported a Doric superstructure, and a few remains of the marble architecture are all that is left. The polygonal masonry further west dates to the late sixth century BC; the architectural plan of this building, which had a courtyard (Figure **31**.8), together with a description of the area by Pausanias suggests that the 'Law Court at the Delphinion' was located here. In contrast there is still no firm information for the interpretation of a large rectangular courtyard (Figure **31**.9) to the south. A small temple was located in it surrounded by columns, of which only the foundations are preserved; the second century AD date of the complex may suggest an emperor cult was carried out here. A further shrine in a separate enclosure (Figure **31**.10) is to be found east of the courtyard complex, with a small temple on a podium of ancient concrete (second century AD). It may be that this Doric temple surrounded by a colonnade is the cult place of Kronos and Rhea mentioned by Pausanias.

The entire Ilissos area was a holy precinct dating back to very ancient times with numerous cults. From the literary sources we know of, for example, a sanctuary of Herakles and another of Aphrodite, which must have been here. The sacred tradition of the area was preserved until late Antiquity, since a three-aisled basilica dating to the fifth century AD, decorated with Early Christian mosaics, has been found on the site of the modern sports centre (to the east; Figure **31**). There are also archaeological remains from two more cult sites. On the south-east side of what was once the valley of the Ilissos, which is now largely dry and has mostly disappeared but was described by Plato as an idyllic wooded area, a rectangular chamber was hewn out of the rock (behind the church of Ayia Photini; Figure **31**.11); there must have been a Pan Sanctuary here (Figures **31**.12; **32**), since in the afternoon raking light a figure of this god can be seen, carved into the rock on the south side. Further up the slope on the other side of the many-laned, traffic laden Leophoros Ardittou are the few remains of the foundations of a terrace for the Temple by the Ilissos which, converted into a Christian church, stood almost untouched until 1778 (Figure **34**). It is a High Classical cult building[125] (perhaps dedicated to Artemis Agrotera), which was very similar to the Nike Temple on the Acropolis (Figure **9**) and probably on the same plan (by the architect Kallikrates), built

Figure 32 Ilissos area, Sanctuary of Pan, rock-cut relief.

soon after 440 BC. Thanks to drawings of the building by the English scholars Stuart and Revett (1751–53) not only are the architectural details of the small Ionic shrine, built of Pentelic marble, well known but also its overall appearance. Parts of the temple, especially the blocks of its relief frieze (of Parian marble),[126] are scattered in museums in Athens, Berlin and Vienna today.

The **First Cemetery** (Figures **2**.12; **33**). The principal Cemetery of Athens containing countless marble grave monuments of the nineteenth and twentieth centuries is situated south of the area of the Ilissos and can be reached from Anapavseos Street (Figures **2**.12; **33**; open 9.00–17.00hrs). The visitor obtains an interesting impression of the influence of Classical Antiquity; many grave monuments call to mind ancient temples, and ancient sarcophagi and grave stelai are imitated. This is exemplified by a copy of the Lysikrates Monument (see pp. 97–8) or by the graves immediately left of the main entrance. Among the latter is the grave of Heinrich Schliemann (1822–90), which was designed by Ziller in the form of a Doric temple on a high podium with a relief frieze (Homeric scenes, scenes of sites excavated by Schliemann: Plate 27).

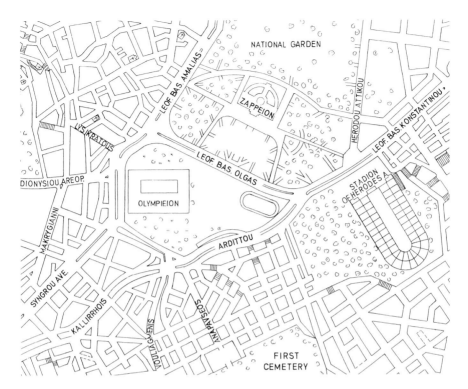

Figure 33 Sketch plan of the area of the Olympieion.

About 100 m along the central path and turning left, the specially enclosed Protestant cemetery is reached; amidst numerous graves of famous Philhellenes and historians the grave stele of the noted archaeologist Adolph Furtwängler (1853–1907) can be seen with a bronze copy of a sphinx he found on Aigina. As well as the pseudo-ancient grave ornaments there are also accurately carved portrait busts, almost life-size representations of whole families and surprisingly abstract modern grave stones to be seen.

In the Greek Orthodox church there are several memorial services for the dead, announced in the different suburbs by invitations stuck onto the house walls; there is a service forty days after death and then a year later and three years later; after the church ceremony the mourners meet at the grave side and eat a sweetmeat made of wheat, raisins and pomegranate seeds.

The **Stadium of Herodes Atticus**. The stadium can be reached from the area of the Ilissos by crossing over Leophoros Ardittou or from the National Garden (Figure **31**). In summer cultural performances occasionally take place here. On normal days sportsmen train on the running tracks or on the paths under the pine trees above the marble building.

Figure 34 Temple by the Ilissos, *c.* 1750 (after Stuart and Revett). Photo DAI Athens (Att 444)

In the years 330/329 BC the Athenian politician Lykurgos had the running track used in the Panathenaic Festival games removed from the Agora to the hollow between two hills east of the Ilissos. The natural valley was levelled by putting in an earth fill and equipped with a 183.30 m-long track and some seats on the slopes. The whole construction was named after the Attic measure for the length of the running track, which was a stade. From now on the athletic contests held during the Panathenaic Festival took place here. After many repairs in the following centuries the rich Athenian Herodes Atticus (sophist, politician and patron of the arts; Plate 65) finally had the whole Stadium[127] rebuilt in Pentelic marble between AD 136 and 140. The slightly curved long sides close into a half-circle at the south end which was surmounted by a stoa; the tiers of seats, which were decorated in Antiquity with reliefs of owls and accommodated around 50,000 people, are divided into two blocks by a gangway running round halfway up; on the west side is a box for dignitaries. The present appearance of the Stadium is due to the Alexandrian Greek, G. Averoff, who had the site restored true to the original using ancient fragments; during this restoration ancient building components were incorporated into the new building (see in the interior the two ancient double herms with the heads of the young Apollo and the bearded Hermes Propylaios). Shortly after the renovation the 1896 Olympic Games, the first of the modern series, took place in the Stadium.

In Antiquity the Stadium was separated from the city by the Ilissos. A large bridge, perhaps also a gift of Herodes Atticus, was put up across it to give easy access to the sports site (Figure **34**). It is certain that Herodes Atticus had two further buildings put up above the Stadium on the two side hills; a few remains have been found. On the west Hill of Ardettos the foundations of masonry on a concrete terrace belonging to a Temple of Tyche can be seen; it was connected to the Stadium by a long staircase. The first priestess of this city goddess was the Roman wife of Herodes Atticus, Regilla. Opposite on the east hill are the foundations of masonry with concrete belonging to a narrow monument over 40 m long. It is thought to be the mausoleum of the dedicator, since literary sources say that after his death in Marathon (AD 177/178) Herodes Atticus was buried here at the Stadium; an altar block with the inscription 'for the hero of Marathon' supports this idea. Alternatively, it is thought that the monument could be the base for the festival ship from the Panathenaic procession of AD 140 sponsored by Herodes, which was later exhibited. An unfinished marble sarcophagus, which perhaps once contained the bones of Herodes Atticus, but which also received a later burial in the third century AD, seems to support the first interpretation. Today the sarcophagus decorated with carved strigils is displayed in a niche on the east side of the upper stadium area. However, the proportions of the foundations, which are unusual for a mausoleum, are more appropriate to the base of a ship.

7   The National Garden, main boulevards, National Museum, Lykabettos, Tourkovounia and the Academy at Kolonos Hippios

The **National Garden** (Figure 2.14). Simultaneously with the laying of the foundations for the royal palace in 1836, a park was laid out on the lines of an English one. Queen Amalia had plants and trees brought from all over the world for this and grew palm trees from datestones; a vegetable garden was also laid. Thanks to a waterwheel, which was set up during the work, the plants could be continuously watered, even during the hot summer months when the population of Athens hardly had enough drinking water. At particular times of day, generally in the hot midday, the park was open to the public. Today the dense foliage of the National Garden with its duckpond, flower beds, arbours, huge shrubs and trees is a welcome oasis of freshness and peace. Walking around it the visitor continually meets traces of Antiquity, such as the architrave of the water reservoir on Lykabettos with a large Hadrianic inscription (Figure **39**), stone seats from the nearby Stadium, columns and Corinthian capitals, a Roman mosaic and the remains of wall courses. The south side of the garden contains a large Neoclassical building for state receptions and exhibitions, the **Zappeion**, which was donated by two brothers called Zappas and built by the architects Hansen and Ziller in 1875–85.

Leaving the National Garden on the west side and crossing the wide Leophoros Amalias the visitor reaches the **Church of Soteira Lykodimou** (the Nikodemos Church). This relatively large Byzantine church was finished in 1044; the oldest inscription dates to 1035. Its attached monastic buildings were destroyed in an earthquake in 1701, while the catholikon was much damaged by the Turks in 1780. In the War of Independence the church was largely destroyed; it was acquired by the Russian government and carefully restored in 1855 by the Bavarian artist L. Thiersch; he also built the four-storeyed belfry in the earlier style and undertook the painting of the interior of the church. This massively proportioned building stands on the foundations of a Roman bath dating to the time of Hadrian; hypocausts and floor mosaics can be seen in the crypt, which follows the plan of the Roman walls. In the interior of the cross-domed church the upper gallery, which can be reached from the narthex, is striking. The dome rests on the columns of this upper floor, which is carried by eight pillars. This plan allows quite a large diameter for the dome and gives the impression of a stoa. On the exterior the careful masonry in cloisonné technique has some brick ornament and, as especial decoration, clay plaques with arabesques and animal representations.

On the east side of Syntagma (Constitution) Square (Figure 2.16) stands the **Old Palace**, in which the **Greek Parliament** meets today (Figure 2.15). It was built between 1834 and 1838 by the Munich architect Gärtner for King Otto; the monotony of the façades is enlivened by marble entrances decorated with columns. The paved area in front of the west façade with the Memorial to the Unknown Soldier is the scene of the popular change of the guard by the Evzones ('well belted'), the former bodyguard of the king, wearing traditional costume.

Syntagma Square, which was originally designed by Leo von Klenze, is framed on the other three sides by large hotels, including the 'King George' and the 'Grand Bretagne', both built in 1867 and steeped in tradition, and by the offices of international airlines and modern highrise buildings. Recently the square has been restored with fountains and flower beds in connection with the building of the new metro; some of the older cafés had to disappear as a result of this; others still invite a pause for refreshment. During the construction of the metro ancient remains were found, especially graves, which lay in the east outside the city walls. The discovery of Roman baths and a classical industrial quarter, including a bronze foundry, is also important. Syntagma Square, together with the circular Omonia Square, is a main orientation point in the city plan of modern Athens. All the important roads and streets running in different directions begin here. The big rallies of the political parties take place here before each election, recalling the proclamation of the constitution in 1843 from the balcony of the palace. Since January 2000 there is a subway station open to the public where some archaeological finds of the excavations during the construction of the 'Metro' are displayed (copies).

East of the National Garden at the rear of the palace in Herodes Atticus Street the **New Palace** stands in a pretty park with large trees; it was built by Ziller for the crown prince. Today it is the residence of the president; here, too, the Evzones in national costume keep watch.

From Syntagma Square **Leophoros Vas. Sophias** (Avenue of Queen Sophia) runs east and then north in the direction of Kephissia. There are noteworthy nineteenth century buildings on this wide road, for example the Egyptian, French and Italian Embassies in the neighbourhood of the palace; there are also the town houses of leading Athenian families, some with interesting art collections, and also larger museums. Only a brief mention can be made here of these buildings and their collections, some of which are worth visiting.

The **Benaki Museum** lies at the corner of Vas. Sophias and Koumbari (Figure **2**.17) in a nineteenth century marble mansion (and in a new annex, opened in June 2000). It consists of the private collection of Antonios Benakis, a rich Greek businessman based in Cairo who collected ancient, Byzantine, Arabic and Chinese art and left his estate, including this building, to the Greek nation.[128] A high point of the display is the modern Greek folk art and objects which illustrate Greek history since the War of Independence. The jewellery dating to several different millennia stands out amongst the antiquities, as well as the works of minor art, which include numerous terracottas. There are important ikons in the Byzantine department dating from the fourteenth to the sixteenth centuries. In addition there is a Greek sculpture display, fabrics and garments from Greek Asia Minor, as well as interesting embroideries and paintings of the nineteenth and early twentieth centuries; a fine shop and a restaurant are also attached. The visitor to Athens should not miss this museum.

Two blocks further east Neophytou Douka runs left up towards Lykabettos. In the new building at No. 4 a particularly interesting modern museum on several floors for Cycladic and ancient Greek Art,[129] the **Goulandris Museum**, is a gift of Nicolas and Dolly Goulandris. It displays a unique collection of Cycladic marble figurines, jewellery and stone vases from the third millennium BC. The timeless appearance of the severely abstract marble figures takes the visitor by surprise; the large number of such Cycladic idols in this collection allows development and changes to be studied. Copies of ancient jewellery, marble plates, etc. can be bought in a shop at the entrance. The Neoclassical building which is connected to this museum serves for temporary exhibitions (for example some archaeological finds of the Metro works) and has an impressive façade on Vas. Sophias.

On the opposite side of Vas. Sophias is the Officers' Club, beside which Regillis Street runs south. On the left side of Regillis is an extensive building plot on which a new museum building for the art collection of another branch of the Goulandris family was planned. During excavation work the foundations of a large building complex have recently been found, the plan of which seems to be a **Greek gymnasium** with a palaestra. Since, according to literary sources, the Lykeion, the school of philosophy formed by Aristotle,[130] should be placed in this area (near the source of the Eridanos), the few building remains have been identified as this building. However, the existing masonry is of a much later date, certainly post-Sullan. This means that, if the identification is valid, there are no architectural remains from the Late Classical Lykeion preserved in the later building. The publication of the excavation should clarify this matter.

Following Vas. Sophias further away from the city on the right is one of the most important Athenian collections, the **Byzantine Museum**. It is housed in a building with a large inner courtyard dating to 1840 and contains architectural components, frescoes, mosaics, sculptures and ikons dating from late Antiquity into the eighteenth century. The museum buildings, which are undergoing a large extension, have recently been newly arranged.

To the east next to the Byzantine Museum is the modern **War Museum** containing exhibits which illustrate the development of weaponry from the Mycenaean period onwards. The highlight of the collection is the history of the War of Independence and the wars of the twentieth century.

The **National Pinakotheke** (Picture Gallery) is located at the big junction of Vas. Sophias with Vas. Konstantinou. It mostly contains pictures by Greek artists of the nineteenth and twentieth centuries, as well as designs for marble sculptures (many portrait busts) by famous nineteenth century sculptors.

F rom Syntagma Square to Omonia Square. The two pivots of Athenian traffic circulation are connected by wide avenues; from Syntagma Leophoros E. Venizelou Street, called Panepistimiou (University Street), carries the traffic down to Omonia, while Stadiou Street takes it up from Omonia to Syntagma. Along and between these important arteries are many banks and offices, some shops, noteworthy buildings and museums.

Proceeding down **Panepistimiou** from Syntagma after a few minutes' walk a large house with balconies supported on columns can be seen on the right. This is the **house of Heinrich Schliemann**, the German excavator of Mycenae, Tiryns, Orchomenos and Troy. He called his house, designed by the architect E. Ziller in 1878/1879, 'Iliou Melathron', that is, Palace of Ilion (= Troy) in memory of his Trojan excavations. The modern High Court of Justice (the Areopagos) met here for many years; the Numismatic Museum is located here today. On the corner of Panepistimiou and Omirou is the building of the influential **Greek Archaeo-logical Society**. Beyond it is the Catholic **Church of St Dionysios** and three buildings in Neoclassical style: the Academy, the University and the National Library. The **Academy** (1859–85; architect Th. Hansen; Figure **2**.18) is built in the Ionic style (influenced by the Erechtheion) and houses the Academy of Athens; its sculptures and (inside) its painted decoration are therefore orientated towards Classical themes: in the pediment the birth of Athena from the head of Zeus, in front of the façade statues of Socrates and Plato, in the interior paint-ings of the myth of Prometheus. The scientific institution 'The Academy' was founded in 1926. The relatively simple building in the middle is the headquarters of the **University of Athens** (architect Chr. Hansen; Figure **2**.19); lectures and seminars have only recently been removed from it to a campus in the suburbs. Today only ceremonies take place in the beautiful halls. Next is the **National Library** (Figure **2**.20), a large rectangular building with a curved outer staircase and a magnificent Doric façade (Plate 28). It was built in the 1890s to a design by Ziller; the reading room with tall Ionic columns and pleasant roof lighting is also impressive. Continuing towards Omonia on Trikoupi Street a few metres up on the left the **German Archaeological Institute** is located in a house built by Schliemann on Ziller's designs in 1888. Right next to it in Pheidiou Street is a much ruined mansion which is one of the oldest buildings of modern Athens. It is the former residence of the Austrian ambassador Prokesch von Osten, who built it in 1836 in the Neoclassical style; at that time it lay outside the city. Later it contained a music school (the **Odeion** where Maria Callas trained); today the ruins are empty awaiting restoration and a new use. Panepistimiou Street ends in **Omonia Square**, a circular area which once had fine houses in the Neoclassical style around it. Today the square, with its peeling façades and with modern build-ings all round, has lost its charm and is no more than a roundabout for the heavy traffic; important avenues run from here to all parts of the modern city. In January 2000 the immense building operations to connect the old and new metros were finished here.

There are monuments worth visiting on **Stadiou Street**, especially in the upper south-east part. For example, the important Byzantine Church of **Ay. Theodoroi** (Figures **2**.21, **35**) on the large Klavthmonos Square on the south side of the street (at the beginning of Evripidou Street). This building, which dates to the early eleventh century, had a predecessor dating to the ninth century, the paving stones of which are preserved under the present church. This cross-domed church with four pillars in antis in the middle has three apses on the east end; on the west end a narthex has been put in front of the central room. The exte-rior of the church is built in the usual cloisonné technique, that is limestone

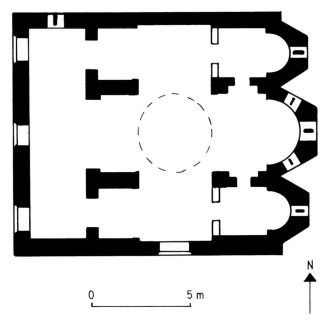

N

0   5 m

Figure 35 Ay. Theodoroi.

blocks framed by vertical and horizontal terracotta bricks, with a clay frieze depicting animals and plants, as well as pseudo-Kufic script on the bricks. An inscribed slab (perhaps reused) over the main door on the west side relates to a restoration in September 1040 (6548 in the Constantine Calendar). The belfry is a later addition; the interior decoration is modern. The **City Museum** is on the south-east side of Klavthmonos Square (Figure **2**.21). It houses documents pertaining to the Bavarian period of the history of Athens; of particular interest is a model of Athens in the last century. A few metres further on going towards Syntagma Square, Stadiou reaches Kolokotroni Square (equestrian statue of Kolokotronis (1770–1843), a general in the War of Independence) with the **Old Parliament Building** (Figure **2**.22). This building, the 'Old Vouli' (earlier the town hall), consisting of a chamber and adjoining wings, today contains the National History Museum which houses mementoes and documents of the history of Greece starting around 1770 and gives information on important personalities of the War of Independence and of the early years of the reign of King Otto. This museum can also be used as a starting point for a stroll through Plaka and to the Byzantine churches of the Old Town.

Just before Omonia Square the wide 28th of October Street (called Patission as it leads to the suburb of Patissia) runs north. The **Technical University** (**Polytechnion**), a building complex in the Neoclassical style, can be reached in a few minutes' walk. A student revolt against the military dictatorship

was suppressed here by tanks in November 1973, an event which is com-
memorated annually on the 17th of November with a demonstration through
the city.

A few steps further north is the **National Archaeological Museum**, the
most extensive and important collection of Greek antiquities in the world, with
rich displays of sculpture, pottery and works of minor arts. The museum was
built from 1866 to 1869 and has been enlarged many times. It has separate
departments: straight in front of the main entrance on the ground floor is a rich
prehistoric collection and an equally rich sculpture department (Figure **34**), as
well as the department of Greek pottery (often closed) on the upper floor; next
to the latter is a small special exhibition of interesting finds from the Cycladic
settlement of Akrotiri on Santorini (Thera), including important frescoes. On
the south side of the museum in Tositsa Street is the entrance to the department of inscriptions (Epigraphical Museum). The numismatic collection has
now moved to the Schliemann House on Panepistimiou. The visitor should
make several visits to the National Museum, if possible, since the collections
are too important to get a good overview in only a few hours. It is also worthwhile on the first visit to find out about the opening times of the Greek pottery
department, which is often closed, so that it can be visited on a second occasion. The most important objects will be briefly described here in the form of
a round tour following the chronological development of Greek art and the
order of find complexes (Figure **36**). (Owing to renovations in the museum
there may be changes to the order of the monuments).

Rooms 1–3. Vestibule with ticket counter, cloakroom, book and postcard stalls.

Room 4. Finds of the Mycenaean period are displayed here, a culture named
after the great palace at Mycenae, lying some 30 km south of Corinth in the
Argolis. Traces of this culture have been found all over Greece. It dates from
c. 1600 to c. 1100 BC. Its discovery is mainly due to H. Schliemann, who excavated from 1876 at several sites, which he located from the tales of Homer. The
objects in Room 4 are not arranged in the showcases chronologically but in stylistic groups and by site (for example: Mycenae: Cases 1, 2, 25, 26). Most of the
artefacts are burial offerings; the dead were buried with objects of daily life
(pottery, jewellery or seals) and also with weapons; at Mycenae the faces of
the dead were covered with gold masks. A close look at the small details
of decoration is rewarding, such as, for example, the ritual depictions on the
gold signet rings, the inlaid decoration with hunting motifs – a lionhunt by armed
Mycenaeans – on the daggers and swords, the high relief decoration on gold
cups, such as bull-catching with nets, or on the amazing gold masks, which in
spite of some individual traits cannot be seen as portraits of Mycenaean leaders.
There are some fresco fragments with hunting scenes or processions of ladies
from the palaces of Mycenae, Tiryns or Boeotian Thebes. Mycenaean art was
initially strongly influenced by the Minoan culture of Crete. Some finds, such as
Egyptian faience or alabaster vases from Crete, bear witness to a far-flung trading
network.

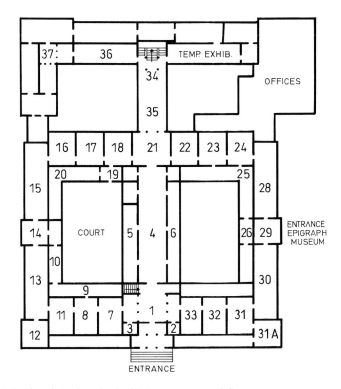

Figure 36 National Archaeological Museum, ground floor.

Room 5. In the narrow left-hand side room objects from the Neolithic period are displayed (6000–2000 BC). Simple pottery with incised decoration is on show, as well as stone implements (choppers, axes, chisels, arrow heads, etc.) and figurines with a very schematic form, which first depict fertility goddesses with steatopygous bodies and later with violin-shaped bodies on which the breasts and sexual organs are emphasised.

Room 6. In this side room objects from the early culture of the Cycladic islands in the Aegean are displayed (third and second millennia BC). The fine marble figurines are striking; they are small, simple and stylised with nose and sexual organs emphasised. A particularly well-known Cycladic figurine is the seated harp player (see also the Goulandris Museum p. 101). The marble or clay flat plates (known as Cycladic frying pans), often decorated with spiral form ornament, are also striking. At the far end of the room are finds from the famous Cycladic settlement of Phylakopi on Melos (plan and photo on the wall); obsidian, a black stone suitable for use as scrapers and blades, was quarried on this island and exported round the Mediterranean.

Room 7. The tour through the Greek sculpture collection begins here on the left next to the ticket booth. The visitor must bear in mind that ancient marble sculpture was always painted, but that today almost nothing is left of the colour (hair, eyes, lips, clothes, etc.); this feature is very important when the overall appearance of Greek sculpture is considered. On the right-hand wall: limestone metopes from an Early Archaic temple (c. 630 BC) at Mycenae with an obscure theme, which is stylistically akin to the contemporary Cretan Daedalic style. On the right next to the door to Room 8: a limestone grave relief of Kitylos and Dermis from Tanagra in Boeotia (inscription); the brothers, or friends, stand with their arms round each other, each with the inner leg forward instead of the usual left leg forward; provincial Boeotian work dedicated by Amphalkes c. 600 BC. On the left next to the door to Room 8: statue of a woman from Delos in a belted robe; it is unclear whether the statue represents the goddess Artemis or the dedicator, Nikandre (inscription on the left side); the tall, block-like figure with shallow carving dating to the mid-seventh century is one of the first life-size representations of European art (given that large wooden statues may have been lost); next to it is a seated woman from Tegea carved from a single limestone block together with her chair; the statue, probably a goddess, wears a long peplos, similar to that of 'Nikandre', with a mantle lying diagonally across it, c. 620 BC; further seated statues are on the left next to the entrance. In the middle of the room is one of the most famous Greek vases, the Dipylon Vase Inv.804 (see p. 61); this enormous amphora is a masterpiece of both potting and Geometric vase painting dating to c. 750 BC; neck and body have bands of Geometric motifs, especially meanders, with two animal friezes in between and a picture, in the handle zone, of mourning men and women by a corpse on a bier covered with a check cloth (a prothesis scene); the vase, which is almost as tall as a man, stood above a grave in the Kerameikos; the bottom of the vase is pierced for pouring libations into the earth for the dead (or for nailing it to the base). In a case on the wall behind the Dipylon vase is a small ivory figurine from a grave in the Kerameikos dating to c. 730 BC and portraying a female figure with polos, a head covering which is often used in depictions of goddesses; the figurine may have been the handle of a costly object, such as a mirror; oriental artistic influence can be clearly seen.

Room 8. Egyptian standing male statues apparently had great influence as models for the production of the Greek kouros statues. The frontal stance, the position of the arms and the left leg forward are all related to Egyptian works. However, the ancient Greeks developed something new from these prototypes by making them nude and altering the proportions. This can be seen especially in the large heads; the statues are freestanding with the weight of the body over the legs rather than leaning slightly backwards against a support, as in the case of the Egyptian statues; the dynamics of the human body and its potential for movement are emphasised by the straining muscles and joints and the proportions of the limbs. The room is dominated by the huge kouros from Sounion (Plate 45) in the middle of it (fragments of similar statues from the same site on the right next to the entrance to Room 11 and left and right behind the big kouros); typical features of the Archaic youth statues are the stance with left leg forward, the hanging arms with fists on the hips, the 'Archaic smile' and the long hair in beaded plaits confined with a band; on the forehead is a wreath of flowers;

the limbs of the body are very stylised, for example, ears, knees and ankles; the stomach is divided into eight muscle compartments, in the typical manner of Early Archaic figures, although six is anatomically correct; the legs are long and muscular to express athleticism; man is portrayed at the peak of his bodily power. The Sounion kouroi are votive statues which were set up in the Sanctuary of Poseidon at the beginning of the sixth century; however, most of the other kouroi come from graves (see below). The obvious orientation to the right of the large Sounion Kouros is not typical, but was perhaps necessary because of the position which took the altar into account. In front of the wall next to the colossal statue is the head of a kouros, 'the Dipylon Head', and on the wall the lower arm of a statue from the Kerameikos, both dating to *c.* 590 BC; the hair arrangement, the artistically knotted ribbon with long curved ends and the ear and eye modelling are similar to the Sounion Kouros, but everything is rounded and more spherically modelled. The limestone kouros head from Ptoion in Boeotia (*c.* 580 BC), on the right of the entrance to Room 9, is in a different style. The shape is angular, the face appears sharper, the mouth narrow lipped and unsymmetrical; the forehead is framed above by plaits combed symmetrically to the temples, while on the back of the head the typical beaded plaits hang down.

Room 9. The next two side rooms, 9 and 10, also contain Archaic sculptures including some statues of korai with richly folded Ionic mantles and a hurrying Nike statue in the Archaic kneeling-run pose. The kouros from Melos at the right end of the long room dates to *c.* 550 BC and the kore from Merenda at the other end to *c.* 540 BC; the statue base, which bears the inscription naming Phrasikleia made by Aristion of Paros, was found earlier built into a chapel; Phrasikleia wears a peplos decorated with incised embroidery motifs (rosettes, meanders); there is jewellery on her neck and ears and a wreath of flowers on her head; she holds a flower bud in her hand; the whole statue was richly painted. She was found together with a kouros (in Room 10). The preservation of both statues is so good because they were hidden in Antiquity (perhaps before the Persians came) by burying them at the site of the ancient grave.

Room 10. It is probable that the kouros in the centre of the room, found in the same grave as Phrasikleia, is also by Aristion of Paros. The youth, whose body parts are stylistically more developed (ears, knees, ankles and eyes) than those of the Sounion Kouros, already has the arms free of the body and slightly raised, although they are still attached to the hips by a small support; the hair falls below the nape of the neck onto the shoulders and is curled on the forehead in front of the band; traces of the original painted decoration can be seen on the pubic hair. As well as the Archaic grave statues, which are well represented by Phrasikleia and the kouros found with her, stelai were also used as grave monuments; a few examples are on show here. They generally depict youths shown as athletes (ephebes) with discus, spear or unguent flask. A plaster model on the right of the entrance illustrates a complete grave stele: a panel with a Gorgon relief supports the figural shaft, which is crowned by a sphinx as a grave guard. Four examples of such Archaic sphinxes are on show; they are hybrid beings with winged lion bodies and female heads. In the back part of the room the Kouros of Volomandra in Attica (*c.* 560 BC) is on show and on the left an unfinished statue still with its protective sheathing (mantle), which comes from the quarries of Naxos. It is apparent that the sculptor had already roughly carved the form in the round, probably for completion in the workshop, but was interrupted (Roman sculptors do not carve round the block layer by layer, but work from the front of the block to the back of it to carve out the body).

Room 11 leads from Room 8 with the Sounion Kouros. The complete four-stepped base for an Archaic statue, of which the feet are extant, is on show here. Next to it is a marble disc, the votive of a doctor called Aineas, according to an inscription on the rim. In front of the side wall are two grave stelai with warriors of which the better preserved from Velanideza near Loutsa is a certain Aristion (*c.* 500 BC); there are traces of paint on his armour depicting, on the shoulder straps, a star and a lion head, and, on the stomach, a meander; ancient repairs can be seen on this stele, a copy of which is set up on the Athenian grave mound at Marathon; the helmet crest, the pointed beard and part of the chiton were added on and are not extant today. Next to the Aristion stele is a grave monument on which the picture was painted only; the remains of paint depict a horseman on a red ground.

Room 12. In this side room adjoining the large Room 13 sculptures from the temple of Aphaia on Aigina (see p. 343) are on show. These were found after the pieces now in Munich and, therefore, were not taken to Bavaria; they consist especially of warrior heads onto which the helmet components and long plaits of hair were separately applied; further fragments are in the wall showcase. Next to this a stele with a running hoplite (*c.* 510 BC); while the legs are depicted in side view (the kneeling-run pose gives an impression of great speed), the torso is frontal, the turn of the upper body being shown by a fore-shortening of the stomach area. In front of the window wall is the statue of a reclining man from Daphni (*c.* 490 BC), probably a pedimental sculpture which was anchored to the pediment by a clamp in the back. The statue of a seated old man wearing a mantle draped diagonally over his body (from Athens, *c.* 520 BC) forms a contrast to the Archaic statues of youths; a once richly painted leopard skin and a leather cover drape his folding stool; the leopard skin suggests Dionysos may be represented. Nearby is a torso with a mantle (compare the Moschophoros on the Acropolis) and a statue with outstretched arms, which was probably carrying votive gifts, found close to the Ilissos (*c.* 500 BC).

Room 13. In this large room some kouroi from Ptoion in Boeotia are on show together with other Late Archaic sculptures. The fragments of a colossal seated statue of Dionysos with a kantharos in his right hand are impressive; this was the cult statue in the Sanctuary of Dionysos on the north slope of Pentelikon (in the ancient Deme of Ikarion, see p. 262); the finely folded garment and the long hair falling from the nape of the neck, which is preserved on the back, are note-worthy. The statue, made *c.* 530 BC, was repaired in Antiquity (probably in the fourth century BC). The head was attached to the body by a girder-like pin and the hand with the kantharos was reworked. The statue of Aristodikos on its base in front of the opposite wall comes from a grave on the Athens–Anavyssos road (by Olympos, see p. 200); a comparison of this Late Archaic kouros (*c.* 500 BC) with earlier statues shows the stylistic development in the sixth century BC clearly; although keeping to the basic Archaic scheme with the left foot forward, the body and limbs are not so severely stylised (ears, knees, ankles, division of the stom-ach muscles in six parts) and the arms are raised and separated from the upper body; a shorter hairstyle has evolved from the long hair of the earlier statues (probably once added separately here in the upper area of the head). The star-shaped pubic hair is typical of Late Archaic kouroi. A comparison of Aristodikos with the grave statue of Kroisos, which is about thirty years earlier and also found near Anavyssos (Plate 44), is interesting. It stands on a three-stepped base with an inscription which is aimed at the passerby: 'Stop and mourn by the grave mon-ument of Kroisos, killed amongst the champions by the wargod Ares'. This man, who fell in battle, had the name of the famous Lydian king. Some of the kouros bases were decorated with reliefs; two such from the Kerameikos (see also that museum) are on show at the end of the room; on their top side the grooves for the statue plinth can be seen. On one, 'the ball game base', there are studies of youths (the details similar to those of Aristodikos) practising athletics on the front and playing a ball game on the left side, while on the right side a fight between a cat and a dog, held on leads by their owners, is depicted; the second base, 'the hockey player base', has a relief of ephebes on the front playing with a ball with bent sticks, while on the sides are chariot scenes with hoplites in armour. Both bases were richly painted, some details, such as reins, etc., having only a coloured finish.

Room 14. The masterpiece of this room is a fragment of a relief stele depicting a boy taking a leaf from the band on his head (the leaf together with some long curls were once added separately in bronze) to dedicate it to a goddess (Athena). The relief, like the Ionic capital next to it, comes from the Temple of Athena at Sounion (see p. 204). It was made straight after the Persian Wars, as shown by the contraposto, and its calm pose is striking. In the middle of the room is a relief fragment depicting a female head on a curving background; the hair is gathered into a snood with only a few loose curls left in front of the ears; the meaning of the relief (Aphrodite?) and its original use are contested (from Melos *c.* 460 BC). Round the walls are some Early Classical grave reliefs (huntsman with dog, youth in a wide-brimmed hat holding a hare, female figures), which come from around Larissa in Thessaly.

Room 15. On the left next to the entrance is the votive stele from Eleusis repre-senting Demeter with a sceptre, her daughter Kore with a torch and the young hero Triptolemos at the moment when Demeter gave the ears of corn (originally added in metal) to Triptolemos; the relief dating to 440/430 BC was so famous that it was copied centuries later (Roman fragment in New York). On the other side of the door are two reliefs of horsemen dating to the mid-fifth century BC (from Thespiae in Boeotia and from Aigina), perhaps grave stelai, perhaps, however, architectural reliefs. In the middle of the room the bronze 'God of the Sea', a High Classical statue found in a shipwreck off Cape Artemision in north Euboia, makes a striking impression; it seems it was to be transported across the sea as booty (together with other statues, such as the Horse and Jockey in Room 21). The bearded, athletic god is poised with an arm raised to throw some- thing; the stance gives an impression of controlled might and power. Whether Poseidon or Zeus is represented can only be deduced by reconstructing the lost weapon: the right hand with its open finger position cannot have held a trident but only the middle of a thunderbolt; also, a trident is a stabbing not a throwing weapon and would disturb the balanced composition of raising and aiming; it is, therefore, a fine original bronze statue of the god Zeus (c. 460 BC). The female roof figure (akroterion) with fluttering garment by the left wall comes from the Temple of Ares in the Agora. In the back of the room is the sacred symbol of Apollo, the omphalos (navel), wound around with wool fillets in relief; a statue once stood on the upper side (traces of feet), and it was earlier wrongly thought that this statue was the male figure exhibited next to it with the result that the many Roman copies were called 'Omphalos Apollo'. The youthful male body clearly shows the innovations of Classical sculpture in contrast to Archaic. The proportions and details of the figure are based on nature, even if idealised. The innovation of Classical sculpture is the differentiation between the supporting leg and the relaxed leg; this causes a curvature of the body, perceptible at the middle of the upper body (linea alba) and the spine; in addition the distribution of the weight gives a corresponding tilt to the hips and shoulders; the head is slightly inclined on the side of the supporting leg; like the bronze statue of the 'God from the Sea', this statue, probably Apollo (found in the Theatre of Dionysos), also had long hair in two plaits wound round the head and knotted above the forehead.

Classical Grave Reliefs. Rooms 16, 18, 23 and 24 contain Classical Attic grave stelai. The obvious stylistic changes in these monuments, which all date from c. 430 to 317 BC, can be used to show a chronological development; they develop from simple stelai crowned with a palmette to architectural imitations of small temples (naiskoi); over the years the reliefs become higher until the framed figures appear almost in the round. The orientation of the figures also changes; in the beginning they are looking at each other, but by the mid-fourth century the dead person looks out of the picture towards the spectator. Thematically there is almost no change; one or more figures, members of a family, stand or sit by each other; women are often accompanied by their servants, men by their fathers or slave boys; adults often shake hands, a gesture indicating family ties, which in the case of children is replaced by the presentation of a gift (birds, other animals). Servants occasionally offer their dead mistresses jewel boxes or their infants; a hint of the cause of death (during birth or in the cot) is given both in childbirth representations and in the scenes of a child being handed to its mother, although the majority of grave reliefs give no hint of the cause of death. There is equally little information given about professions; men are mostly represented as Athenian citizens in public life, for example leaning on a knotted stick; only in a few cases are they depicted as priests with a long robe and a sacrificial knife; women are almost always in a domestic context, sitting on a stool or on a chair, or accompanied by their families. The grave stelai could be ordered in advance or on the occasion of the death of a family member; relatives still alive could then be portrayed and their names added when they died, or again a stele with a picture of the recently deceased was put up on the family plot, so that the same person could appear several times on a grave. Earlier grave stelai were often reused, perhaps on economic grounds; new inscriptions were added or the picture was altered by a sculptor. This reuse of Classical pieces still took place in the Roman period, when new grave stelai were set up again in Attica. As well as relief slabs there were also grave reliefs in the form of marble vases, especially colossal lekythoi, which were typical grave vases; these carried small, very low reliefs on the body. In addition the graves were often bordered by guard figures (dogs, lions, sirens, servants, or even archers). The reasons for the blossoming of Attic grave reliefs *c.* 430 BC (under the influence of the Parthenon sculptures) are unknown; perhaps there was some reason after the plague of 429 BC or the state grave monuments fostered a need for representation among private citizens and, with the end of the great Classical building programme, the sculptors found a new field of operation here. In contrast it is known from literary sources that a decree of Demetrios of Phaleron in 317 BC forbade grave sumptuousness and with it the ever increasing use of luxurious grave reliefs; the figural stelai were replaced by simple columns or blocks (trapezai) on which only the names of the dead were inscribed. Below (Rooms 16, 18, 23, 24) only characteristic examples illustrating this general description are noted.

Room 16. In the middle of the room on the left side of the entrance to Room 17 is a stele from Salamis or Aigina, *c.* 430 BC, crowned with a lotus-palmette frieze; a young man is depicted with a bird in his left hand, which he has taken out of a cage; a cat sits on a column and a small boy stands in front of it. The artistic influence of the Parthenon frieze is apparent. A huge marble lekythos found in Syntagma Square depicts a family (left) from whom the god Hermes, as the guide of the souls (Psychopompos), leads away a female inscribed as Myrrhine. Next to it the base of a lost marble lekythos with reliefs on three sides; on the front a man picks fruit from a tree which a woman opposite him collects in a fold of her garment; on one side is Hermes in a petasos (wide-brimmed hat) and on the other a priest in a long robe with a knife.

Room 17. In the left half of the room, finds from the Heraion of Argos are displayed (pedimental sculptures, metope reliefs with battles of Amazons, fragments of the cornice with lion head water spouts and a lotus-palmette frieze with birds on it as well as the head of the so-called Hera of Argos *c.* 420 BC), while in the right half some Classical votive reliefs dedicated to different gods are on show. On the left, near the door is a relief for Apollo who sits on a tripod, and next to him is an assembly of gods ending with a bull-bodied river god; the relief was dedicated by a woman named Xenokrateia and was found in a sanctuary in Phaleron (c. 400 BC). Opposite the entrance is a double relief stele from the same temple with pedimental and roof ornament; on one side Hermes is driving a four-horse chariot with the hero Echelos and the nymph Basile (inscription on the architrave) and on the other side Artemis before an indistinct god, with the horned river god Kephissos facing outwards and three nymphs; the inscription below the pediment says 'Hermes and the Nymphs' (c. 410 BC; the poros bases of both dedications are in Room 21). On the right near the door is a seated female from the pediment of the Temple of Poseidon in Sounion. In the right corner is a dedicatory relief to Dionysos who is reclining on a couch (kline) with a griffin rhyton in his right hand and a phiale in his left; in front of him sits a woman turning towards three actors with mask and drums (c. 410 BC, from Piraeus).

Room 18. The masterpiece of this room is the naiskos stele of Hegeso (opposite the entrance). The young woman, clad in chiton and mantle, sits on an elegant stool with her head covered holding in her hand a piece of jewellery, once painted; she has taken it out of a jewel box offered by her maid who is wearing a long robe. The composition is clear, the execution of the best quality and the framing of the scene strong and simple. The stele, found in the grave plot of Koroibos in the Kerameikos (see p. 67), is a prime example of a High Classical grave relief (c. 420/10 BC). A further good example of that period is the small stele of Ktesileos and Theano (on the left by the Hegeso stele). Theano sits on a stool with turned legs (symbol for a household setting) and pulls a fold of her robe forward with her right hand, a frequently recurring gesture of departure and mourning; her husband Ktesileos, in a mantle, stands in front of her, with his hands clasped in front of him (also a mourning gesture) leaning on a staff (once painted and now no longer evident), which he has pushed in his armpit; this stance is often seen on depictions of men speaking in public, for example, in the Agora (see also the Parthenon frieze with the picture of the Panathenaic procession); thus, on the one hand the man is depicted as if in a public situation, which does not fit with the woman, but on the other hand the connection of the pair through grief, which is so apparent in the picture, is clear. Further grave monuments, all dating to the late fifth and early fourth centuries, offer the usual themes: seated woman with servant (stele of Phrasikleia on the window wall); servant offers seated mother a baby (next to Phrasikleia stele). On the right of the passage to Room 21 is a small relief on which a ship's bow with battering ram is depicted; above it, sunk deep in grief, sits a man in a simple chiton next to his weapons; the relief probably decorated a grave for Demokleides who fell in a naval battle. Some whiteground lekythoi in a wall case allow comparison with the shape of the large marble lekythoi in the room. The clay vases were used in a cult of the dead at the grave and, therefore, carry brief sketches of the survivors in front of stelai, which stand on many-stepped bases and are decorated with ribbons and wreaths; often the dead person appears on the other side of the grave monument, occasionally being led away by Hermes. In the middle of the wall is part of a state grave monument which was found on the side of the Dromos in the Kerameikos. It is the crowning piece of the grave monument for the fallen horsemen in the Battles of Corinth and Koroneia (394 BC); the names of the dead are inscribed below the ornament (Plate 29), including Dexileos, whose relatives built him a cenotaph in the Kerameikos on the family plot (see p. 68; Plates 20, 31); the symmetrically composed anthemium decoration of the crowning piece with lotus blossoms and rosettes belongs to the best quality ornamental work of the Classical period. The relief next to the crowning piece, under which the names of the dead are listed again, arranged by tribes, also comes from this grave monument; the fragmentary depiction (Plate 30) calls to mind the Dexileos stele (Plate 31): a galloping rider fights a hoplite.

Rooms 19 and 20. From Room 17 the visitor can enter the L-shaped Rooms 19–20, which give access to an inner courtyard with a garden and a café. The L-shaped room contains some Classical Greek sculptures and some Roman copies of Classical works. At the left end of the room is a headless female torso in a belted chiton, with a mantle draped round its hips. It is a small copy, found in Athens, of the cult image of Nemesis of Rhamnous; the original cult image (see p. 246) is known from numerous marble fragments and its relief decorated base, which was found in the temple and restored. The seated statue of a goddess, perhaps Demeter (*c.* 430 BC), is next to the torso on its left. In front of the goddess is a roof figure from the Agora, comprising a Nereid sitting on a leaping dolphin. Right next to the entrance is a votive relief to Pan (*c.* 410 BC); an inscription gives the name of the dedicator, Archandros. It was found on the south slope of the Acropolis and depicts the donor himself in front of an altar, the god Pan in a rock cave and three figures of Nymphs. On the right of the entrance is a votive relief to Apollo (sitting on a tripod), with his mother, Leto, (right) and sister Artemis (*c.* 410 BC). Next are three Roman copies of a famous Apollo statue, called the 'Kassel Apollo' after the place where the best preserved copy is kept. The life-size head near the window, the large torso and the statuette opposite it in front of the wall are all copies of this Classical work, which is assigned to an early work of Pheidias. Two small figures of a windswept Athena dating to *c.* AD 140 come from the Asklepieion of Epidauros; the inscriptions on the bases were not carved until AD 300 and 304. The large relief pillar of an Amazon copies a Classical statue type assigned to Pheidias; this copy served as a Caryatid in the Villa of Herodes Atticus near the Monastery of Loukou in Arcadia (near Astros). On the left, next to her, is a copy of Athena Promachos; the huge bronze original by Pheidias stood east of the Propylaea on the Athenian Acropolis (see p. 23). On the shelf to the side of the statuette are miniature copies of figures from the west pediment of the Parthenon, which were found in Eleusis and probably decorated a Roman temple there. The following statuettes give an idea of the Athena Parthenos, the 12 m-high chryselephantine statue by Pheidias displayed in the Parthenon; on the smallest copy (the so-called Lenormant Athena) the shield and base reliefs can be seen, whereas the well preserved, but uninspired, Varvakion Athena (Plate 15) dating from the late second century AD does not give these details; this 1:10 reduced copy does, however, give a good idea of the draperies, the Nike on the outstretched hand and the particularly rich helmet decoration; the remains of painted decoration are clearly recognisable (for example, the eyelashes). By the window is part of a slab from the frieze on the High Classical Temple of Apollo at Bassae depicting an Amazon; the relief frieze, which was once on the inside of the cella, is now in the British Museum, almost complete.

Inner Courtyard. Next to some Attic grave reliefs, Roman relief decorated table supports and a large garlanded sarcophagus (late second century AD) with figures of Dionysos, Satyr and Eros, the remains of marble statues are on show which were found in a shipwreck off Antikythera (see also the bronze statue in Room 28). The figures have been much eroded by seawater and molluscs, where they were not covered with sand. They are marble copies of lost Classical and Hellenistic originals: horses from a team, the Greek heroes Diomedes and Odysseus and a Satyr asking a Maeniad to dance. The Museum Café can be reached from this garden.

Room 21. This central room of the sculpture collection gives access to the Mycenaean Room 4 and, via the back rooms (Rooms 34, 35), to the Karapanos Collection (Room 36) and the special exhibition rooms (Rooms 44–47), as well as up the stairs to the Vase Collection rooms and the Thera exhibition.

In the centre is the galloping bronze Horse and Jockey, whose crouched pose captures the tension of the horse race. The group, which was found in the shipwreck off Cape Artemision together with the 'God of the Sea', is a Hellenistic work. Opposite it is the marble statue of an athlete tying a band on his head (the Diadoumenos); it is a fine Hellenistic copy of a work by the Classical sculptor Polykletes of Argos, which is a prime example of the contraposto of the supporting and the relaxed leg and the corresponding tilt of hips and shoulders; like the famous spear carrier of Polykletos this figure, too, is known from numerous Roman copies. This marble copy of the Diadoumenos, dating to *c.* 100 BC, which was found in an ancient villa on Delos, has an addition consisting of a support on which a quiver is hung; this suggests that the athlete's statue was very probably interpreted here as a representation of Apollo. Left of the entrance to Room 4 and next to the door to Room 18 are two female figures closely wrapped in mantles, copies of the same Late Classical original; they belong to a type known as the 'Small Herculaneum Woman', which has been much copied. These two copies allow a comparison of the details. The fine Late Hellenistic copy (*c.* 100 BC) is contemporary with the Diadoumenos, which also comes from Delos (green painted decoration is preserved on the borders of the garment); the other figure, which is broader and heavier, was found in Aigion on the north coast of the Peloponnese and dates to the second century AD (see also the late second century AD copy in Room 32). Next to the statue from Aigion is a Roman copy of another statue type, the 'Large Herculaneum Woman'; this is a copy of a fourth century BC original; the mantle on top of the chiton is drawn over the head and falls in fine folds, producing sharp diagonally running creases;

the present example combines the statue type with the portrait of a Roman lady of *c.* AD 140. In front of the wall to Room 22 is an idealised naked male statue, probably a god or hero; a cloak is folded across his shoulder from whence it hangs down to be draped round his left arm (Roman copy of a fourth century BC original). Next to this statue is a Classical Attic grave relief on which three grave vases with reliefs are depicted (that on the right is restored) below bands and alabastra: on the loutrophoros in the centre is a young rider next to his horse, equipped with two spears and a wide-brimmed hat (petasos), with an old man in front of him, perhaps his father, and a boy; on the left-hand lekythos is an ephebe playing with his hoop; the grave relief (*c.* 380 BC), to which the group of the figured grave stele with the marble vases belongs, decorated the grave of a certain Panaitios, son of Amaxanteus, in the Kerameikos.

Room 22. Sculptures and architectural elements from the Classical Temple of Asklepios at Epidauros (390–370 BC) are on show here, especially the pedimental figures. The theme of the west pediment was the Amazonomachia, the Battle of the Greeks against the Amazons; the leader of this band of female warriors, Penthesileia, forms the centre of the composition on a rearing horse in the middle of the pediment. Only a few fragments are extant from the east pediment, so the interpretation as the sack of Troy is not certain. The sculptor of these figures was perhaps Timotheos, one of the best artists of the fourth century BC. According to inscriptions of accounts he was paid a lot of money for models. The roof was crowned by riding Nereids or Aurai ('Breezes').

Room 23. In this room are Attic grave reliefs dating to the mid-fourth century BC. A huge marble lekythos stands in the centre of the room. In front of the wall on the left of the entrance to Room 24 there is a very fine relief, the 'Ilissos Stele': on the left a youth in heroic-athletic nakedness with legs crossed leans negligently against a low pillar in front of which a small boy crouches; opposite the athletic huntsman, recognisable from his throwing stick and hunting dog, his old father is depicted in a long himation leaning on a stick; he has his right hand on his chin in a gesture of mourning and looks broodingly at his son; in contrast the latter is facing out of the relief looking aimlessly into the distance. The work is ascribed to a prominent sculptor of *c.* 340 BC; his design was also used as a model of some less important imitations (see the relief to the left and stelai in the museums of Marathon and Piraeus). On the window wall is the grave relief of an armoured warrior (his head, which was made separately, is missing) together with a bearded old man and a small boy; it comes from Salamis and dates to *c.* 340 BC. To its right are two hunting dog reliefs, also from Salamis, perhaps once decorative slabs for the base of a grave monument, and to the left a lion grave guard, carved in the round. Next to these is the fragment of a Doric frieze with a relief decorated metope depicting three mourners. The marble block may once have belonged to a building on which other reliefs with similar themes were to be seen, which were not really to be interpreted as true to life but rather as scenes from tragic plays; in this case the building could have been a choregic dedication, since the block was found not far from the Street of the Tripods. Sirens, mythical figures with the lower body of a bird and the torso and head of a female, famous for their seductive song, were used as guards in cemeteries, similarly to the grave lions and dogs; they, too, were often set at the edge of the grave terraces on the sides; there are two examples in this room, one holding a kithara in its hand. From Room 23 the L-shaped neighbouring Room 25 can be reached; it contains document and votive reliefs.

Room 24. The Attic grave reliefs in this room are late examples. The naiskoi (architectural frames in temple-like form) have a noticeable depth and in some cases an extensive breadth, so that the figures appear to be carved almost in the round. Examples of this feature are to be seen on the right near the entrance from Room 23 and on the opposite wall, where the relief of Prokles and Prokleides (from the Kerameikos, *c.* 325 BC), depicting a man in armour, an old man seated opposite him and a woman in the background, is to be seen; its huge base is also preserved; the different lettering of the inscriptions on the roof beams (epistyle) show clearly that there are later additions to the monument. By the window wall are two very different grave dogs: on the right an attentive, upright, slim, elegant hunting dog, on the left a fatter reclining dog. Between them is the stele of a warrior with his shield, to whom a boy offers his helmet. A further form of grave custodian, in addition to lions, dogs and sirens, is the kneeling archer, to be seen in this room. These figures with their large quivers once bordered a grave of an ambassador from the Orient which was situated next to the grave plot of Dionysios of Kollytos in the Kerameikos. Right next to the entrance to Room 24 a grave lekythos and a small relief are on show, which have similar motifs, scenes of childbirth; the mother is depicted reclining on a couch, with servants and other women surrounding her; the depiction, which is not usual on Attic grave reliefs, hints at the cause of death. Before visiting Room 25 with votive reliefs it is worth looking at the last Attic grave reliefs in Room 28.

Votive and Document Reliefs. **Rooms 25–27**, which are L-shaped and make up two sides of a second inner courtyard, contain votive and document reliefs, mostly dating to the fourth century BC. The first group consists of marble slabs, dedicated to particular gods in their sanctuaries by ancient pilgrims; they depict the god in question, often with the dedicator or a group (family) of worshippers. Most of the reliefs are architecturally framed; others, for example, Pan and Nymph reliefs, have irregular forms suggesting caves. The names of the dedicators are often known from inscriptions. The document reliefs consist of marble stelai which are officially displayed; in the lower part decrees are inscribed, while in the illustrated area above it the two parties to the contract are usually symbolised by personifications or by gods (Athens is symbolised by Athena). The inscriptions refer to the eponymous archon in office which means the reliefs can be accurately dated.

Room 25. Entering from Room 23, on the right in front of the wall are eight votive reliefs of Pan and the Nymphs, some of which were found in the different caves dedicated to these gods (Phyle, Vari, Eleusis; see also Room 35). The reliefs mostly take the form of natural caves, on the edges of which animals, but also river gods or hunters, can often be recognised; only one, on the right of the entrance from Room 23, a dedication to Trophonios in Levadhia, has a rectangular frame: Pan is displayed here accompanied by numerous gods and heroes (Kybele, Dionysos, Kore, Trophonios, Kouretes, Dioskouroi) who surround an altar; the four members of the family of the dedicant appear on the right-hand side of the relief. The votive relief, opposite between the windows, for Apollo (with kithara), Leto (with sceptre) and Artemis (as huntress with a stag) comes from Pharsala in Thessaly; the dedicatory inscription of a certain Gorgonilla (or Gorgoniska) is a later addition below the figures. Next to it is a heavy slab depicting Dionysos and a woman before an incense burner. Opposite the door to Room 23 is a votive offering base, the front side of which displays a charioteer in a quadriga in front of which the tripod victory prize is depicted. A little way down on the left of the door are two examples of document reliefs: on the left (1467) a treaty between Athens and Kerkyra (Corfu) dating to 375 BC with a picture of Athena, the personification of the island and the Athenian Demos; on the right on the shelf (1479) a fragment of a decree text from the Acropolis: the account of the 'treasurers of Athena' and the other gods is partly preserved below the relief of Athena shaking hands with Hephaistos (or the Demos); he is handing over the treasury at the end of his year in office 397 BC. On the wall opposite, next to the corner of the room, are three more document reliefs: on the right, the alliance (362 BC) between Athens and some west Peloponnesian cities with the picture of Athena, Hera and Zeus; in the centre, a decree in honour of three kings (shown on the relief) of the Bosporian kingdom (neighbourhood of the Crimea) dating from 346 BC and left, a decree in honour of Euphron of Sicyon (Peloponnese), dating from 318 BC; he is shown in the relief in a chiton and chlamys, accompanied by a boy holding his horse, and is being presented with a wreath given to him by the Demos of Athens in the presence of Athena. In the corner of the L-shaped room are four statues of girls dating from c. 300 BC, which were displayed as votive figures in the Sanctuary of Eileithyia, the goddess of birth; they are similar to the statues of 'bears' (arktoi) at Brauron (see p. 223). In the right angle of Room 25 most of the reliefs on show are dedicated to Asklepios and Hygieia and were found in the Asklepieion on the south slope of the Acropolis. They are works of simple sculptors dating to the late fifth and fourth centuries BC, but nevertheless bear striking witness to lively religious practice. The gods stand or sit, towering over the small adorants. An altar often separates the world of the gods from that of the humans; it can also be put over the corner in three-quarter view. Asklepios is regularly accompanied by his sacred animal, the snake, which twists up round the stick on which he leans or is coiled next to his chair. Statuettes were found depicting the god, in addition to numerous reliefs and the figure of a naked boy sitting on the floor. In the centre of the room is the upper body of an impressive Asklepios from Piraeus; the missing limbs were carved separately and the eyeballs made of another material; the statue, which dates from the second century BC, was found in the Asklepieion of Mounychia near Zea Marina.

Room 26. On the window side of the room is the famous votive relief from the Amphiareion near Oropos, dedicated by Archinos to Amphiaraos (*c.* 380 BC): on the left, the healing god is depicted leaning on a stick, treating the shoulder of Archinos; next, the dedicant lies on a bed covered with drapes and is 'bitten' by a snake in his sleep, a symbol of healing through the god, and far-right, he is seen standing by a relief stele; thus, three episodes have been compressed in this small picture. On the window wall there are further Asklepios reliefs; four child figures and two Asklepios statuettes opposite come from Epidauros. On the left, next to the door to Room 27, is a votive relief fragment on which the goddess Artemis is depicted with a long torch accompanied by a dog; to her left the contour of a mountain and a fleeing stag can be seen. On the right of the passage is a fine votive relief to Asklepios from Loukou in Arkadia; the god is in the middle leaning on his stick, with his left hand resting on his hip; behind him stand his two sons and three daughters (the Asklepiadai), while a family of adorants with gifts and a sacrificial pig appear before him from the left. The find spot, one of the large villas of Herodes Atticus, shows that he had the Attic relief, which was already *c.* 500 years old, transported as a religious artistic object from Athens to his private villa; it was one of the many objects furnishing the villa, which was richly decorated with Classical and Hellenistic originals, copies of such artworks, new artworks and portraits, mosaics and paintings.

Room 27. In the last of the votive relief rooms is a large statue of Hygieia, a Roman copy dating to the second century AD after a Classical Greek original. On the window wall is an interesting relief with a picture of the washing of the feet of Odysseus; the hero, recognisable from his felt hat (pilos), returns home after 20 years' absence and is recognised by his nurse Eurykleia; behind the seated Odysseus stands his wife Penelope with her loom; the relief dates from the mid-third century BC, perhaps copied from an earlier painting. On the opposite wall are some small votive reliefs to Cybele; the mother goddess is seated in a naiskos, flanked by lions and holds a drum in her hand. Next to it hang examples of banquet reliefs: a god, for example, Asklepios, reclines on a couch with a goddess sitting at its foot; in the background there is usually a tree with a snake and a horse. A marble circular base from the Agora (early fourth century BC) shows the remaining eight of the twelve gods, with figures set far apart from each other: a goddess in front of seated Poseidon, Demeter, Athena, seated Zeus and Hera, Apollo with kithara and the remains of another figure.

Room 28. The right-hand narrow wall of this room is dominated by the grave relief of Aristonautes from the Kerameikos; the warrior is portrayed in full armour in rapid motion with his mantle billowing out behind him; mantle and shield are connected to the back of the relief, while the figure is otherwise carved fully in the round; this dynamic picture is one of the last grave reliefs before the law of Demetrios of Phaleron against grave luxury. Next to this grave monument are narrow slabs with very low reliefs which once made up the side walls of large naiskoi, also grave lions and (right) the so-called last Attic grave relief, a matronly female figure closely wrapped in a mantle; the details of the mantle, such as deep folds and creasing, are often seen on later Hellenistic cloaked figures. The date and meaning of a large and striking horse relief next to the window is uncertain; a young negro tries to control with bridle and stick a stately horse whose back is draped with a panther skin; the complete picture is not preserved and it is also not known whether it is a very unusual burial monument (in which case it must date before 317 BC, which is improbable from the style of the horse's body) or an official city monument, perhaps the decoration of the large statue base of a Hellenistic ruler (in which case it must date to the third century BC); unfortunately the location of the find, near the Academy, does not decide the question. In the next part of the same room halfway down, the sculpture of a baby stands on a high plinth; it was once held on the arm of a matronly female figure wearing a robe reaching to her feet; the statue, which is known from Roman marble copies, depicts the goddess of Peace (Eirene) with her son, Ploutos (Wealth), and a cornucopia and was an official dedication by the city of Athens; the sculptor Kephisodotos made it to exhibit in the Athenian Agora in 375 BC (fine copies in the Munich Glyptothek and the Metropolitan Museum in New York; representations on Panathenaic prize amphorae). Diagonally opposite Ploutos is the armed Aphrodite of Epidauros, a Roman copy of the original dating to c. 400; the garments, the closely fitting chiton slipping from the shoulder and the mantle with deeply separated folds emphasise the shape of the body more than they hide it, a stylistic phenomenon which is also to be seen on the reliefs of the Nike parapet, the prime example of the Rich Style (see p. 46). The goddess probably held her weapon, which she has drawn from the sheath attached to her sword band, in her raised left hand. Next to her in the centre is the bronze statue of an ephebe, who once held an object in the palm of his left hand, while his right hand makes a movement as though warding something off (perhaps it held an oil-containing vase); the statue dating to 340–320 BC was found in the sea near Marathon. The bronze statue of a hero or a god in the centre of the room was found in a shipwreck off Antikythera. The position of its fingers suggests the athletic figure, which is probably an original dating to c. 340 BC, was holding either an apple or a Medusa head in its raised right hand; this means it has to be Paris or Perseus. Behind this large bronze figure is the head of a bronze bearded boxer from Olympia, whose profession is clear from the cauliflower ear, the broken nose and the scarred, bloated face in dramatic contrast to the fine, rich curly beard and hair; he once wore an olive wreath on his head, a symbol of his victory in the ring (c. 350 BC). Further works in this room comprise some female heads dating to the fourth century BC, including the excellent 'Head from the South Slope' of the Acropolis with soft face, large, deep eyes and curly hair held by a wide ribbon (on the right next to the entrance to Room 29). At the end of the room are some fragments from the pedimental decoration of the Temple of Athena at Tegea (Peloponnese) depicting themes from the myth of the Calydonian boar with the hero Meleager; some heads of warriors and hero figures and the remains of a boar are on show from this group by the sculptor Scopas, one of the most famous artists of the mid-fourth century BC.

Room 29. This room is dominated by the 'Themis of Rhamnous', a votive statue to the goddess of law, which was once displayed in the treasury next to the Temple of Nemesis (see p. 248); it is the dedication of a man from Rhamnous, called Megakles, made by the sculptor Chairestratos, who worked c. 300 BC. The high belting of the crumpled chiton and the contrast of the light material of the under-garment to the heavy mantle is typical of the style of this time. Opposite Themis are three copies of a Greek hero head, the Eubuleus, an Eleusinian god of the underworld; the type has recently been assigned to the hero Triptolemos (the best copy with the attachment for the chiton comes from Eleusis). On the right near the door are three relief slabs from a monument known as the 'Base of the Muses from Mantinea' (Peloponnese); together with a missing fourth slab they were probably the decoration of a base on which a three-figured statue group comprising Leto and her two children, Apollo and Artemis, stood, which, according to Pausanias, was made by Praxiteles; the reliefs depict the musical contest between Apollo and the satyr Marsyas, which the god naturally won; as a punishment for his arrogance in competing with Apollo Marsyas was skinned by a Skythian. On the reliefs are the Muses, the companions of Apollo, the god with kithara, the Skythian, whose knife already indicates the result of the contest, and the satyr blowing the double flute. In the centre of the room is the Hellenistic marble figure of a barbarian war-rior from Delos and to the right behind it many sculptural fragments from the cult image group from the Temple of the Great Goddesses in Lykosoura (Peloponnese; a picture gives the reconstructed arrangement of the figures). The colossal heads of Demeter, Artemis, and the Giant Anytos are preserved; the chair is richly decorated with figures of small tritons. Of particular interest is a garment fragment, on the right of the entrance to Room 30, with figured relief decoration, which pre-sents pictures as though embroidered in the material. The group is a work of the Hellenistic sculptor Damophon, who also repaired the Pheidian chryselephantine statue of Zeus in Olympia. On the left next to the passage to Room 30 is a Roman copy of a portrait head of Demosthenes, the famous Athenian orator and politician leader of the opposition against Macedonian rule in Greece (the original, dating from 280 BC was in the Greek Agora in Athens).

Room 30. A collection of Hellenistic sculpture, including some small grave reliefs from the Aegean islands and some late Hellenistic portrait heads, is on show here. On the left of the entrance in two show cases are the bronze fragments of the statue of a philosopher in mantle and sandals; the bearded head with piercing eyes, the wild hair and the wrinkled asymmetrical straining forehead make a lively impression. The statue was part of the cargo of the ship sunk off Antikythera (c. 200 BC). Standing near the window wall behind two Hellenistic figures of children are the two thrones from the Themis 'Temple' (treasury) in Rhamnous, dedica-tions of a certain Sostratos to Themis and Nemesis (fourth century BC). The colos-sal figure of Poseidon from Melos dominates the centre of the room; while his left hand holds his gathered himation on his hip, his raised right hand probably held the trident; the interpretation of the figure as Poseidon comes from the dol-phin on the side. A small figure (in a showcase on the right in front of Poseidon) is the same kind of Hellenistic statue type; here a chiton has been added to the upper body and a dedicatory inscription on the base says that Timokles, son of Timokleides, has dedicated the work to Sarapis who is then depicted with this statuette. A Hellenistic marble rider dominates the end of the room; the general or leader clad in armour and a marshal's mantle sits on an impressively arranged horse, whose body is supported by a pillar carved from the same marble block. In the right-hand corner at the back of the room are two parts of the Zeus cult image from Aigeira (north coast of the Peloponnese), consisting of a worried countenance with pathetic open mouth and massive beard and a huge arm; the seated statue was put together from many hollowed out pieces, partly to lessen the weight, and clamped to the back wall of the temple cella. On the right next to the passage is the famous so-called 'Slipper Slapper' group dating to c. 120 BC found in a large house on Delos, in the quarter of businessmen from Beirut; the goddess Aphrodite is defending herself with her sandal in her raised right hand against an insistent goat-legged Pan, while a small Eros flies over her shoulder and has grabbed the horn of Pan. Amongst Hellenistic grave reliefs characterised by naiskoi with large figures closely wrapped in mantles, the Hellenistic portraits of a married couple (from a grave monument in Izmir, Turkey) and two male heads (one is designated as a priest from the myrtle wreath in its full hair, from Athens) are arresting, impressive works dating to the second century BC. Next to the door to Room 29 is the torso of a female statue from a monument, which stood on the ancient road from the Dipylon to the Agora and is described by Pausanias; according to him it was a statue group for Dionysos, a work of the sculptor Euboulides dating to c. 200 BC. The torso preserved belongs to a Muse, whose body was clamped to the back wall of the monument; the head of Athena on show next to it, which was earlier assigned to the same monument, must be later for stylistic and technical reasons and so cannot have belonged to the Euboulides monument.

Rooms 31–33. These rooms have been completely rearranged and mostly contain works of the Roman Empire, especially portraits, grave stelai and sarcophagi, which show the development of Greek sculpture under the Romans in chronological order (31 Late Hellenistic sculpture and works of the first century AD; 32 works of the second century AD; 33 works of the third century AD up to late Antiquity). In Room 31A, the corner room, sculptures connected with Attic ephebes, that is the military training of the male youth, are collected, especially reliefs with lists of names of 'recruits' and decrees of these young men in honour of their superiors, the Kosmetes, whose portraits are set on herm pillars with inscriptions. Roman imperial portrait sculpture was originally dominated by likenesses of the emperor himself, which were used as a prototype; private citizens usually imitated the style and fashions, especially the hair and type of beard, of the emperor of their time; these portraits, therefore, can be accurately dated. In the first century AD the beardless type of emperor portrait, which came into vogue following Alexander the Great, was still extremely popular; the beard appeared as a widespread fashion on male portraits in the time of Hadrian (AD 117–138); to begin with it was trimmed and short, but with successive emperors it became increasingly longer. A characteristic of the art of portraiture (although not universally practised in Greece) is the custom from *c.* 130 AD onwards of incising a fine ring on the eyeball to mark the iris and also of making a bean-shaped depression to show the reflection of light.

Room 31. In front of the wall on the left of the door as well as in front of the opposite wall there are Late Hellenistic likenesses, for example, the portrait of a man (320) making a momentary movement of his head, the head of a priest (437), which is similar to the likeness of C. Julius Caesar, as well as an old man with a realistically carved face and a mouth twisted up on one side (331). The large marble statue near the door to Room 31A comes from Delos and depicts a man in a majestic pose, naked like an athlete. Next to it stands the figure of a young boxer wrapped in a mantle (the boxing gloves cast aside decorate the statue support), which was found in the Gymnasion in Eretria on Euboia together with its inscribed base. On the next wall some likenesses of the Julio-Claudian imperial family are displayed (beginning with Augustus [3758] followed by his heir apparent C. Caesar [3606], a portrait of Caligula damaged by fire [3590a] and a head of Claudius decorated with an oak crown [430], as well as a statue in the pose of Jupiter, of which the head – once added separately – perhaps of Claudius, is unfortunately missing; there are also a few portraits of the emperors' consorts). The bronze figure in the middle of the room is a fragment of a high-quality statue of a mounted Augustus, which was brought up out of the Aegean by fishermen. The decoration inlaid in copper on the fringes of the general's mantle and the decorative stripes (clavi) on the tunic can be seen. On the other side of the door there is a likeness of the emperor Domitian (345), which is unfinished in the area of the upper head and the back of the head, and a portrait of his father Titus (originating from Smyrna, once with separately added eyes; 348). Some family grave reliefs are displayed on the fourth wall of the room, amongst which a three-figured group comprising Amaryllis, the devotee of Isis, between her parents makes a particularly life-like impression (231). The figure of a man on the left edge of the relief, which was originally interpreted as her father, has now been assigned to her brother, Mousaios; this emerges from the inscription carved in the sunken surface above him. Her mother on the right has the typical hairstyle of the time around AD 100 with the Flavian coiffure with corkscrew curls.

Room 31A. This room is given over to likenesses honouring the kosmetes. These were officials elected for a year who were reponsible for the training of the ephebes. At the recruitment of the young men (aged about 18) their names were marked on stelai, which have almost all been found in the Archaic Agora on the north-east slope of the Acropolis, where they swore their oath to Athens. Most of the male portraits in this room come from that find spot. They are arranged in chronological order and offer a wide range of representations of the trainers of the ephebes. As a few preserved examples show, the heads belonged to herms on which the name of the kosmetes and his year of service were inscribed. Among the men portrayed there are some very impressive personalities, as well as sculptural work which is often of very high quality, as can be recognised, for example, in the fine drilling of the individual hairs on the head and the beards; some of the men, whose likenesses have probably often been set up at the end of their term of office as memorials in their honour by the ephebes, even have cauliflower ears, that is their ear muscles are portrayed as thickly swollen, as happens with injuries from blows in boxing; the former sportive training of the dignitaries now functioning as kosmetes can thus be determined.

Room 32. This room contains portrait heads of the second century AD. The large marble likeness of the Emperor Hadrian (3729) dominates the left wall; his oak crown is decorated with a cameo (the eagle depicted recalls the honorary title given to him of 'Olympios'). On the left near this head is the bust of a contemporary private citizen and on the left of it is Antinoos (417), the favourite of Hadrian, whose portraits were distributed throughout the whole Roman Empire in very large numbers, after he drowned in the Nile in AD 130. On the right next to Hadrian is the much damaged likeness of his wife, the Empress Sabina (419), who has the typical turban hair style of that period (see also the private citizen portraits next to the door to Room 31; although the likeness of an older woman [3550] with a hair style which looks like a croissant is quite different from the others). On the opposite wall, beyond the over-life-size likeness of a priest (356), the gallery of second century AD emperor portraits continues with the heads of Antoninus Pius (5421), Marcus Aurelius (572) and Lucius Verus (3740); the drilled masses of hair and the beards of ever-increasing length illustrate the development of portraiture. The highly polished likeness of Commodus (488) was once interpreted either as Athena (with helmet) or as Herakles (with a lionskin), since the sides and back of the head were added on separately and are now missing. Next to Marcus Aurelius the fine bust of his wife Faustina (4536) is eye-catching; her hair style illustrates the new fashion of setting the hair in waves to form a chignon on the nape of the neck. The bust of Herodes Atticus in philosopher's robes (Plate 65) can be seen beside the door to Room 33, and that of his pupil Polydeukion (both busts from Kephissia; Plate 66) as well as the votive relief of a youth as Achilles (Plate 68), which, from its likeness to the Greek hero and its provenance from the villa of Herodes Atticus near Astros in the Peloponnese, can be interpreted as the second pupil of Herodes Atticus, who was called Achilles. In the centre of the room is the sculpture of a Maenad sleeping on a panther skin, a statue type which is also often used for Hermaphrodite. The pillar (which supported a table) with the baroque looking Dionysiac group in the neighbouring show case is an example of the high quality of sculptural art of that time: the carving of the fine, pierced marble components, the polish of their surface and the painting is worthy of a great master. Opposite there are more family grave reliefs (for example, the devotee of Isis, Alexandra, wearing a fringed stole tied with the typical knot in front, or the youth Artemidoros chasing a boar), as well as an ossuary with different mythological scenes, the figures of a dead husband and wife and a large sarcophagus with scenes of the Calydonian boar hunt, which was closed by a gabled lid with incised roof tiles.

Room 33. This room exhibits examples of Greek portraiture dating from the third to the fifth centuries AD. The excellent head of a young man with long hair in the middle of the room, which dates to *c.* AD 200, is a prominent work; the support of the bust, preserved in pieces, was carved in the form of palm and acanthus leaves. The over-life-size likeness near the door to Room 32, which had the eyes once added separately in another material, could represent the emperor Septimius Severus; it dates to the same period as the youth, but the likeness and the fashion calls the portraits of the Antonines to mind, emperors who were claimed as family ancestors by Septimius Severus, even though there were no family connections. The opposite wall of the room is dominated by a large sarcophagus (*c.* AD 230), which is carved like a bed (kline) with curved fluting between the legs; the lid, which is no longer the gabled roof of the second century AD, has the form of a mattress with a cushion, on which the figure of a man reclines; the bundle of writing rolls next to his torso was carved out from the figure of a second person; this is clear by comparison with other sarcophagi; for sarcophagi of this type were mostly mass-produced, leaving the portrait uncarved until the sarcophagus was sold; in this case the male figure was removed to make way for the bundle of rolls and the man was worked out of the unfinished female figure. In front of the right wall are portraits of men and women, whose faces are characterised by formal, but nevertheless very expressive features; the physiognomy is emphasised by wrinkles to indicate exertion and power, as well as a firm gaze looking upwards from beneath highly arched brows. In late Antiquity this formality is exaggerated almost to the point of caricature. However, amongst the later likenesses there are marble works of quality, such as the bust of an official (423) wearing the low folded toga with flat hair on top of his head and a voluminous mass of curls at the sides.

Rooms 34 and 35. The large hall with stairs to the upper floor is supposed to create the impression of a sanctuary with its contents. It contains some Greek dedicatory sculptures and votive reliefs from different Greek sanctuaries. In the middle is a large altar for Aphrodite and the Graces, found in the road between the Agora and the Kerameikos. On the right-hand side of the room is an architrave decorated with wreaths; it belongs to the choregic dedication of Thrasyllos on the south side of the Acropolis and was part of the façade architecture on the rock high above the Theatre of Dionysos (320/319 BC, see p. 52). Also in the middle of the room is the upper torso of a High Classical statue of Aphrodite, which was the cult image in the sanctuary at Daphni (see p. 151). The sacred birds of the goddess of love, the doves, also from the Aphrodite sanctuary at Daphni, can be seen in the wallcase next to the sculpture. At the end of the room on each side of the staircase stand two Classical grave loutrophoroi with relief depictions of the dead; this form of grave monument was mostly used for those who died unmarried. On the left side of the large chamber some votive reliefs are on show: at the back are three votives to Herakles; the hero either stands in a colonnade or is lying on a rock. At the front of the room is a votive to Zeus, depicted with other gods and heroes (Herakles, the river god Acheloos as a mask, Hermes with his staff, etc). Next to it are two votive reliefs for Pan and the Nymphs (from the south slope of the Acropolis and from the Pan Cave on Pentelikon; see p. 54, 262); Pan appears with other gods, on the first relief next to the entrance, with Apollo and Hermes in front of the Nymphs, while beyond them six pilgrims are shown at the right side as adorants; on the second relief beyond it Pan is seen with the Nymphs and Hermes in a cave-like framed picture.

Room 36. In this side wing a large collection of small bronzes is on show (Karapanos Collection), most of which come from Dodona (near Ioannina, Western Greece), and works of Early Greek to Classical art (eighth–fourth centuries BC). Other bronzes come from excavations in Olympia, Samos and the Cabirion near Thebes. On show are parts of weapons, bridles, inscriptions and, of especial interest, eyelashes and eye fragments which were put into the eyeholes of bronze statues. There is also the moulded leg of a tripod, parts of weapons and statuettes (Zeus, Pan); the cheek piece for a helmet with an embossed relief picture of a warrior above a fallen man is remarkable. A folding and a flat mirror, bronze jugs, statuettes of gods (Eros, Hermes) and representations of animals are also to be seen. The Archaic bronze flute player in a long robe was found in Dodona. The following showcases have terracotta statuettes from a sanctuary of Artemis on Corfu, depicting the goddess with her bow, deer and birds. Also on show are bronze statuettes, pins, a hydria (water jar), arm bands and a strigil, that is a scraper for athletes to scrape sand off the body. The reconstruction of a Roman chariot with bronze decoration (from Nikomedia in Turkey) can be seen next to marble reliefs and a Hellenistic cloaked figure. At the end of the room Greek grave reliefs, Roman portraits and Hellenistic heads are displayed; the high quality (the polishing of the marble) of a female portrait (c. AD 130) with a 'turban hairstyle', in which the plaited hair is laid on the head in a nest, is striking. The following showcases have bronze vase handles and moulds for statuettes of deities (Athena, Sarapis); a Late Archaic statuette of Zeus also comes from Dodona. Metal ornaments, pins, swords, leaves from wreaths and a fine actor statuette fill the next showcase. There are also vase feet in the form of claws, armbands, an Archaic runner statuette from a vase and bronze tripod legs. In the last small showcase a high quality statuette of a rider from Dodona is displayed, part of a pair, of which the other one is in the Louvre; the fine working of the horse's mane can be seen (c. 560 BC).

Room 37. There are showcases containing many small bronzes round the walls, including many Geometric works. A quite large statuette of a musician playing a double flute from the Heraion on Samos (mid-sixth century BC) is of interest.

The Upper Floor

Special **Exhibition of frescoes and finds from Akrotiri** on Thera. Akrotiri, a Cycladic town with strong Minoan influence, has been uncovered on the Aegean island of Thera (Santorini); it was buried under lava and pumice, just as Vesuvius buried Pompeii; the well preserved frescoes on the walls of the houses, which are still standing with windows and doors intact, are unique works of art dating from *c.* 1520 BC. Photos in the vestibule give an impression of the excavation. In the main room some showcases contain objects from the excavation; pottery decorated with figures of animals (dolphins, octopuses, horses, goats); a lion-shaped vase; a tripod offering table and the plaster cast of a bed, obtained by pouring plaster into the hollow left in the pumice by the rotted bed. The frescoes are exhibited in the backroom. The walls of the houses and cult rooms were painted with almost life-size pictures: monkeys in a rocky landscape, swallows above lilies, antelopes, boxing children, a fisherman with his catch, a priestess with an offering dish and female figures in the typical Minoan/Mycenaean ritual garb of flounced

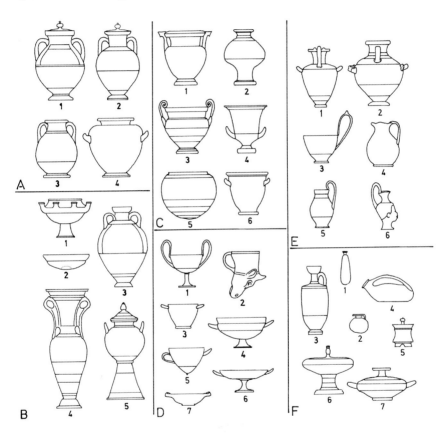

Figure 37 Shapes of Greek vases (not to scale).

A: storage vessels: 1: belly amphora; 2: neck amphora; 3: pelike; 4: stamnos.
B: cult vessels: 1: kernos; 2: omphalos bowl; 3: Panathenaic amphora; 4: loutrophoros; 5: lebes gamikos (wedding vase).
C: mixing vessels: 1: Kolonetten krater; 2: psykter (for cooling); 3: volute krater; 4: kalyx krater; 5: lebes; 6: bell krater.
D: drinking cups: 1: kantharos; 2: rhyton; 3: skyphos; 4: black-figure painted cup; 5: mastos; 6: red-figure painted cup; 7: attic kothon.
E: scooping and pouring vessels: 1: hydria; 2: kalpis; 3: kyathos; 4: oinochoe; 5: olpe; 6: head-vase.
F: anointing vessels and boxes: 1: alabastron; 2: aryballos; 3: lekythos; 4: askos; 5: pyxis; 6: plemochoe; 7: lekanis.

skirts with tight jackets which leave the breasts bare (compare with the procession of women from Thebes in the Mycenaean Room 4). There are also miniature frescoes which give interesting views into daily life at that time; a river landscape is depicted with animals and palms, a settlement in a bay with a harbour and in front of it large and small decorated ships and battle scenes with armed soldiers and bodies of drowned men drifting in the sea.

Vase Collection (Rooms 49–56; since the earthquake of September 1999 much restoration work has to be carried out especially in this part of the museum; it is not known when it will be re-opened). This little-visited collection of Greek pottery gives a unique chronological overview of the different pottery styles in Greece from the Bronze Age (including Mycenaean) through the Geometric period to the famous Athenian Archaic and Classical vases, Hellenistic vases and the colourful terracottas of Attica and Boeotia (Figure **37** gives the names of the vases, their shapes and their usage). In the historical period the vases were not painted with colour but with watered down clay; where this slip was put on, the firing gave rise to a dark red-brown to black pattern according to the thickness of the slip. In the Geometric period the vases were decorated with compass drawn circles, plants, maeanders, bands, and other Geometric motifs, which were sometimes hatched; gradually the severe arrangement of the decoration was enlivened with

Figure 38 Depiction of a vase painter at work (inside an Attic cup, Boston, MFA).

stylised figural representations (animal frieze) and small pictures (the dead on a bier, a funeral procession, daily scenes, later also myths). In the seventh century BC Corinthian pottery dominated the Greek market; it is easily recognisable from its decoration in purple-red and pale pink on a very light background; the figures are buried in countless filling motifs, especially rosettes. In addition to the two main centres of Greek vase production, Corinth and Athens, there were many other pottery workshops which developed their own style (for example, the islands Melos, Naxos, Samos, Lemnos or Euboia and the production of relief amphorae in Boeotia, etc.). These can only be studied in all their particulars in the Athenian collections. In the Archaic period the Attic workshops took over the Greek market. The vases were decorated with pictures in black on a red ground; in this technique interior lines had to be added by incision after firing; additionally a covering colour could then be added (red and white, the latter especially used for the skin of female figures), which has often flaked off today. Between 530 and 520 BC the painting technique was changed. The motif was reserved, the background painted with a thick slip – it became black on firing – and the interior lines of the clay coloured figures, that is the robes, muscles, faces, hair, etc., could be drawn as thin brown lines (Figure **38**); through this the figures became more lively, the total impression was more three dimensional and the appearance of the red figures on the black backgound was closer to life (called 'red figure' style as opposed to the earlier 'black figure'). An important dating context comes from vases from the Acropolis, which were burnt in 480 BC in the Persian destruction and buried in the Persian destruction fill. The Classical white-ground lekythoi depicting scenes of mourning comprise a particular group of vases. The figures are drawn with few lines on a light background and given coloured robes; these swift but excellent sketches are particularly striking (see Room 18). Pottery is an important medium for an excavator for dating the levels. Vases broken into sherds are found in large numbers in every excavation; a good academic knowledge of this abundant material allows it to be dated to within a few years (in historical times); the painter and potter of Classical vases, who have often both signed the vase, can be recognised from their 'handwriting' and their style, and their development can be followed. The visitor interested in Greek daily life should make a point of looking at these vases; the vases also offer a wide variety of scenes from a large number of myths to those interested in Greek mythology. A detailed description of the exhibits is not possible here because of their large numbers.

Sale of plaster casts. There is a shop in the basement in which plaster casts of antiquities (reliefs, statues, terracotta statuettes, etc.) from Athenian and other Greek museums can be bought, as well as catalogues, postcards and books.

Lykabettos. The highest city hill in Athens is Lykabettos ('Wolf Mountain') at 277 m above sea level (Figure **2**.24). In clear weather its summit with the Chapel of Ay. Georgios is a very good place from which to look at the panorama over the sea of houses in the city to the Saronic Gulf (café and restaurant). The visitor can quickly regain the orientation lost walking between all the similar blocks of flats. Myth says that Athena tore the rock from Pentelikon and dropped it on her way to the Acropolis.

Several paths snake up Lykabettos between the sparse pine trees and the large agave plants; there is a carpark on the west side to the north below the summit (an open air theatre, located in a modern quarry here, is used for performances in summer). There is also a cable car on the south side (in Aristippou Street at the end of the steps on Ploutarchou; signposted).

I n the south below Lykabettos is the quarter called '**Kolonaki**' ('little column', named after a column standing there), with shops, street cafés and bars. The centre is the busy Kolonaki Square with its numerous cafés, where international newspapers can be bought at the kiosks (Greek: periptero). The square is actually called 'Philikis Etairias' (= the society of friends), derived from a secret lodge of the last century, which planned to free Greece from the Turks. About 200 m metres up the hill (136 m above sea level) are the remains of a **Roman water reservoir** called 'Dexameni' (Figure 2.23), which supplied the ancient city with water from the time of Hadrian and exerted the necessary pressure in the piping system. The façade of this cistern was decorated with four Ionic columns and an architrave, on which an inscription named the

Figure 39 Eastern city gate of Athens (*c.* 1780) with the epistyle of the Hadrianic water reservoir (*c.* 1800).

dedicator of the installation. It was still almost intact in the fifteenth century, but the marble components were torn down in 1778 and built into one of the gates of the city wall (Figure **39**). Today one of the inscribed architrave blocks is in the National Garden (see p. 106); the cistern is used by the city water company; there are only a few wall remains to be seen at the site and some column bases on which the façade complex once stood.

The **Gennadios Library** is also to be found on the south slope of Lykabettos, a few hundred metres east of the water reservoir; it has a lavish façade of Naxian marble. It belongs today to the American School of Classical Studies opposite and is the gift of a former Greek ambassador to London (1922). The library, which is open to the public, houses a collection of international importance consisting of all the books in every language on the subject of modern Greece. Occasionally parts of the holdings are displayed in a changing exhibition.

The **Monastery of Petraki** (eighteenth century) is two streets downhill in Gennadios Street; it is the seat of the synod of bishops; within its walls is an old Byzantine church (tenth century) of the cross-domed type with four columns in the main room. The frescoes (1719) were painted by Georgios Markos, who painted many Attic churches in the first half of the eighteenth century. There are many marble fragments in the pretty flowering courtyard of the monastery, including, built into the belfry, a Classical anthemion stele, a Late Hellenistic grave relief, from which the picture has been recut and turned into a lion head, and a statue base used as a water trough.

One of the main streets of Athens, Leophoros Alexandras, runs along the plain between Lykabettos and Tourkovounia; the stadium of the well-known Athenian football club, Panathenaikos, is to be found here. A few steps southeast of the stadium in A. Tsocha Street, the restored Middle Byzantine cross-domed church of **Ayion Panton** (All Saints, also called Homologiton) lies between the modern blocks of flats. Many earlier ancient and Early Christian stones are built into its walls, including a Classical boundary stone (OPOC); two columns of marble from Karystos have been used in the interior while more spolia lie next to the small church; they originate from ancient marble architecture – parts of columns from a Classical temple of the amphiprostyle type similar to the Temple of Nike on the Acropolis[131] – and an earlier, perhaps Early Christian, predecessor to the church.

Tourkovounia. From the summit of Lykabettos a low hill lying in the middle of the sea of buildings can be seen in the north. It is the 'Turkish Mountains', the Tourkovounia, an almost treeless chain of hills running north–south, which is oddly fissured with modern quarries; in Antiquity this mountain was probably called Anchesmos. Fine villas on its east side house some of the foreign embassies; their personnel live in this garden quarter, which was systematically planted between the wars. An ancient altar was found on its northernmost peak, *c.* 330 m above sea level,[132] from whence there is a good view over the suburbs of Athens lying on the slopes of Parnes and Pentelikon. There was a cult place here as early as the eighth century BC. After a temporary cultic decline in the sixth century, cult was renewed and the site was architecturally

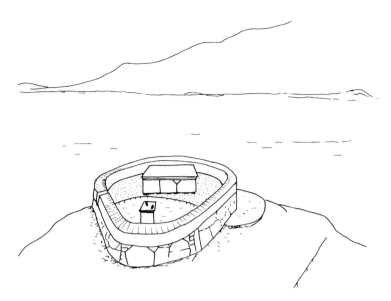

Figure 40 Sanctuary of Zeus on Tourkovounia, reconstruction (by Lauter).

enhanced with an oval enclosure wall, within which a small altar stands on a slightly raised plateau; next to it there may have been a statue (Figure **40**). This simple rustic installation dating from the late fourth century BC, which covered an earlier cult place inside its wall, was probably dedicated to Zeus Anchesmos, according to Pausanias, but it could also have been for the worship of an unknown hero.

To reach the north end of Tourkovounia it is easiest to drive in the direction of Kephissia on Leof. Kephissias and then turn left, either by the sign 'Philothei' and follow the main street until the suburb below the north peak is reached, or to turn later at a wide crossroads to the west (sign Nea Ionia) and at the first opportunity (traffic lights) again left and follow this street to the north peak. A concrete path snakes up from the last houses to the altar. If, after the turning from Leof. Kephissias the visitor continues in the direction 'Nea Ionia' after some kilometres several tall pillars belonging to a former **Hadrianic aqueduct**, and repaired in the Middle Ages will be reached. A few kilometres further west are two more similar aqueducts. The road runs between these pillars (the area is called Kalogreza) and bends left to the foot of Tourkovounia in the direction 'Galatsi'. A few hundred metres further on, on the west side of the road, the Omorphi Ekklesia, after which the wide avenue is named, stands in an open area.

The **Omorphi Ekklesia** ('Beautiful Church') lies to the west below the cult area on Tourkovounia. It stands on a site which had already been built on in Antiquity; polygonal masonry on the south side of the church bears witness to large Greek architecture (Plate 37). This interesting Byzantine

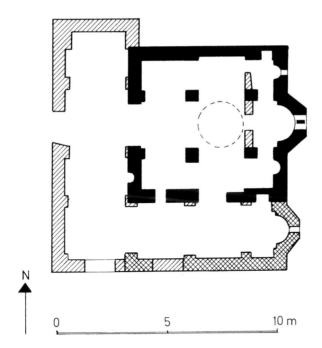

Figure 41 Omorphi Ekklesia at Kalogreza.

church (Figure **41**) was built in the eleventh or twelfth century. The main room belongs to the type of cross-in-square domed church. The walls are built of the typical cloisonné masonry; the corners of the octagonal dome were emphasised by marble columns on the exterior and its windows by marble arches above them. An adjacent church dating to the thirteenth or fourteenth century is connected to the south side of the central building. In the west a narthex was built in front of the total width (fifteenth or sixteenth century). The remains of frescoes in the interior (normally closed, keys in the Byzantine Museum) date to *c.* 1300.

The **Academy** and the **Kolonnos Hippios**. The area, known today under the general name of 'Academy' and particularly famous for the school of philosophy founded by Plato, was dedicated to the hero of this site Hekademos (or Academos); this is known from ancient sources and from a boundary stone dating to the sixth century BC found at the site.[133] Several other sanctuaries on this site were combined with the worship of Hekademos: Eros, Hephaistos and Prometheus, the Muses and, especially, Athena, the goddess of art and wisdom, the patron deity of the Academy. The torch race of the Panathenaia, which led over the Dromos to the Kerameikos, began in this area, which lies some 3 km outside the city. A sacred olive grove stood in the precinct of the Academy. The oil from its olives was put into special vases, the Panathenaic prize amphorae, and given to the victors as prizes in the athletic contests at the Panathenaia.

Only a few, not very appealing, ruins have been excavated in the area of Hekademos. They include remains of the prehistoric and Geometric periods, of which nothing can be seen today except a few mudbrick walls under a protective roof in the south-west of the area. What can be seen are the foundation walls of two gymnasia, in which young athletes could train; they are large rectangular areas with some bases for colonnades along the inner wall; one of the gymnasia also has a large water basin (in the north-east of the area). Although Classical blocks are built into these installations, the present buildings date to the Late Hellenistic or Early Roman period.

The simple Athenian suburb with the ruins of the Academy is best reached by car. Leaving Omonia Square in the direction of Corinth, after crossing the railway line turn right into the sixth street (the wide Palamidiou Street) to the Church of Ay. Georgios on the Square of Akademias Platonos and from there left into Platonos Street; follow this to the eleventh street on the left (Tripoleos) and then go left to a green area on the right-hand side in which the ruins are situated. For Kolonos Hippios the visitor continues along Tripoleos Street in a north-easterly direction.

The private house of Plato, in which he established a school of philosophy and learning, the famous 'Academy of Plato', lay between the ruined area of the gymnasium and the hill of Kolonos Hippios to the north-east. The modern academies are based on this ancient establishment as meeting places of eminent scholars, the first being the Academia Platonica of Cosimo de' Medici founded in 1470 in Florence.

The Kolonnos Hippios,[134] which is a hill set today in a simple suburb with a park and a modern open-air theatre, was dedicated in Antiquity to Poseidon, the protector of horses (hippos = horse), and Athena; the sea god had a sacred cave here. According to myth the cult site of the Eumenides was in this neighbourhood; blind Oedipos fled to them, before he disappeared into the Underworld. Today a visit to the hill is only worthwhile if the visitor wishes to visit the graves of two great historians; the German Carl Ottfried Müller, professor at Göttingen (1840) and the French archaeologist Charles Lenormant (1859) are buried on the highest point. Müller's grave is decorated with an imitation of an ancient anthemion grave stele, Lenormant's with a marble grave vase on a plinth.

8   Piraeus and Daphni

Piraeus[135] was and is the harbour of Athens, the most important unloading place for merchandise in the whole of Greece and one of the country's most prominent industrial areas. A visit to this densely settled city is not pleasing on the eye, since the view is made up of wharves, warehouses, business offices, shipping lines, administrative buildings, shops and modern concrete buildings. However, the busy atmosphere of the large modern harbour with its arriving and departing passengers, and, in the early evening, the view of the boats leaving for the Aegean islands and the intrepid small ferries and 'flying dolphins' going to and from the nearby islands of the Saronic Gulf does have some charm. Zea Marina and the Small Harbour (Mikro or Tourkolimano: Plate 34), both lying south-east of the main harbour and bordered today by fish tavernas, are quieter, since they are yacht harbours. There is little tangible evidence of the important role Piraeus once played in the ancient history of Athens, because it is densely covered with modern buildings.

A day trip to Piraeus is sufficient for a good overview. If the visitor wishes to see other sites as well as the museum and harbour, then a car is necessary, although parking is difficult. Those who do not care to walk through the city can take the metro to the terminus and from there take a taxi to the Archaeological Museum, which is the most practical beginning for a visit. Another taxi to reach the north-east city gate is also a good idea.

Initially the hills of Piraeus were islands separated from the mainland. Even in the Archaic period they were cut off from the later Athenian harbour by marshes; shipping for the city moored on the beach at Phaleron. The most important and highest hill of Piraeus (Figure **42**) was the Mounychia Hill in the south-east (87 m above sea level); as early as 512 BC the Peisistratid Hippias wanted to build a fortification here, since he had noticed the particular importance of this site for controlling Athens. The Greek philosopher Epimenides (seventh century BC) referring to the rock, known today as 'Kastella', apparently said, 'If the Athenians knew how much sorrow this hill will bring to the city, they would remove it with their teeth'. He was right because, after the extension of the harbour and the fortification of Piraeus by Themistokles (from 493 BC), the possessor of the hill could also take over Athens: the Spartans in the Peloponnesian War, the successors (Diadochs) of Alexander in the Hellenistic period and the Venetians of Morosini (1687).

The rise in importance of the ancient harbour (Figure **42**) began with the establishment of the Athenian fleet against the Persians under Themistokles (Archon 493/492 BC). He had the Munychia Hill and two other high points (Eetoneia in the north-west and Akte in the south-west) fortified with a wall; in the three bays below these hills harbour installations were constructed for merchant ships and shipsheds for the war triremes (Plate 87). The largest bay, the Kantharos Harbour, where the island ferry boats moor today, faces west with the smaller adjoining Kophos Harbour on its north side. A colossal marble lion was set up at the harbour entrance, from which Piraeus aquired the name of Porto Leone in the Middle Ages; Morosini took the lion to Venice at the end of the seventeenth century; it stands there today in front of the Renaissance porch to the Arsenal; a cast has recently been put up on the south side of the

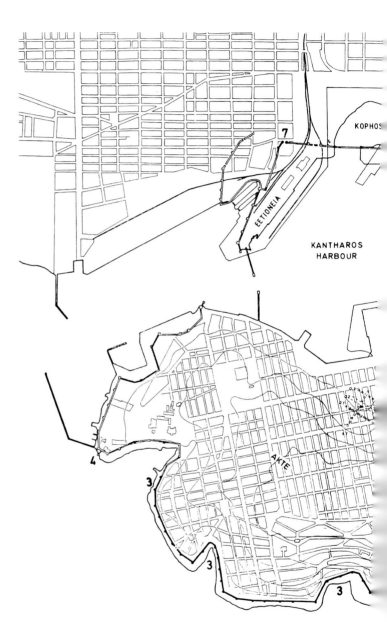

Figure 42 Piraeus, map of the ancient and modern town (after von Eickstedt).

ZEA HARBOUR

MOUNYCHIA

MOUNYCHIA HARBOUR

0   500 m

harbour, next to the large customs building. On the south coast two further harbour bays lay below Munychia; to the west was Zea Marina (Pasha Limani) with *c.* 196 shipsheds for triremes (remains of the buildings were found in the last century and at present are still visible in basement), and to the east was the Munychia harbour, which was called Phanari (Lighthouse) in the Middle Ages and then Tourkolimano and, since 1967, officially Mikrolimano. On its west side on a rock rising high over the sea, in the area of the modern yacht club, the ruins of a sanctuary to Artemis were found which was in use from the seventh century BC into late Antiquity; today no remains are visible in this area.

The most impressive ancient ruins, which can be seen today, are the **fortification works** (Figure **42**.3). There is almost nothing left of the Themistokleian walls, since they were destroyed after the Peloponnesian War; most of the preserved wall dates to the early fourth century, when the Athenian Konon renewed the fortifications. In the south the *c.* 3 m-wide wall runs along the coast (Plate 32), its outer surfaces of ashlar blocks filled with a rubble core. There were bastions at regular intervals to which stairs led up on the inside. In several places in front of the walls clear traces of quarrying provide evidence of the economising of material necessary in the construction of the wall. An unfluted column stands on the westernmost cape of Akte, inside the Naval Academy today. It marks a rectangular enclosure in which sarcophagi are exhibited. A late inscription on one of the blocks of the compound says that the grave of Themistokles was here (Figure **42**.4); Pausanias also mentions this in connection with this building. The style of lettering and a mistake in the name of his father suggest that this assignation is not original, especially as Themistokles died in exile in Magnesia in Asia Minor (*c.* 459 BC) and the enclosure with the nearby column was first erected in the fourth century BC.

On the land side in the north and east the fortification wall is not well preserved; the ruins of the city gates lie here: the 'Gate between the Long Walls' with a large courtyard, the Asty Gate with rectangular towers on earlier round foundations and the 'Eetoneia Gate' with two round towers built round a rectangular construction (Plate 33). These gates also belong to Konon's renovations of the city wall.

The Asty Gate (Figure **42**.6) can be reached from the main harbour by going along Gounari Street to Hippodameia Square to the junction with Pylis Street; the ruins of the gate are located here in a fenced-off area; continuing from here along Kodrou Street, after a crossroad, there is an open area to the east in Zanni Street in which the Gate between the Long Walls (Figure **42**.5) has been excavated. The Eetonia Gate (Figure **42**.7; Plate 33) is on the west side of the main harbour; it can be reached by going along Akti Kondyli to the west and turning left (south) into Kanari Street after crossing the railway lines; 500 m further on the gate can be seen on a small hill where new excavations are carried out.

The Gate between the Long Walls was the entrance to Piraeus from Athens. Both cities were joined by these two walls which formed a corridor, so that traffic between harbour and city was protected from possible enemies. There are only a few remains of the Long Walls visible (for example, just south of the metro in the suburb of Kallithea).

Because of modern buildings in Piraeus little is known of the layout of the ancient city within the walls. The dwelling quarters were laid out on a grid plan system with streets crossing at right angles. This so-called Hippodamic system, named after the ancient architect Hippodamos of Miletus, is known from literary sources and also in detail from the excavation of some of the housing insulae; the excavations reveal that there must have been at least two planning systems which met together at an obtuse angle. However, the public buildings of the city, the Agora, the administrative buildings and the large sanctuaries, have mostly not been found. The centre of the city may have lain north of Zea Marina. However, in 1988 Greek archaeologists found a building which belonged to the harbour installations, namely the foundations of the north entrance to the **Skeuotheke** (Naval Arsenal; Figure **42**.8) of Philo (in a modern building plot between Ypsilantou Street and Kountouriotou Street north of II Merarchias Street, and a short walk from Zea Marina and from the Archaeological Museum). It is a huge, three-aisled warehouse in which the tackle, oars and other equipment of warships were stored; this arsenal was designed and built about 330 BC by the architect Philo, who also designed the vestibule of the Telesterion at Eleusis (see p. 275). Until 1988 the building was only known from a very detailed inscription found on the northside of Zea Marina, with the design, in which all the details of the arsenal from the complete measurements to the particulars of windows and doors and internal divisions are exactly listed, so that a reconstruction by modern architects was possible at the end of the last century (Figure **43**). The building remains as excavated, that is the foundations, partly of earlier building material, and some fragments of the Doric superstructure, match the details of the inscription exactly. It was typical of Attic democracy that the arsenals, including the Skeuotheke of Philo, were regularly opened to the public; they could thus survey the state of the naval equipment and also examine the basis of Athenian sea power at first hand.

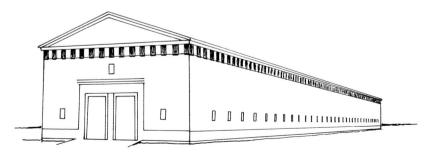

Figure 43 Piraeus, Skeuotheke of Philo, reconstruction (after Travlos).

One of the two ancient **theatres** of Piraeus has been found next to the Archaeological Museum (in Char. Trikoupi Street; Figure **42**.9). There are a few remains of seats and of the stage building; from the street a few blocks of the theatre can be seen on the slightly rising slope. It is quite a small theatre dating to the late second century BC. A larger theatre, the so-called Old Theatre, was found many years ago on the west side of Mounychia Hill, but was reburied and built over with modern housing blocks. Nothing is, therefore, known of its layout, but it can be reconstructed as a rectangular installation. The Athenian Assembly sometimes met in that theatre.

The **Archaeological Museum** contains only a small part of the finds from Piraeus; many other monuments are in the National Museum.

On the ground floor in the left side room there is a huge grave monument, reconstructed from many fragments which were found during building operations in Kallithea (east of Piraeus). It consists of a square podium with a frieze of Greeks fighting against Amazons (there are traces of colour), with a naiskos on top of it in which the statues of an old man and two youths are displayed; this superstructure is also decorated at the base with a relief frieze (animal representations). Two of the figures are named in an inscription: The grave monument, one of the largest in Attica dating to the Classical period, belongs to a man from Histria on the mouth of the Danube. Important grave reliefs are displayed on the walls of this room, including a copy of the 'Ilissos Stele' (see p. 122) and a huge, narrow anthemion stele with a relief of a grave vase and a battle scene (the rider reminds one of Alexander the Great) in the style of the Dexileos relief (see pp. 68 and 120). In the central room at the foot of the stairs is a huge figure of a lion from a grave monument. In the right-hand room there is a series of relief slabs of high quality depicting dancing nymphs and battle scenes of Amazons and Greeks. The latter are copies at original size of the relief scenes on the outside of the shield of the Athena Parthenos, but here the complete Classical representation is reproduced in separate panels. The Early Roman marble copies were apparently to have been transshipped, as they were found in the harbour; the parts not covered by sand were partially eroded by sea water and molluscs. Some Classical grave stelai and sculptures in the round are also displayed here, including portraits of Roman emperors. On the left-hand wall is a small bust of Claudius in armour AD 41–64, but his likeness has been recut from one of Caligula (37–41 BC); next to it is another portrait of Claudius and a large, high quality portrait of Trajan (AD 98–117); opposite this on the other side of the room is the upper part of a colossal statue of Hadrian in armour (AD 117–138); at the front end of the room another portrait of Hadrian and the cloaked statue of the Emperor Balbinus (AD 238) can be seen. On the upper floor on the left is a room with many funerary stelai, including a relief of two young warriors, one of whom, like the famous Doryphoros statue of Polykleitos, has a spear on his shoulder. In the back rooms of the upper floor are four large bronze statues; Athena dating to the fourth century BC, a youth in the style of Archaic kouroi, but with the right leg forward (wrong in comparison with real Archaic kouroi, therefore an archaistic work), and two figures of Artemis. In the small room in front of the Bronze Room are two herms from the same cache and next to them a headless Archaic maiden (kore) in the Samian sculptural style and a kouros from the Aphaia sanctuary on Aigina. In the back room on the right of the stairs are finds from the Cybele sanctuary in Moschato, north-east of Piraeus, consisting of an early fourth century BC statue of the goddess enthroned in her temple and many votive reliefs depicting this fertility goddess from Asia Minor with her lions. At the head of the stairs is a wooden coffin and a large, shallow metrological relief giving the standard length of an arm, a yard, a foot and a hand, the measurements used in Antiquity (from Salamis).

It is worth climbing the **Mounychia Hill** for the view from certain places: to the south Mounychia harbour can be seen (Mikrolimano; Plate 34) and beyond it the west coast of Attica with Hymettos; on the east side modern Piraeus, then the centre of Athens with the Acropolis; behind, Lykabettos can be seen in clear weather and Pentelikon; to the west is the main harbour and Salamis. There are only a few remnants of the ancient architecture which must once have existed on the hill; there are some house walls in a park on the summit and, in the rock, traces of quarrying and some steps of later houses are visible. On the north-west side of the summit, a few steps below the park, there are the high walls of a fortification; the masonry style and the use of earlier blocks date this fortification, which once went round the whole summit, to the Macedonian Empire.

Daphni: the Monastery, the Cave of Pan and the Temple of Aphrodite

The famous Byzantine monastery of Daphni lies on the pass over Mt Aigaleo, which separates the Athenian from the Thriasian plain; it is located near the modern National Road, which roughly follows the ancient Sacred Way through the pass, on the site of an ancient sanctuary of Apollo, which Pausanias mentions in his travel guide. Nearby, on the south slope a Cave of Pan has been found and a few hundred metres further west on the right near the National Road, the Classical Temple of Aphrodite.

The easiest way to reach Daphni from the centre of Athens is to take the road to Corinth which is signposted from Omonia Square (c. 11 km). Just before the top of the pass turn left to the monastery (signpost). In front of the entrance to the monastery follow the path through the woods in a westerly direction c. 250 m to the Cave of Pan, which is visible above the trees. For the Temple of Aphrodite continue along the National Road towards Eleusis and park a few hundred metres west of the monastery at the first turning on the right.

The **Monastery of Daphni** (Figures **44**; **115**; Plate 35). In Antiquity a
temple, which according to Pausanias was dedicated to Apollo Daphnios,
stood at the top of the pass of Aigaleo where the monastery stands
today, about halfway between Athens and Eleusis. It was destroyed in AD 395
by Alaric the Goth. In the fifth century an Early Christian monastery was built
on the same site, covering an area with an enclosure of 100 m by 100 m; cells,
porches, dining and guest rooms were built alongside the inner walls. A basilica
was erected in the middle of the courtyard; a few remains of its foundations
can be seen west of the present church. The foundations of the rooms and
porches, which are still visible in the north, and the enclosure itself, date from
this period. Since the monastery was in a strategically important position and
controlled the Aigaleo pass, the fortification was repaired and rebuilt in the
sixth century under Justinian.

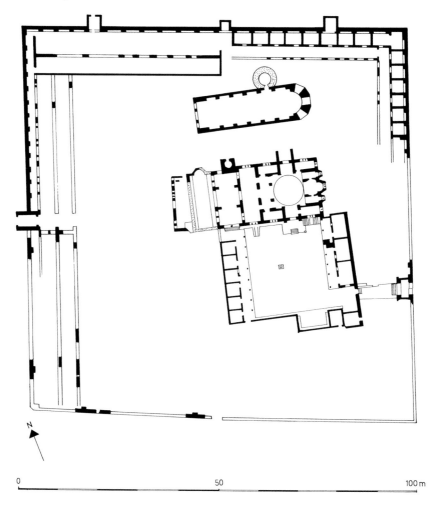

0	50	100 m

Figure 44 Monastery of Daphni (*see also* Figure 115).

In the so-called Dark Ages the monastery, like so many other Early Christian churches, was abandoned and fell into ruins. In the eleventh century it was refounded, the buildings were repaired and the catholikon, dedicated to the Dormition of the Virgin, was put up on the site of the basilica in 1080 and, with small alterations, is still to be seen today (Plate 35).

The well-articulated lines of the building with its impressive dome are immediately apparent from the exterior. The lower part of the wall consists of large blocks arranged in cross-like patterns and the upper courses are of carefully executed cloisonné masonry. Terracotta bricks emphasise the curve of the two- and three-part bay windows, a simple zigzag frieze decorates the wall, running horizontally round the outer wall and including the windows; a double one runs round the drum of the dome. The apse behind the bema is emphasised both in colour (through the use of terracotta bricks) and also ornamentally (by a maeander frieze). The church belongs to the cross-domed type with eight pillars and a narthex, which in this case supported an upper floor; the latter was reached by a tower with a spiral staircase built onto the north side; the monastery library was probably located here, or a room for the abbot. A few years after the refoundation at the beginning of the twelfth century an outer narthex was added, the arches of which were supported by ancient Ionic columns; both narthexes underwent alterations in later times. With one exception the ancient columns were taken to England by Lord Elgin.

Today the church is entered from the south. Eight pillars arranged in a square support the dome which rests on four squinches. This system allowed a larger dome diameter in comparison with the four-pillared type, so that the entire inner room in front of the bema, prothesis and diakonikon (sacristy) lies under the curve of the dome. The architecture around the sixteen windows of the drum is particularly impressive. The extremely rich interior decoration is only fragmentarily preserved. The floor was originally covered with different coloured marble slabs with geometric motifs and the side walls were covered with marble right up to the decorated cornice; this was destroyed in the Turkish period and replaced by frescoes in 1650. Above the cornice, however, many of the original fine, gold-ground late eleventh century mosaics are preserved, an important testimony to the art of that period, which has rightly made Daphni so famous. The figures in the pictures are tall and slim; their elegant forms are repeatedly compared to ancient designs. This 'Classicismus' appears not only in the garments of the figures but also in the rendering of the folds and in the movements of the personages. The art of the mosaics is enhanced by careful details, for example in the garden of Anna or at the Birth of Christ; the severity of the picture of Christ (Pantocrator) in the dome is in complete contrast to these charming mosaics.

Leaving the catholikon, to the north of the church further evidence of the Middle Byzantine period can be seen in the form of the foundations of a large refectory with apse.

The luxurious life of the monastery, which was famous for its wealth, came to a sudden end in 1207 as a result of the Frankish occupation. The Greek Orthodox monks were driven out and in 1211 Cistercian monks moved in.

The sarcophagi, seen next to the ancient and Early Christian finds in the south courtyard, date to the time of Burgundian rule. Alterations were carried out in the church; the upper floor of the narthex was removed and the west façade of the outer narthex was decorated with Gothic pointed arches in Frankish taste; the turreted fortification enclosure wall was also renovated.

The Cistercians were driven out by the Turkish invasion in 1458. There are signs that the monastery was once more occupied by Orthodox monks in the sixteenth century. South of the church, low cells with arcades in front of them were built round the paved courtyard and the east gate, which is still the entrance to the monastery today, was added to the enclosure; the original entrance was on the west side.

During the Greek War of Independence the monastery was used as a refuge, for example, for the metropolitan bishop of Athens, Bartholomew, who hid there from the Turks in 1770; the resistance fighters under Tasos Mavrovouniotis had their headquarters here, but were betrayed by a monk called Paisios, so the Turks took over Daphni and set fire to the church to melt the gold of the mosaics. After serving as a barracks for Bavarian soldiers in 1838–39 and as a lunatic asylum in 1883–85, the first restoration work began on the deserted monastery in 1889 with the renovation of the dilapidated dome. Extensive renovation work was necessary after the earthquake in 1981; the mosaics were restored and cleaned and now glow in their original colours. But the earthquake of September 1999 again caused damage.

The **Cave of Pan**. The Classical shrine of Pan is established in a small natural cave on Aigaleo. It had four small rooms, partly divided from each

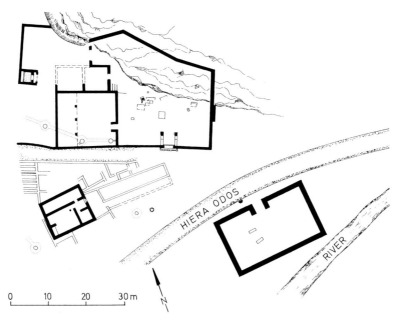

Figure 45 Daphni, Sanctuary of Aphrodite.

other by walls, and a long terrace in front of it, retained by two walls of field stones. Figurines and vases, found in excavations in 1932, date the beginning of the cult of Pan here to the fifth century BC (see also the north slope of the Acropolis, Vari, Marathon – Oinoe, Phyle), that is after the intervention of the god at the Battle of Marathon.

The **Temple of Aphrodite**[136] on the Sacred Way to Eleusis (Figure **45**) was more important than the Cave of Pan. Today the numerous carved niches on the rock face for votive reliefs and offerings are clearly visible (Plate 36). In front of the rock is an enclosure with a small entrance, on the west side of which large foundation blocks indicate a building; a few metres further south there are the remains of a small building. In Antiquity the Sacred Way ran in front of both these buildings; on the other side of it a rectangular house with foundations of irregularly cut blocks is visible; the excavator has suggested it was a guardpost. In late Antiquity two graves lay here. Many sculptures were found during the excavations: the upper torso of the Classical cult image and some doves (see p. 131) and a large number of votive reliefs with representations of different parts of the body, which show that Aphrodite was called upon as a healing and protective goddess (just as on the north slope of the Acropolis, see p. 54) and that after recovery a votive was given to her in thanks.

9   Kaisariani and the monasteries and quarries on Hymettos

'All around all the fat and soft earth is washed away and only the lean skeleton of the land remains.' The problem[137] which Plato described at the beginning of the fourth century BC, affects Hymettos, the local Athenian mountain, even more today. The bare mountain range extends east of the city over 18 km in a north–south direction, from the Athenian suburb of Ay. Paraskevi to Vouliagmeni, where it ends at Cape Zoster. The Pirnari gorge divides the range in two. There is a radar station on the peak (1,026 m above sea level) which is a prohibited military area. In Antiquity a sanctuary of Zeus Ombrios (the cloud gatherer) was located here. Pausanias (I 32, 2) mentions a statue of Zeus and an altar. Indeed between 1923 and 1939 the remains of an altar were found a little below the summit; with it was pottery which scholars have suggested shows continuity of cult from the Mycenaean period into late Antiquity. Some sherds dating to the seventh century BC have scratched letters on them, naming Zeus.[138]

Geologically, Hymettos consists of layers of slate (for example, the characteristic green Kaisariani slate) from limestone formations and crystalline marble; both types of stone were quarried from as early as the sixth century BC into late Antiquity. The so-called Kara limestone was used for the foundations of large buildings and the white Hymettian marble for sculpture, inscribed stelai and architecture. From the late fourth century BC the blue-grey marble was also used for these. Even today there are huge marble quarries in operation on Hymettos.

Hymettos has many caves; in total 78 caves open to daylight are known today. Two of the most interesting stalactite caves are Koutouki near Paiania and the Cave of Pan and the Nymphs near Vari (see pp. 194 and 233).

There are numerous springs at the foot of Hymettos, but in spite of this abundance of water the erosion of the mountain continues. Negligence or arson nullify the careful forestry work which has been carried out continuously for decades. In 1988 a huge part of the forest was burnt almost up to the monastery of Kaisariani. The times of Pindar or Ovid, or even the writers of the Middle Ages, who all describe the mountain as covered with many kinds of plants, blooming shrubs and dense woods, seem to have passed.

To reach Hymettos it is best to go along Mesogeion Street, turn right in front of an underpass (signpost to airport) into Leoforos Katechaki Alimou and follow this to the ascent to Kaisariani. Here it meets the road that leads from the suburb of Kaisariani up to the monastery (it is signposted in the town near the War Museum). The asphalt road goes past the monastery and winds (with superlative views over the city) up the mountain. Above the Monastery of Asteri is a mountain saddle (with OTE station) which gives a wide view over the Mesogeia in the east up to Porto Raphti. From here the road, which continues up the west side of Hymettos below the military zone, is closed.

The **Monastery of Kaisariani**. According to popular tradition the monastery is named from an alleged water installation, a gift of the Emperor ('Caesar') Hadrian, which carried water to Athens from this district with its many springs. However, there are no traces of such an aqueduct, so the nomenclature is not entirely convincing. There is an interesting hint that 'Kaisariani' is connected to the name of Saisara, a daughter of Keleos, a mythical king and priest of Eleusis; according to Pausanias, Saisara was also a priestess of Demeter. An inscription in the area of the monastery indicates a Demeter cult, which names an Eleusinian high-priest (hierophant). It is possible that the site is named 'Saisariane' after the daughter of Keleos.

The neighbourhood of Kaisariani has three springs: the monastery spring, which is perhaps to be identified with the ancient Kallia, a spring south-west of the monastery near a simple chapel and the spring of Kalopoula c. 300 m to the north-east. The spring Kallia lay (according to a tenth century report by Suidas) by a sanctuary of Aphrodite and was famous for curing sterility, a belief handed down to the present time.

Archaeological remains in the area of the monastery comprise buildings dating especially to the Roman period. On the peak of Ay. Markos, which lies south-west of the monastery and can be reached after a 15 minute walk, there was an important building, probably a temple, dating to the second century AD, from which many architectural fragments exist; they can be seen in the monastery garden and as spolia in the monastery buildings and in the church on the hill itself. A three-aisled basilica with three apses was built on the peak, with its splendid view of the plain of Athens, in the fifth century as a successor

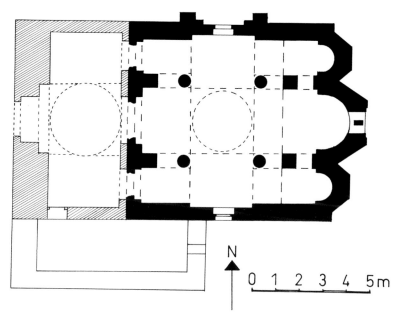

N

0 1 2 3 4 5m

Figure 46 Kaisariani, church of the Taxiarchs.

to this Roman building; its foundations can still be made out east of the later church of the Taxiarchs. The choir screen and other parts of this Early Christian church were built into the catholikon of the monastery. During the 'Dark Ages' the church decayed and was replaced in the tenth century by a Byzantine church (Figure **46**), dedicated to the Taxiarchs. Only a small part of its walls is left, but its plan shows the transition from basilica to cross-in-square domed church, for example, in the size of its stepped angular apses and a nave wider than the transept; the dome, supported on pendentives, must have been oval. Ancient and Early Christian spolia were also much reused in this church. During the Frankish period the one-aisled chapel of Ay. Markos was built onto the south side of the church of the Taxiarchs, and a Catholic church service was held in it. Much of the walls and the barrel-vault is preserved today. Later the hill was used as the monastery cemetery, which was moved in the eleventh century to a more protected place. A small chapel dating to the Turkish period was used as a charnel house. Interesting ancient architectural fragments can be found, especially in the west wall of this small church, which was also dedicated to the Taxiarchs, including a marble block with a plant frieze decorated with animals; another part of this frieze is in the monastery garden.

To the north-east below the hillock new monastery buildings were put up in the eleventh century right next to a spring, which perhaps supplied a nymphaion in the Roman period (remains east of the catholikon); only the church and bath house belonging to these buildings are extant. The catholikon (Plate 38), dedicated to the Presentation of the Virgin, was built as a cross-in-square

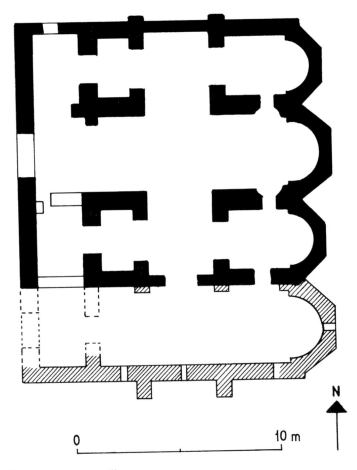

N

0   10 m

Figure 47 Kaisariani, catholikon.

domed church soon after AD 1000 (Figure **47**). The careful cloisonné masonry, partly obscured by later repairs, was only enlivened by plain brick decoration over the window arches and a horizontal running zigzag frieze below the dome; the three entrances were emphasised by marble thresholds and lintels of spolia. In the interior the choir screen from the Early Christian basilica and the fine marble paving catch the eye. The dome, which has a very high drum, is supported on four ancient pillars. The frescoes of the main room, which follow the usual themes, date from the eighteenth century (according to the Byzantinist Chatzidakis), but are painted in a style derived from the Cretan School of the sixteenth century. The oldest painting is on the former south exterior wall of the church; it can be seen today in the side chapel of Ay. Antonios where it has deliberately not been plastered over. It consists of a hardly recognisable representation of the Virgin as mediator; it dates to the fourteenth century. The narthex of the catholikon is a seventeenth century addition like the side chapel and the belfry; the simple masonry of its exterior distinguishes it clearly from the original church complex. Its paintings date to 1632, as an inscription over the entrance together with the details of the fresco painting bear witness. They were commissioned by Ioannis Venizelos, who had taken refuge in the monastery from the plague in Athens. Moses and Aaron with the twelve tribes of Israel can be seen above the inscription, the tree of Jesse on the north wall, and Jesus with his disciples on the south wall, in a representation of the parable of the workers in the vineyard. The painting was executed by the Peloponnesian artist Ioannis Hypatos.

Part of the bath house with its fine dome (Plate 38) also belongs to the original monastic building (eleventh century). It encloses a natural spring, which had an unusual embellishment in front of the east exterior wall of the monastery: the water gushed out of an Archaic marble ram head which came from the 'Old Temple of Athena' on the Acropolis (copy). The division of the interior of the bath house follows that of the traditional Roman baths (sudatorium, caldarium, frigidarium); next to the sudatorium are two dayrooms. A circular marble bench, to be seen in the monastery garden, originally belonged to the bath house. In the Turkish period the bath house was turned into a mill; millstones and an olive press in the interior indicate this.

The remaining monastic buildings date to the sixteenth and seventeenth centuries, such as the cella with loggia (which adjoins the bath house) in which the living tower of the Venizelos family is integrated, as well as the refectory with kitchen, pantry and dining hall.

Up until the eighteenth century the monastery, which was also known under the names of Seriani and Syrgiani, was famous for its olive groves, vineyards, bee-keeping and remedies made of herbs from Hymettos. During the Turkish period it was the spiritual centre of the neighbourhood and its highly educated abbots taught in the Athenian schools. As a result of its clever political management Kaisariani always occupied a special position and had tax exemption, whether it was from the Catholic Church, the Turks or the Byzantine patriarchate. The decline of the monastery began at the end of the eighteenth century; its autonomy was removed and the famous library was partly sold to the English and partly used as fuel for fires on the Acropolis during the Turkish seige. During the reign of Otto I a nunnery was temporarily lodged in Kaisariani. After that the monastery was abandoned and the buildings decayed. Restoration of the monastery buildings was first accomplished on the initiative of Kaiti Argyropoulou, who, in conjunction with the 'Friends of Trees', set up an extensive reforestation programme (financed today by the WWF) in the monastery area. A monument on the hill south-east of the monastery commemorates the woman to whom the renovation of this idyllic site is largely due.

The **Monastery of Asteri** (Figure **48**). The uninhabited Monastery of the Archangel (Moni Taxiarchon), better known by its local name of Asteri, lies at a height of 545 m above sea level on the slope of Hymettos. The origin of the name, according to legend, is that Asteria, the sister of Leto, hurled herself from a rock here to escape the pursuit of Zeus and was turned into a quail. The name more probably derives from Ay. Loukas of Steiria, who stayed in

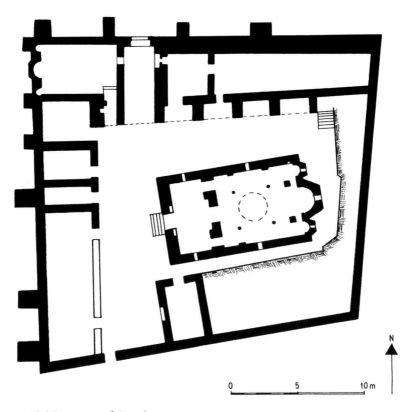

0　　　　　5　　　　　10 m

Figure 48 Monastery of Asteri.

Athens during his religious instruction and withdrew into the mountain world of Hymettos. Thus, the Christian tradition of the monastery reaches back at least into the early tenth century; an exact date for its foundation is not known. The monastery church was built in the eleventh century, a cross-in-square domed church with narthex, which is preserved today. The typical cloisonné masonry can only be recognised around the octagonal drum. The dome is supported on the interior by four columns with Ionic capitals. The frescoes date from the sixteenth century. The entrance building, the later refectory with apse and a fine fresco dating from the seventeenth century, the kitchen, the earlier refectory, the cella and the fountain house in the south also survive from the monastery precinct, which is enclosed with a high wall. The former Greek queen, Frederica (wife of Paul I and mother of Constantine II), lived here for many years; central heating was installed in the old rooms for her. The entire complex was restored a few years ago.

The Monastery of Asteri is generally closed; there are no regular opening hours. It can be reached by continuing up the asphalt road 3.5 km above the monastery of Kaisariani. The ruins of a living and defensive tower dating to the Turkish period are located 2.5 km along the road; such towers were used by famous Athenian families as places of refuge in unsafe times. A branch of the road near this tower leads down to the suburb of Papagou and the monastery of Ay. Ioannis Theologos (see p. 159).

The **ancient quarries** on Hymettos (Figure **49**). Marble began to be quarried on Hymettos[139] from the sixth century BC. At first only the white marble was used for making sculptures, inscribed stelai and architecture, but from the fourth century BC until late Antiquity blocks of blue-grey stone were also quarried; these were generally used for Athenian architecture and not for sculpture. Wherever the white or grey-blue marble layers appeared on Hymettos in good enough quality, deep gouges, which can still be seen today, were made into the hillside to quarry them out. The tool marks from carving the blocks can still be seen on the quarry walls, which may be quite high (see p. 259; Figure **84**). Discarded or broken columns and other building material, which was not transported to its destination, can be seen in some quarries. A 'dragon house', unique in Attica, lies above the quarries on the slope (above a large quarry located near the top). In spite of its bad preservation this round house of large, coarse, marble blocks is clearly related to the similar well-known 'dragon houses' of south Euboia. This house was used as accommodation for the quarry workers and can be dated to the Roman period from a graffito (the name Kethegos can be read) in the quarry behind it. A path running almost horizontally round the slope, straight above and south of the Kaisariani monastery, offers a walk high above the city with wonderful views of Athens and the islands of the Saronic Gulf; there are numerous ancient quarries further up the slope; many types of wild orchids and other wild flowers, such as daffodils and anemones, grow around them and on the surrounding slopes, enlivening the bare mountainside in spring.

To the west next to Katechaki Street and south of the road to the suburb of Kaisariani (about opposite the ancient quarries just described) is a hill which has two huge modern quarries cut into its north-east and south sides. It is called **Fox Mountain (Alepovouni)** and is important for archaeologists and epigraphists because boundary inscriptions are carved in many places on its rocks. American scholars (J. Ober, M.K. Langdon)[140] have found more than twenty of these rock-cut inscriptions, which perhaps demarcated areas of bee-keepers from each other; for Hymettos was famous in Antiquity for its bee-keeping which produced high quality honey. South-east of Fox Mountain, Katechaki Street meets a street coming from the suburb of Vyron (traffic light); here the visitor can go left (to the east to the slopes of Hymettos) and then left again to a sports area. Paths, signposted in red, run from there up Hymettos to the ancient quarries, which can be clearly seen from below. The next turn from Katechaki Street southwards is that to Kareas.

The **Monastery of Kareas** lies above the southern suburb of the same name in a hollow on the sides of which ancient quarries with dumps of marble fragments can seen.

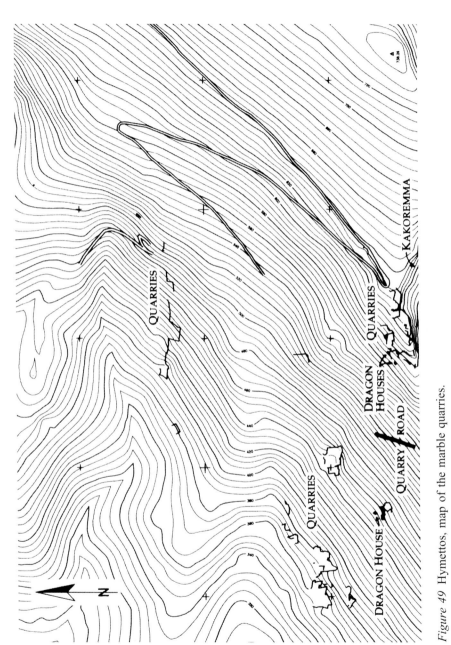

Figure 49 Hymettos, map of the marble quarries.

The visitor should take the Kareas exit from the wide eastern ringroad, Leof. Alimou Katechaki, which runs along Hymettos, and follow the main road Leof. Ay. Ioannou Karea through the suburb uphill; before it turns right downhill, a road lined with cypress trees leads left to the monastery (open 7.30–12.30; 15.00 to sunset).

A notable Byzantine church belongs to the well tended modern convent. According to ancient sources a predecessor stood here as early as the ninth century, and some finds even suggest an Early Christian building. The present catholikon dates to the eleventh century, although the original cloisonné masonry is hardly recognisable as a result of alterations and renovations; an idea of its early quality can best be obtained in the area of the apse. The cross-domed church originally had four columns on the interior, one of which was later replaced by a pillar. The walls today are not decorated and fresco remains can only be seen in the apse. A plaque over the entrance mentions an endowment in 1769; afterwards, in the nineteenth century, the monastery declined. In 1971 it was reconsecrated and given to an order of Greek Orthodox nuns for missionary work.

A wide earth path runs southwards from the monastery keeping to the same height along the slope. After 15 minutes' walk it widens on the west into an area with benches. Some rock-cut inscriptions have been found in this area,[141] which are not easily explicable; perhaps they bordered a small sanctuary or perhaps they mark an ancient water pipe. The path, which already existed in Antiquity,[142] was the crossing for walkers who wanted to go over Hymettos and down into the Mesogeia on the shortest route to Koropi (Sphettos) and Merenda (Myrrhinous), as well as to Sounion.

The **Monastery of Ay. Ioannis Theologos** lies at the north-west foot of Hymettos, on the edge of the modern suburb of Papagou.

From Mesogeion Street, which goes to Raphina, turn into the suburb of Papagou opposite the Ministry of Defence onto the wide Kyprou Street; follow this to a modern church square with a park, go halfway round this and then turn right into the next street (Leof. Stratarchou Papagou). The tenth street is the wide Anastaseos, which must be followed about 300 m to the right out of the suburb. Soon after the last houses a sign pointing to the right leads to the monastery (open 7.00–12.00, 15.00–18.00hrs).

The monastery was founded in the thirteenth century; the catholikon belonging to the cross-in-square dome type also dates to this period. Two of the four interior columns are decorated with Ionic capitals. The frescoes date to the sixteenth century. In the fifteenth century a narthex was added to the front of the church, which is embellished with a modern veranda porch today. Only parts of the refectory, the porter's lodge and a watch tower, which is built into the enclosure wall (seventeenth century), are preserved from the other old buildings of the monastery. Seventeenth century frescoes can be seen in the refectory. The church is shaded by large pine trees and is surrounded by a small, well-tended flower garden. North-east of the monastery, at the side of the road, is the small whitewashed church of Ayia Eleousa dating to the sixteenth or seventeenth century, which is the cemetery church of the monastery. The source of the River Ilissos is located nearby. During new road construction works this area unfortunately has lost its once idyllic appearance.

The (Philosopher) **Monastery of Ay. Ionannis Kynigos**. In the far north of Hymettos, high above the valley between it and Pentelikon, lies the Monastery of St John the Hunter, also known as the 'Philosopher's' Monastery (Plate 39).

Follow Mesogeion Street out of the city to the suburb of Ay. Paraskevi. Turn right before the square of the same name with the modern church, go round the square and then follow Ay. Ioannou Kynigou uphill to its end, turn left there and at the first opportunity again right. The narrow winding road goes up to the monastery. (open 7.00–12.00, 15.00–17.00hrs).

T he monastery, which has a tradition going back to the tenth century, lies behind a high enclosure wall at a height of 330 m above sea level on the north-east slope of Hymettos. The names of 'Kynigos' and 'Philosopher' derive from the founder or dedicator of the monastery, which is a convent today. The church, which is consecrated to St John the Baptist (Prodromos), is particularly interesting; two building phases can be made out (Plate 39). The earlier building complex comprises a small cross-domed church dating to the twelfth century, which was restored in the thirteenth century (inscription). The walls, carefully constructed of cloisonné masonry around the drum, are noteworthy for the use of large marble blocks in their lower courses. In the interior the dome is supported by two pillars and two huge, unfluted columns crowned with ancient Ionic capitals. There are two more similar columns in front of the south side of the church. The two later (seventeenth century) building phases can easily be separated from the Byzantine because of the careless masonry on the exterior. The large narthex with the belfry and the low west dome belong to these phases. The undamaged frescoes on the interior also date to the Turkish period; in the right side arm of the catholikon there are a few remnants of earlier paintings, which have been wantonly destroyed. Later additions to the church have been largely removed; only a small colonnade dating to the eighteenth century with an ancient Doric capital has been left. On the south side of the courtyard dilapidated remnants belong to earlier monastery buildings; they have recently been replaced by new buildings. The remaining buildings are all more recent.

The remains of ancient quarries can be seen near the monastery (south and east) and an ancient road, which crossed the ridge of Hymettos from the Athenian plain to the Mesogeia, to Paiania.[143]

Plate 1 Athens from the west (Stademann 1835).

Photo DAI Athens (AthVar 985)

Plate 2 Athens, Acropolis and Olympieion with the Ilissos and the Mouseion Hill: view from the stadium of Herodes Atticus, *c.* 1900.

Photo DAI Athens (Akr 409)

Plate 3 Model of the Athenian Acropolis, *c.* 480 BC (Mus. Makrygianni, design M. Korres). Photo DAI Athens (87/940)

Plate 4 Model of the Athenian Acropolis, *c.* AD 180 (Mus. Makrygianni, design M. Korres). Photo DAI Athens (87/949)

Plate 5
Athens, Acropolis:
Propylaea, east
façade; in the
background the Hill
of the Nymphs,
c. 1900.

Photo DAI Athens
(Akr 24)

Plate 6 Athens, Acropolis: Temple of Athena Nike from the east.

Photo DAI Athens (Akr 2430)

Plate 7 Athens, Acropolis: foundations of the Old Temple of Athena and Erechtheion.

Plate 8 Athens, Acropolis: Erechtheion, west façade. Photo Robertson (1854)

Plate 10 Athens, Acropolis: foundations of the Old Parthenon in the south.

Photo DAI Athens (Akr 112)

Plate 9 Athens, Acropolis: snowy view from the Propylaea to the Parthenon.

Plate 11 Athens, Acropolis: Parthenon from the north-west, *c.* 1900.
Photo DAI Athens (Akr 280)

Plate 12 Athens, Acropolis: restoration works of the Parthenon, 1998.

Plate 13 Athens, Acropolis: Parthenon, west frieze.

Photo DAI Athens (Hege 2545)

(a)

Plate 14 Athens, Acropolis: Parthenon,
(a) slab VIII of the west frieze (photo 1930)
and (b) part of a cast made at the time of
Lord Elgin.

Photo DAI Athens (Hege 1744, 2286)

(b)

Plate 15 Copy of the statue of
Athena Parthenos, ten times reduced
in size (Athens, National Museum).

Photo DAI Athens ((NM 5149)

Plate 16 Athens, Acropolis: two
Archaic korai in front of the
Parthenon. The photograph combines,
unhistorically, monuments of two
different epochs which were never to
be seen simultaneously. The Korai lay
buried in the Persian destruction fill
of the Acropolis when the Parthenon
was finished. The picture gives,
however, a good impression of how
Greek sculpture looked in the
sunlight.

Photo Wagner

Plate 17 Athens, theatre of Dionysos and the Museum Makrygianni, *c.* 1890.
Photo DAI Athens (Athen Bauten 119)

Plate 18 Athens, theatre of Dionysos: throne of the priest of Dionysos.
Photo DAI Athens (Hege 1063)

Plate 19 Athens, Kerameikos: overview from the east with the Pompeion.

Plate 20 Athens, Kerameikos: Street of the Tombs.

Plate 21 Athens, Agora: overview from the west.

Plate 22 Athens, Plaka with Roman Market and Library of Hadrian: view from the Acropolis.

Plate 23 Athens, Tower of the Winds.

Plate 24 Athens, little Metropolis Church.

Plate 25 Athens, choregic monument of Lysikrates, so-called Lantern of Demosthenes.

Plate 26
Athens,
Olympieion
and
Acropolis.

Plate 27 Athens, First Cemetery, mausoleum of Heinrich Schliemann.
Photo DAI Athens (Athen Bauten 573)

Plate 28 Athens, National Library.
Photo DAI Athens (80/655)

Plate 29 Anthemion of a state burial monument to the horsemen fallen at Corinth and Koroneia in 394 BC; one of them was Dexileos of Thorikos (Athens, National Museum).
Photo DAI Athens (NM 4600)

Plate 30 Fragment of a stele of a state burial monument to the war dead at Corinth and Koroneia in 394 BC; under the heroic depiction of the fight there are some names listed by tribes (Athens, National Museum).
Photo DAI Athens (Hege 1692)

Plate 31 Stele of Dexileos, a member of the cavalry fallen in the war of 394 BC (Athens, Kerameikos Museum).

Plate 32 Piraeus, southern part of the city wall, *c.* 1890.

Photo DAI Athens (Pir 46)

Plate 33 Piraeus, tower of the Eetoneia Gate west of the main harbour.

Plate 34 Piraeus, Mikrolimano with remains of the ancient mole.

Plate 35 Monastery of Daphni from the south-west.

Plate 36 Daphni, Sanctuary of Aphrodite.

Plate 37 Athens – Kalogreza, Omorphi Ekklesia.

Plate 38 Monastery of Kaisariani, catholikon and bath.

Plate 39 Monastery of Ay. Ioannis Kynigos, catholikon from the south-east.

Plate 40 Vouliagmeni, Sanctuary of Apollo on Cape Zoster.

Plate 41 Vouliagmeni, rock-cut boundary inscription on Kaminia Hill, in the background Cape Zoster.

Plate 42 Cave of Pan near Vari, main chamber looking towards the entrance.

Plate 43 Elympos, apse of Early Christian basilica.

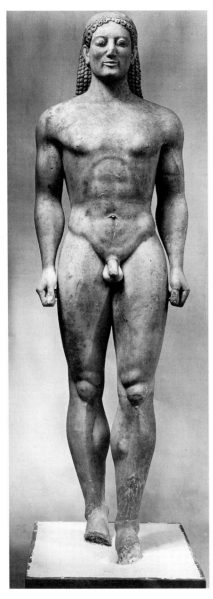

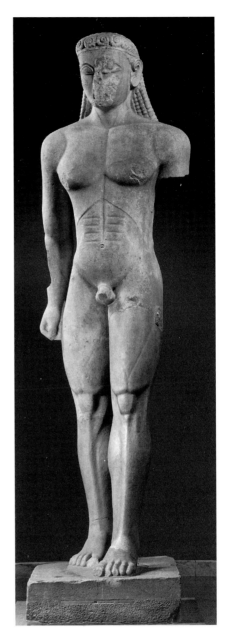

Plate 44 Statue of Kroisos found on a grave at Anavyssos (Athens, National Museum).

Photo DAI Athens (NM 4262)

Plate 45 Statue of a kouros found at the top of Cape Sounion (Athens, National Museum).

2 Attica I: From Athens to Sounion and in the Mesogeia

1 Glyphada, Voula, Vouliagmeni, Vari and the south-west Attic coastal sites

E very visitor to Greece tries to see the Temple of Poseidon at Sounion. The site is justly famous both for its shining white ruins and for its impressive position on the southern tip of Attica. An excursion to Sounion is also very worthwhile because there are some sites of interest and beauty to visit on the road from Athens to Sounion (the so-called Apollo Coast, with many good beaches), which decisively round off the picture of Attica, although they are less well known. They include small ancient local sanctuaries, a sacred cave, country villas, Early Greek settlements, etc., all set in the picturesque landscape of south Attica with its juxtaposition of coastal coves and high rising mountains.

The route out of the city may appear to some to be tedious, since the mass of buildings stretches endlessly along Vouliagmenis Street towards the airport. It is difficult to imagine that a few decades ago, and right back into Antiquity, the settlement consisted only of isolated farmsteads or small villages. The visitor gets the same impression if he leaves Athens via Syngrou Avenue and turns in Phaleron onto the coast road going southwards.

The ancient deme of Halimous lies north of Hellenikon airport; its name survives today as 'Alimos'. Various excavations have been carried out in this suburb from the last century onwards. One such excavation on a small peninsula, called **Ay. Kosmas** today after its chapel, but probably called Cape Kolias in Antiquity, uncovered an Early Helladic settlement (2500–1900 BC) with houses known as corridor houses, which had rooms one behind the other. The cemetery belonging to the settlement lay on the Mainland; it contained cist graves lined and covered with stone slabs. The finds suggest that the inhabitants may have been closely connected to the Cyclades. Later there was a Mycenaean settlement on the same site with houses of megaron type. There is almost nothing to see of these ancient remains on the cape today. However, the sports centre in the park just to the north might be of interest to some tourists; there are tennis courts and facilities for every type of ball game; it is also possible to learn diving in a special pool.

A few kilometres inland to the east a small **theatre** was found in 1975 **at Trachones**,[144] which must have been used as a meeting place by the inhabitants of the neigbourhood, the deme of Euonymon. It is situated on Archaiou Theatrou Street (Street of the Ancient Theatre), which turns off west from Vouliagmenis Street about 100 m north of Alimos Street. The excavations of the last few years have uncovered a small stage building of ashlar limestone blocks with stucco decoration, an oblong orchestra and rows of seats correspondingly laid out on a rectangular plan on a slightly hollowed and gently rising natural slope. In a second building phase six large thrones of Hymettian marble were put in front of the original first row of marble seats, which consisted of slabs with letters on the front for the dignitaries (prohedria). The finds, which date the construction of the theatre to soon after 400 BC, include, in particular, two archaising figures of Dionysos, which were set up at the sides of the orchestra. The small theatre is particularly important, since it persuasively supports the results of new research that the Greek theatre first had a rectangular form until the mid-fourth century BC and then was developed into a circular form. At any rate, all the Early Greek theatres known up to today have a rectangular plan – another one has just been excavated some kilometres to the west – while the circular form called by us 'Classical' is first found in the mid-fourth century BC.

On a small hill in the vicinity of the theatre a three-aisled Christian basilica, which lay above a Greek sanctuary, was discovered and excavated in 1929. The remains of the church have completely disappeared; however, its existence shows continuity of settlement into late Antiquity in the district around Trachones.

In the area of the Hellenikon airport there was once a **Classical cemetery**; when the landing strip was constructed a particularly large grave plot of ashlar masonry was moved into the adjoining private airclub to the south-west, where it can be seen today between the eucalyptus trees from the wide coast road (Leof. Vas. Georgiou II'). The expensive suburb of **Glyphada**, which is known in Athens for its many clubs, restaurants, golf course and watersporting installations, lies south of the airport. The remains of a large **Early Christian basilica**,[145] which was apparently built to commemorate the visit of St Paul to Greece, are to be seen right on the waterfront next to a small yacht harbour (west of the crossroads of Leof. Vas. Georgiou II' and Lampraki Greg.; Figures **50**; **51**.1). The church had three aisles with a large apse at the end of the central one. There is little left of the external masonry and the interior columns, but an idea can be gained of how impressive the basilica must have looked in its location right next to the sea looking towards a small green peninsula in the south.

The suburb of Voula[146] lies south and east of Glyphada. Vouliagmenis Street forks here; a newly constructed main branch leads directly to Vouliagmeni (see below), while the other branch – called Kalymnou – goes off to Vari and Varkiza (Figure **51**). About 2 km along this side road behind a long right-hand

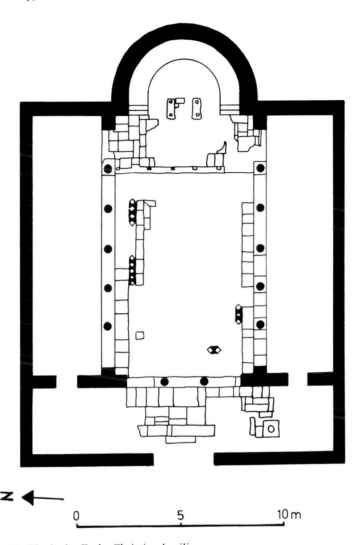

Figure 50 Glyphada, Early Christian basilica.

curve a large open space (called Kalambokas) lies on the right (west) of the road (Figures **51**.4; **52**), on which numerous, at first apparently muddled, wall remains can be seen. However, when the visitor goes up an elevation on the west to look over this ancient settlement and runs an eye along the separate lines of streets, then the house plans can easily be made out. The complex has an irregular town plan with wide main streets and smaller alleys; in the north-west of the area a large building block, which has a round tower with a diameter of 8 m in the centre, can be seen very clearly; on its north side is a bathroom with a waterproof floor which has been renewed many times. One of the two known sanctuaries is situated on a street fork about 30 m south,

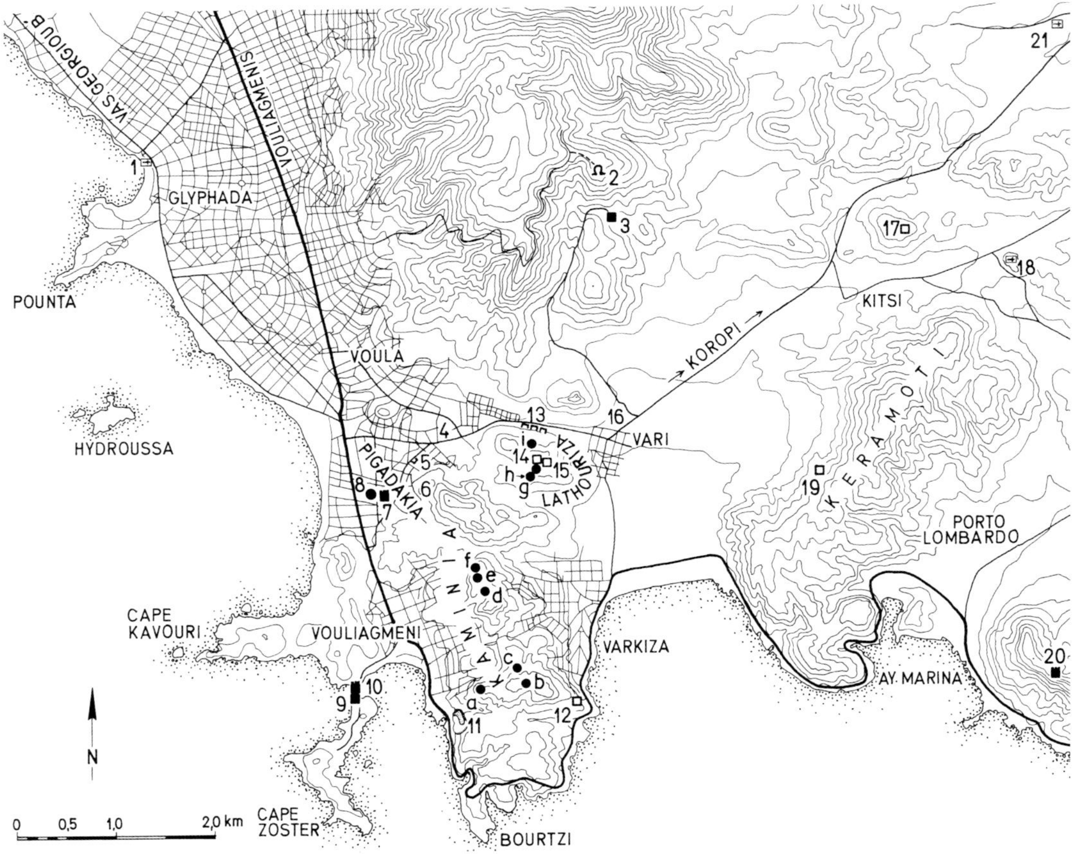

Figure 51 Map of the area of Voula, Vouliagmeni and Vari

1: Glyphada, Early Christian basilica; 2: Cave of Pan; 3: Classical farmstead; 4: Kalambokas: Classical settlement; 5: Classical grave plot (Athinon st.); 6: Kastraki Hill: fortified acropolis; 7: farmstead with tower; 8: Heroon (Eleftherias st.); 9: Sanctuary of Apollo; 10: farmstead with tower; 11: Lake Vouliagmeni; 12: sanctuary above Varkiza; 13: grave plots; 14: Lathouriza, fortified settlement with temple; 15: Lathouriza, Geometric settlement; 16: ancient cemetery of Vari; 17: Kiapha Thiti 18: Panagia Thiti; 19: Early Helladic settlement; 20: watchtower of Ay. Demetrios Hill. Rock-cut inscriptions: a: Sotimides graffito; b–f: boundary inscriptions; g–i: ZW/BA-boundary inscriptions.

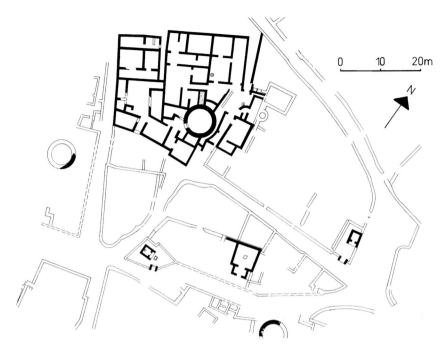

Figure 52 Voula, Kalambokas, Classical settlement.

surrounded by a temenos wall with a miniature propylon. It consists of a small temple in antis with an altar in front of the east side; its interior was decorated with a pebble mosaic. The excavations have revealed part of a large Classical village, which is perhaps to be identified with the centre of the ancient deme of Halai Axionides. House, grave and sanctuary remains found in recent years, which have been uncovered in separate building plots south of Kalambokas on the other side of the large Vari–Vouliagmeni main road, also belong to this settlement. This part of Voula, called **Pigadakia**, has been densely built over in recent years; during the building operations ancient ruins have been found everywhere; some have been built over and others left exposed. They include, in the centre of the quarter, a large farm house with a square tower (Figure **51**.7), which has the ashlar masonry of the lower wall and the threshold well preserved; a street with a large drain a few metres south-west of this (corner of Eleftherias and Kariotaki); a street fork with a heroon consisting of a temple-like building under a mound of earth surrounded by a wall (behind a tall block of flats next to Eleftherias 38 (Figure **51**.8) and an impressive grave terrace (in Athinon, corner of Kavalas: Figure **51**.5), now used as the retaining wall of a garden; these are some examples from this Classical settlement, which, with its mixture of town and country architecture with graves, has an obvious suburban character. The hill **Kastraki** (Figure **51**.6), on which the acropolis belonging to this settlement was probably situated, towers over all in the east.

Kastraki Hill can be reached by continuing a few hundred metres further from Kalambokas and turning right (west) at the T-junction, which goes left to Vari and right to Vouliagmeni and has heavy traffic. The pine-clad hill of Kastraki ('small fortress'; Figure **51**.6) can be seen south of this road, before the next wide avenue. An easy path through the pine woods leads up to the highest point in the west for those who are interested in climbing up the 132 m-high hill and who have the time. The observant visitor can recognise a few ground plans of small houses dating to the Classical period there on the surface and, on the south slope, the wall of a Hellenistic fort, for the most part destroyed. This was probably used as the camp of the Athenian opposition to the Macedonian occupation of Piraeus in the early third century BC. To the west below this acropolis is the district called Pigadakia (see above).

T he mountain, known today as **Kaminia**, which extends north–south south of Kastraki and divides Vouliagmeni from Varkiza, formed the boundary between two demes in Antiquity. This is known from two series of inscriptions (Figure **51**.b–f),[147] which are cut into the rockface on the ridge about 300 m apart and mention the word OPOC (= boundary; Plate 41). Similar boundary inscriptions are found in other places in Attica. They follow obvious landmarks and generally lie on hill ridges, which acted as natural dividing lines between two demes; these were fixed as boundaries in the late fourth century BC by means of the inscriptions.

Turning left (east) at the above mentioned T-junction in the direction of Vari, the visitor drives through a long valley lying between the foothills of Hymettos in the north and smaller hills in the south. The road is bordered by numerous tavernas, the so-called Vlachika, which serve different types of grilled meat and other typical Greek dishes.

B efore the road runs into **Vari**, a large **Classical grave plot** (Figure **51**.13) can be seen at the end of the row of tavernas to the south by the road; it is surrounded by a wall of large ashlar blocks, which is constructed of polygonal masonry.[148] There was an earth mound in the interior, which was apparently included in the Classical grave enclosure. There are smaller grave plots beside it and some undecorated marble sarcophagi on the ground (which have been brought here from other find locations).

The hill of **Lathouriza** (Figure **51**.14–15) lies to the south behind this cemetery; traces of an ancient settlement and a sanctuary enclosed by a wall have been found in different places on it.[149] A small shrine, which has been dated to the Geometric period, is situated close by on the north slope. On the peak the badly preserved foundations of an oblong double temple can be seen with an altar in front of the east side (Figures **51**.14; **53**). The fortified installation around this sanctuary,[150] which dates to the late fifth century BC, consisted of a wall on three sides while on the fourth side, on the west looking towards Kastraki, the sheer rocky hillside gave natural protection. Rooms were built on

(a)

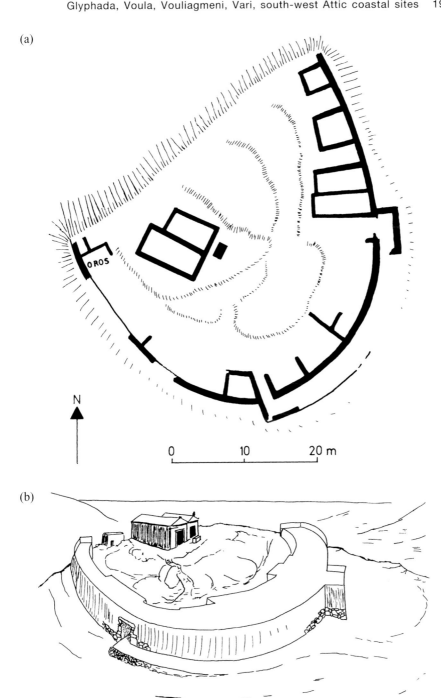

(b)

Figure 53 Vari, Lathouriza, Classical fortified settlement: (a) plan;
(b) reconstructed view from south-east (after Lauter).

the inside of the wall. On the edge of this west slope there are three ancient rock-cut inscriptions (Figure **51**.g–i),[151] probably of late date, with the word ΟΡΟΣ and above it the angular letters ΖW and below it the letters ΒΑ; their exact meaning is still unknown; perhaps they were the boundary markers between Cape Zoster in the west and an Imperial property east of Lathouriza which dated to the Roman period. They are located halfway up the west slope on the north side, in the south next to the double temple and in the southern adjoining hollow on an eminent ridge.

Turning from this hill to the south-east, an excavation of considerable inter-est (Figures **51**.15; **54**) is located on a saddle below.[152] It consists of several rounded, apsidal or rectangular rooms which are partly built adjoining each other and partly detached. This unique Attic settlement, which was occupied from the eighth to the fifth centuries BC, that is from Late Geometric to Archaic, also contained, according to the latest research, cult rooms with benches, which were built onto the walls, and lodgings for pilgrims. A circular area enclosed by a wall, inside which a place of burning with numerous terracotta figurines was found, is of particular interest; it is a small open-air sanctuary with an altar; the slabs with rectangular slots for posts, now lying inside the stone circle, once framed the entrance to the sanctuary, which was located in the south-east of the surrounding wall; they were not used as socles for roof supports, as some schol-ars previously thought. The entire complex was probably a settlement and early sanctuary belonging to the deme of Anagyrous, which adjoined the deme of Halai Axionides to the south-east and included the modern area of Vari and Varkiza. Graves, which have been found in the neighbourhood of the Lathouriza Hill (near the petrol station in Vari by the road to Koropi) and date to the same period, show that the area was densely populated.

This supposition is also now supported by a number of rock-cut inscriptions which have been found on the surrounding hills. Most of them are name graffiti dating to the sixth century BC. In one case several rock-cut inscriptions by the same person called Sotimides (Figure **51**.a) make it clear that simple shepherds carved longer texts, partly in verse, while watching their flocks. This also presents interesting evidence of the high standard of education of the rural population of Attica, which was of course also a necessity for participation in the running of the Athenian democracy.

Two other sites can be reached from the suburb of Vari: the **Vari Cave** and the **Vari House**.

Route: going from Vari in the direction of Koropi after a few metres turn left (at a petrol station; to the west an Archaic cemetery was excavated, Figure **51**.16) into a narrow side road running north-west; at a fork at the end of this follow the asphalt road, bearing right into a valley cutting, up to several abandoned concrete houses on a hilltop. The Vari House (Figure **51**.3) can be seen from there on the other side of a valley to the east. Following a dirt road up the side of Hymettos, the entrance to the Vari Cave (Figure **51**.2; covered with a new metal grille, so at the present time it is not accessible) is reached about 250 m above the Vari House; the ruined house lies almost directly below to the south.

(a)

(b)

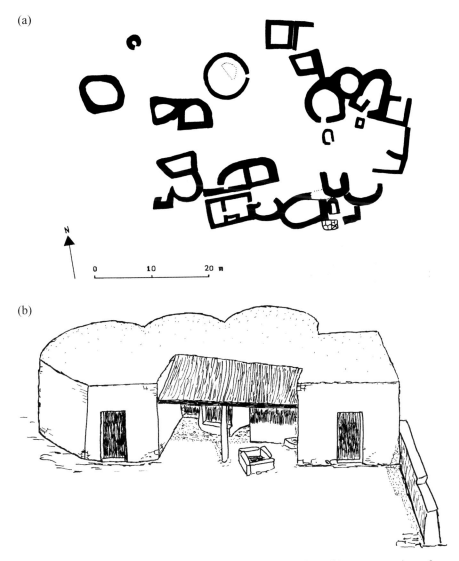

Figure 54 Vari, Lathouriza, Geometric settlement: (a) plan; (b) reconstruction of the north-eastern house (after Lauter).

The Vari Cave can also be reached by car in the following way: from Vouliagmeni Street 4 km south of the exit to Hellenikon airport go left at a traffic light into a side road and then, a few metres later, turn right; then continue up the mountain and at the junction with a street coming from the west go left; follow this about 4 km up Hymettos past the Voula Cemetery (Νεκροταφείον Ανω Βούλας) to a high tension pylon; there walk *c.* 500 m along a dirt road downwards to the right and then go right at the fork. The entrance lies 290 m above sea level, a little below the path, which then continues down to the Vari House.

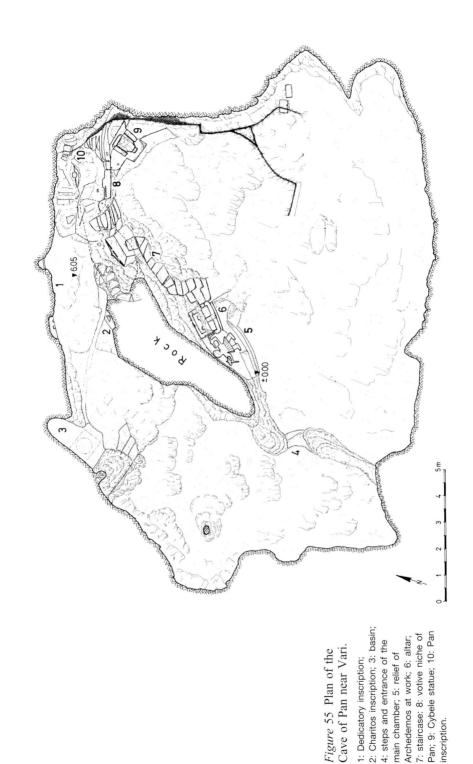

Figure 55 Plan of the
Cave of Pan near Vari.

1: Dedicatory inscription;
2: Charitos inscription; 3: basin;
4: steps and entrance of the
main chamber; 5: relief of
Archedemos at work; 6: altar;
7: staircase; 8: votive niche of
Pan; 9: Cybele statue; 10: Pan
inscription.

The **Vari Cave** (Figures **51**.2; **55**) is a stalactite cave with two chambers, one above the other, in which there was once a spring; in Antiquity there was a sanctuary to Pan, the god of herdsmen, and to the Nymphs here.[153] The entrance consists of a natural opening through which the visitor can descend to the first landing by means of 12 steps cut into the rock (recommended only for those who do not suffer from vertigo, are steady on their feet and have sensible shoes). At this point the first inscriptions and votive niches are cut into the rock (Figure **55**.1–2). The floor of the smaller, upper chamber (a torch is necessary) curves slightly and has a few steps left from a staircase in the middle of it; at the far end it descends into the larger chamber below. At the other side of the large chamber there is a narrow stair, which runs down from the entrance (Plate 42); on its right is a house-like niche with a Pan inscription (Figure **55**.8) and a seated figure (the head is missing) on a throne carved out of the rock (Figure **55**.9). It is probably a representation of Kybele, the mother-goddess from Asia Minor. On the high projecting wall which divides the two chambers the sculptor, Archedemos of Thera, has portrayed himself in life-size relief (Figure **55**.5) with his implements, hammer and mason's square or chisel, in his hands (Plate 42). Apparently it was he who decorated the cave for the worship of the Nymphs, for in an inscription next to the entrance steps he has described himself as 'Nympholeptos', that is bewitched by the Nymphs. The finds, which include fine marble votive reliefs dating to the mid-fourth century BC, show that these goddesses were worshipped here for centuries together with the Muses, the Charites, Apollo and Pan. This heathen cult was ended by the Christians in late Antiquity; however, they themselves continued to use the cave: lamps with signs of the cross bear unequivocal witness to this. After that the place was abandoned and forgotten until 1765 when the English traveller R. Chandler found the cave again for later generations to investigate.

The **Vari House** below the Vari Cave is interpreted as a country house, which was the centre of a farming area in the valley (Figures **51**.3; **56**). This is indicated by numerous terrace walls in the neigbourhood as well as the architecture of the building. Six rooms lie on the north and east side of a colonnaded courtyard while a massive tower was erected on the south-west corner; this was normally used for stowing away the agrarian implements, while the airy upper floors could be used for storing the crops; the tower also offered a good view over the surrounding countryside and could be used as a refuge in the case of a hostile attack. The English excavators found gardens right next to the house on different terraces fenced by walls.[154] In recent years similar farms have been investigated in south Attica (see p. 210), which support the identification of the Vari House as a country house with a farming business. These other examples also have small country cult places for deities close to them, which were connected to nature and worshipped by the country folk; in the case of the Vari House it consists of the Pan Cave, in the case of the house on Cape Zoster, an Apollo sanctuary (see p. 197).

South-west of Vari and Varkiza three promontories stick out into the sea (Plate 41); the whole peninsula is called Lambarda today, but in Antiquity it

(a)

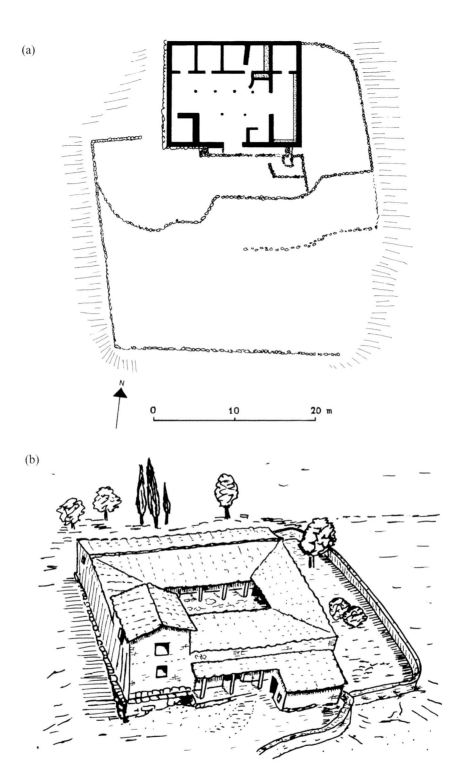

0   10   20 m

(b)

Figure 56 Farmhouse near Vari; (a) plan; (b) reconstructed view from the south (after Jones).

was called **Cape Zoster** (Figure **51**). The foothills of Hymettos run down to the sea here to form four big bays, which are very popular today for water sports. The suburb takes its name, Vouliagmeni, from a collapsed sinkhole, a cave eroded into the limestone ('Vouliagmeni' means 'the sunken'; Figure **51**.11), which can be seen east of the modern road near the coast; its high vertical walls are floodlit by night and make an impressive location for the restaurant which has been established in it. The basin of the sinkhole is filled with warm sulphurous water utilised by the thermal bath (24°C water temperature in summer and winter) which has been installed on its edge.

At the narrowest point where Cape Zoster joins the mainland, an ancient villa (Figure **51**.10)[155] and, a few metres further along on the beach (on the property of Astir Beach, entrance free on demand), the remains of a temple[156] have been excavated (Figure **51**.9; Plate 40). According to Pausanias the **temple** was dedicated to **Apollo**, **Artemis**, **Leto** and **Athena**. Three cult statue bases and a sacrificial table can be seen in the interior of the temple, of which the first building phase dates to the late sixth century BC; the throne of the priest was found near the entrance to the adyton. The fourth century BC colonnade was probably no longer standing by the Roman period. In contrast the base of the oblong altar in front of the east side is preserved. The large building north of the temple is often interpreted as a lodging for priests or pilgrims, but it is in fact a **country house**. It had (only recognisable from the foundations) a courtyard framed by many rooms, which lay behind a colonnade (very similar to the Vari House, see above, Figure **56**), while the massive foundation on the south-east corner suggests a tower was located here. More rooms were added to the courtyard later and the original colonnade was integrated into their walls and, thus, made superfluous.

The road from Vouliagmeni to Varkiza winds along the cliffs with a fine view to the west to Aigina and the east Peloponnese. Shortly before Varkiza the foundations of a **rural sanctuary** (Figure **51**.12)[157] lie on a ridge, which rises in the south-east about 100 m above sea level; it was visited and in use, with interruptions, from the eighth century BC into late Antiquity. The terrace wall belonging to the remains of the architecture on the east side is particularly visible today. In Varkiza, which is a bathing resort with a long sandy beach, the main road from Vouliagmeni meets up with the road which went along the Vari valley, like the ancient road from Athens to Sounion. The road then follows the coast southwards passing numerous bathing bays and holiday resorts until it reaches the southern tip of Attica and Cape Sounion.

Those especially interested in the history of ancient settlement may wish to make a detour from Vari to the north-east to visit some interesting sites which are not well known. Only *c*. 2 km out of Vari on the right of the road going to Koropi there is a high hill rising from the plain called **Kiapha Thiti** (Figure **51**.17), on which numerous traces of ancient settlement can be seen. The small hill was once enclosed by a Mycenaean fortification wall, while a few metres beneath the summit there are the ruins of a small Early Christian church, which was even furnished with a balustrade decorated with figures. Excavations by German and

Canadian archaeologists in recent years have revealed evidence of a Late Classical and Hellenistic settlement.[158]

About 1 km south-east of Kiapha Thiti a hilly ridge extends southwards, from which a single hill is separated by a narrow valley on its north side. The small eighteenth century chapel of **Panagia Thiti**, which has ancient spolia built into its walls, stands on this hill (Figure **51**.18).[159] A few years ago a Doric capital dating to the Classical period was found here. This may have belonged to a cult building which was dedicated to Dionysos or Aphrodite; for the plateau on the small rocky hill, which can only be reached from the north-west side, held an ancient sanctuary, which was marked off by some boundary inscriptions carved into the rock. On the south-west, north-east and south-east sides the large, deeply carved letters HO can be seen in several places; they represent a shortening of the word for boundary (ΗΟΡΟΣ; they still have the Archaic-Early Classical H as an aspirant). In the north below this sanctuary a few remains of architecture can be seen on several terraces, as well as stelai sockets cut into the rock; it may be the assembly place of the deme of Lower Lamptrai which was attached to a sanctuary. The plain below the hill was settled in Antiquity and used for farming; the most important find from here is a fourth century BC grave plot with sculpted decoration: a male statue and a fine relief of a lion decorated the grave of a rich family (in the Brauron Museum storeroom).

The high ridge south of Kiapha Thiti acted as an ancient (Trittys?) boundary. This is known from a row of **boundary inscriptions** cut into the rocky ground, which follow the line of the ridge until it meets the valley of Porto Lombardo in the south.[160] Four letters separated by a diagonal slash can be read ΟΡ/ΠΜ; they can probably be translated as 'Horos Paralias Mesogeias'; that is the 'boundary' between a deme or a trittys lying 'beside the sea' and one 'in the Mesogeia (inland)'.

Continuing a few kilometres further along the coast road from Varkiza to Sounion and rounding the rocky height of **Keramoti**, on which numerous rock-cut inscriptions and a Late Neolithic/Early Helladic settlement (Figure **51**.19) have recently been discovered, the small bathing bay of **Ay. Marina** is reached. Prehistoric building remains were discovered here on a tiny island, which is joined to the coast today by a concrete fill. At the next village beyond Ay. Marina, which is called Ay. Demetrios, a small road turns off inland; a wooded site with a spring is located on it about 700 m along. The church, which was built here in the eleventh or twelfth century, is dedicated to **Ay. Demetrios** (Figure **57**). While the long northern side and half of the apse belong to the original building, the southern part was renovated in the post-Byzantine period following the early plan. This can be clearly seen from the different masonry, although repeated whitewashing is increasingly obscuring the fine details of the building technique. In the north wall the fine brick decoration, which is typical of the Middle Byzantine period, can be seen: it consists of simple geometric decorative bands and complicated arabesques (Figure **57**). South of Ay. Demetrios a high ridge, the Demetrios Hill, runs along the coast. It is worth the climb (which is not too difficult on the east side, although the west side is rugged) to its north peak where the orthostate blocks of a **Classical watch tower** are preserved

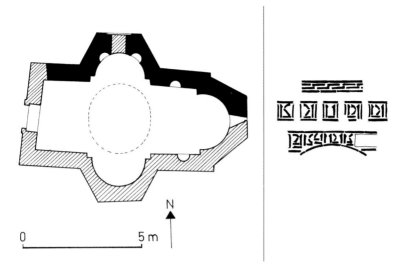

Figure 57 Ay. Demetrios near Lagonisi.

(Figure **51**.20).[161] The tower was probably part of a larger installation, of which some remains of foundations can be seen a few metres to the east on the slope below. The strategically favourable position of the site will be immediately clear to anyone standing at this point: the Saronic Gulf lies far below it with the bays of Porto Lombardo, Ay. Marina and Varkiza; in the north-west the foothills of Hymettos can be seen with the Vari Cave and the Classical Vari House; Lathouriza, which lies opposite this site, is visible and the high ridge of Kaminia, which separates the bay of Vari and Varkiza from Cape Zoster at Vouliagmeni. In fact there is an impressive view over the entire series of monuments described in this chapter.

2 From Anavyssos to Sounion

The Sanctuary of Poseidon on the southern tip of Attica with its Classical temple, and its white columns rising high above the blue sea, is a traditional must for every traveller to Greece. Those who do not wish to visit this impressive and interesting place in the company of a huge number of tourists from all over the world should go in the early morning (open from 10 to sunset) or at least before midday; towards evening many busloads of tourists wait there to see the sunset.

Cape Sounion lies about 70 km south of Athens, by car about 1½ hours non-stop. The road (see p. 185) leaves Athens by Vouliagmeni Street in the direction of Voula and then goes past Vari, Varkiza and the bathing beaches of Ay. Marina, Lagonisi, Palaia Phokaia and Legraina.

Anavyssos lies a few kilometres inland on this drive to Cape Sounion. Four different ancient demes lay in the neighbourhood of this village, one of which, Anaphlystos,[162] is reflected in the modern name. The archaeological remains were particularly studied in the last century, but most of the settlement remains from this area, which was once densely inhabited from the Geometric to the Early Christian period, have disappeared today. The district is famous because of some very high quality Archaic sculptures which were found here and are now in New York, Berlin, Munich and the National Museum, Athens. In Room 13 of the latter, Kroisos (*c.* 540 BC, Plate 44) and the Late Archaic Aristodikos are displayed, each standing on a base inscribed with his name (see p. 116).

On the north edge of Anavyssos, a large Archaic cemetery marked by a row of cypress trees has been excavated to the south of an adjoining road to Keratea and east of the main road; the finds have been taken to Brauron. The small church of Ay. Panteleimon, a typical post-Byzantine (seventeenth century) building, also lies north of Anavyssos on the right of the road to Keratea and about 3 km from the sea. The interior of this simple building is decorated with frescoes dating to the eighteenth century. The reused ninth or tenth century architrave adds a pretty detail to the furnishing; it emphasises the main entrance of the iconostasis and is decorated with palmette tendrils.

The administrative area of **Elympos** (also Olympos), where there is a cemetery church worth visiting (east of the village on the right of the road to Anavyssos), lies north of Anavyssos. The church dates to the post-Byzantine period and is called Panagia Mesosporitissa. The building, which is very unusual in its interior divisions, is built on a foundation of carefully laid ancient blocks. The identity of the ancient building, which once stood on this site and from which the spolia in the masonry come, is unknown. In addition stones with Early Christian motifs are also built into the walls of the church. The frescoes in the interior date to 1772, according to the inscription relating to their commission. The ruins of a large Early Christian basilica in Elympos, which are more important than the cemetery church, can best be reached from the eastern entrance to the area; here at the fork of the asphalt road a dirt road branches off; the excavation area lies *c.* 150 m along it on the left (signposted). It is a three-aisled basilica, which has its foundations, column bases and marble panelled floor preserved, as well as mosaics in the choir with inscriptions and geometric motifs (Plate 43). The position of the altar, which was surrounded by a four-columned baldachin, can also be seen in the floor. This particularly large basilica with its transverse narthex dates to the fifth century. The agrarian installations in a small annex on the south-west corner of the church are also interesting; they consist of an olive crusher to separate the flesh from the stones and a press with a basin to catch the squeezed oil. Driving on from Elympos a few kilometres further in the direction of Lagonisi, a steep hill can be seen north of the road in the level area in front of the

Paneion mountain ridge which, together with the surrounding area, is called **Trampouria**.[163] In the Hellenistic period there was a sanctuary here on a small terrace. In front of the site the trained eye can see: steps hewn out of the rock-face (on the SE side), a few large limestone blocks which are the remains of walls (on the edge of the area in front of the eastern altar), the base of the altar with a rectangular sacrificial pit (bothros) cut in the rock below it and the foundations of the temple (dated to the Hellenistic period) on the peak (marked by a modern spot height); the pit below the altar indicates that the goddesses Demeter and Kore could have been worshipped here. Finds from houses that were to be seen in the last century down in the plain show that the entire area was settled and farmed in Antiquity; until recently this was also clear from the fragment of a Classical grave relief depicting a loutrophoros, which was built in over the door of the church below the Trampouria hill, but is now no longer there.

The mountainous **Patroklos Island**, called Gaidouronisi today,[164] lies a few kilometres west of Sounion. It has a few Hellenistic walls preserved which belonged to a fortress used by the Ptolemaic admiral, Patroklos, as a base against the Macedonian garrisons in Piraeus and on Cape Sounion. Today the fortress is largely in ruins; only the remains of a Classical farm tower, which have been incorporated into the later Hellenistic installation, are preserved.

Going past Patroklos Island the next turn off on the left is an asphalt road running north-west into the **Charaka valley**.[165] In the 1980s numerous ancient terraces were discovered in this valley, which were made in the fifth and fourth centuries BC and used for farming. Parts of the walls can still be found on the north slope of the valley (levelling operations for weekend houses have recently increasingly disturbed the ancient terraces) and the artificial terracing can be seen almost everywhere on the slopes. In addition a few remains of farms have been found, one with an olive press, which was hewn out of the rock, on the east slope on the other side of a stream bed, and another with two towers on the saddle adjoining the valley in the west. A grave plot right next to the road east of the entrance to the Charaka valley can be clearly seen; the lowest courses of its enclosure wall are extant, behind which a simple sarcophagus was found, still in its original position. The grave, which was built over by a house in the Late Roman period, must have belonged to a farm which lay a little further north, where numerous potsherds and large stones are scattered over the soil.

On the north-east side of the valley a deep gorge opens to the sea. The plateau above this gorge, the plain of Ay. Photeini, was also intensively farmed in Classical Antiquity, as ruins of farmhouses bear witness. On the high ridge, which terminates this plateau in the east above the valley of Legraina, five boundary inscriptions were found in 1981, carved in the rock along the line of the ridge. They mark the boundaries between two demes, 'Atene' in the west and perhaps 'Amphitrope' in the east in the valley of Legraina.

The valley of **Legraina**, which extends northwards beyond Ay. Konstantinos, also contains interesting archaeological finds. A few hundred metres north of the village, on a small hillock in the middle of the valley, the ruins

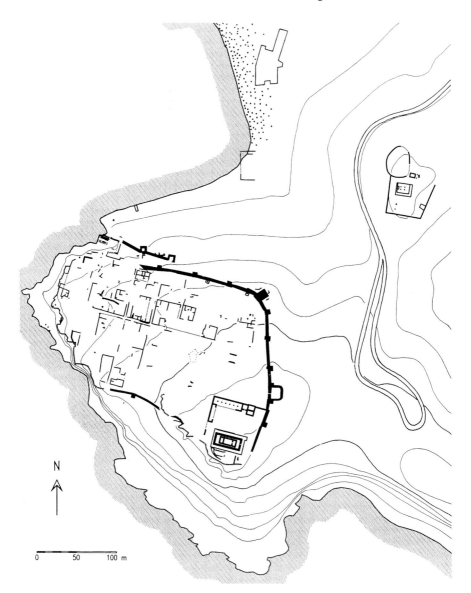

Figure 58 Map of Cape Sounion with the sanctuaries, the town and the harbour area.

of two large Classical farmhouses were found,[166] which were situated in a field with the apt name of 'Palaia Kopraissia', that is 'old dungheap'. Further down the valley (to the north) beyond Ay. Konstantinos the earth road passes a site, excavated by Belgian archaeologists in the district called Megala Pevka, which has Classical furnaces for the smelting of silver ore. And again further north, to the south-west below a very obvious red limestone rock, the few remains of a Classical villa and a bath can be made out; it is an overgrown excavation, which is difficult to find today, named Poussipelia[167] after the field where it is located.

When the visitor has passed Legraina and the last turn-off before **Cape Sounion**, the Sounion peninsula can be seen falling steeply in the south. Behind the sheltered bay (ancient harbour) the settlement can be made out rising towards the summit, which is surrounded by a wall, topped by the shining white columns of the Temple of Poseidon (Figures **58**; **60**; **61**).

'On the Greek Mainland Cape Sounion rises in Attica opposite the Cycladic islands and the Aegean; there is a harbour, if (coming from Asia Minor) one has gone round past the foothills, and on the tip of the cape lies the temple of Athena Sounias'. Pausanias begins not just his chapter on Attica but his entire travel guide to Greece (*Periegesis*) with this description. As a result all scholars previous to this century identified the temple, long known and partly plundered, on the peak of the cape with that of Athena. Today the High Classical temple (Plate 46) is known to belong to Poseidon. Some inscriptions found near this temple and the discovery of a further temple about 400 m north on a level hilltop allow the conclusion that Pausanias has passed on false information. It is, however, understandable when one bears in mind that in his time the temple of Athena had been transferred (see p. 86) and was no longer visible and the cult of Athena had probably been moved to the temple of Poseidon on the cape.

Prehistoric remains have been found on the hill of Cape Sounion[168] and the cult of Poseidon was already practised here in Homeric times; votives (vases and sculptures, such as the huge Sounion Kouros, National Museum, see pp. 113–114; Plate 45) illustrate the growing interest in the sanctuaries of Poseidon and Athena. According to our present knowledge, apart from an altar on the summit of the cape, there seems to have been no large architecture until the end of the sixth century BC; a temple was not constructed until the Late Archaic period; this was destroyed by the Persians in 480 BC and its building components of poros limestone are partly preserved in the foundations of the new Classical building (Plate 46). During the time of the Parthenon (*c.* 440 BC) a new temple was built of white Agrileza marble, the remains of which we see today (Figure **61**). It lies on an artificial terrace with two stoas in the north and west (Figure **60**) to which a gate gave entrance; next to this propylon was a room, perhaps for a guard. During the Peloponnesian War, in 413/412 BC (after the attack of the Spartans on Dekeleia; see Thuc.VIII.4), the sanctuary and the settlement were protected on all sides by a wall with ten towers (Figure **58**); the position of the entrance is unknown.[169] This fortification must have been renovated and repaired many times in the course of history; for example, in the third century BC a massive outer wall was built on the north side, using marble blocks which had been removed from grave terraces in the neighbourhood, to protect a newly built shipshed on the north-west corner of the town (Plate 47).

On arriving at the cape the first site is that of the **sanctuary of Athena** (Figure 59). It lies on a terrace scarcely 40 m high, which is surrounded by a wall. In the centre there was a large temple of which only the foundations are preserved; further north a small Classical shrine can be seen with an altar in front of it and the base for a marble statue on the interior; this small temple is connected by tradition to the Homeric hero Phrontis, whose grave mound was identified as a tumulus north-west of the temple. Similarly, some floor slabs on the west side of the cella still indicate clearly the position of the cult statue in the large temple of Athena,[170] in front of which are four stones which once carried the inner columns of the building; the cult statue was separated from the rest of the room by a balustrade between the western inner columns. This mid-fifth century temple is interesting for two reasons. Vitruvius, the Augustan architect, emphasised its unusual ground plan: the building had only two outer rows of columns, that is on the east and the south sides, where the entrance to the temple probably lay, since the foundations of the altar, also unusually on the south side, can be seen there on a levelled area with bases of stelai. Moreover, the fate of the temple is curious. After its destruction, probably during the Mithridatic wars, but possibly as part of a planned programme in the framework of imperial Roman religious politics, parts of its architecture (including eight columns) were carried to the Agora of Athens and reused in the building of an Early Roman temple, the small Southeast Temple (see p. 86); columns and capitals from this building have been found in Sounion and in Athens, the latter marked with mason's marks.

The **Temple of Poseidon** (Plate 46) lies about 400 m to the south on the summit of the cape (Figure 58). The present path takes the visitor over the former fortification wall northwards past a large bastion built from spolia (Figure 60) to the side of the propylon of the temple (Plate 47). The entrance to the sanctuary terrace is built of two materials: poros was used in the interior, which was then dressed with white marble from Agrileza on the exterior in a second building phase. The terrace was crowned with a High Classical temple standing on a podium-like substructure (Figure 61), which shows a close relationship in its plan and elevation and in many details to the Hephaisteion (Figures 22; 111) and the Temple of Ares in Athens (the earlier Temple of Athena Pallenis, see pp. 81, 236–7) and to the Temple of Nemesis at Rhamnous. Some of the very slim columns of the 6- by 13-column peristasis were carried off to the parks of European castles (for example Klein-Glienicke in Berlin, Venice, south England). They are recognisable because, apart from their typical marble, which does not have the warm patina of Pentelic marble because it lacks the iron content, they have only 16 wide and shallow flutes instead of the usual 20 flutes of the Doric column. Besides these unusual architectural details other peculiarities of the temple have set a trend: the architrave of the pronaos was extended beyond the sidewalls of the cella up to the entablature of the peristasis (as on the east side of the Hephaisteion) and decorated with an Ionic frieze

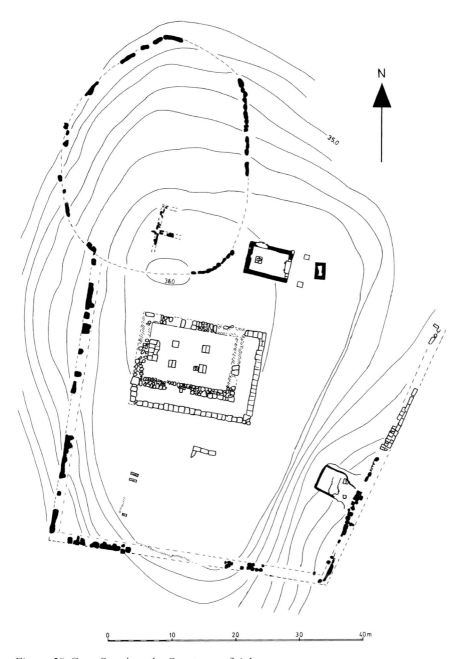

Figure 59 Cape Sounion, the Sanctuary of Athena.

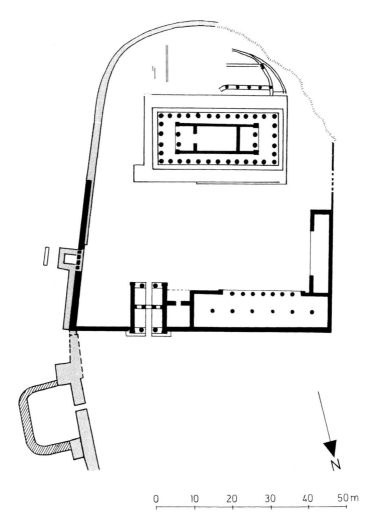

0   10   20   30   40   50 m

Figure 60 Cape Sounion, the Sanctuary of Poseidon and part of the fortification wall with the Hellenistic bastion.

with mythological battle scenes; the pronaos was thus turned into a separate compartment, which led in turn to the façade being more sharply differentiated and emphasised. As in the case of the Hephaisteion, the west side mirrored the east side with a relief frieze which only extended across the width of the cella. Two other peculiarities are unique in Greek temple architecture and illustrate a new conception of space: the back porch with the relief frieze was made deeper than the pronaos and the ancient architect abstained from dividing the cella with internal columns (which had Late Archaic antecedents); through this the space was decisively widened.

As a result of these observations, that is the very slim, almost 'Ionically' proportioned columns, an Ionic frieze of Parian marble and other oddities,

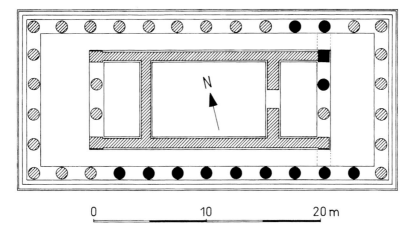

Figure 61 Temple of Poseidon (black: the columns and the anta still standing before the restoration works).

scholars of ancient architecture have suggested that an architectural workshop from the Ionian islands was operating in Sounion, although under Athenian supervision. The unprecedented building activity in the High Classical period of Perikles' time, which must have occupied many stonemasons in Attica simultaneously, may have made the employment of foreign craftsmen necessary (see also Figure **13**).

Up until now only a few excavations have taken place on the steep area of the cape (Plate 47) to the north below the Poseidon Temple. Some well built houses with marble thresholds were found, which, when considered together with other house remains evident in the area, can be interpreted as **town** buildings (Figure **58**); quarters also had to be found for pilgrims and travellers, who were perhaps compelled to stay in Sounion because of unfavourable winds in the Aegean. The housing quarters were planned with streets crossing at right angles so that the whole town (with one exception in the north-east) extended on a grid pattern;[171] the houses had a ground plan of 50 × 50 feet (*c.* 16 × 16 m). We know of other sanctuaries inside the town wall from inscriptions, as, for example, an Asklepieion which was founded in the later third century BC. On the north-west corner of the fortification behind a bastion built of reused material the remains of a **Hellenistic shipshed** for two ships are preserved (Figure **58**); the incisions cut into the rock for the keels of the ships can be clearly seen; the sides of the shipshed, which was over 20 m long, were dressed with spolia blocks of Agrileza marble; a roof must have stretched over them. The shipshed was evidently a special part of the natural harbour with its sandy beach, perhaps for the small, swift rowing boats of the Athenian garrison stationed here. A little further north (outside the fence) a much smaller boat house cut into the rock can be seen. The massive foundations of an almost square warehouse (Agora) are located at the fence, where the rocky coastline runs into the sandy beach (the ancient harbour mentioned by Pausanias).

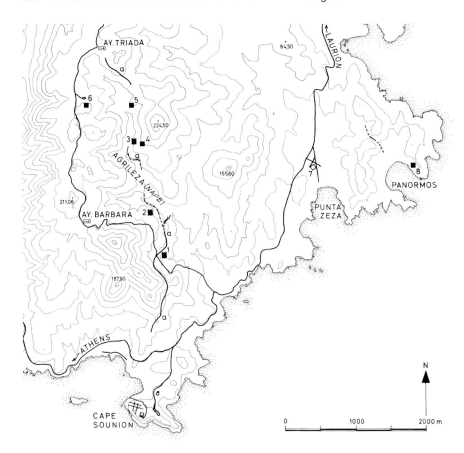

Figure 62 Agrileza valley north of Sounion.

1: Princess farm; 2: Cliff farm; 3: Golden Pig Tower; 4: excavation of ore washeries (British); 5: excavation of ore washeries (Greek); 6: excavation of ore washeries with tower (Greek); 7: Agora of Punta Zeza; 8: smelting furnaces at Panormos; a: ancient road.

The sanctuaries of Poseidon and Athena and the fortifications constructed around the town were naturally not cut off from the hinterland. Rather, they were parts of the deme of Sounion to which a large area of the Lavrion, the mountainous district to the north with intensive silver mining, belonged, together with the settlements located *c.* 4 km further north at **Pascha Harbour** and in the Panormos bay (Figure **62**). In the bay of Pascha Harbour[172] an installation bordered with numerous rooms (*c.* 81 m × 56 m in side length; Figure **62**.7) and some house remains have been found; in addition, on the east side of the beautiful neighbouring bay of **Panormos**[173] (signposted on the Sounion–Lavrion road to the east), several workshops with smelting furnaces for silver working (Figure **62**.8) have been discovered, as well as a harbour mole. In the last century a relief of Herakles was also found in this district, which can be connected to a Herakleion mentioned in an inscription for the deme of Sounion (see p. 83); the same inscription also mentions farming in the Classical period on the large

Pounta Zeza peninsula, a fact which is also supported archaeologically by long walls around plots of land and Classical farms with towers. All the ancient remains and the epigraphical information give a very good indication of the position and extent of the deme of Sounion; still more large farmhouses and silver mines with their washeries in the hills lying to the west also belonged to this Attic country district (see pp. 210–15), as well as the fortified town with the sanctuaries on the cape and others in the neighbourhood and Classical graves with marble façades – removed to build the Hellenistic fortification wall on the cape – set along the highway to Athens.

3 Lavrion, Thorikos, Porto Raphti and Brauron

The area from Cape Sounion to Thorikos was the centre of silver mining, particularly in the Classical period, and, therefore, contributed decisively to the might of Athens. Ores were mined here, especially silver which was used for the coins, the 'owls of Athens' (Figure **67**). The mountainous countryside in this southern part of Attica, which is little visited, has its own charm: light pine forests are intermingled with huge heaps of slag; an interested walker can find numerous ancient industrial installations, houses and cisterns, as well as remains of Classical farms and the quarries which produced the shining white Sounion marble. The view from some hilltops can encompass the Saronic Gulf on one side and the nearest Cycladic islands (Makronisos, Kea, Kythnos and Serifos) on the other side.

Agrileza and Souriza.[174] The valley of Agrileza and that of Souriza (Figure **62**) perhaps give the modern visitor the best impression of the ancient industrial use of the area. They offer an interesting excursion, particularly for those who are able to gain an idea of their former appearance from only a few architectural remains and at the same time like to wander around looking for antiquities which are almost unknown even to archaeologists.

Both valleys can be reached from two sides by car: either turn off the Sounion–Lavrion road 1.1 km north of the crossroads at Cape Sounion right next to the taverna 'Syrtaki' into a narrow road and follow this up to a dirt road signposted north to Agrileza (the Princess Tower lies here next to the road); continue further along the asphalt road passing a chapel (Ay. Varvara) and some partly ruined houses to where, after about 5 km, an asphalt road branches off right (east) into the Souriza valley (see below). Or turn off on the north edge of Lavrion to Ay. Konstantinos (former Kamariza) and turn just before this place to the south (Chaos, Ay. Triada, Sounion); this road, which is bordered on both sides by slag heaps and galleries, has a military area a few kilometres along it followed by the chapel of Ay. Triada, behind which an asphalt road on the left (east) about 250 m wide leads to a parking place. A well-excavated industrial quarter lies below to the south, while the Souriza valley slopes down to the east and then curves south to join the Agrileza valley.

The Agrileza valley lies about 2 km north of Cape Sounion (Figure **62**) and could be reached from there by a wide, ancient road, which crosses the saddle next to a large modern house (on the site of a Classical grave plot). The valley is relatively flat in the south but becomes steeper and narrower to the north, on the slope of Mont Michel. In the middle at the place where a valley branches off to the west, some small houses have been built in recent years, which can be reached by a dirt road that is tarred further on. From here one can go in a north-westerly direction round the foot of Mont Michel and meet the Souriza valley, which rises to the west, at its end. At the beginning of the valley in the south the ruins of a round tower can be seen by the road,[175] the so-called **Princess Tower** (Figures **62**.1, **63**, **64**). It comprises the main building of a small farm, which has its enclosure wall with attached rooms preserved together with a large, flat, round threshing floor further east. The lower part of the tower wall was built of quite small marble blocks, only the door frame being of large blocks; the upper floors were built of mudbrick, which today makes up a large part of the packing round the tower. For safety reasons the entrance did not lie at gound level, but half a storey up accessible by a wooden ladder. The necessary farming implements were stored in the tower, which dates to the early fourth century BC, and the harvest was kept on the dry upper floors; the top floor was certainly furnished as living quarters. The fine architectural remains, which lie to the west of the tower on the other side of the ancient road, also belong to this farmstead; they are parts of a grave plot, which the owner of the farm had built for himself and his family and which could be admired by those journeying along the road from Sounion to Athens. An inscription found here names the owner of the farm as a certain Timesios; he is perhaps identical, or at least related to, a silver mine contractor and the owner of a second farmhouse, which lay *c*. 1 km further north (the so-called Cliff Tower; Figure **62**.2).

There are several similar farms with towers in the Agrileza valley. In the case of **Cliff Tower**[176] (Figure **62**.2) the owner is known from rock-cut inscriptions, which also give evidence of simple rural sanctuaries or belong to graves. A certain Timesios, probably the man who also owned the Princess Tower farm, received this farm in payment for a debt; with it he acquired almost the whole Agrileza valley, together with the side valley to the west, for farming and animal grazing. The few remains of the Cliff farm, consisting of the ruins of a small house and a round tower as well as two large threshing floors, lie above a quarry, which has a steep slope (the Cliff).

There are numerous **quarries**[177] on the slopes of the Agrileza valley running to the north (Figure **62**.2), which produced the marble for the buildings in Sounion (Plate 48); also, in the valley itself, there are some terraces for houses and graves built from this material, as well as large rectangular or small pear-shaped cisterns, in which water for the inhabitants and workers of the district could be collected from the house roofs. In some quarries rounded incisions in the marble rock show where column drums were extracted for the Poseidon Temple at Sounion.

On the south side of Mont Michel, British and Greek archaeologists have excavated a large Classical **ore washery**[178] to which several cisterns and a

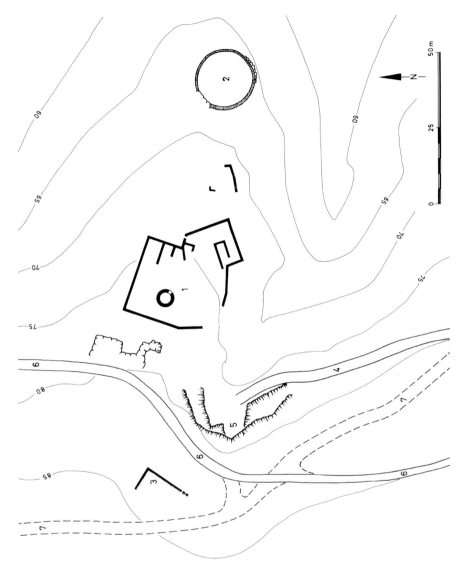

Figure 63 Agrileza, Princess farm, plan.

1: tower and courtyard with attached rooms; 2: threshing floor; 3: grave plot; 4: ancient access to the farmstead; 5: quarry; 6: ancient road; 7: modern asphalt road.

large house with two courtyards belong (Figure **62**.4); to the west of this large building complex there are more, smaller washeries (the Greek Archaeological Service has recently excavated a small washery a little north of the earth path) as well as a rectangular tower lying above the valley (Figure **62**.3; **Golden Pig Tower**); the latter was separated from the washeries by a boundary inscription cut into the rock to the east of it. The reuse of older masonry with regular grooves suggests that it was of later date than the fourth century washeries, perhaps built in the Hellenistic period; it could have been a watch tower on the road from Sounion to Athens. The carving of the letters on the south door block, which can be restored to a name ΔΙΟΔ (-ορος or -οτος), is of interest.

Briefly the mining of silver was carried out in the following way: silver ore was mined in underground galleries and brought to the surface over steps and haulage shafts. The ore, which was crushed small and then finely ground, was then washed in an installation with settling tanks to clean the used water (Figure **65**), in other words, the sandy component was separated from the ore; finally the washed, argentiferous lead ore was smelted in a furnace, generally built by the sea because the wind would blow the gas vapours away and because of the need for large amounts of wood, since imported wood could easily be landed here (see p. 208); during this process the slag was separated from the silver lead (Figure **66**). In a final stage the lead was separated from the silver by cupellation in refining furnaces; after another refining the silver could then be used for minting coins (Figure **67**). A typical large washery can be seen on the south-west corner of the English excavations, as well as numerous rooms, partly built of mudbrick, which were used as workshops. Many similar installations are located in a large excavated area c. 1km further north (at the junction of the Souriza and Agrileza valleys: Figure **62**.5), which have been investigated by Greek

Figure 64 Agrileza, Princess farm, reconstructed view from north-east (after Jones).

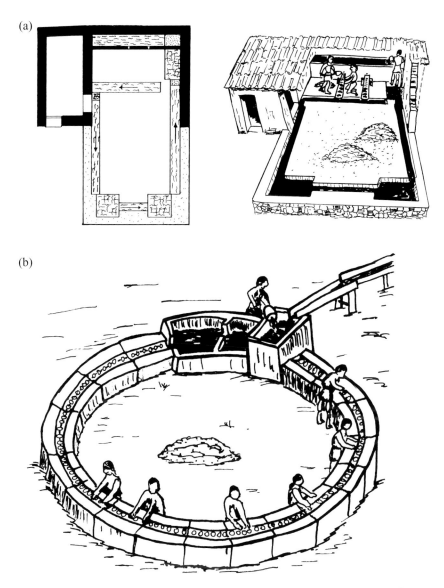

Figure 65 Types of Classical ore washeries: (a) plan and reconstruction of a square ore washery (b) circular (or heliozoidal) ore washery (after Jones and Conophagos).

scholars; many cisterns can be seen here, as well as rooms used as workrooms and living quarters including washrooms lined with watertight plaster; the bathroom on the south edge of the excavation with a double terracotta bathtub would probably have been used by a high ranking supervisor. In a house on the northwest corner of the excavation an inscription was found in which a certain Simos is described as the contractor of a mining plot called Ἀσκαλεπίακον; he is known from other fourth century BC inscriptions which are all connected to silver mining in Lavrion. The silver mines were leased by the state to private individuals; they undertook the exploitation of the silver mine using slave labour at their own risk. We know something of the organisation of the silver mining from the treatise *Politics* by Aristotle: in the case of already operating pit shafts the length of the lease was only three years and the price relatively high; in the case of a new plot, where shafts and galleries had to be dug and the risk was correspondingly higher, the city of Athens gave a licence for ten years. Some Athenians became very rich, particularly if they employed a mining specialist; for others the risk was too great and they ruined themselves. In the late fourth century BC, both the yield from Lavrion dropped sharply and the 'world price' for silver fell (partly because of the treasures from the east brought to Greece by the army of Alexander and the intensive mining in the Pangaion range). From that time onwards hardly any silver mining took place in south Attica.

I n the **Souriza valley**, which rises to the west of the Simos workshop, the trained eye can see many similar industrial areas with cisterns, amongst which lies another tower with red plaster decoration on the interior walls (the so-called Red Tower). An area with washeries, cisterns and house remains, which lies close to the hilltop (to the south below the asphalt side road: Plate 49), has been well excavated and restored. On the hill slope to the south some shaft entrances can be seen, some very deep (*c.* 100 m). A few metres above to the west are the walls of a square tower (the Hilltop Tower; Figure 62.6), which was built on top of a rectangular washery that had gone out of use. It is, therefore, surrounded by further small cisterns, dug into the rock and lined with watertight plaster. This tower, too, had an entrance high above the ground, on

Figure 66 Reconstruction of cupellation furnaces (after Mussche).

its south side, which could only be reached by a wooden ladder which could be drawn up.

The district must have been densely inhabited in the Classical period. Many people were employed in the silver mines and the industrial installations; they lived there in the district and had to be looked after (the sources mention more than 20,000 slaves). The farms, which were apparently fertile in south Attica in Antiquity, could supply some food (there is also evidence of similar farms in the Charaka valley north-west of Cape Sounion, see p. 201), but they were mostly dedicated to producing olive oil which was traded for corn from the Black Sea area. Another business factor, but of less importance, was marble quarrying. The most important factor for Athens was the state organised silver mining in the Lavrion.

The Athenian 'owls', the famous silver coins of the city (Figure **67**), were prized throughout the whole ancient world because of their high silver content. Themistokles financed the fleet for the Battle of Salamis with them. The silver of the Lavrion had been discovered much earlier in the Early Helladic period; the intensive, almost industrial, exploitation of the ore began in 493 BC. From then onwards the famous silver coins with the little owl on one side and the head of Athena on the other were minted in Athens for centuries. In 1860, work was renewed at the mines and continued for about a hundred years; companies of different nationalities shared in mining the lead ore. At the same time the first observations on the ancient remains were made, but systematic research in Lavrion began only a few decades ago.

Lavrion. The harbour of this small town on the south-east coast of Attica is the port of departure for the Cycladic island of Kea. In this unattractive town there is an archaeological museum, which will be opened to the public soon (the most important monuments here are the frieze of the temple of Poseidon on Cape Sounion, made of Parian marble, and some grave stelai), and a small mineral museum (located to the north-west of the big square next to a school in a small Neoclassical building). Numerous fine minerals from the Lavrion mines are displayed here together with a few archaeological finds.

Figure 67 Early Classical 'owl' silver coin of Athens.

Thorikos. Belgian archaeologists, who have been excavating for many years in Thorikos, are deeply involved in the research of the industrial use of Lavrion. They have discovered parts of a town with dwelling houses, washeries and workshops; there were industrial areas in between the houses and situated next to a large theatre.

About 2 km north of Lavrion an asphalt road branches off north to a large power station; c. 400 m along it there is a fish taverna from which a small dirt road leads to the left to the foot of the hill below the theatre of Thorikos.

Ancient Thorikos (Figures **68–70**) lies on the slopes of Velatouri Hill[179] which has a characteristic double summit which can be clearly seen from the east and the west. In the saddle between the two summits, in which traces of settlement going back to the Neolithic period have been found, are the oldest visible remains on the site (Figure **68**.5), a Mycenaean tholos tomb with an oval chamber (9 m × 3.5 m) and an encircling wall. South of this is a fifteenth century BC grave, also with an enclosure wall. On the east side of the hill there is another, partly restored, tholos tomb dating to this period (Figure **68**.4; Plate 50); these remains suggest there must have been an important Mycenaean centre here; its ruler is called Kephalos in mythology.

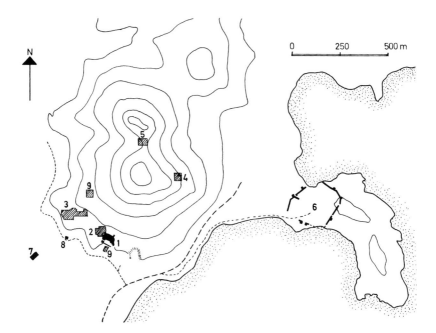

Figure 68 Thorikos, plan.

1: theatre; 2: quarter with workshops; 3: quarter with workshops and dwelling houses;
4, 5: Mycenaean tholos tombs; 6: fortress; 7: Doric temple, so-called Telesterion; 8: watch tower;
9: cemetery.

On the climb up the Velatouri to the excavations, terraces can be seen on the slope of the higher southern peak, the acropolis; numerous houses must lie here unexcavated. Two large town quarters have been excavated up until now; they date from the sixth to the fourth century BC. One (Figure **68**.2) lies west next to the theatre and has a large well-restored washery between numerous small house foundations (Plate 52). The washery has a basin from which water flowed through several holes over ridged boards and so cleaned the ore of earth and other loose components (see p. 212; Figure **65**). Since water was precious, it was caught in channels arranged in a square with a deep settling tank on each corner in which sand particles sank down while the clear water was removed. The cleaned ore was laid out to dry in the empty area in the middle of the square. Next to the restored washery at Thorikos an entrance closed by a grille leads into a gallery which goes deep into the mountain. Further west round the Velatouri there is a second settlement quarter. It is interesting that in this living and industrial complex there were also houses which had a high tower as part of their building plan (Figure **68**.3). The whole settlement had an irregular plan following the natural lie of the land; it was not enclosed by a wall, but instead, there was a separate fortress, which could be used as a place of refuge, on the east peninsula, which protruded into the sea. An isolated tower probably belonged to a watch and signalling system, the remains can be seen on the south-west side of the settlement (Figure **68**.8). On the west slope above the larger settlement zone are the remains of a cemetery (Figure **68**.9) in which a few grave plots can still be recognised; oblong blocks with rectangular slots, in which Classical grave reliefs were once clamped, also belong to it. A second, much larger, cemetery lies below the theatre (see below). In the Adami river valley,

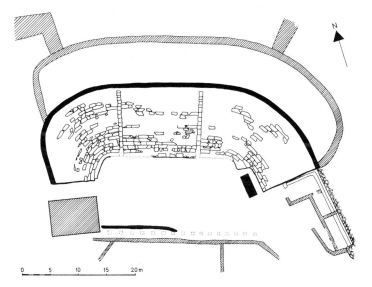

Figure 69 Thorikos, the theatre and the Temple and altar of Dionysos (black: Late Archaic; hatched: Classical).

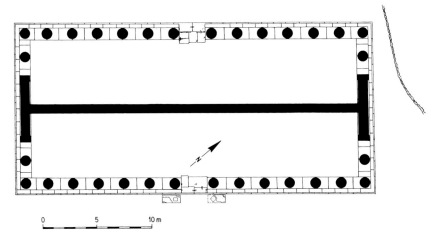

0   5   10 m

Figure 70 Thorikos, Doric temple, so-called Telesterion.

there is a very unusual Doric building (Figure **70**; Plate 51)[180] made of Agrileza marble dating from the fifth century BC (Figure **68**.7). It may have been dedicated to the 'two goddesses', that is Demeter and Persephone, according to an inscription which perhaps belonged to it; this suggestion is supported by the fact that the seventh century Hymn to Demeter relates that the goddess entered Attica at Thorikos. The High Classical Doric building has 14 columns and an entrance on each long side; it is most odd that there was no canonical cella, but the interior was divided into two halves by a wall down its length, while antai protruded on each narrow side in front of which there stood an extra column on each side followed by the corner column of the long sides. This unusual sacred building with its unique plan is unfinished, as a mantle (bosses) on the columns and steps indicates; parts of it were taken to Athens at the beginning of the Roman period and built into the South-west Temple in the Agora (see pp. 78, 86). Today most of what is left of the temple at the original site is visible, after having been excavated three times (1893, 1964 and since 1994), if it has not been covered with mud after heavy rain. Further investigation of the monument, and the uncovering of the temenos wall, of which only a short stretch is visible on the north side, might clarify the numerous architectural and religious problems arising from the building.

The largest monument at Thorikos is the theatre (Figures **68**.1; **69**; Plate 52)[181]. Its oldest structures (the terrace for the orchestra) seem to date back to the sixth century BC. In the Late Archaic period, the oblong, almost rectangular, bottom row of stone seats (with letters added later on the lowest blocks for the dignitaries, bases for wooden thrones) was built onto the slope and the stage (orchestra) was widened into an extended elliptical form; an original stage building must have been of wood since there are no traces of it; some large blocks with post holes certainly belonged to the foundations of such a wooden building; they lie below the orchestra today. On the west side a temple of Dionysos was erected, which can only be recognised from cuttings in the rock; its terra-cotta roof decoration, which has been excavated, dates it to the Classical period; on the east side an altar stood in a niche left for it in the seating, east of which there is a room hewn out of the rock, which was perhaps used for the storage of stage props. In the fourth century BC the theatre was widened in the north and surrounded by a high retaining wall with regular courses; two buttresses, in the western of which a gate with a pointed arch has been constructed, acted as an additional support to the upper section and functioned as entrance ramps to the upper rows. The Thorikos theatre is important, because its early date indicates that the Greek theatre developed from a rectangular to a circular plan (see Trachones p. 186). To the south below the theatre there are several rectangular stone constructions which belong to a cemetery with impressive decoration (Figure **68**.9). The excavators uncovered Archaic and Classical burials, which, surprisingly, lay right next to the living quarters. This has given rise to the suggestion that perhaps the important personalities of Thorikos were buried here. However, it is also possible that the town boundary lay near the back wall of the stage, so that the cemetery actually lay outside the settlement. Further investigation is needed in this area for a final explanation (on the edge of the excavation there are fine marble blocks suggesting the presence of an important monument).

The remains of a fortification[182] have been found on a peninsula east of the Velatouri (Figure **68**.6). Today only a few wall remains can be seen belonging to it; they run north and south of the chapel of Ay. Nikolaos and have also been excavated on the hill lying *c.* 300 m west, where there are still two towers with an entrance built between them. Similarly to the walls on Cape Sounion, the fortress was built during the Peloponnesian War (413/412 BC after the attack of the Spartans on Dekeleia; see Thuc.VIII.4) to serve as a protected place for the population of the unwalled settlement and to guard the two harbours flanking the peninsula. These harbour bays were probably also the reason why Thorikos became a centre in the Lavrion so early on; on the one hand it had always offered the possibility of easy sea transport for the material needed to get silver (the beginning of metal working is dated back to the third millennium); on the other hand its position was ideal for trade with the nearby Cyclades, Crete and the rest of Attica.

Porto Raphti. Today two roads connect Lavrion with the large plain of the Mesogeia, the harbour of which, Porto Raphti, is also called 'Harbour of the Mesogeia' (Limani Mesogeias).

The first is a winding road going over the mountains to Keratea and Markopoulo; the second, which is more recent, runs through a valley further east directly to the west foot of the Thorikos Mountain and along the old railway line to meet the first road shortly before Keratea; a new bypass begins here from which a small road leads off a little north of Keratea east to Kouvaras; from there Porto Raphti can be reached directly by a pretty rural road which passes some modern monasteries and runs over wooded hills. Another connection from Keratea to Porto Raphti goes via Markopoulo.

The harbour of Porto Raphti lies in a deep, well-protected bay, which is enclosed by a peninsula and two tiny islands. On the larger island of Raphtis a high stone foundation is set on the tip on which a colossal, headless, **Roman seated statue** of a man (Plate 53), probably an Antonine emperor, in a general's mantle (paludamentum), is set up.[183] Originally it was interpreted as a woman or as the personification of the inhabited world (Oikoumene), but the male dress permits its identification as an emperor. This statue gave the harbour its name: the inhabitants described it as a tailor (= raphtis) sitting at his work. In calm weather one can ask a fisherman in the harbour to go over to the island; a little clever bargaining and a suitable reimbursement will arrange a fine boat excursion lasting about one and a half hours (including a visit to the island). As late as the eighteenth century a statue also stood on the smaller island of Raphtopoula; it is lost today.

On the peninsula south of the harbour bay opposite Raphtis a fortification and a settlement called **Koroneia** (today Koroni)[184] were built in the late fourth and third centuries BC. The remains of the enclosure wall made of field stones can still be seen and in some places the foundations of houses, with terraces built in front of them on the sloping hillside, in which the civil population of the neighbourhood lived, as well as the barracks in which a military garrison was quartered. Finds of pottery and Ptolemaic coins have enabled American and German archaeologists to date the fortification to the first decades of the third century BC; the military garrison was stationed here from 267 to 262 BC, when the Egyptian admiral Patroklos, who supported the Athenians against the Macedonians occupying Piraeus, had many military installations erected in Attica (see Patroklos Island above p. 201). However, the large dimensions and elaborate façades of the terrace houses have no military character; they must be older and were already dwelling houses for the local population in the Late Classical period.

By using the peninsula of Koroni as a naval stronghold the Ptolemaic admiral had taken the most important harbour in east Attica; it had been used since ancient times as a point of connection between the Mainland and the Cyclades. The Athenian delegations usually left from here for the Apollo sanctuary on Delos. The early connections of the Cyclades with Attica are attested from archaeological remains on the north side of the bay. There, on the hills of Perati a late Mycenaean chamber tomb cemetery (twelfth–eleventh century) has been found. The burial gifts give evidence of far-flung trading connections and bear witness to the importance of this safe harbour already at that early date. Unfortunately, the settlement belonging to this important site has still not been found. Finds from the Classical period (fine grave reliefs, today in Brauron Museum), the Roman period (remains of baths on Themistokles Street) and the Early Christian period (basilica 150 m east of the baths) illustrate the long history of the area.

Brauron.[185] The pretty and well-preserved sanctuary of Artemis of Brauron (Plate 54), which was excavated just after 1948 and partly restored, lies in a quiet isolated valley between Porto Raphti and Loutsa (Figure **71**). Artemis, the goddess of the hunt, was worshipped here from very early on; in the

Hellenistic period the Erasinos River, which flows through the valley, flooded and covered much of the sanctuary with mud, turning the surroundings into a marsh; however Roman reliefs (the hero relief of Polydeukion, the pupil of Herodes Atticus, is an example) show the cult place was still functioning, because the temple was situated on higher rocky ground and an artificial terrace. The importance of the cult, which reached its acme in the fifth and fourth centuries BC, is shown by the founding of a Brauroneion on the Acropolis of Athens, perhaps as early as the late sixth century BC; the Peisistratids, who came from the area of Brauron, had probably brought 'their' goddess to the centre of Attica. Apart from the Artemision archaeological evidence shows settlement in the area dating from the Neolithic period onwards; in the Mycenaean period the acropolis on a hill to the south had a wall built round it, while the dead were buried in chamber tombs at the foot of a mountain to the east. An Early Christian basilica some 500 m west of the sanctuary on the slope above the road (Plate 55) is the latest building belonging to the ancient habitation of the area; according to inscriptions a settlement must have belonged to it, which has still not been found.

Brauron can be reached by a small, well-made road from the north side of the bay of Porto Raphti or from the main Markopoulo–Porto Raphti road or from Loutsa. The site is signposted on all the roads leading to it. (If the site is closed to visitors, it can be seen quite well from the fence; the museum has normal opening hours.)

As well as a cult place the Sanctuary of Artemis functioned as a 'boarding school' for girls who, as children over ten years old, were sent there to live in a kind of convent group for some years and were brought up and prepared for adult life including motherhood. Every five years there was a large festival in honour of the goddess, the Brauroneion, when the girls danced in saffron coloured robes dressed as bears (arktoi), while other worshippers of the cult journeyed in a procession from Athens. The goddess was worshipped as Artemis–Iphigenia, for according to myth Iphigenia came from Tauris to Brauron and started the cult. Euripides mentions in *Iphigenia in Tauris* that the grave of Iphigenia was here and that the robes of women who had died in childbirth were dedicated at it.

The excavations at the sanctuary (Figure **71**; Plate 54) have uncovered numerous finds which support and fill out the literary sources about the cult. Thus, the origin of the cult seems to have been in a cave on the south-east corner of the excavation, which later collapsed and was replaced by a small shrine; perhaps this place is to be identified with the 'grave of Iphigenia' mentioned by Euripides.

The actual Temple of Artemis next to the chapel of Ay. Georgios (fifteenth century) stands partly on a terrace and partly on the natural rock. It was a temple in antis opening to the east, of which the cella consisted of a room divided by columns and a further closed part, the adyton (unenterable). Today

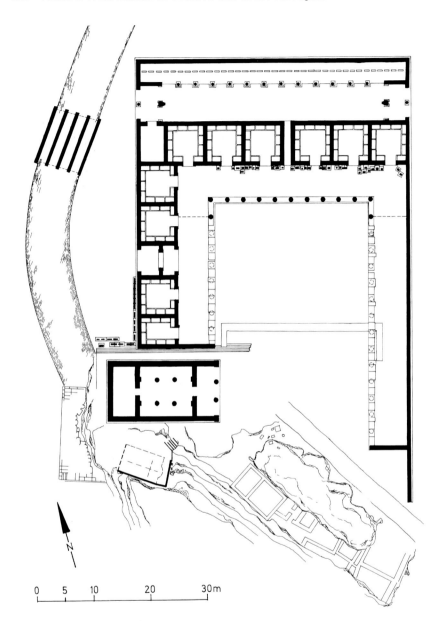

Figure 71 Brauron, Sanctuary of Artemis.

only a few remains of the foundations of this fifth century BC building can be seen in the shade of a large pine, together with some fragments of Doric architecture.

We know of two names for the temple from inscriptions, of which one was 'Parthenon'. Scholars have assigned the two names to the two parts of the cella. However, it is clear that a second smaller cult building stood next to the large Doric temple, that is in the area of the chapel of Ay. Georgios. The rock cutting here is much older than the chapel building; this can be seen from stelai cuttings along the edges of the niche as well as from the lines of the foundations inside the church. It seems probable that an earlier temple stood here next to which a larger, later cult building was erected, supported by higher retaining terraces.

The well restored colonnaded courtyard with its attached rooms makes an impressive picture (Plate 54). These buildings made of soft limestone were erected at the end of the fifth century BC; only the capitals, metopes and the lintels and thresholds were of marble. The building consists of a rectangular yard which was supposed to be framed on three sides by a peristyle; however, only the north stoa and one column each on the east and west sides was put up; the rest remained unfinished. On the north and west sides of the yard lay ten almost square rooms, in which couches (klinai) were set up round the walls; their attachments are preserved as clamp holes with a lead fill in the poros stone floor; also, in the north wing, some of the tables can be seen, which were once set up before the couches; the size of the couches is for the normal adult, so they must also have been used as resting couches at the Brauroneion for those who had travelled to take part in the festival. In the south in front of the entrances to the dining rooms, in the actual stoa of the courtyard, stood small statues of youths and maidens (often with gifts in their hands, see Museum); they are presents from grateful parents to the goddess Artemis–Iphigenia, under whose protection pregnant women placed themselves; thus it is not strange that there are statues of youths as well as maidens; it was not limited to statues of girls as 'bears'. Today many stone bases, generally in the form of pillars, can be seen here; they carried reliefs and sculptures; there are also inscriptions on some of the bases. On the west side the row of dining rooms is interrupted by the main entrance, through which carts also seem to have come; this is shown by wheel marks, which also go diagonally across the bridge over the Erasinos in the west, and by the abraided building corner. In the north a stoa was built onto the courtyard behind the northern rooms; it could be entered on both short sides through wide doors set in the middle, which could be locked. Offerings were hung up (perhaps the saffron robes?) in this stoa, perhaps on wooden pegs; at any rate something must have been displayed here in an unusual way set into a long row of clamp stones.

In Antiquity the Artemis sanctuary at Brauron could be reached in two ways. A road from Athens ran to Brauron and crossed the Erasinos a few metres west of the large courtyard by means of a bridge supported on five pillars. A second road, which almost follows the modern path to the museum, ran from the sea along the slope to the cult place.

Museum. The museum contains mostly the finds from Brauron, but there are also some from the neighbourhood. The votive offerings found in the Sanctuary of Artemis are particularly interesting: statuettes of children with gifts for the goddess, reliefs with representations of Artemis and pilgrims worshipping her and votive reliefs to other gods (Apollo, Leto); these sculptures almost all date to the fourth century BC (Room II and III). In the vestibule and in the courtyard (with a good view over the bay of Brauron) are Classical grave reliefs, many of them from Merenda, the ancient deme of Myrrhinous (see p. 230); the missing upper part of a fine grave stele depicting three people (in the vestibule, found at Porto Raphti) is now in a private collection in New York. Other rooms have show cases of pottery from the neighbourhood dating from the Neolithic to the Geometric period (Room IV) and small votive gifts from the Artemis sanctuary (vases, implements, necklaces, gold jewellery with fine granulation and a bronze foil statuette on a wooden core dating to the seventh century; Room I). A relief depiction of Polydeukion, the pupil of Herodes Atticus (c. AD 165; compare Plate 66), lying on a couch like a Greek hero, hangs in the passage between Rooms III and IV.

To the north of the road to Athens some 500 m west of the Artemis sanctuary a large **Early Christian basilica** is located (Plate 55); it was built in the sixth century AD using older building material and was probably no longer standing by the seventh century (Figure **72**). It was entered from the west via a courtyard with buildings round the side through the outer narthex fronted by five columns and the narthex. The interior of the church is divided into three aisles of which the middle one, wider than the side ones, is distinguished by a large apse with seats for the clergymen. Later side buildings were added to the side aisles: in the north a small choir, in the south a complete chapel. A round baptistry with a font was built onto the south front, which could be reached from the side aisle. The large church was elaborately decorated with different marbles: the columns are of Euboian cipollino; the floors

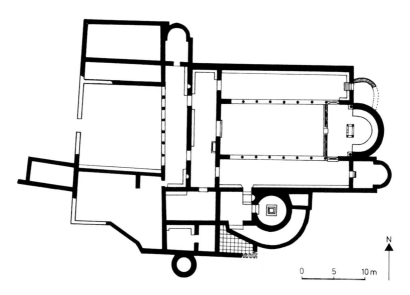

Figure 72 Brauron, Early Christian basilica.

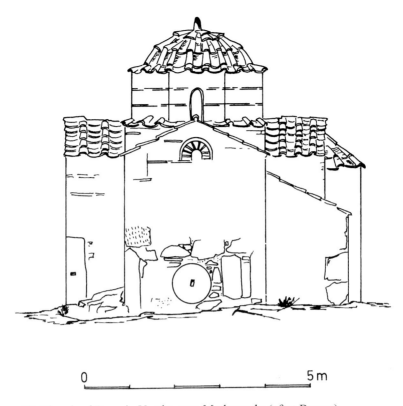

0   5 m

Figure 73 Church of Panagia Varaba near Markopoulo (after Bouras).

and walls had marble revetment. After the church was abandoned in the seventh century a small chapel was built in the basilica, which was perhaps the cemetery church belonging to some graves which have been found in the narthex.

About 2 km west of the bay of Brauron, in the plain of Mesogeia, a high Frankish tower is located on a small hill; the place is named after it **'Pyrgos of Kato Vraona'**. It stands on a site which had already been settled in the prehistoric period, as sherds and a double encircling wall round the hill testify.

A few kilometres further south-west in the vineyards on the right of the road from Porto Raphti to Markopoulo several courses of large limestone ashlar blocks can be seen on a rock rising a few metres above the plain. A closer look shows these ancient (Classical) building components belong to an oblong tower-like building (the so-called **Limiko Tower**),[186] which is surely the remains of a large agrarian centre.

Another 2 km to the west (about 2 km north of Markopoulo) the small chapel of the Virgin Mary (**Panagia**; Figure **73**) stands on its own in the countryside in a field called Varaba. The plentiful use of ancient spolia (on the south side a large column drum strikes the eye; it comes from Brauron), the style of the masonry and the proportions of the low, octagonal dome date the pretty church to the thirteenth century. The frescoes on the interior date to the eighteenth century.

4 The Mesogeia: Loutsa, Raphina, Spata, Markopoulo, Koropi and Paiania

The large plain east of the Hymettos range, bounded in the north by Pentelikon and in the south by the foothills of Paneion, is called 'Mesogeia', the 'inner land', to which Porto Raphti and Brauron also belong (see pp. 219–25). The plain was intensively farmed in Antiquity and densely populated. Today the area is mostly abandoned and ugly; only in the area round Markopoulo, the centre of Attic retsina production, can cultivated vineyards be seen. The final step in the destruction of this once important cultural area is the construction of a new airport, which will be opened in March 2001. Nevertheless, there are some sites worth visiting, especially small Byzantine churches, which are scattered widely across this extensive area.

Loutsa. North of the coastal site of Porto Raphti, also called the 'Harbour of the Mesogeia', and of Brauron lies Loutsa, a village with a long sandy shoreline, which has spread extensively along the coast in the last few years. At the north end of the village directly on the beach the remains of a large **temple**[187] and, a few steps further south, a further small prostylos with a cult pit (bothros) have been excavated. The large cult building was dedicated to Artemis Tauropolos; Euripides mentions it in his *Iphigenia in Tauris*. It had an adyton behind the cella, in which the cult image was placed, as is often the case with temples of Artemis (Brauron, Aulis). Although only the foundations are extant (these have been excavated several times, but they are covered with sand after each time), the temple can be reconstructed as a wide Doric peripteros with 8 to 12 columns; a further unusual feature of the building plan is that the columns have only 16 flutes, as in the Poseidon Temple at Sounion. The temple must have been the centre of a big festival, the Tauropolia, which took place here every year; contests were also organised in connection with Dionysos. The mention of a festival of Dionysos in an inscription dating to 341 BC suggests the presence of a theatre, but it has not been found until now. In contrast the remains of the late Antique settlement have been found; it includes an Early Christian basilica with three apses; this has, however, completely disappeared.

Raphina. The harbour town of Raphina lies in the north-east corner of the Mesogeia. One can now sail from here to Euboia and the north Cyclades (Andros, Tinos) and also to almost all the other Aegean islands by ferry boat or hydrofoil. The modern harbour is very active; freshly caught fish are sold here and are also served in the simple tavernas on the quayside.

The site of Raphina has a long history; the old deme name of Araphen lives on in its name. It was already settled in the prehistoric period, by those who traded with the Cyclades and worked with copper and lead, because of its attractive harbour situation in two sheltered bays. On a hill 2 km south of the harbour (called **Askitario**[188] today) and above the large harbour two Early Helladic settlements have been found, similar to that of Ay. Kosmas on the west coast of Attica. Further excavations about 1 km further inland revealed numerous traces of Roman walls, which have not yet been explained; the only certainly recognisable building was a bath built of small stones, bricks and mortar (next to the entrance to the village on the main road from Athens on the north side opposite a BP petrol station). The centre of the deme of Araphen probably lay here.

   Monastery of Daou Pentelis. A few kilometres west of Raphina the road to the monastery, which lies on the south-east foothills of Pentelikon, branches off from the Athens-Marathon road (Figure **74**). The monastery was founded as early as the Middle Byzantine period (eleventh/twelfth century) and then completely renovated in the sixteenth century and in 1949. It has a quasi-rectangular

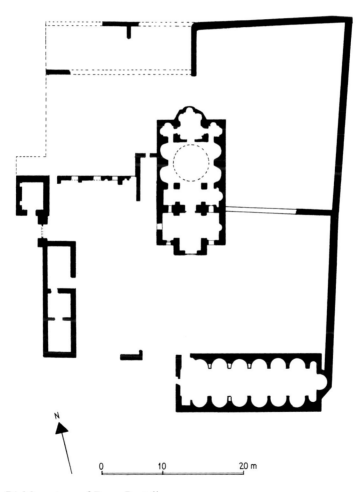

Figure 74 Monastery of Daou Pentelis.

enclosure wall, onto which the cells (on the east side), the refectory with many apses (in the south-east) and stables (on the north side) have been built. The large catholikon (Plate 56) which is divided into three parts, the naos and the inner and outer narthex, stands in the centre of the courtyard. The plan of the main building is unique in Greece. The church has a hexagonal plan resulting from the addition of two extra dome supports on the north and south sides, which can also be seen on the upper storey, where women could take part in the church service. Small apses were added onto the corners of the hexagon, which is inscribed in a rectangle; the side rooms carry octagonal domes. The prothesis and the diakonikon (sacristy) are small three-apse side chapels. The architectural scheme of the main church derives from Armenian and Georgian ecclesiastical antecedents; the present appearance of the church dates to the second half of the sixteenth century, but may copy its Middle Byzantine predecessor. The esonarthex (inner narthex), two-storeyed like the main part of the church, was built at the same time as the naos. In contrast the three-storey outer narthex, also crowned with a dome, which appears as a massive tower in front of the façade of the main church, was built later, probably in the mid-seventeenth century. Some fine marble fragments of ancient grave monuments have been built into its walls.

Pikermi and **Spata**. The Marathon road, also called 'Mesogeion', which runs from Raphina to Athens, passes the village of Pikermi. There must have been a densely settled deme here, but up until now only a few traces of settlement have been found.

They consist in particular of several Archaic and Classical cemeteries; in addition there are two **Early Christian basilicas** known in this area, of which the foundations of one, Ay. Vasilios, (signposted in the Vourva field from the road from Spata to Pallini on the field path to Ay. Spiridon, south of Pikermi) can still be clearly seen today. Its main room was divided into three aisles by two rows of columns, of which the middle one ended in a semicircular apse; a narthex and an exonarthex lay in front of the west side across its entire width, while the north side was flanked by four rectangular rooms. The name Vourva is also known to archaeologists because of an extensive cemetery with large grave monuments with mudbrick walls; nothing is left of it today.

Pikermi, however, is not famous for its archaeological remains, but is known worldwide for its important palaeontological finds. Animal bones dating to the beginning of Pliocene eight million years ago have been collected from the stream bed of Megalo Revma, which gathers the water from Pentelikon and flows down to Raphina. They belong to animals which need a savannah climate and which are normally connected with Africa: monkeys, giraffes, antelopes, etc. The finds are an important support for the theory that the continents of Africa and Europe were connected in the prehistory of the earth before they eventually drifted apart.

Spata lies a few kilometres south of Pikermi, roughly in the centre of the Mesogeia; it is a small town of winding streets, in which the finds from the region used to be collected. Driving through it today, the visitor should not miss a fine

Classical grave relief with many figures, which is built into the wall of a corner house on the north side of the main street; it dates to the early fourth century BC. There is nothing left today of a once famous Mycenaean chamber tomb on the south slope of the settlement hill. Leaving Spata and following the road south-east to Merkouri and from there in a south-westerly direction to Koropi, one passes the church of Ay. Petros. It was probably built at the beginning of the fifteenth century and is an example of the transition from the Late Byzantine to the Turkish period in building techniques. It is a cross-in-square domed church with two types of columns and has many ancient and Early Christian spolia built into it, as is common in Attica.

The area of the new Athens airport lies south-east of Spata. Archaeological excavations took place before the levelling for the runways and the buildings and produced village structures dating to the Classical period and a street grid with many branches. North of the airport on the other side of the road from Spata to Loutsa there is a long hill called **Zagani**, which had to be levelled for the safety of the incoming flights. This is the more unfortunate because one of the most important Attic settlements dating from Late Neolithic or Early Helladic has been found here. A rescue excavation revealed many houses, some of which were constructed of herringbone masonry, inside an enclosure wall. In the Late Classical period, when nothing of the prehistoric settlement was apparently visible except the enclosure wall, five boundary inscriptions belonging to the usual Attic type (OPOC), were incised along the ridge of the Zagani hill, which probably marked the boundary between two districts (the inscriptions were cut out of the rock before the hill was removed).

Markopoulo. This town is known in Attica as a centre of wine production; the large factories which produce retsina and unresinated wine can be seen lining the road to Athens. In the town itself there are some churches worth visiting, particularly the **chapel of Ioannis Prodromos**, which lies on the right of the main road as it runs from the main square to Keratea. The building, which has a plain yellow plastered exterior, is richly decorated on the interior with frescoes ascribed to the well-known artist Georgios Markos of Argos, who worked in Attica in the first half of the eighteenth century. A fine grave relief dating to *c.* 380 BC is built into the wall on the exterior near the entrance. The scene, a servant girl in front of a seated female, was probably given a new meaning here as the Annunciation.

More churches worth visiting lie outside the town at the sides of the main roads. **Ay. Triada**, dating to the post-Byzantine period, lies *c.* 2 km north-east of Markopoulo on a small hill on the right of the road to Porto Raphti (the entrance and the enclosure wall of the earlier monastery can be seen from the road behind a garage). It is a double church with two apses and two narthexes and is of interest not only because of its numerous Early Christian spolia, which come from a basilica which stood here, but also because of its well preserved frescoes dating to the eighteenth century; they are ascribed to the school of Markos, who combined traditional Byzantine elements with the 'modern' conception of form (the Limiko tower is located a few metres further on in the direction of Porto Raphti on the left, north of the road, see p. 225).

On a small hill (east of the road) on the southern edge of Markopoulo a tower dating to the Middle Ages can be seen next to the ruins of a small chapel. Below the tower is a Middle Byzantine **church of the Taxiarchs**. Its original twelfth century cross-domed building is shaded by a huge, very old olive tree. In the interior the cloisonné masonry typical of this period can be seen on the arches of the cross dome; the remains of the original frescoes, which date to the twelfth century, are also preserved (some of them painted over many times) next to the iconostasis, which contains ancient marble columns. In two later building phases first a vestibule supported on two arches was added in front of the core of the church and then a long narthex; at the junction of these two annexes an ancient column stood on three steps, with a capital consisting of an earlier column base. A few metres north of this pretty church of the Taxiarchs the wall of another chapel can be seen, on which the faded remains of an angel fresco are preserved.

A few kilometres south of Markopoulo the eighteenth century **Ay. Demetrios** is located 200 m west of the road to Keratea; it comprises a one-aisled chapel with a narthex added later in front. The church is of interest for its Early Christian spolia and well preserved eighteenth century frescoes, which have a very individual style.

A little further south, on the side of the mountain of **Merenda** lying east of the road and marked today by a huge quarry, a large cemetery (dating from the Geometric to the Hellenistic periods) was excavated at the side of an ancient road three decades ago. It belonged to the deme Myrrhinous, the name of which lives on in the modern field name Merenda. Some temples stood here (for Artemis, Athena, whose cult image and temple were restored by Herodes Atticus, etc.) according to ancient sources and inscriptions. Two famous Archaic marble statues[189] which come from here are Phrasikleia and a young man, on display today in the National Museum (Rooms 9 and 10; see p. 114); the statue base of the maiden had long been known, since it had been built into a nearby chapel of the Virgin (**Panagia**). It gives her name as Phrasikleia and the sculptor, who made the figure *c.* 540 BC, as Aristion of Paros. The church of the Panagia, which lies south of the road running round the Merenda mountain from Markopoulo to Kalivia Kouvara, still has the foundations of an earlier basilica on its south and east sides. The high building, into which some ancient architectural elements have been built, has pointed arches on the interior.

K oropi. The town of Koropi lies on the south-west edge of the Mesogeia. There are many churches worth visiting in its neighbourhood, which often have ancient and Early Christian spolia. West of Koropi in the Classical deme of Sphettos two ancient sites are also worth visiting.

The Church of the **Metamorphosis** in Koropi dates to the tenth/eleventh century and still has its original frescoes. Turning off in the town to the west at the small square with the statue of King Constantine the church of **Ay. Petros** can be seen 500 m along on the left; the simple barrel-vaulted seven-teenth century church stands out because of its particularly well-preserved contemporary frescoes. **Ay. Asomatoi**, lying on the same street 500 m further on, is a small cross-domed church, which was built in the seventeenth century with ancient spolia from the sanctuary portico at Brauron. About 250 m west of Ay. Asomatoi opposite the 'Kastro tou Christou' (Bethlehem Monastery) a low hill with a medieval tower can be seen and, 50 m east of it, the simple long building of **Ay. Athanasios**, which was constructed in 1768 according to an inscription. The remains of the walls in the neighbourhood belong to the medieval town of Philiati. Numerous ancient spolia and Early Christian blocks by the church bear witness to the cultural continuity of this site. The modern Bethlehem Monastery can be reached directly from Koropi (signposted). On the hill (**Kastro tou Christou**) are the remains of a Mycenaean fortification wall made of large irregular blocks of rock. The relatively close succession of small Mycenaean fortifications outside Athens can be appreciated here, since only a few kilometres southwards, on the hill of Kiapha Thiti (north of Vari, see p. 197), a further citadel dating to this period is known (see also Thorikos p. 216). The site was also important in the Hellenistic period, since in the north below the monastery, just behind the entrance and next to a small chapel (with ancient columns of Euboean marble in the interior), many rock-cuttings for votives can be seen, as well as traces of an enclosure wall. The find of a statue base with an inscription in honour of Demetrios of Phaleron shows the impor-tance of this rural sanctuary in the Early Hellenistic period.[190]

On the eastern foothills of Hymettos, north-west above the Kastro tou Christou, from the plain a whitewashed church, which is dedicated to **Prophitis Ilias**, can be seen in the saddle.

To reach the church and sanctuary follow the road from the Bethlehem Monastery to the west. The asphalt ends after a few hundred metres and turns into a dirt road; at the next opportunity go on foot to the right (north) and climb up the slope following a narrow winding path.

After a climb up a donkey track on the south side of the mountain a small plateau lying in a hollow is reached (510 m above sea level). It was surrounded with a rubble wall in Antiquity and served as the sanctuary containing at least two temples. One lay on the site of the church, which was built from countless ancient blocks; there is a wonderful view from here over the plain to Porto Raphti. The second temple, built of fine polygonal masonry, lies a few metres further west. Both cult buildings have been dated by Greek excavators to the sixth century BC, but they could have been built later, in the Classical period; the cultic contents are unfortunately unknown.

North of the hill with the church of Prophitis Ilias a valley runs west up the slope of Hymettos. The modern way follows an ancient road connection, the 'Sphettia Odos', which led from Athens past the Monastery of Kareas across the mountain ridge and finally reached the Mesogeia west of Koropi, the ancient deme of Sphettos. A signpost in the form of a herm stood there in the sixth century BC, dedicated by Hipparchos, the son of Peisistratos (in the storerooms of Brauron Museum today); on its shaft is an inscription giving the name of the dedicator and the distance from the city. Ancient sources tell us that such monuments were also set up by Hipparchos at other important road points, such as at forks or crossroads.

The church of **Ay. Anargyroi** can be seen about 2 km along on the left following the old road eastwards from Koropi to Brauron. The church attained its present form with supporting pillars in the eighteenth century; thick layers of plaster and modern painting have made the masonry unrecognisable. However, in spite of the many alterations the semi-hexagonal apses of the central and northern side aisle still indicate a Middle Byzantine core building, probably a cross-domed church. Ancient and Early Christian spolia were also used here as special decoration (columns in the interior, others in the front yard). Only 100 m further east on the right of the road the church of **Panagia** can be seen, a one-aisled seventeenth century building with interesting frescoes of the same date and many ancient spolia, including a fragment of a fourth century BC grave stele.

Two eighteenth century churches must also be mentioned. **Ay. Georgios** lies on a hill north of the Koropi-Markopoulo road, about half a kilometre outside Koropi. The narthex of the long building must have belonged to an older church. The small cross-domed church of **Prophitis Elias** is situated one kilometre south.

The ridge of Kondra lies south of Koropi. The church of **Ay. Nikolaos** is situated about 1 km along a road running south-east from the town towards this mountain. The unusual three-apse building is modelled on a Middle Byzantine cross-domed church (tenth/eleventh century), while some details of the superstructure show characteristics of the Turkish period (changes to the windows, the entrance, etc.). The long narthex was added on later.

The chapel of **Evangelistis Loukas** is particularly worth seeing. Some kilometres south of Koropi a road branches off westwards from the Koropi-Vari road to a large quarry (on the T-junction a chapel with ancient columns); the monastery of Ay. Triada lies 200 m along it. To the east next to this monastery the Loukas Church is situated in a fig plantation in the field **Lambrika**; this name recalls the ancient deme of Lamptrai,[191] which was divided into two parts; this is Upper Lamptrai (see p. 81). The chapel, which is the cemetery church of the monastery today, was built in the twelfth/thirteenth century; some ancient spolia can be seen on the outside of the unplastered walls. The unusual form of the chapel is the result of many conversions. The high narrow narthex with added side entrances exhibits characteristics of Frankish building techniques, while the long main building with a high crossroof probably received its present appearance as a result of a seventeenth century alteration. The interior division does not reflect the outer appearance; the nave has blind arches in its disproportionately thick north wall, which are neither reflected in the long south wall nor do they correspond to the roof. The frescoes in the main room date to the seventeenth and eighteenth centuries. A fourth century BC grave stele decorated with rosettes and an anthemium bearing the name of a family from Lamptrai, has been built in over the door between the narthex and main church; the anthemium, which probably goes with the stele, was placed above it. Other antiquities which come from this site include a votive inscription to Apollo and the crowning monument of an Archaic grave stele with the relief of an armed rider on the front (National Museum, Room 8).

P aiania. The next village north of Koropi is Paiania, which was earlier called Liopesi; the present name derives from the ancient deme Paiania, which lay here. It is known as the birthplace of Demosthenes (384–322 BC), who committed suicide on the island of Poros by taking poison when he was condemned to death by the Macedonians. Many small churches have also been built here, some of which were painted by Georgios Markos of Argos.

In the town itself there is a private museum, the **Vorres Collection** (signposted), which is worth a visit. The owner of the museum, which is open to the public, has displayed modern Greek art in a well-lit museum building on the west edge of Paiania; the collection offers an interesting overview of post-war Greek art. The perseverance of Vorres in trying to preserve lost Attica as it once was in this small area is particularly impressive. His large old house, which is built in the traditional style, could also be considered a museum; it has folk art, beautiful furniture, embroideries, and also, here and there, antiquities which come from the neighbourhood. Everything is lovingly looked after and carefully displayed. The garden surrounding the house is a particular gem. Several gardeners are employed full time both to look after the Greek plants, which have been specially sought out and many of which can only be seen here, and to keep the garden in a tidy but natural condition. The property will eventually be given to the state.

O n the east slope of Hymettos, above the Vorres Museum, the stalactite **cave of Koutouki** lies at 510 m above sea level (signposted from the main road 'Cave of Peanias'); the entrance, from which there is a good view over the Mesogeia, can be reached by car. The large 3,800 square-metre cave is well lit (with coloured lights) and furnished with a comfortable walkway, which takes in all the stalagmites and stalactites worth seeing. Finds from a prehistoric use of the cave are documented.

On the foothills of Hymettos, north-west of the site (access from Ay. Triada Street at the end of which go right and then take the first street left) the small cross-domed church of **Ay. Triada** is located alone on a small cypress-covered hilltop. The original Byzantine building (twelfth/thirteenth century) apparently underwent many conversions and even the narthex was added later. Only the Pantocrator in the dome survives from the older fresco decoration; the remaining paintings date from the Turkish period or are modern.

In the west part of Paiania is the church of **Ay. Paraskevi** (Spyr. Angeli Street), which stands on the site of an Early Christian basilica. In addition to numerous ancient architectural fragments, some built into the building, which dates to the Turkish period, and some lying in the courtyard, the choir of the basilica is preserved as the apse of the present day chapel. The side chapel dedicated to Ay. Charalambos was built after the Turkish period. The church is decorated with interesting frescoes, some copy pictures of the Palaeologue period, for example the forty martyrs in the upper area.

East of the centre of the town (from Plateia Davari follow Papageorgiou and Sp. A. Papaspirou streets) the **Panagia** church lies hidden in a pretty courtyard with tall flowers. The three-aisled building with a saddle roof has three semi-hexagonal apses on the east and a side chapel on the south side. In the church-yard the walls of an earlier building can be seen as well as spolia built into the west side of the entrance as decorative elements.

Ay. Athanasios is a particularly interesting building. It is located on the south edge of Paiania, some 200 m north of the fork to Markopoulo or Koropi, just east of the Stavros–Markopoulo road (Figure **75**). The asymmetric three-aisled church with semicircular apse is completely built into the choir of an Early Christian basilica; part of the wall of this earlier building is still extant in the area

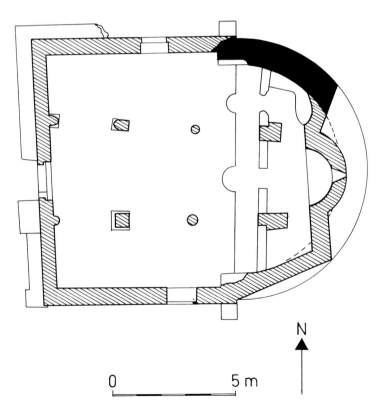

N

0   5 m

Figure 75 Paiania, church of Ay. Athanasios.

of the north-east wall. The present church dates to the Turkish period and, in addition to Early Christian spolia, also contains ancient blocks (capitals, grave inscriptions, fragments in the courtyard). The painting of the iconostasis (1773) must also be mentioned; it imitates the original appearance of a marble chancel screen.

The Karelas field lies just south of the district of Paiania (on the drive up to the stalactite cave, do not turn right uphill after the last houses, but continue straight on south). The church of **Ay. Georgios Sklepios** dating to the Turkish period stands here a few hundred metres east of the narrow road in an olive grove some 1.5 km distant from Paiania. Many ancient architectural components were used in the construction of the one-aisled building with (converted) dome; there are also many ancient blocks around the church. Inside an ancient marble basin is displayed in the north corner in front of the apse. The name of the church together with the existence of the spolia might suggest an Asklepios sanctuary stood on the site of the present church.

Continuing southwards along the road the twelfth century cross-domed church of **Ay. Nikolaos Chalidou** lies on an S-bend a few kilometres further on. The frescoes in the dome and in the zone below it date to the Middle Byzantine period; other paintings are assigned to the Markos School. The side chapel dedicated to Ay. Savvas was added much later. The entrance is flanked by seats of ancient marble; further marble fragments are scattered round the courtyard.

Stavros (Kantzas). On the return journey from Paiania to Athens north of the village on the right of the road a hill rises up and is crowned with a high cross. In Antiquity there was a temple on the hilltop, as rock-cuttings make clear. Besides these an inscription cut in large letters in the natural rock can be seen. On the north slope below the hilltop, there are numerous additional cuttings in the rock for walls, which, together with pottery lying around on the surface, suggest the existence of a small ancient settlement.

Continuing towards Athens, north of the village of Glyka Nera is a hamlet comprising the village of Stavros named after the large cross roads with the Mesogeion bridge. Just south of the electricity station at Stavros by a large 'AB' supermarket (known as AlphaVita) a small road branches off east to Spata 500 m along which another small road turns off left to the power station; the chapel of **Ay. Nikolaos** lies here. The area was earlier called Kantzas (also Leontari today) and was known for its huge **marble lion**.[192] A local tale is attached to this: a wild lion, which lived in a cave on the east slope of Hymettos, annually ate the most beautiful girl in the district; he was eventually turned into marble by Ay. Nikolaos and tied to the ground by his paws. The marble lion lay in front of the church with its stomach on the ground until a few years ago (Plate 57) so the tale was immediately comprehensible; recently it has been set up on a concrete plinth under a protective roof. This impressive late fourth century BC animal sculpture with its head turned to the side was probably an imposing grave guard in a cemetery from which further remains have been found and excavated close by (see also the fine anthemion framed by sphinxes, which crowned a stele, in the west wall of the Ay. Nikolaos chapel). Some blocks from the enclosure wall of this once impressive grave plot are also extant. The attribution of the grave to the family of Demosthenes must unfortunately remain hypothetical, although it is known that the ashes of the politician were brought to Athens in a hydria after his suicide on Poros; perhaps they were buried in his home deme.

The church of the **Palaiopanagia** not far from the lion is worth a visit. Go east from the lion of Kantzas, then continue east on the road to Papangelaki crossing a newly built road; the church lies 700 m along the road in a modern monastery. The remains of a Middle Byzantine church have been integrated into a church of the Turkish period with a saddle roof. The semi-hexagonal apse facing north shows that it was one of the few three- or four-apse buildings in Greece; for the apse must have been repeated on the east, south and perhaps on the west sides. The careful masonry of the north apse supports the dating. Inside the apse there are frescoes dating to the Byzantine period; the remaining wall painting of the church dates to the eighteenth century.

On the return journey from Kantzas to Athens a visit to the Monastery of Ay. Ioannis Kynigos on the north slope of Hymettos can be made (see p. 160).

A short deviation into the district north of the Mesogeion Road, which one crosses coming from Paiania to Penteli, leads to **Gerakas** (part of which includes the ancient deme of Pallene). Many remains of ancient buildings were found here in the last century as well as in 1998 during excavation works. In this respect the small cemetery chapel of **Ay. Georgios**[193] is of special interest (most easily reached by driving in the direction of Penteli to a crossroad going right with the sign 'BDF', following this to the factory and then going south *c.* 1 km; the cemetery then lies east of the road). The small chapel has a fine Classical anthemium with tendrils and a loutrophoros grave relief set over its entrance (Plate 58). A large corner triglyph has been built into the interior; it comes from a Late Archaic temple, which must have stood not too far away. It must have preceded a **High Classical peripteros**, the foundations of which were excavated a few years ago on the south slope of a hill a few hundred metres north of the large Stavros crossroads (the excavation site can be reached from the crossroads with its high bridge by following the road to Penteli and Chalandri a few hundred metres north to its fork and then turning right (east) here into a small side street and then immediately left again; the foundations, which are fenced off, lie just below two new houses and close the small street). The measurements of the substructure of the temple,[194] which is made of limestone blocks, are exactly the same as those of the Temple of Ares in the Agora of Athens; since, apart from this foundation, not a single marble building component belonging to the superstructure has been found at Stavros, it is very probable that it was this building which was carefully taken down, marked and transported to Athens where it was re-erected as the Temple of Ares (see p. 81). The cult building on this original site in the ancient deme of Pallene was dedicated to the goddess Athena Pallenis. We know quite a lot about this important sanctuary from ancient sources and from inscriptions. It played a role in Peisistratios' rise to power (546 BC), as the decisive battle between the supporters of his family and the Athenian opposition took place here. Later Euripides mentions the hill with the Athena sanctuary, and inscriptions from the Acropolis state that the sanctuary of Athena of Pallene had to pay tax to the city goddess of Athens. We also know of an ancient cult association from inscriptions; citizens from the three neighbouring demes of Pallene, Paiania and Gargettos (located north on the slope of Pentelikon) belonged to it. as did those from the deme of Acharnai on the slope of Parnes, where an important cult of Ares and Athena was located. This ancient cultic connection of Athena Pallenis with Ares makes the rededication of the temple after its removal quite possible; however, Athena was not banished from the cult building, since Pausanias mentions a statue of the goddess in the Ares Temple in the Agora. Whether the cult continued in the older Archaic temple after the removal of the Classical peripteros cannot be known without research into that building or knowledge of its original site.

3 Attica II: The plain of Marathon and north-east Attica

1 The plain of Marathon and the Battle of Marathon 490 BC

The plain of Marathon[195] lies on a broad bay with long sandy beaches, which are much used by Athenians in the summer. The beaches extend over many kilometres from Ay. Andreas in the south to Schinias in the north; the sea here becomes warm very quickly because the water is very shallow. At Schinias light pine woods stretch almost into the sea and offer welcome shade. In the north the bay is bounded by a narrow peninsula, the Kynosoura ('dog's tail'), on which the remains of fortification walls have been found; in the west the foothills of Pentelikon border the wide plain. This fertile area is intensively farmed today; next to the usual silver-green olive trees, vegetable fields and many greenhouses and mushroom farms can be seen.

A good view of the plain of Marathon can be obtained from the south-west coming out of Athens and driving over Pentelikon (over Nea Penteli or over Dionysos) to north-east Attica. The Mesogeion road, which runs between Hymettos and Pentelikon via Raphina and Nea Makri from Athens to Marathon, has fewer curves.

The Battle of Marathon, when the Athenians defeated the enormous Persian army in autumn 490 BC, is famous; this feat was the foundation of the prominent position Athens achieved in the Classical period. It much enhanced the national self-confidence of the Greeks, and does so even today. The Athenians achieved the victory with the help of the Plataians; the Spartans who had been summoned by a fast runner arrived after the battle. The fortunate outcome of the battle was based mostly on the speed of the attacking battle line (phalanx) of heavily armed men, who ran below the dangerous arrows of the Persian archers. A stratagem, which was perhaps devised by the Athenian Miltiades and used after many days of hesitation, was also decisive; he increased the numbers on the sides of the phalanx and ordered the weaker centre of the line to retreat. The Persian centre could then be attacked from the sides. The enemy, apparently surprised by the speed and force of the attack, turned in flight and were pursued to their ships in the north of the bay. Even the intervention of the Persian cavalry came too late. The fallen Greeks were buried in two tumuli, according to current research. The 192 Athenians were buried together with funerary gifts in a tumulus somewhere close to where they met the enemy, while the Plataians lay further west (on the present dead-end road to the Museum), perhaps at the place where they rounded off the left wing of the battle line. This means that the Greeks attacked the Persians from the south-west.

Both grave mounds with their burial offerings, consisting of weapons and especially pottery, have been excavated by Greek archaeologists (some scholars doubt that the known grave mounds are those of the fallen soldiers of the Battle of Marathon). Perhaps it was the general Miltiades, the leader of the attack, who dedicated his helmet to Zeus at Olympia; at any rate a Corinthian helmet was found there engraved with his name. Marble stelai with the names of the fallen once stood on the grave mound of the Athenians (fragments of a similar list, perhaps a copy, were recently found in Athens); the present grave relief displayed at the foot of the mound is an imitation of a grave stele which was actually made around 510 BC (stele of Aristion, National Museum); it comes from another site and illustrates only the armour of a hoplite (heavily armed man).

The Greeks set up a victory trophy, a tropaion (turning point), at the place where the enemy host turned in flight. The probable remains of the Marathon tropaion are built into a medieval tower, which stood roughly in the middle of the plain, by the church of Panagia Mesosporitissa (today accessible from a field path, which branches off right from the road to Rhamnous behind a long row of cypresses and leads to a chapel; next to it a mushroom farm). The victory monument, an unfluted column, supported a large Ionic capital (today in Marathon Museum) on which, perhaps, weapons gained as booty were displayed, or perhaps a statue of Nike, from which a possible fragment, of Parian marble, with the remains of folds is preserved (in the Museum garden). The remaining large square blocks of the medieval tower have long carved lines on their original outer side suggesting they are spolia from an Attic grave terrace (see below Rhamnous), but they did not belong to the tropaion.

There are two further consequences of the Battle of Marathon, which are still influential today. The tale tells of a runner who brought the news of victory to Athens and collapsed there and died of exhaustion. The Olympic contest of the Marathon run introduced at the 1896 Olympic Games is based on this story. However, the historicity of the run is doubtful, since the historian Herodotus, writing at the time of the event, mentions a Spartan runner, but says nothing about a Marathon runner. Also the dramatic embellishment of a heroic death resulting from the run, which is first mentioned in later sources, raises doubts as to the truth of the event. The length of 42.195 km for the Olympic contest was fixed in 1908, when the starting point was at Windsor Castle and the end at the king's box in the London stadium. In contrast the *c.* 260 km long run to Sparta, which is little known today, certainly took place. One can also connect the touching story of the first victor in this Olympic contest to the new monument at the entrance to Marathon, where the course of the first modern Marathon started. Due to his lack of entry qualifications a simple Greek shepherd, Spiridon Louis, after whom the modern Olympic stadium in Athens is named today, was excluded as a competitor by his native land and won the contest in 1896 as a member of the American team.

2 The Marathon Area

T he **Museum Area** (**Tsepi** and **Vrana**). Turning left (west) off the main Athens–Marathon road to the signposted Marathon Museum the visitor passes the prehistoric cemetery of Tsepi and the Tumulus of the Plataians. Right next to the turning there is an Early Helladic cemetery with many graves made of slab lined cists with heavy covering slabs. They were covered with low earth mounds and are protected today by corrugated iron roofs. All the mounds continued in use into the Mycenaean period. The settlement to which they belong lies *c.* 400 m further south. An almost contemporary cemetery north of the museum is very similar; it also has a protective roof. In contrast a Mycenaean tholos tomb south-east of the museum (the guards must be asked to accompany one and open it) has a much more impressive appearance: a 25 m long entrance (dromos) leads to a door with a relieving triangle above the lintel; behind it lies the burial chamber in which two burials with offerings, including a gold cup, were found. Two symmetrically arranged horse burials found during the excavations in the dromos suggest the dead belonged to a leading family.

The Marathon **Museum** contains many finds from the neighbourhood: the burial offerings from the cemeteries just described, from other graves and from the grave mounds fill most of the showcases, to which (in Room A) the finds from the Cave of Pan at Oinoe are added. The tropaion of the Battle of Marathon with an Ionic capital and many inscriptions from sanctuaries, which are important for the reconstruction of the battle, are on show. The surrounding showcases contain pottery, including that from the Athenian mound; some of it is much older than the battle and suggests that the grave mound was already standing as a family grave, when it was reused to bury the fallen hoplites; another explanation suggests that the earth of the mound was taken from older grave mounds in the neighbourhood and that this accounts for the presence of the older finds. The adjacent rooms contain Classical grave reliefs (fourth century BC), including two monuments in the form of Panathenaic prize amphorae with reliefs of a priest and his family, and finds from the Roman period, such as portraits of the emperors, which probably once decorated the villa of Herodes Atticus[196] on the plain of Marathon (he himself is portrayed as a bearded head which is very worn; compare Plate 65). In the portrait room there is also a marble couch with a man lying on it, a grave monument from the villa of Herodes Atticus.

The statues, indicative of Egypt, come from the sanctuary of the Egyptian gods in Brexisa (on the south edge of the plain), and comprise a statue of a young man as Pharaoh (another such statue from the same site is in the National Museum) and a goddess, both also belonging to the estate of Herodes Atticus; they are to be connected with an Egyptian-style lintel with a solar disc framed by two snakes (known as uraea in Egypt), which once spanned the sanctuary porch (in the Museum courtyard). Further architectural pieces and seated statues also come from the properties of Herodes Atticus; there are parts of an entrance arch from his villa with an inscription (it is dedicated to the unity of marriage partners) which names the owner and his wife Regilla; it was found together with the severely damaged statues of a woman and a man seated on thrones, perhaps the representation of the owner of the villa himself. Two herm pillars once carried portraits of pupils of Herodes Atticus, the one a portrait of Memnon, a coloured man from Ethiopia who was called the 'small topaz' because of his dark skin (Plate 67), the other his pupil Achilles (Plate 68); below his name a curse formula is inscribed, to prevent the destruction of the work.

O**inoe**. Ancient Oinoe lies in an isolated green valley with gushing springs between high deciduous trees some 3 km west of modern Marathon.

It can be reached from the southern entrance to Marathon, turning off left from the main road near the monument for the running contest into a narrower road (straight on), staying on the left at a T-junction and following this road for *c.* 3 km west to a high medieval tower.

B eneath the medieval tower, which has several storeys, the remains of Roman baths were found when pipes were laid. The bathing rooms and the brick supports which carried the floor and allowed the circulation of hot air (hypocaust) can be recognised.

To the east of these ancient remains on the edge of an area with many springs there is a strange installation of large marble blocks which has still not been explained today (Figure **76**): square pillars define a courtyard which has a row of oblong blocks set at right angles to its sides; these have a slightly concave upper surface and grooves on the sides in which sluice gates were apparently set (Plate 59). The courtyard is lined with watertight plaster; the whole installation, which is surrounded by a corridor, must be connected functionally to the abundance of water in the area. Above this installation are the remains of an exedra to which steps are leading up. The marble parts were erected in the Roman period to which the brickwork, which is also extant, dates; perhaps the building was a nymphaion; from evidence from inscriptions and finds of sculpture it was part of the property of Herodes Atticus, who had it constructed on this site.

On the north slope of the hill above the tree-ringed springs (a fine grassy path leads round the slope) the entrance (now walled-up) to a stalactite cave

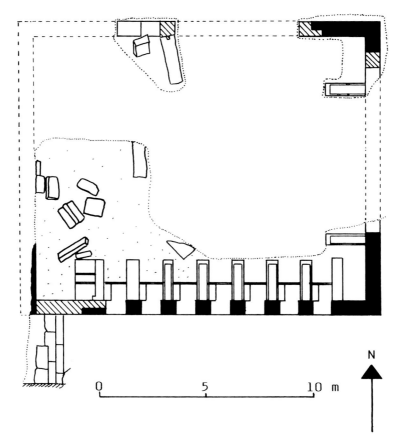

Figure 76 Marathon – Oinoe, courtyard installation of the villa of Herodes Atticus.

was found in 1958, which is also mentioned by Pausanias in his travel guide to Greece: 'The entrance is narrow, but inside there are chambers and small lakes and the so-called herd of Pan, rocks which in most respects look like goats' (the stalactites look like goats' beards). The finds from the interior date to the Neolithic and the Mycenaean periods; further inside, Classical vases, lamps and figurines were found. These, together with the terrace in front of the entrance, can be connected to the celebration of the cult of Pan, which was set up here after the Battle of Marathon in 490 BC because the god himself had helped the Greeks by instilling 'panic' in their enemies.

Nea Makri. Before the turn off to the Athenian burial mound on the road from Athens to Marathon the Temple of Isis of Brexiza is located on the east of the road on the sea (on the beach next to a large hotel and behind a military barracks some 2 km north of Nea Makri; Figure **77**). Marble building components, which once decorated the entrance, comprising parts of the lintels with uraea and solar discs, are now in the museum. The entrance led into a court-

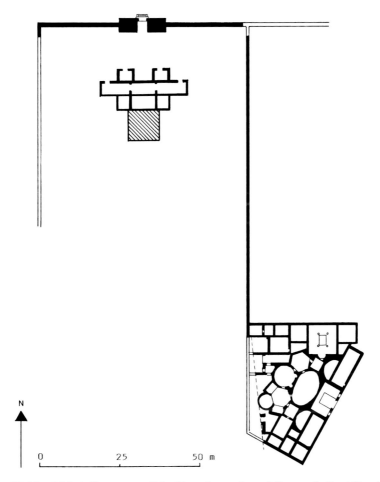

Figure 77 Nea Makri, Sanctuary of the Egyptian gods and Roman bath at Brexiza.

yard with a paved floor; the temple stood on the south side on a socle with many steps (recalling a pyramid). Today all that can be seen of this sanctuary are the foundations of the walls, the courtyard and the temple socle; parts of the walls are now not visible because of levelling in 1991. A little to the south the foundations of a neighbouring bath (Figure 77) can be seen; they comprise round and hexagonal rooms with heated floors, which were grouped round a large oval pool; the brick walls had marble revetment and the floor was also laid with costly slabs. The clay pipes, which heated the rooms with warm air, can be seen in the breaks in the walls. In Antiquity this bath house right next to the murmuring sea with its sandy beach must have made a very luxurious impression. The portrait busts of the emperors Marcus Aurelius and Lucius Verus and that of Herodes Atticus, which are kept in the museums of Paris and Oxford today, come from this area. The finds and the literary sources (*Lives of the Sophists* by Philostratus), which mention a sanctuary of Kanobos near the villa of Herodes Atticus in Marathon, give rise to the conclusion that the sanctuary of the Egyptian gods was dedicated by Herodes Atticus (and probably also the baths connected to it).

In recent years still more traces of ancient settlement on the plain have been found in the neighbourhood of Marathon. There is now evidence that the damp, sometimes marshy, land was in use from the prehistoric period into the Early Christian. A prehistoric to Archaic settlement has been found on the coast east of the tumulus of the Athenians; two Early Christian basilicas in the same area illustrate the long continuity of settlement. Remains of houses and different sanctuaries, for example to Dionysos, Herakles, Hermes and the Charites, are known, mostly from inscriptions and literary sources. A high point in building activity was apparently in the second century AD as a result of the generosity of the family of Herodes Atticus, as portraits, herms and inscriptions, which name family members of Herodes Atticus (Plates 65–68), bear impressive witness. The monumental decoration of the neighbourhood was strongly supported by Herodes himself.

The **Marathon Dam**. North-west of Marathon lies a dam, which serves the water supply of Athens; watersports and swimming are therefore not allowed in this lake. The roads leading up to it, which wind through the mountains of Marathon or of Ay. Stephanos, offer many views of the once thickly forested countryside on the north side of Pentelikon, which is now almost bare due to yearly forest fires. The lake is the result of a 285 m-long and 72 m-high dam wall, which was constructed in 1926–31 with the help of the USA. It can be crossed on foot or by car. The pump house is particularly worth seeing. It was built as a copy of the late Archaic Athenian treasury at Delphi, but without the sculptural decoration of that building. It is situated below the wall far down in the valley with paths running down to it through pretty gardens.

Varnava. North-east of Varnava there is a Classical tower worth visiting near a chapel of Ay. Paraskevi with a gushing spring (Plate 60).

At the south-east entrance to Varnava (from the direction of Grammatiko) follow a road branching right (to the north) 450 m to a cemetery, there turn right into a field way and then turn off after 1.4 km; the chapel is situated *c.* 150 m further on; the spring rises under the choir.

A few steps above the chapel there is a roughly square tower[197] of large blocks, which is still well preserved; only one side is very damaged. Inside the beam holes for the upper storeys can be seen and the former attachment of the wooden door, which was probably heavy, can be made out on the partly overgrown south side.

The tower was already visited at the beginning of the last century by the German historian, C.O. Müller. The east side shows that it is not a watch tower because there are foundations here of neighbouring buildings and the fields to the north have numerous potsherds and roof tile fragments, which date the tower and the buildings round it to the Classical period (the careful masonry also supports this date). It seems to have been an ancient farmhouse with a tower for safety. It is possible that soldiers were quartered here as a watch post on the north boundary of Attica at times of crisis, but unfortunately it cannot be proven.

Aphidnai. West of the Marathon Lake there is a hill on which there was an ancient fortress, called Aphidnai in Antiquity and which belonged to a series of Attic boundary fortresses (from Aigosthena over Oinoe, Panakton, Phyle to Rhamnous; Figure **88**). Its history goes back to pre-Mycenaean times; Theseus is supposed to have hidden the captive Helen here, until she was freed by her brothers the Dioskouroi. In the Mycenaean period Aphidnai was an important site which commanded the neighbourhood and its fertile plain (south of the modern Kapandriti). Even in the fourth century BC there was still an important fortress here, but today almost nothing is left of it (on the south-east side part of a tower). On the summit there is a flat area (with a modern chapel) on the west side of which a few traces of walls are still visible; stone heaps belonging to former house walls, which were built on terraces, can be seen here and there on the slopes. The real charm of the place lies particularly in its rural situation; pretty grass paths run up the cone-shaped mountain between small oaktrees; the almost untouched countryside blooms with a sea of brightly coloured meadow flowers, daffodil and wild orchid, especially in spring. There is also a wonderful view of Parnes, Pentelikon, the Marathon Dam in the valley and the fertile fields around. This idyllic place can be reached from the road from Kapandriti to Varnava, from which field paths lead south to the hill.

3 Rhamnous

Ancient Rhamnous is located in north-east Attica at the end of a dead-end road right on the sea opposite the island of Euboia. Attica is still relatively unspoilt here; the fields are cultivated as vineyards and the countryside is not yet inhabited. The remains of an important Classical sanctuary are set in wonderful surroundings with a fine view to Euboia. In Antiquity a street, bordered by elaborate grave plots, ran south of the sanctuary coming from Athens to the temple and then going on to the settlement, which lay on a hill near the sea fortified with strong walls. The area north of the sanctuary, which has been continually excavated since 1975, is not open to visitors. Meanwhile a good view over the area can be obtained from the temple terrace (Plate 61).

Rhamnous lies some 20 minutes' drive from modern Marathon. Turn off east-wards from the main Athens–Marathon road *c.* I km south of the village (Schinias and Ay. Marina signposted for ferry boats; a small road turns off a little further on the right to Schinias beach) and follow this side road *c.* 8 km. Behind the village of Kato Souli, but before Rhamnous, a small road goes right to Ay. Marina, a harbour from which boats cross to south Euboia (Styra). A little later the road forks; the left fork goes to the Rhamnous excavations. The remains of a round tower lie in the fields on the right (east), which once belonged to a Classical farm, now eradicated by modern houses.

During the course of the intensive excavations of recent years[198] the fenced-off area has been much enlarged (Figure **78**). Turning behind the ticket office straight left (west), the southern street of tombs is a few metres away. First a (partly restored) circular grave can be seen; this is a common building type in Attica; it looks like a tower at first glance. However, the narrow foundations and the small diameter leave its identification as a tomb in no doubt, especially in its connection with a road framed with tombs. Long, high grave terraces (generally reconstructed with blocks found at the site, but sometimes with new blocks) run along the street to the north; the front sides have fine, impressive marble blocks facing the viewer on which Classical grave reliefs stood. Some 50 m south of the temple area west of the street of tombs are the foundations of a large house with numerous rooms grouped round an open courtyard; the entrance lay on the south side, where the masonry mixed with small stone slabs can be clearly seen.

'The houses on the sea belong to men; a short distance from the sea lies the Sanctuary of Nemesis, who is the most inexorable of all the gods with regard to criminals'. Thus Pausanias describes the position of the two excavated areas and adds a story about the arrogance of the Persians at Marathon. Above, at the end of the valley which runs from the sea into the fertile plain (Plate 61), the sanctuary of the vengeful goddess Nemesis is situated on an artificial terrace on a long retaining wall (Figures **78**.1, **79**). Her temple is largely destroyed, partly because the poor quality local marble used erodes easily, and partly because, since Antiquity, there has been man-made destruction, burning the marble in limekilns. Nevertheless, it has been possible to obtain an almost complete picture of the building and its cult image; different scholars have been able to restore the relief decorated base from thousands of marble fragments together with parts of the cult image of the goddess, made by Agorakritos of Paros, a pupil of Pheidias, as well as large parts of the temple up to the roof. The results of this precise work are housed in the storerooms of Rhamnous (not open to the public). On the site of the temple itself the stepped substructure (measurements 21.38 m × 9.95 m) can be seen on the terrace with the foundations for the cella and some column drums (6 by 12 colonnade), which still have their protective covering (mantle; only the columns of the pronaos were finished with fluting). The building was unfinished, since work stopped at the outbreak of the Peloponnesian War (431 BC). Numerous parallels in the plan and in details of the layout and proportions suggest the temple must have been constructed only a little later than that of Poseidon in Sounion, the Hephaisteion in Athens and the Ares Temple in the Agora (the earlier Athena Temple in Pallene), thus in the decade after 440 BC. In the mid-first century AD the cult building of Nemesis was dedicated to Livia,

Figure 78 Rhamnous, sketch plan of the street of tombs, the Nemesis Sanctuary (1) and the fortified town (2) with its harbours (3–4); E: ticket booth at the entrance.

the deified wife of the emperor Augustus, as an inscription on the east archi-trave attests. A temple must have stood here before the Classical period, for older limestone building components were discovered in the foundations of the marble temple; they must have belonged to an Archaic predecessor, which probably fell victim to the Persian sack of 490 BC.

Right next to this High Classical temple, orientated on a slightly different axis, stood a smaller, older building which was probably erected as the first shrine for a statue of Nemesis soon after 480 BC; for this goddess was closely connected to the victory at Marathon as the avenger of the presumptuous Persian invasion. Later the statue of a youth, the figure of a priestess and the statue of Themis, the goddess of law for men and gods, were set up in the small building, of which the exterior walls were of large polygonal blocks and the interior of small stones; the statue of Themis was an early third century BC dedication (now in the National Museum, see p. 127). The building had no columns, but it was closed even on its façade, which could only be entered through a narrow door; it was probably a treasury. In the vestibule there were two thrones (copies today) next to the cella door, dedicated by a certain Sostratos to Themis and Nemesis in the fourth century BC; they prove that both goddesses were worshipped in Rhamnous.

The other areas of the ancient town (Figure **78**) are not accessible to the public because of excavation and restoration work. From the northern end of the temple terrace there is a view of a few white marble socles belonging to large impressive grave monuments on both sides of the road leading down

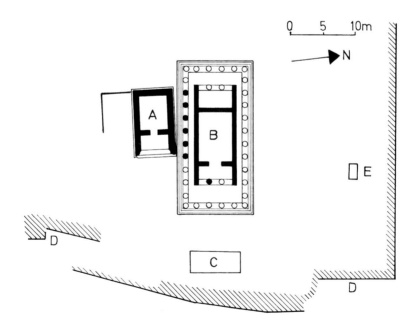

Figure 79 Rhamnous, Sanctuary of Nemesis.

A: treasury; B: Temple of Nemesis; C: altar; D: terrace wall with propylon; E: bothros (votive pit).

to the town.[199] Below on the coast there is an isolated, somewhat steeply rising hill which is surrounded by a massive wall with towers and at least two entrances (Figure **78**.2; Plate 61); on both sides of the hill there are small bays which were used in antiquity as harbours (Figure **78**.3–4). There was a town in this fortress with a military garrison on the 'acropolis'; thus Rhamnous can be considered as the easternmost of the Attic border forts. After the first investigations in the last century, excavations have been carried out here, and also on the slopes of the valley above the street of tombs, since 1975, to investigate the houses, the public buildings (for example, a rectangular theatre with many altars and an oblong large gymnasium area) and the acropolis. The well preserved east gate, in front of which small altars and marble seats with an incised board game were set up, is particularly impressive; next to the gate is a niche in which a relief, lost today, was placed; below it a dedicatory inscription was carved on the wall. The excavated area inside the gate has several houses on a small, winding, stepped street (the walls have been restored to a certain height with Antique stone material), among which is a sanctuary of Aphrodite with walls of very fine marble masonry. There are drains everywhere, lying partly under the street surface and partly running under the houses. In a house near the large (southern) main gate a once restored herm was found; a casting of this is set up again today in its original position. A small Classical sanctuary lies on the slope opposite, outside the south gate of the fortress; it was dedicated to the healing god Amphiaraos. A small shrine stands on a terrace with many gifts to the god in an open courtyard.

An impression of the fortress can also be obtained from a distance, if the visitor follows a path south of the fence around the excavated area, which crosses the valley to the west and runs along that side of the mountain slope; a branch to the right leads to a popular nudist bathing bay with a pebble beach.

4 The Amphiareion of Oropos and Avlona

Before leaving Attica on the way from Athens to Boeotia or Euboia, the visitor should not miss a visit to one of the most beautifully situated sanctuaries in this part of Greece, the Amphiareion of Oropos (Figures **80–81**; Plate 62). It lies in an isolated, thickly wooded valley and has some monuments of both archaeological and technical interest. The visit to this sanctuary can be combined with a trip to Euboia, for which one crosses to Eretria on the ferry boat from Skala Oropou.

Leaving Athens on the National Road in the direction of Lamia/Thessaloniki turn off either at Kapandriti to Kalamos and go from there to Markopoulo Oropou, or take the road to Skala Oropou one exit later on the National Road, from which a side road at Markopoulo leads south to the signposted Amphiareion. It is about one hour's drive from Athens. A visit to Rhamnous and the Amphiareion on the same day is only possible if made very hurriedly and with a very early start from

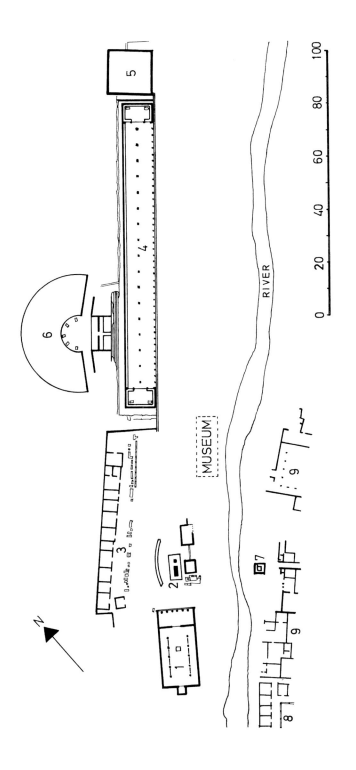

Figure 80 Amphiareion (Oropos).
1: temple; 2: altar; 3: agora with statue bases; 4: stoa; 5: bath; 6: theatre; 7: klepsydra; 8–9: dwelling houses.

Athens, because of the unfavourable road connections (a little south of Rhamnous a new asphalt road leads to Grammatiko; from there Varnava, Kapandriti and the National Road can be reached).

In **Markopoulo Oropou** the small church of Zoodochos Pigi is worth visiting; it lies on the mountain side and its dome, which is almost 10 m high, can be seen from far off. The high rising octagonal drum sits on four slim columns set far apart so that the inner room is very light. The disunity of the building is noticeable on its exterior, into which some spolia (ancient and Frankish) have been built; however, in comparison to other contemporary churches of the Turkish period, the detail is very carefully executed. Frescoes were painted on the interior on the upper walls above a whitewashed socle in the late eighteenth century.

Ancient **Oropos** lay on the site of the modern town of that name (Skala Oropou), as a few settlement remains – most important a Geometric settlement[200] – which have mostly been revealed in the course of modern construction work, and ancient cemeteries bear witness.[201] An oracle and a healing shrine dedicated to Amphiaraos belong to this site. Amphiaraos, according to myth, was one of the Seven against Thebes; during the general flight at the end of this war he and his chariot were engulfed by a split in the earth, which Zeus had opened with his thunderbolt. Amphiaraos is said to have reappeared at a spring, actually at the site where his sanctuary is, and he was worshipped here from the late fifth century BC (when the Asklepios Sanctuary was also founded in Athens) as a divinity connected to the earth (= chthonic) and as an interpreter of dreams; during this the healing sleep, which was part of the cure in the Amphiareion, seems to have played an important role. The site of the oracle (Plate 62), the attached site and the whole district called Oropos, which is clearly separated from Attica by mountains, was a continual source of strife between Athens and Boeotia, because of its position on the Attic–Boeotian border. After the Battle of Chaeronea (338 BC) the area came under Attic rule; later it seems to have attained a certain independence.

The high point of the sanctuary falls in the Late Classical and the Hellenistic periods (fourth–first century BC); most of the numerous statue dedications from kings and Roman generals belong to the latter period.

One enters the wooded valley from the south-west and goes down to the stream bed (Figure **80**; Plate 62). On the right below the path the large temple of Amphiaraos can soon be seen; it was built in the fourth century BC on a high banked-up terrace (Figure **80**.1). Its oblong cella was divided by two rows of columns into three aisles, in the central one of which the base of the cult image and also an arm belonging to the huge statue of the healing god can be seen. Whether columns stood in front of the cella façade is not entirely certain, but, in contrast, it is clear that the temple had no peristasis (colonnade). An unusual feature is a room built onto the back side, which was connected to the interior of the temple by a door; it must have been an adyton (the unenterable) related to the chthonic character of the cult. In front of the temple the large foundation of an altar can be seen (Figure **80**.2), where, according to Pausanias,

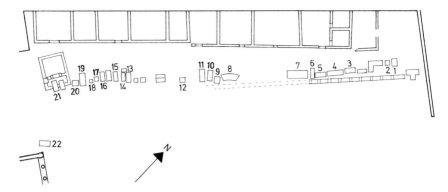

Figure 81 Amphiareion, agora with statue bases.

1: Philonautes; 2: Boidion, daughter of Philonautes; 3: Ptoion and his wife Aristonike; 4: the priest Theodoros and his son Theodoros (late third century BC); 5: the priest Diodoros and his wife Phanostrate (late 3rd century BC); 6: Appius Claudius Pulcher (54 BC, s. Eleusis; pedestal: late 3rd century BC); 7: Queen Arsinoe, wife of Ptolemaios IV. Philopator (late 3rd century BC); 8: Diomedes (*c.* 275 BC) and the priest Timarchos (*c.* 150 BC); 9: Paulla Popillia, wife of Gn. Calpurnius Piso; 10: Gn. Calpurnius Piso (100–50 BC); 11: Brutus, the murderer of Caesar (*c.* 43 BC); 12: the poet Heraklitos (*c.* 30 BC); 13: the general C. Scribonius Curion (*c.* 80 BC); 14: a man from the island of Andros (*c.* 300 BC); 15: ? (early 3rd century BC); 16: M. Vipsanius Agrippa, general and son-in-law of Augustus (27–12 BC); 17: Adeia, sister-in-law of King Lysimachos (306–281 BC), 18: ?, the sculptor was a certain Sosis (*c.* 250 BC); 19: Gn. Cornelius Lentulus (*c.* 70 BC); 20: Megakleides of Oropos (300–250 BC);
21: P. Servilius Isauricus (74–44 BC), 22: Sulla and his wife Metella (88–86 BC).

sacrifices were made not only to Amphiaraos but also to some other gods: Zeus, Herakles, Apollo, Hestia, Aphrodite, Athens and Hygieia, as well as Pan and the Nymphs and other divinities. The ceremonies could be watched by ancient visitors to the sanctuary from some slightly curved steps on the north side, described in an inscription as 'theatre by the altar'. The sacred spring lay below the altar, that is very close to the stream bed, east of a small bath.

The path to the theatre is lined on the north side by many statue bases behind which groups of rooms framing the area can be made out (Figure **80**.3, **81**). The inscriptions on the pedestals illustrate the interest of the leading men of the Hellenistic period in the oracular site; they include, next to local priests, for example, the following personalities: Adeia, sister-in-law of King Lysimachos of Thracia and Macedonia (306–281 BC; Figure **81**.17) and Ptolemy IV of Egypt (221–204 BC) with his wife Arsinoe (Figure **81**.7) and Roman generals and governors, such as Sulla (Figure **81**.22), C. Scribonius Curio (Figure **81**.13), Gn. Calpurnius Piso (Figure **81**.10), Gn. Cornelius Lentulus (Figure **81**.19), Brutus, the murderer of Caesar (Figure **81**.11) and Marcus Vipsanius Agrippa, the general and son-in-law of Augustus (Figure **81**.16). Many of the bases carried statues of Greeks unknown today, perhaps of more kings; later the pedestals were altered and new inscriptions added naming the Romans mentioned (and perhaps statues were altered too; occasionally, for reasons of cost only the portrait heads may have been changed); in addition it is clear from the different heights of the foundations of the marble bases that some were replaced and displayed anew, while the foundations of earlier statue pedestals sometimes rise above the more recent ones.

Next to these rooms to the north-east and behind a staircase to the theatre a two-aisled stoa extends over more than 100 m (Figure **80**.4); it had Doric columns on the exterior and Ionic on the interior, covered in plaster; surprisingly the two rows of columns do not correspond with each other. This fourth century BC stoa, which was furnished with benches along the back wall, has square rooms on both ends. The athletic contests, which took place regularly in the flat area between the stoa and the stream bed in a stadium (not excavated), could probably be watched from here. Next to the north end of the stoa are baths with several rooms (Figure **80**.5).

Behind the stoa on the natural slope of the valley a small theatre for about 3,000 people was constructed (Figure **80**.6). It is particularly famous because of its well preserved Hellenistic stage building, which can be reconstructed in many of its details. Supporting pillars with half-columns carry a Doric entablature, on which a fragmentary dedicatory inscription stands; pictures could be set up inside the door openings, which are noted in the architrave inscription just mentioned; the slots for hanging them are preserved; they are not present in the middle because there was a door here which connected the stage building and the orchestra. The chorus and the actors originally performed in the circular orchestra. Later performances took place on the first floor of the stage building (skene). For this reason a new stage building was erected above the lower wings, which again had Doric architecture as a background, in this case with at least three doors; it can be dated to the mid-second century BC from an inscription on the architrave (in it the stage building and the doors are mentioned; parts lie on the ground behind the proskenion). The five marble chairs with their beautiful tendril decoration, dedicated in the first century BC by the priest Nikon, were most unsuitable for watching the performances. The simple steps higher up the slope, almost completely lost today, were better seats. Two building phases can also be made out from the few surviving conglomerate blocks of these steps, since the curved foundations of a circular theatre koilon were later worked into the original straight seats (probably arranged in trapezoidal form). It is probable that the theatre with straight rows of seats went with an early wooden form of stage building, which can be understood from stone and post holes right behind the skene wall of poros blocks.[202]

Less magnificent but nevertheless important buildings for a spa have been excavated on the south side of the stream bed, connected in Antiquity by a bridge to the large buildings; they are partly hidden today between scrub and trees; they comprised pilgrim and healing houses for lodging guests, administrative buildings and taverns (Figure **80**.8–9). In contrast, the high-ranking personnel of the sanctuary, the priests, had no quarters in the Amphiareion; according to the sources they lived in Oropos and came in from there.

These building remains include a particularly interesting and well preserved monument: a water clock (klepsydra; Figure **80**.7). A square shaft was filled with water during the course of 12 hours, which then ran out through a hole

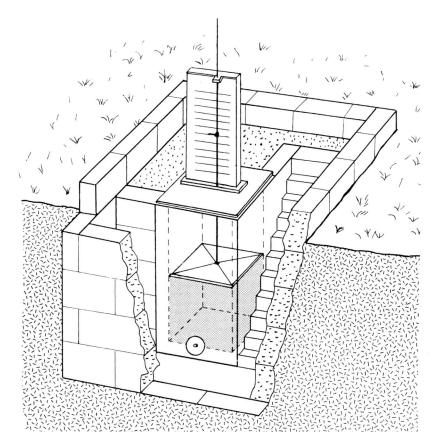

Figure 82 Reconstruction drawing of the klepsydra in the Amphiareion.

during the following 12 hours. A float connected to a dialhand lay on the rising and sinking water surface, which showed the time (hours only) on a board (Figure **82**). The technical problem of such clocks still to be solved, of which a further example has been found in the Athenian Agora, is the regulation of the in and out flow of water, since the Greeks divided the time between sunrise and sunset into similar parts; thus in summer the hour was 75 minutes long during the day and 45 minutes at night; in winter it was reversed. The outflow opening for the release of the water is well preserved on the Amphiareion klepsydra; going down the stairs on the side of the water shaft, one can see a bronze disc with a small central hole let into the block, which allowed the water to flow out to the stream bed opposite an opening; however, no mechanism has been found which controlled the opening or the shutting of the bronze exit hole.

The small **museum** in the sanctuary has long since been emptied and is closed. However, a look under the concrete roof round the building is worthwhile; on the south back side the north-east corner of the temple entablature is displayed; there are painted remains of maeander decoration on the fine plaster of the limestone blocks. There are, in addition, many components of the stoa architecture and three tripod bases, gifts from victors in musical contests. On the other side of the building there are some statue bases and the grave relief of a family, which dates to *c.* AD 120; father and mother stand on each side of their daughter.

From Oropos a narrow road goes south-west to **Avlona**, a small village on the slopes of Parnes on the other side of the National Road. At the north-east entrance to the village there is a villa in a small park, the Zygomala Museum. It contains an interesting folk art collection of textiles and embroidered clothes (for opening hours call 0295–42012 or 41096).

4 Attica III: Pentelikon, Parnes and the Thriasian plain

1 Pentelikon and Dionysos

The marble mountain Penteli or Pentelikon was called Brilessos in Classical antiquity. An Athenian suburb lying further south called 'Vrilissia' has kept this ancient name, which is known from Thucydides. Under the Roman Empire (Pausanias) the name Pentelikon seems to have become usual; it derives from the name for the marble (Pentelic stone) already used in the Classical period.

The mountain lies north-east of Athens and is separated from the range of Mt Parnes by a valley. From Athens it looks like a low cone covered with numerous light patches, which mark the many quarries and marble dumps on its slopes; there is a military radar station on the summit of the 1,109 m-high mountain. One can nevertheless drive by car on a good asphalt road almost to the highest point and enjoy, especially in clear weather, a wonderful view over the sea of houses of Athens to the Saronic Gulf and Aigina and into the Peloponnese; to the east one can look over the plain of the Mesogeia, the other side of Hymettos. A trip to Pentelikon also gives an opportunity to visit ancient and modern marble quarries and the Sanctuary of Dionysos on its north slope.

Drive up: by car from Athens take Penteli Avenue via Chalandri to the village of Penteli or drive to Kephissia on the Kephissias Avenue in order to turn off via Ekali in the direction of Marathon to Dionysos. (Above Ekali the fort of **Kastraki** is located on a steep rocky hill, the slopes of which have been built up in recent years; from the main road to Dionysos turn off east into Ismini Street and follow this to the end in order to go up the mountain to the left. The top of the mountain is enclosed by a rubble wall;[203] in the interior a few remains of houses can be seen and roof tile fragments can be found. This small fortress, which probably dates to the Hellenistic period, guards the pass from the plain of Athens to the north and has visual contact with most other fortresses [Aphidnai, Dekeleia, Katsimidi] and with Athens itself). Continuing on the drive to Dionysos a few kilometres to the east at Ay. Petros a road bends right (south) and runs along the south slope of the mountain to Penteli, Kephissia, and Chalandri. In Penteli turn to Nea Penteli and from there follow a signpost behind a large square to the left to 'Monastiri Ay. Panteleimonas'; an asphalt road goes to the left to the monastery after some curves past a road shrine, while the road to the right goes to the summit with many S-bends. Some 500 m after the fork to the modern Panteleimon Monastery a dirt road branches right, by which, after taking the right-hand road at a further fork 1.5 km further on, the ancient quarries for the Acropolis buildings are reached; these are best arrived at by walking. Another access route to the village of Penteli goes over the Athens–Marathon Road ('Mesogeion') up to the turn-off to Sounion at Stavros (see p. 236); there turn off the wide main road and go beneath it at a traffic light to the left (north) in order to drive up the slopes of Pentelikon to the village (the site of the temple of Athena Pallenis is located nearby). Those who wish to return from Marathon over the mountain to Athens can turn off a few kilometres south of the famous grave mound of the Athenians, still to the north of Nea Makri, to Dionysos and Ekali (to the west).

On the way out of Athens on Kephissias Avenue the green suburb of **Chalandri** lies on the right (east). Here (a little south of the wide Palaiologou Street) behind a large modern church lies the small chapel of **Panagia Marmariotissa** (on the street of the same name, which turns off east from Ethnikis Antistaseos; Figure **83**; Plate 63).[204] It is converted from a Roman marble mausoleum, which is thus well preserved today. Its valuable building material gave the church its name and shows that the grave was built for a rich inhabitant of the ancient deme of Phlya, which was located on this site. Since the mausoleum building is a contemporary copy of another in Kephissia (Plate 64), of which the owner is known to be Herodes Atticus, it is very probable that here also the rich, famous Athenian from Marathon was the builder. If one asks the guard of the modern church, it may be possible to look into the impressive interior of the grave building; the barrel-vault could once be entered from the east, where the church apse is built today; in contrast the west side, which has a door today, was closed in Antiquity. The floor of the mausoleum lies several metres below the earth; its wall socle, which is above earth, rests on a high profile and probably once gave the impression of an altar.

Passing the modern Olympic stadium and through the suburb of Amaroussion, in which many potters from Siphnos offer their wares, **Kephissia** is reached on the wide avenue of the same name. The famous rich Athenian, Herodes Atticus (AD 101–178),[205] had one of his country villas here; portraits of him (Plate 65) and one of his pupils and protegés, Polydeukion (Plate 67), other sculptures, many inscriptions and a bath house have been found in it. Rich people lived in Kephissia in Antiquity, and even today there is a suburb of villas here with many Neoclassical houses in large gardens. The **Roman mausoleum** (Plate 64) dating to the second century AD in the main square of Kephissia (Platia Platanou) can be reached from the terminus of the metro; it is surrounded by a modern protective building with windows and still contains four marble sarcophagi, some of which are piled on top of each other today.

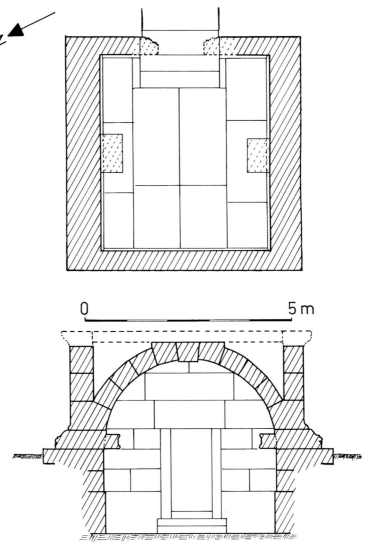

Figure 83 Chalandri, Panagia Marmariotissa: plan and section of the Roman mausoleum.

They have simple reliefs, for example, Erotes, bulls' heads and female figures killing bulls (Nikes), caryatids, scenes from myths and garland decoration; one of the sarcophagi has a relief bust on its narrow side, of which the portrait head is not finished, but roughed out. The lids of the sarcophagi are like house roofs and reflect the idea that the sarcophagus is the house of the dead; later, in contrast, lids were made in the form of a bed (kline), which so to speak served the deceased as a couch at a feast; the grave in Kephissia can be ascribed to the family of Herodes Atticus because an inscription on one of the wall blocks of the entrance, a mourning epigram composed by Herodes himself, testifies to the ownership of the mausoleum. The building itself consisted of an almost square chamber lying below the ancient road level into which a stair descended from the east. Everything was made of marble blocks; the finds of curved stones suggest the small mausoleum must have had a barrel-vault, just as that preserved in the same way in the Marmariotissa in Chalandri (Figure **83**; Plate 63). Parts of the mausoleum were reused in the mosque with a minaret dating to the Turkish period built right next to it (today the ruin is almost unrecognisable as a mosque).

As already mentioned, traces of the country villa of Herodes Atticus have been found in Kephissia, mostly consisting of remains of the baths and some stray finds, such as the portraits mentioned above of himself and one of his pupils (in the National Museum: Plates 65–66; see p. 130). The villa, in which the sophist often retired to relax by studying rhetoric and philosophy, must have been unusually elaborate. He also received guests here with similar interests, such as the Roman author, Aulus Gellius (*c.* AD 145 in Athens to study philosophy), who describes the wealth of the house in his *Attic Nights*.

Kephissia lies *c.* 300 m above sea level on the slopes of **Pentelikon**, which is particularly famous for its **marble quarries**.[206] The Greeks used the fine-grained shining white marble for all their buildings from the late sixth century BC, since its hardness made it particularly well adapted for them, while the softer Greek island marbles (i.e. from Naxos or Paros) were better for sculpture; however, many statues were also worked from this material. For example, the Classical Acropolis buildings with their rich sculptural decoration are of Pentelic marble; it is a stone which gains a fine yellow-brown patina in the course of time from its iron inclusions. The occurrence of high quality marble veins, that is those without impure inclusions, was already almost exhausted in the second century AD, according to ancient sources; Pausanias mentions that after the building of the stadium of Herodes Atticus (AD 140) Pentelikon was almost completely robbed out. This comment is, of course, exaggerated since even today at Dionysos large amounts of marble are quarried daily (quarrying on the Athenian side is now forbidden). However, this material is often streaked with green or grey flaws and therefore of lower quality, as is also the case in works of late Antiquity; in the meantime there are problems in finding completely clean pieces of large size for the restorations on the Acropolis, material which for aesthetic and static reasons cannot contain impurities.

The large ancient quarry called **Spilia**, from whence the marble for the Classical buildings of the Acropolis comes, lies at a height of *c.* 700 m on the south-west side of the mountain (Plate 69). It consists of a hole in the rock of about 50 m length falling vertically on two sides, which terminates in a deep cave opposite the entrance (this cave was further excavated by the military a few years ago). The high marble walls show clear marks of the chiselling by which the blocks of roughly the same height were separated from each other by channels (Figure **84**). Oblong holes were made in the stone on the underside of the blocks running parallel to the veins of the marble into which wedges were pushed. The latter were made either of metal and split off the block,

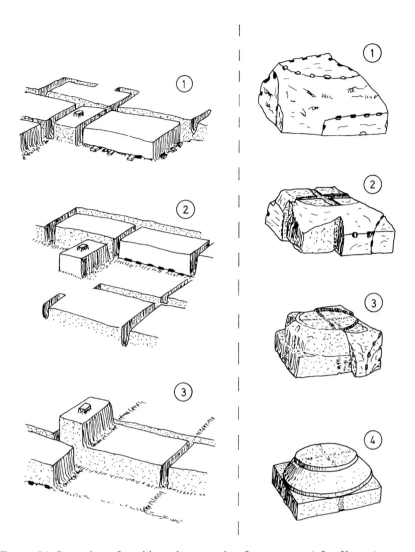

Figure 84 Quarrying of marble and preparation for transport (after Korres).

or of wood, which had been wetted with water to make it swell up, so that the thrust of the stretching wood freed the marble block from the rest of the rock. Lastly the block was worked into almost final form while still in the quarry; only a mantle a few centimetres thick, remained, which would be removed at the final building site or display place (Figure **13**); this system made the pieces as light as possible for transport. On the left next to the cave entrance the oblong holes into which the wedges had to be struck can still be seen a little above the ground at different stages of working. The rock wall allows the lengths and heights of the blocks to be seen clearly, because the tool marks running in different directions are differently structured.

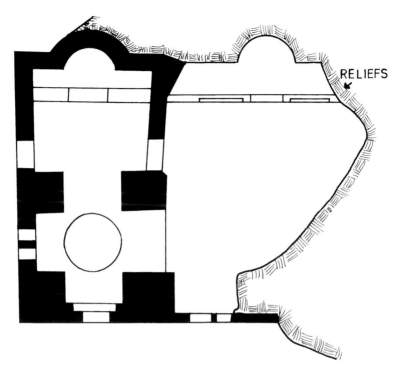

RELIEFS

Figure 85 Pentelikon, Spilia, the chapels at the entrance of the cave.

Some of the crude blocks were damaged in transport or left in the quarry for other reasons, where they have been occasionally found even in this century. However, most of the pieces were transported on sledges. On both sides of the road, which begins in front of the quarry, there were rectangular holes cut into the bedrock; they were for wooden stakes on which ropes were tied and untied in order to reduce the acceleration of the sledge as it slid down the slope with the marble block. Then the blocks were put on wagons and brought to the construction site for their final use and working (the Acropolis for example is 18 km away) or into a workshop. Most of the marble components were pulled up the Acropolis over a ramp on the west side; when the Propylaea was finished cranes had to be used; the girders which supported them were clamped into the rock on the south slope.

There is a small, pretty, double chapel (for Ay. Nikolaos and Ay. Spiridon) in the entrance to the cave in the large quarry (Plate 69), which is built partly into the marble quarry wall and partly in front of it (Figure **85**). It dates to the eleventh or twelfth century and contains the remains of Byzantine frescoes; on the south wall of the cave there are simple reliefs of angels, which have been worked straight onto the marble surface; they can be dated to the Early Byzantine period from their hairstyles, which call to mind late Roman portraits, together with inscriptions cut here; unfortunately it cannot be ascertained whether they are the Christian successors to an ancient shrine. The small dome of the chapel with the remains of frescoes is damaged by cracks, which are due to the sinking of the foundations after excavations by the military.

Although there were no signs of worship of the ancient gods in the cave used by the Christians, a little further up the slope of Pentelikon a small collapsed cave in the shape of a round chamber was found in 1952. Inside pot-sherds and two inscribed votive reliefs were found (today in the National Museum, Room 34–35) which show that the Nymphs and the god Pan were worshipped here from the fifth century BC for over 700 years. Apart from these divinities Athena must also have been worshipped on Pentelikon, since Pausanias mentions a statue on the summit of the mountain; the site of this can perhaps be identified with an artificial platform built south-east below the radar station. Nothing is left of the statue itself, which was probably made of bronze. However, archaeologists and marble workers have found other works of art at different times, which were unfinished and for reasons unknown today were left behind in Antiquity; for example, there are two lion sculptures and, only a little below the summit, a huge seated statue, which was perhaps planned as an image of Dionysos; this god was worshipped at a known cult site on Pentelikon.

The **Sanctuary of Dionysos** lies on the north side of the mountain.[207] It belonged to the ancient deme of Ikarion, as an inscription, which was found in the ruins of the church of Ay. Dionysios in the sanctuary, tells us (Figure **86**). The origins of the cult place go back at least to the sixth century BC, as the marble fragments of a large Archaic seated statue show. They are on show today in the National Museum (see p. 115); Dionysos wears a fine pleated robe and sandals on his feet; in his right hand he holds a large kantharos (drinking cup) like a sceptre, as a sign of his intoxicating powers.[208]

The small sanctuary lies in a grove on a dead-end road which branches off from the Ekali–Marathon connection (signpost); the surrounding wooded valley was particularly charming; most of it was burnt down in 1998.

The little-visited site has some badly preserved, but still interesting, building remains set in a small precinct (Figure **86**). A simple theatre in the south, two temple-like buildings in the north and a stoa and a semicircular monument on the north-east are arranged around an empty level area; all the buildings, except for the monument, which was once used as the apse of the church, are only recognisable from their foundation walls. A retaining wall for the earth fill and seats are preserved from the theatre; in addition there are some marble double seats for the dignitaries. The theatre is not only important for its rare rectangular stage plan (today no longer visible; see, however, p. 180: Trachones), but also for its relatively early date in the sixth century BC, that is at the time of the introduction of the cult of Dionysos to Athens. The inventor of ancient tragedy, Thespis, must have first performed his works here (c. 534 BC), and perhaps even came from Ikarion.

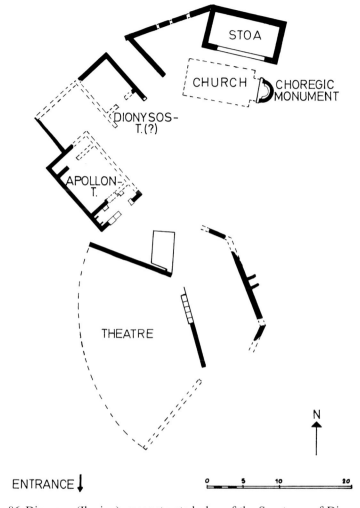

Figure 86 Dionysos (Ikarion), reconstructed plan of the Sanctuary of Dionysos.

Political meetings took place in the theatre as well as dramatic performances. Three victorious financers (choregoi) of such a performance set up the semi-circular monument here in the Hellenistic period and had their names inscribed on the roof beam. They placed their victory prize on the roof of the monument, while a bench on the interior of the niche invited those visiting the site to sit and rest. The separate components of this small choregic monument are almost completely preserved and lie scattered around its site for a future restoration.

Apollo was also worshipped in Ikarion (Dionysos) together with Dionysos; the oblong building on the west beside the theatre belonged to him, as American archaeologists (1888/89) have ascertained from an inscription on the threshold;

votive reliefs[209] were once clamped onto some base blocks in front of the façade; several examples of these have been found. The building lying diagonally behind the Apollo temple is perhaps that of the god of wine; but nothing certain can be said about it, as it has never been excavated. The extensive damage to the buildings, which makes an exact attribution difficult, is largely the result of the reuse of numerous ancient stones for the construction of a Christian church here. Its site can be made out from a collection of worn marble blocks with Christian symbols and ornaments. The small sanctuary of Dionysos was probably the religious and cultural centre of the deme Ikarion. Almost nothing is known of the ancient settlement of the neighbourhood; however, part of it seems to have lain to the south on the other side of the road, where sherds and rock-cuttings have been found. An extensive grave plot with marble decorative sculpture (a marble grave vase on a high column was an obvious monument) could be seen a few decades ago. On the main road from Ekali to Marathon, west of the turn off to Dionysos, some ancient building components can also be found, consisting of monolithic columns right next to the road and larger blocks in the wood west of some ruined barns. However, these observations do not give a uniform picture of the ancient settlement in this area.

In **Stamata** lying further north an Early Christian church was excavated in 1976. Greek archaeologists have investigated several large farmhouses with towers and a small sanctuary in recent years in the hilly country further northwest, in the mountains above the plain of Marathon. The discovery of a Classical goatpen in which architectural furnishings for milking the animals were found is unique.

Continuing a few kilometres further along the winding road the turn-off to Penteli and Athens is reached at Ay. Petros, where there is a simple country taverna; there is a fine view over the plain of Marathon from here.

Penteli village is reached by means of a good asphalt road which runs along the south slope of Pentelikon, from which many paths with picnic places branch off; the village square is surrounded by tavernas. Following the road in the direction of Nea Penteli and Chalandri the Penteli Monastery lies about 1 km to the right. It was founded in 1578, but most of the buildings are more recent. The oldest part, which was partially already standing before the construction of the monastery, is the church, in the narthex of which, paintings dating to 1233 are preserved. The building on the north side of the monastery, the old people's home (Gerokomeion) is particularly worth seeing. Two ancient works of art have been used at the side of the west entrance: a small Kybele relief and an unfinished relief depicting Herakles. In the crypt-like, lower part of the monastery there are small rooms which are said to have been used as a 'secret school' for Greek children during the Turkish period. Here, too, some ancient building elements (a High Classical Ionic column base which bears witness to an Ionic temple here, probably looking like the Ilissos temple [see p. 101], Corinthian capitals) are displayed.

The cemetery chapel of Ay. Nikolaos dating to 1578 (from an inscription in the narthex over the door to the naos) lies outside the monastery walls amidst high cypresses to the south-east on the other side of the road. The main room with a barrel-vaulted roof has double blind arches on its long side. The east side ends in two apses, which cut across each other and belong to two building phases. The chapel was completely restored in 1936. During this work some ancient blocks were built into the courtyard wall in front of the entrance.

An oblong church building with a high dome, called Ay. Trias tou Nerou (of water) after a gushing spring nearby, stands on Penteli Square amidst some tavernas. The original core consists of a squat cross-domed church with a narrow narthex; later a longer exonarthex was added to the original construction, which dates to the fourteenth or fifteenth century. During the construction of the monastery it is suggested that the church must have served as living quarters for the abbot at the beginning of the seventeenth century.

An observatory has been set up on the top of a hill opposite (south of) Penteli Monastery. The hill has been increasingly covered with houses in recent years, some of which have a fine view over the plain.

The charm of the area of Penteli once lay in its dense forests, but in the summers of 1996 and 1998 the forests were almost totally burnt down, and with them the Aleppo pine trees (pefke) which are almost the only examples of their type extant on Pentelikon.

2 Parnes with Phyle and Menidi

West of Pentelikon the extensive mountain range of Parnes (Parnitha) closes the Athenian basin to the north. It is the largest and highest mountain in Attica (1,413 m), with only a few passes leading over it to Boeotia. On the other side of the Aigaleo mountain chain it continues, under the name of Pastra, further on to the range of Mt Kithairon, which it joins; here it forms the boundary of the Thriasian plain with Eleusis on the coast. Its particular charm lies in its wooded hills and valleys, which are a favourite trip for Athenians in summer because of the cool air and in winter for winter sports. On the south slope a cable car runs up from the foot of the mountain to a large hotel with a casino. In addition an asphalt road winds up with many curves to a height of *c.* 1,000 m and then runs in a huge loop round the entire summit; it offers many beautiful views: southwards into the Attic plain, northwards into the Boeotian basin and westwards to the high plains of Skourta.

Ascent: leave the city centre to the north on Liossion Street in the direction of Acharnes and follow the well-signposted 'Parnitha'. Or go along the National Road in the direction of Lamia and turn off at the exit 'Acharnes' for the drive to Parnes. The road to Phyle ('Phili') also runs via Liossion Street to Ano Liossia, where one turns off for Phyle, crosses the village and finally drives up the mountain on a good asphalt road with many curves to a fork where the way goes left to the Monastery of Panagia ton Kliston (Virgin Mary in the Valley). The road continues left up the mountain (a good view of Eleusis and Salamis) to another turn-off (after *c.* 7 km), at which one continues another few metres straight on. The next field path to the left (orientation point: high tension line) leads to the ancient fortress of Phyle after a ten minute walk.

The drive up to Parnes passes through the suburbs of Acharnes and Menidi. Ancient **Acharnai** was the most highly populated deme in Attica in the Classical period; Thucydides mentions that it supplied a large number of heavy infantry. According to Aristophanes in *Acharnians* (*c.* 425 BC) many inhabitants worked as coal burners on Parnes. In the settlement, the centre of which lay on a hill west of **Menidi**, there was a series of important cults, including the famous one to the god of war, Ares, and Athena Areia (the High Classical temple of Ares, which was removed to the Agora and which archaeologists originally thought once stood here, actually came, as we now know, from Pallene).

In addition to the settlement remains on the hill just mentioned there is a Mycenaean tholos tomb in Menidi, the so-called Tumulus of Acharnai (*c.* 1300 BC), which is of interest. It lies on the road from Menidi to Acharnes (signpost: Tholos Tomb of Menidi) and was investigated by German archaeologists in 1879. A 26.52 m-long passage (dromos) runs to the door of the tomb, which is prevented from collapsing by four wide cross slabs set above it with hollow spaces between. It is one of the largest tholos tombs in Attica (see Thorikos, p. 216; Plate 50) with a diameter of over 8 m; the height of the banked-up earth tumulus is over 10 m. It is interesting that in front of the entrance, high up in the earth fill of the dromos, cult activity took place centuries later; the Mycenaean heroes were still thought of and sacrificed to in historical times.

A little outside Menidi the church of Ay. Ioannis lies to the west. It is the smallest cross-in-square domed church with four columns in Greece with a length of 6.25 m and a width of 4.75 m. The chapel with its round drum dates to the fifteenth or sixteenth century; a wooden narthex was added on later than the main building.

A road goes up the slope of Parnes from Acharnes, which rises gently at first. At its foot there are many tavernas, as on all the mountainsides round Athens, in which lamb, goat and other meat from the grill are offered as specialities. North of the tavernas the road winds up the south slope.

On the highest peak of Parnes, **Karambola**, Greek archaeologists found by chance the remains of a sanctuary, which Pausanias describes as belonging to Zeus Ombrios, the cloud gatherer and rain bringer (compare with Hymettos and Tourkovounia). It is an ancient cult place with pottery dating from the eighth and seventh centuries BC.

A **Cave of Pan**, which can be reached after an energetic scramble, lies to the south-west below the peak.

It can be reached by following the road westwards from the mountain terminus of the cable car and then turning left at a fork with the sign 'Spileo tou Panos 5 km'. From here a wide dirt road with a fine view runs at the same height along the north slope to a barrier (c. 2.5 km), behind which it goes into the valley which lies to the north; a few metres before the barrier a narrow path turns off right into a valley lying to the north, along which (at a fork after 250 m to the right) one goes another 3 km to its deepest part. Here the way crosses a stream (cars must be left here), which must now be followed going along a shady path to the west; a few 100 m further, marked with red dots, the path runs up along the left slope over an outcrop of rock; finally one climbs up the rock which has steps cut into it like a ladder to a small natural terrace in front of the cave entrance. The stream bed can also be reached from the other side, by following the mountain path from the spring at Phyle and keeping right at the turn-offs.

The entrance to the cave is a c. 2 m-wide fissure in the mountainside widening inside to a broad stalactite cave, which gets lower as it gets deeper (torch necessary). Late Mycenaean sherds were found in it; in the fifth century BC the Pan cult was introduced here and continued until Christianity replaced it. The place had a long continuity of cult, the high points of which are shown by fine votive reliefs with representations of Pan and the Nymphs and very many lamps with Christian symbols. The votive reliefs, which are in the National Museum today, were originally set into niches in the rock at the sides of the cave entrance, as is known from many other cult places (see Acropolis north slope, Aphrodite sanctuary at Daphni, etc.); the many lamps, which were needed to light the dark cave, gave it its local name of the 'Lamp Cave'. From the natural terrace in front of the entrance one can see into the gorge of Phychte and hear the water cascading over the smoothly washed rocks, as it flows west to the monastery of Panagia ton Kliston. It enables many deciduous trees to flourish; they are mixed in this area with pines and other conifers.

Although the monastery of Panagia ton Kliston lies not far distant, it can only be reached directly from the Pan Cave by practised mountain walkers. However, there is a good road from the village of Phyle, from which the monastery, which was founded in the fourteenth century, can be visited. Today alterations and new buildings have completely transformed the original core of the building. Its charm comes more from its fine situation 500 m above the sea: below it lies the Phychte gorge, where many images of saints and Christian votives were hung in a low niche on the rocks opposite.

The deme settlement of ancient **Phyle** lies about 7 km further up; its remains are thought to be by the small chapel of Ay. Paraskevi next to a spring (terracing on the slope). A few metres further up the road, which more or less follows the ancient pass (with one turn off at which a small shrine was found), goes over a narrow mountain saddle to the boundary **fortress** dating from the early fourth century BC (Figure **87**). It lies on a hill at a height of 680 m overlooking a deep valley. On the south-west side the rock is so sheer that an artificial

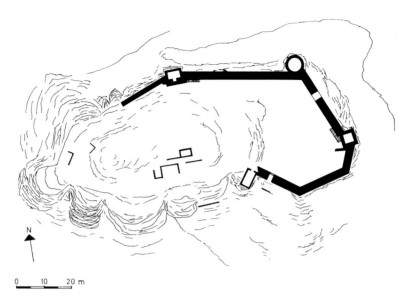

Figure 87 Phyle, fortress.

fortification was not necessary; in contrast, on the other three sides, high impressive walls of ashlar masonry, with two rectangular towers and a round one, protect the fortress. It can be entered by a gate on the east side, while a small postern gate was constructed on the south side descending to the gorge (Plate 70); the door sockets of the latter and the holes for the attachment of the cross beams on the interior can be studied. Steps lead up to the towers of the *c.* 110 m-long and 35 m-wide fortress. At the time of construction in the Classical period there was only little accommodation in the interior; the men would have lived in the towers or in tents or wooden huts. The garrison in the fort – which must have had a predecessor in the late fifth century – had to maintain, guard and keep safe the pass, which went from Athens over Parnes and the Skourta plain to Boeotia.

The fort was one of several posts[210] along the Parnes passes; on the south edge of the Skourta plain the border fort of Panakton lay on a peak 718 m high (south-west above the present village of Prasino) and other forts followed to the west to protect the ancient roads between Attica and Boeotia (Oinoe, Eleutherai, Aigosthenai: see p. 316–19; Figure **88**; Plates 80–83). While Phyle was built at the beginning of the fourth century BC, Panakton already played a role in the negotiations between the Athenians and the Spartans before 421 BC, as Thucydides tells us. In spite of its great age the fort at Panakton is not impressive for its architecture (the fortification wall is of small irregular rubble badly coursed and only preserved to a low height; there are only a few remains preserved of the walls of ashlar blocks in the south and south-west), but rather for its wonderful position above the high plain of Skourta, over which in the

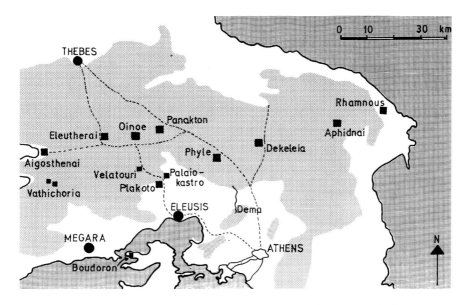

Figure 88 Sketch plan of some Attic fortresses at the border to Boeotia (grey: over 500 m above sea level).

east the peak of Parnes can be seen and in the north Mount Dyrfis beyond Chalkis in the centre of Euboia; wooded valleys lie to the west, and to the south in the distance Eleusis, the bay of Salamis with the ships lying at anchor and the island itself with its stacked mountain ridges can be seen. Recently new excavations were begun here in Panakton, which, from inscriptions found right at the beginning, were able to confirm the fact that the fort belonged to Attica and its identification (long in dispute) as Panakton.[211]

The cemetery chapel of Ay. Paraskevi stands on the north-west edge of the modern village of Panakton. It consists of a small one-aisled chapel dating to the Turkish period with a modern concrete roof. The fine marble iconostasis, which comes from an earlier twelfth century building, is worth seeing; its decoration is similar to the iconostasis in the monastery of Sagmata near Thebes.

The royal palace of **Tatoi**, in which the Greek kings had their summer residence, lies east of the sites described above on the south slope of Parnes (also signposted from Acharnes). The area, which is administered today by an admiral, is closed to the public except for a park. In Antiquity a well-known settlement, the deme **Dekeleia**, lay in its district, to which another border fort belonged; this was built by the Spartans during the Peloponnesian War in 413 BC to cut off the Athenian grain supplies from Euboia.[212] In later times the fort was used to secure the frontier to the north. Finds from the area of Dekeleia were collected in an annex to the palace, which burnt down in 1916. Only a practised eye can see the faintest traces of the fortification wall of the fort. It encircled the hill on which the graves of the Greek royal family are situated today, partly in a mausoleum built like a Byzantine church.

If the visitor follows the road from Tatoi to Malakasa over a pass, a high wooded plain with a modern barracks is reached a few kilometres further on. At the top of the pass a road turns off left (west); at its highest point (after *c.* 200 m) one turns left again onto a small footpath in order to reach the high **Katsimidi** Mountain with its Classical fort.[213] The guard post controlled both the larger camp and the most important pass of Dekeleia into the Oropia. On the peak of Katsimidi there are the remains of a *c.* 800 m-long encircling wall, which went round the narrow almost elliptical plateau; at most places only the foundations of the fortification are preserved, while the stones of the superstructures (seldom hewn into square blocks) lie fallen on the hillside. On the top about in the middle of the whole watch post (next to an antenna station) are the ruins of a Classical tower made of large ashlar blocks. In clear weather there is a wonderful view from the Katsimidi peak, rising to 850 m above sea level, which clarifies the topography of Attica: the pass, which runs north through the high plain, can be clearly seen 200 m below; on a peak in the north-east, called **Beletsi**, there is another outlook enclosed by a rubble wall; in the east the plain round Aphidnai (Kapandriti) can also be seen; in the south behind Dekeleia stretches the plain of Athens bordered by the high ridge of Hymettos, the Saronic Gulf and Aigaleo, while the view to the west offers the green mountain tops of Parnes.

3 Eleusis

The famous Sanctuary of Demeter at Eleusis is one of the most significant sites in the ancient world, important both for its archaeology and for its religious significance. As a result of 100 years of excavation by the Greek Archaeological Society, remains have been found dating from prehistory to late Antiquity; monuments belonging to every period can be seen on the excavation site (Figure **89**). If the bay of Eleusis had not been destroyed by industry with its refineries, shipyards and cement works, the site would have been one of the most beautiful of the Greek sanctuaries. However, if the visitor ignores the unlovely surroundings, the extremely interesting and well preserved remains of one of the most fascinating cult sites of the ancient world are to be seen, as well as a small museum with finds from Eleusis, which is little visited as it lies on the edge of the routes used by the tour groups.

Access: the sanctuary of Eleusis is reached from Athens by the National Road going to Corinth, which goes past Daphni (see p. 147) and north round the bay of Eleusis. The signposted exit goes under the National Road (there is an ancient bridge in front of it) into the town, where a small side street turns left from the main street (sign) to the entrance to the excavation site.

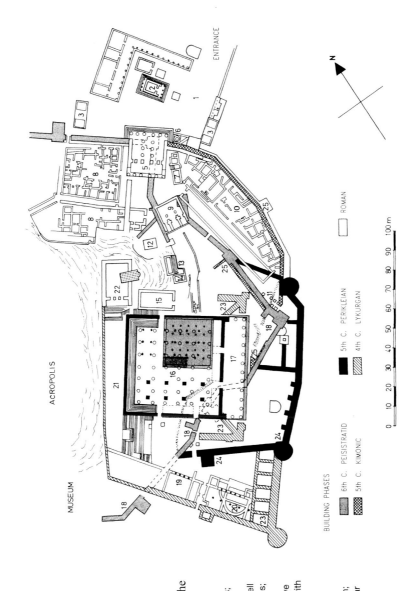

ACROPOLIS

MUSEUM

ENTRANCE

N

ROMAN

BUILDING PHASES

6th C. PEISISTRATID   5th C. PERIKLEIAN

5th C. KIMONIC   4th C. LYKURGAN

| 0 | 10 | 20 | 30 | 40 | 50 | 60 | 70 | 80 | 90 | 100 m |

Figure 89 Eleusis, plan of the Sanctuary of Demeter and Kore.

1: courtyard; 2: Temple of Artemis; 3: triumphal arches; 4: fountain house; 5: Greater Propylaea; 6: well of Kallichoros; 7: cistern; 8: houses; 9: Lesser Propylaea; 10: houses; 11: barn for grain storage; 12: cave (Sanctuary of Pluto); 13: terrace with a rectangular niche; 14: temple; 15: treasury (?); 16: Telesterion; 17: stoa of Philo; 18: Peisistratid wall; 19: portikus; 20: Bouleuterion; 21: terrace; 22: temple; 23: circular tower of the Lykurgan wall; 24: Perikleian fortification; 25: Pre-Persian wall.

The history of the cult of the sanctuary of Eleusis[214] is closely bound to the myth of Demeter. The goddess of agriculture and, therefore, also of fertility, had a daughter by Zeus called Persephone (also Kore = maiden). She was carried off by Hades, the god of the Underworld, who made her his wife. During her despairing search for her daughter Demeter came to King Keleos of Eleusis, who kindly took her in and made her the nurse of his son, Triptolemos. This youth flourished under the care of the goddess and was later commanded by her to bring ears of corn in a winged cart with snakes to the people and to teach them agriculture. His father, Keleos, had to build a sanctuary to Demeter and founded the Mysteries. At the bidding of Zeus, Persephone was finally allowed to live in the world with her mother during growing, ripening and harvest time, while in the time of aridity she had to go down to Hades in the Underworld. The myth of Demeter and Persephone mirrors the nurturing character of nature; the cult and the Mysteries expressed a plea for fertility in every aspect.

The two divinities were worshipped as goddesses of Mysteries twice a year in Athens and in Eleusis: the Lesser Mysteries took place in Athens towards the end of February (Anthesterion) south of the Olympieion on the Ilissos; they probably included cleansing rites and were particularly used for the preliminary selection of people wishing to undergo the initiation (mystai). The Greater Mysteries, which led to the final induction in two steps with a year between them, were the high point of the cult with a large seven-day festival, which took place at the end of September/beginning of October (Boedromion). The central cultic ritual of this festival is not exactly known, because those taking part in the mysteries took an oath of silence, which was indeed kept absolutely. The interpretations of Early Christian authors must be treated as pure speculation, since these were clearly written after the repression of the heathen rites. When it is borne in mind that during the whole of Antiquity, over 1,000 years, very many Greeks from all parts of the land were inducted, including highly educated men, such as Perikles, Aristotle, Plutarch, or the Roman Emperors Hadrian, Antoninus Pius, Marcus Aurelius and Commodus, who were all impressed by the religious fascination of the Mysteries, then it is obvious that the cult had a particular influence on people. Its characterisation as an unimportant or offensive ritual by the Church Fathers is, therefore, not convincing.

The festival, which lasted several days, included rites in different phases. On the first day after the full moon of the month of Boedromion the sacred cult implements were brought by the priestesses in woven baskets, the cistai, to Athens to the Eleusinion in the Agora. Simultaneously the initiates assembled in the Agora and were once more examined and registered for their spiritual qualification; then they had to pay the chief officials, whereby the costs of the sanctuary and the priests and cult helpers were defrayed. On the second festival day a ritual sea bathe took place on the beach at Phaleron. In addition the initiates were sprinkled with pig's blood, and the meat of the animals was finally consumed in a suckling pig feast. The third and fourth days were used for private sacrifices and for spiritual meetings at home. Then there followed the procession from Athens to Eleusis. All the initiates together with the priestesses with the sacred baskets and the cult personnel and numerous accompanying people, escorted by soldiers, under the leadership of the god Dionysos, whose image was carried in front, walked in procession over the Sacred Way to the Sanctuary of Demeter which is *c.* 20 kilometres away. They wore myrtle wreaths and branches with woollen threads tied on. During the procession songs were sung and Dionysos was worshipped with 'Iakche' (Bacchic) cries. The procession went from the Sacred Gate in the Kerameikos over the Aigaleo pass at Daphni, past the Temple of Aphrodite, down to the bay of Eleusis. On the bridges which the procession crossed a particular event took place: men with covered heads called to acquaintances in the procession with obscene remarks and mocked them. This custom, called 'gephyrismos', took place on a small bridge in the area of a lake on the right of the road on the east side of the bay of Salamis and again on a bridge over the Kephissos (it is disputed whether the Athenian river or the river at Eleusis with the same name is meant). Finally the procession reached the Sanctuary of Demeter where the initiation took place on the following day. This act lasted from evening through the whole night in the central cult room, the Telesterion (Figure **89**.16), in the presence of the initiates, who sat on the seats at the side. The ritual, which apparently made a great impression on the initiates in the huge room only lit by torches, was separated into the 'oral', that is a kind of revelation of a secret lesson, the 'act', probably a ritual act by the priests, and the 'vision', the revealing of the sacred cult implements by the Hierophant, the chief priest, who brought them out from the inner sanctum (adyton or anaktoron). Further details of the initiation rites are not known. After the initiation lasting the whole night long, a water sacrifice took place on the following day with special vases, the meaning of which is not clear. Finally the initiates dedicated the clothes they had worn the previous day to both goddesses; this custom suggests that after the religious rites the clothes could not be worn again for secular occasions; they stayed in the sanctuary.

The area of the Eleusinian sanctuary underwent many changes during its long life (building phases of the Telesterion: Figure **90**), which reflect its importance. These have been divided by scholars into eight large periods, as a result of excavations and investigations into the history of the buildings.[215]

a   The hill of Eleusis is situated not far from a coastal bay sheltered by Salamis on the edge of a large plain and, therefore, from prehistoric times was suitable for settlement; sherds bear witness to this early phase of settlement. House remains from the Middle Helladic period have been found on the acropolis and a megaron was built in the Mycenaean period in the area of the later Telesterion (Figure **89**.16), which was probably the palace of the rulers of Eleusis, the Eumolpids; perhaps they had already built a shrine in the area of their houses. It is remarkable that the later adyton (unenterable) of the initiation rooms always remained on the site of the former megaron (dark grey on plan Figure **89**); in addition the Homeric Hymn of Demeter shows that the goddess ordered a sanctuary to be founded exactly on that place, the terrace below the Acropolis, a tradition which suggests there might

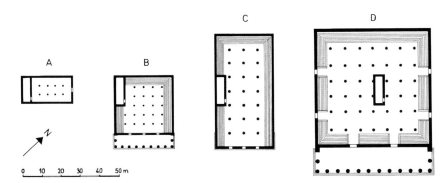

Figure 90 Eleusis, the architectural development of the Telesterion.
A: before 560 BC; B: *c.* 525 BC; C: *c.* 470 BC; D: *c.* 320 BC, stoa *c.* AD 160

be a historical core to the idea that a cult was set up in the palace. The rulers of that time would then have been simultaneously priests of the cult. After the separation of the sacred site from the kingdom the house of the priest was removed.

b In the Geometric period a terrace was put in front of the megaron by the construction of a retaining wall and the small shrine was separated from the town by another wall.

c In the time of Solon in the first half of the sixth century, when Eleusis was finally united with Athens, the extensive refurbishing of the cult area began. A long Telesterion was built 14 × 24 m. The superstructure of mudbricks carried a gabled roof which was decorated with finely painted terracotta tiles. The megaron was now the adyton of the sanctuary, which had rows of seats on the long sides for the initiates to sit. The courtyard east of the assembly rooms was broadened by means of a polygonal terrace wall (dotted on plan Figure **89**).

d Under the rule of the Peisistratids in the second half of the sixth century BC the cult of Demeter spread all over Greece. Corresponding to the growing interest the Telesterion must have been further enlarged to double its original size, so that it then became almost a square with sides over 25 m long (Figure **89**.16, grey area), of which the interior was entered through a vestibule with three doors on the east side; the roof was supported by five rows of five columns each. The foundations were of coarse limestone blocks and the walls of fine poros; on the corners of the roof wonderful marble ram heads (in museum) project over the cornice. The whole sanctuary was protected by strong walls which were fortified with towers (Figure **89**.18).

e Already before the destruction of Eleusis by the Persians, immense restoration and extension works were begun. The Telesterion achieved an oblong plan of 50 m length through the addition of an annex on the west. Then the town walls built of alternating low and high ashlar blocks were widened on the east and renewed in other places with bricks put in front of them (Figure **89**.25). In front of the north entrance the Kallichoron well (Figure **89**.6), where the initiates danced on arrival, received its regular stone enclosure.

f   In the High Classical period under Perikles a new Telesterion was constructed in tune with the importance of Athens (Figure **89**.16, black); Iktinos, the architect of the Parthenon, planned a square building with a side length of 52 m with seats all round the walls. The stoa was surrounded by walls of large rectangular blocks. Its roof was meant to have been supported on a few columns set far apart, but the plan ran into static problems; therefore, finally seven rows, each with six columns, were put up, by which the old adyton remained in the centre with an opening in the roof. The construction is very similar in its plan to a contemporary secular building, the Odeion of Perikles, next to the Theatre of Dionysos in Athens (see p. 53, Figure **6**.31). Other building activities included the widening of the sanctuary by the construction of new walls on the south and east sides (Figure **89**.24). In the north-east corner underground barns with high pillars were constructed (Figure **89**.11), which served for the storage of the corn necessary for the cult. And in the north a large impressive door was built into the city wall with a tower set back on the east side and protruding on the west side (Figure **89**, under 9); this entrance must have been the 'Propylon of Demeter and Kore' mentioned in inscriptions.

g   In the first half of the fourth century BC large extensions to the central stoa were started, as two huge diagonal arrow-shaped foundations at the side of the east vestibule bear witness (Figure **83**.23); however, this project was not carried out. Instead, towards the end of that century the large vestibule (Figure **89**.17) was planned, which had already been decided upon in 352/351 BC and which is connected with the architect Philo (see the Skeuotheke in Piraeus); recent investigations have shown that the building components existing today, which are partly unfinished (bosses on the columns), actually belong to the time of the big building phases in the Antonine period. Besides these, some further buildings were constructed in the sanctuary and outside the walls: a council chamber (Bouleuterion, Figure **89**.20) in front of the south wall and a treasury north of the Telesterion (Figure **89**.15), a small temple (perhaps to Hecate, Figure **89**.14), a rock terrace with steps (Figure **89**.13) and the Sanctuary of Pluto in a niche in the rock (Figure **89**.12); west of the Propylon houses were built for the priests, the officials, heralds and other personnel (Figure **89**.10). The walls were also strengthened and improved (Figure **89**.23) and a separate fort was built on a hill lying further west, on which there was also a Cave of Pan. Outside the sanctuary walls a theatre, a stadium and perhaps a Hippodrome were also built, and, further north, an Asklepieion. The cemeteries of Eleusis, where the dead were buried from the prehistoric to the Roman period, lay to the west below the Hellenistic fortifications.

h   During the period of Roman rule over Greece the Sanctuary of Demeter at Eleusis was at its architectural acme. As a result of Roman interest in the Mysteries there were numerous dedications, which today contribute greatly to the whole appearance of the sanctuary with their fine marble architecture. First the Roman proconsul, Appius Claudius Pulcher, a famous Roman politician and a friend of Cicero, erected a new gate of Pentelic marble (Figure **89**.9) on the site of the old Perikleian propylon; this so-called Lesser Propylaea was begun after 50 BC and finally finished by the son of the proconsul *c.* 30 BC (Plate 71). It consisted first of a large central entrance, beside which, on the interior of the building, two huge female figures with baskets on their heads (caryatids) were set up to support a protruding entablature (one in the museum, the other in Cambridge, UK); in the second century AD the side walls next to the main entrance were broken for two side entrances. In the first century AD several buildings were put up outside the enclosure wall in the south: a large market stoa (agora), a temple of Mithras and some houses. A huge building boom during the reigns of the emperors Hadrian to Marcus Aurelius (*c.* AD 125–180) finally resulted in extensive changes to the entrance area (Plate 72). The Greater Propylaea[216] was built of Pentelic marble (Figure **89**.5); it is an entrance building, which imitates the middle part of the entrance to the Athenian Acropolis in detail, but it is built all on the same level; huge shields with busts of the ruling emperors were added to the pediments above the entrance: on the outside Marcus Aurelius and on the inside probably (today destroyed) Lucius Verus; these suggest that the Propylaea was finished in the years AD 170–180. In front of this building a square was paved with marble slabs on the right and left of which a large triumphal arch (Figure **89**.3) was set up with statues of the emperor's family;[217] the harbour could be reached through the eastern arch by going along the outside of the sanctuary walls, past some small buildings; the western arch gave access to the road to Megara. A large fountain house (Figure **89**.4) by the east arch offered the visitor fresh water and, opposite it on the north-west side of the square surrounded by colonnades, stood a temple to Artemis (Figure **89**.2) and an ash altar.

In the sanctuary itself the Telesterion (Figure **89**.16) was extended again on the west side. A broad terrace was constructed above it (Figure **89**.21), from which some steps led up to the large Temple of New Demeter (Figure **89**.22), which was perhaps dedicated to Sabina, the wife of Hadrian. The final building operations in the sanctuary necessitated extensive working of the outcropping rock. The Bouleuterion (Figure **89**.20) in front of the south wall was renovated and a stoa (Figure **89**.19) was built to the west of it to round off the south side. After this architectural zenith, the sanctuary continued in use into the late fourth century AD; the only real alteration was the construction of a new fortification wall, which was probably put up against the Herulian invasion in the mid-third century AD. Apparently it never had to prove its worth. In 395 AD the sanctuary was plundered by Alaric the Goth and the cult was extinguished.

Round tour (Figure **89** and Plate 72). The entrance to the Sanctuary of Demeter is on the north side across the large paved courtyard (Figure **89**.1), which contains the Temple of Artemis (Figure **89**.2), the triumphal arches on left and right (Figure

89.3) and the fountain house (Figure **89**.4). The Pentelic marble architectural members are mostly lying in front of the foundations of the buildings to which they belonged. The temple and the altars in the square are not well preserved, but, in contrast, the triumphal arches with their many statue bases on which the names of the members of the imperial family are carved, and the Greater Propylaea (Figure **89**.5) can be well reconstructed. The bust of Marcus Aurelius in armour, set in a round shield, must have been impressive, as it looked over the courtyard from the centre of the pediment of the large entrance building. The circular Kallichoron well, which lies on a lower fifth century BC level (Figure **89**.6), can be seen on the left beside the Propylaea; the initiates danced in front of it on their arrival from Athens; the enclosure wall of the well precinct is of polygonal masonry dating to the fifth century, but the rectangular ashlar blocks of the tower beside it are Roman. Passing through the Greater Propylaea with its double row of interior Ionic columns, there is a Roman cistern (Figure **89**.7) on the left below the path, with a stair leading down to it. To the west of the entrance building the remains of priests' houses and dwellings of further cult personnel (Figure **89**.8) are located in an impenetrable area of the site. To the south on the left below the Inner or Lesser Propylaea (Figure **89**.9) a path leads to a long interior courtyard, some dwelling houses (Figure **89**.10) and finally to the barn for storage of grain with its five pillars characteristic of this type of building, which dates to the time of Perikles (Figure **89**.11). The different types of masonry and stones, which enable the separate phases of the enclosure wall and the Telesterion to be differentiated, can be clearly seen from this point, as well as the massive foundations of the stoa of Philo. Returning to the entrance area one goes through the Lesser Propylaea of Appius Claudius Pulcher (Figure **89**.9) on the Sacred Way; its entablature is decorated with relief representations of the typical symbols of the cult of Demeter consisting of round baskets and bundles of ears of corn with bulls' skulls tied with wool and rosettes between them; below these symbols the dedicatory inscription of the Roman proconsul can be read (Plate 71). The cave with the Sanctuary of Pluto (Figure **89**.12) is located on the right above the Lesser Propylaea with a terrace next to it hewn out of the rock into the form of a rectangular niche (Figure **89**.13); the remains of some statue bases stood on the steps. Continuing along the Sacred Way there is a small temple on the west side (Figure **89**.14) and, a little up the slope, the foundations of an oblong building (Figure **89**.15), perhaps a treasury; small copies of figures from the west pediment of the Parthenon were found here. The visitor now enters the large Telesterion (Figures **89**.16; **84**); its present appearance is that of a huge square lying in bright light, but the visitor must imagine it in its original state, which was very dark with a roof supported by countless columns. It probably once had seats all round it, but today only the seats on the rocky west side and those on the north and south sides, which reach as far as the entrances, can be seen. The separate building phases of the initiation hall and of its enlargement are difficult to make out in its present condition. The earliest phase visible, in a deep hole roughly in the middle of the square, consists of a curved wall of large, coarse, irregular stones which belongs to the Geometric megaron complex (eighth century BC); a little further south part of the Solonian wall appears. Next to it, below a fallen slab supported by modern bricks, the fine polygonal masonry of the Peisistratid wall socle (sixth century), which cuts diagonally through the southern corner of the Perikleian Telesterion, can be seen. The two fifth century BC phases are visible on the east side; they consist of pseuo-isodomic masonry (alternately low and high courses of ashlar blocks) and isodomic masonry (short and long blocks in courses of the same height, which are finely dressed with drafted joints; Perikleian). The long stoa (Figure **89**.17) extending in front of the Telesterion dates to the second half of the fourth century BC, at least according to the stratigraphy; its marble columns are fluted on the lower edge only, while the rest of the column is still covered in its protective mantle (bosses); according to recent research these marble components date to the Antonine period. Leaving the central initiation hall on the south side there is a muddled area on the left cut by the remains of the Peisistratid wall (Figure **89**.18), with the Roman portico (Figure **89**.19) beyond it on the south side and the council chamber (Bouleuterion, Figure **89**.20) next to that. The rock, which has numerous steps and niches cut into it, rises up to the west to a long terrace (Figure **89**.21) below the acropolis; this terrace leads to a large temple (Figure **89**.22) lying on a higher level in which the chapel of Panagitsa is situated today. The south end of the terrace leads out of the sanctuary; downhill the fourth century wall with its impressive exterior and a round tower (Figure **89**.23) can be reached; the lower stone courses, covered in scrub, are of rusticated masonry, that is the surface is scarred by vertical chisel marks, which catch the sunlight from the side; above this are tooled blocks where parts of the wall were renovated in the late Antique period. Continuing further round the wall, the Perikleian fortification is reached (Figure **89**.24); its round tower is also well preserved. The ashlar blocks here have coarse protruding bosses. Where the wall curves back towards the entrance Roman cisterns built of bricks can be seen.

Museum. Outside the museum, which is situated above the Telesterion to the south-west, some building components (including capitals from the Lesser Propylaea) and statues, are displayed on the terrace, as well as an Attic marble sarcophagus depicting the myth of Meleager and the boar hunt. A High Classical statue of Demeter (*c.* 420 BC) is on show in the vestibule together with a plaster cast of the famous Great Eleusinian Relief (original in the National Museum; *c.* 440 BC) depicting Demeter with a long sceptre in her left hand standing in front of Triptolemos, to whom she is giving the ears of corn, while Persephone/ Kore stands on his other side holding a torch. The votive relief is not only one of the best known works of Greek art today, but it was also so famous in Antiquity that copies were made of it. Fragments of a large dedicatory relief given by the priest Lakrateides shortly after 100 BC are on the back wall. In the entrance to the room on the right there is a marble piglet; its dedication can be connected with the purification rites of the second day of the festival. In the adjoining room are some dedicatory reliefs, mostly fourth century, as well as the statue of a running girl dating to *c.* 480 BC; in addition parts of the roof decoration of the Peisistratid Telesterion are on show, among which a marble ram head is particularly noticeable (it is similar to the one in Kaisariani monastery which came from the Acropolis). The proto-Attic amphora is also famous; it depicts Odysseus and his comrades blinding Polyphemos and the pursuit of Perseus by the Gorgons (c. 650 BC). In the third room amongst the sculptures (statues of Dionysos, including ones with Archaic mantles) a statuette of Poseidon leaning forward with his elbow supported on his bent knee stands out; it is a copy of a famous fourth century BC work. High shelves on the right display some Roman portrait heads, which indicate the importance of the sanctuary in the Roman period; two portraits of youths wearing myrtle wreaths can be connected to the Eleusinian Mysteries. In the next room are two statues of emperors (Claudius and Nero) in the usual Roman costume, the toga, as well as a statue of Antinoos, the favourite of Hadrian. Two fine models of the sanctuary illustrate the different building phases; the first shows the enclosure wall and the Telesterion in the late sixth century BC during the time of Peisistratos, while the second depicts the appearance of the sanctuary at the end of the second century AD, when it had reached its zenith (Plate 72). The next room contains, in addition to the fragment of the huge caryatid from the Lesser Propylaea, some grave assemblages (including a bronze vessel with partly cremated bones, c. 500 BC) and pottery; a clay kernos is important; it is a ritual vase with many small round declivities into which different gifts to the divinity were put. Hung on the wall are the remains of a stole, one of the few preserved examples of material found in Greece. The last room is used for pottery groups of all periods; they are arranged in the show cases in chronological and topographical order.

Outside the area of the excavations there is very little more to see in the modern town of Eleusis (for example some poor remains of Roman buildings south of the archaeological site); archaeology has suffered greatly at the hands of modern industry; for example, the Hellenistic fortification on the hill to the west, on which there was also a Cave of Pan, was removed in 1953 during demolition for the construction of a cement works. However, the small church of **Ay. Zacharias**, which has numerous ancient architectural remains built into it, still exists on the town square a few steps east of the sanctuary. One of these spolia, which is no longer in place today but on display in the National Museum, comprised the Great Eleusinian Relief. The chapel is located on the site of a Christian basilica which was erected on the Sacred Way in the fifth or early sixth century AD using a lot of ancient material as spolia. It illustrates the survival and the religious conversion of the ancient cult site.

The bridge over the Kephissos (Plate 73) mentioned above on which, perhaps, the rite of gephyrismos took place, that is the mocking of the initiates, is located one kilometre east of the sanctuary next to the overpass above the National Highway. With its four arches of regular large ashlar blocks it is one of the most impressive ancient bridges in Greece. According to a late Roman source Hadrian had it constructed after the Kephissos was flooded and made it difficult for the procession to cross over to Eleusis in AD 124. The previous bridge had been dedicated between 320 and 315 BC by one of the richest Athenians, the politician Xenokles of Sphettos, who was a political friend of Lykourgos.

4 The Thriasian plain

The Thriasian plain, which lies to the north of the bay of Eleusis and Salamis, is surrounded by three mountain ranges: to the east lies Aigaleo, to the north Parnes, and to the west Pateras, a high ridge which makes up the border with the Megarid. The area takes its name from the Attic deme of Thria, which was located here. In Antiquity, as also today, it was connected to Athens by only two passes. The first one, the Sacred Way, crossed Aigaleo at Daphni; the second way led further north through a valley lying between the foothills of Aigaleo and Parnes; its route lies roughly along the present asphalt road from Aspropyrgos to Ano Liossia.

If one takes the National Road to Corinth in order to reach the Thriasian plain and Eleusis, a few metres west of the exit to Aspropyrgos there is a disorderly collection of large ashlar marble blocks north of the road (carried on a flyover). These were, as spolia, once built in a tower (**Aspropyrgos** means 'white tower') which was moved aside during construction works for the National Road; they belonged to a Roman imperial mausoleum. A close look at the marble blocks reveals an inscription on one block and on another a relief depicting a large wreath of leaves with a ribbon fluttering in the wind.

The Thriasian plain is crossed by turning off from the National Road to Aspropyrgos and going towards Ano Liossia. From Antiquity up to this century this fertile area produced cereal crops and olives and was an unspoilt landscape. It was watered by springs, while Eleusis had a pipeline from Parnes. There are traces of settlement round the edges of the plain dating from the Neolithic period onwards. Today it is an abandoned area, much spoilt by small industries and gravel pits.

On the west side of the plain the remains of a fort called **Plakoto** (Figure **88**) are located on a low hill near Magoula, lying west of the road to Kokkini (Plate 74). It consists of an inner Classical enclosure with a round tower, which is preserved to about three metres high, and a stronger, exterior fortification wall, which was probably built later and which has masonry set in careless courses. This small fort[218] guarded the whole plain as far as Aigaleo and protected a road which ran from Eleusis to the north through the valley of Sarandapotamos into Parnes and further north to Boeotia. Opposite it, on a slope to the north-east with a water canal winding round it, a further Classical building called **Palaiokastro** is located; it is called a fort in spite of its curious building plan. It can be visited by turning down right onto a dirt road a few metres north of the entrance to a large cement works, following this to the water canal, and then continuing along the canal round the mountain to a bridge from which the hilltop can be reached. The building has a circular plan with a very large diameter which suggests it was not roofed. The entrance is on the south-west side and beside it a stair goes up the wall. Palaiokastro also offers a good view over the neighbourhood; indeed the view to the west into the Koundoura valley and to the Velatouri tower (see p. 319) is better from here than from Plakoto. Perhaps Palaiokastro acted as a connection between the separate border forts, since the dwellings in the interior of the enclosure were of impermanent material, which would be unlikely if it were a watch post.

On the north-east corner of the Thriasian plain, a little east of another cement works at a railway crossing, a long ancient wall can be seen left and right of the road on the ridge of the hill. It is called the **Dema**,[219] but it is not clear from whence this modern name comes (Figure **88**). The Dema connects Parnes with Aigaleo, covering a distance of over 4 km following the water shed between the Attic and the Thriasian plain (Plate 75). Investigations by British archaeologists have shown that this barrier closing the pass was probably constructed at the end of the fifth century BC. It is composed of many separate sections of walling, the joints of which allow many passages. In it, there were two large, built entrances which also enabled wagons to pass. The separate long sections are built of different wall techniques and have varying widths; sometimes they reach a width of 2.80 m, but at other places they are only 1m thick; in Antiquity their height was probably limited to two metres. This wall was to prevent, or at least make difficult, the entrance of enemies of Athens over the northern pass, because in 431 BC, the first year of the Peloponnesian War, the Spartans marched unhindered into Attica at this point. A small fort with a round watch tower on a hill in the middle also belonged to the whole defensive complex.

Near the road next to and in front of the Dema a house[220] has been excavated which is mistakenly called a priest's house by some scholars, since it has a similar plan to the one by the Apollo sanctuary at Cape Zoster and to the Vari House excavated below the Vari Cave (see pp. 194 and 197), which were also interpreted as buildings for cult personnel. Other more convincing interpretations show they are farm houses. Nothing is now left of this building as it lies beneath a dump.

A few kilometres to the west, between Parnes and a yard for dustbin lorries (signed as 'skoupidotopoi'; from here a field path runs c. 500 m north), on the other side of a newly built trunkroad at the foot of the mountain there are the remains of a second house. Its back wall is cut into the protruding rock of the foothill. Two rooms can be clearly seen; one had a support in the middle and the other a small right-angled niche in the wall in which, perhaps, a small statue was displayed. This house, which extends further to the south and west (a few foundations), is most probably also a farm house. Its position at the foot of Parnes on the edge of the plain supports this interpretation, since in this way valuable fertile land was not built over. A few steps further west a large installation with stone circles of rubble masonry has recently been excavated. This important structure, explained by the excavator as an installation for breeding animals, which may have been connected to the nearby farm house, must await the publication of the finds.

Again a few metres further west below the new trunkroad on the edge of the plain the remains of a **Mycenaean bridge**[221] can be seen; little is left but, nevertheless, the details are impressive. It crosses a stream bed which carries water from a rocky gorge on Parnes down to the plain during rainfall. A few remains of the former road can be made out at the side of the bridge. The bridge is made of massive rough stones which were hewn and aligned so that they once made a firm, pointed corbelled arch.

On the slopes of Parnes a large concrete water canal winds at quite a height, sometimes carried on a high embankment, which brings drinking water to Athens from a fair distance, since the same concrete canal can be seen below Delphi. The canal leaves the mountains towards Panakton, which can be reached from the Thriasian plain (exit Mandra from the National Road) via Kokkini, Stephani and Prasino (see p. 268). In contrast the pass through the Dema wall goes to Ano Liossia and from there either to the north to Phyle (see p. 267) or to the south via Acharnes and Menidi (see p. 266) to Athens.

Plate 46 Cape Sounion, Temple of Poseidon, *c.* 1890.

Plate 47 Cape Sounion, Sanctuary of Poseidon and fortified town.

Plate 48 Agriliza valley, marble quarry for column drums of the Temple of Poseidon at Cape Sounion.

Plate 49 Souriza valley, workshops, ore washeries and cisterns at the Classical silver mines. Photo Loxias

Plate 50 Thorikos, Mycenaean tholos tomb on the east slope of Velatouri Hill.

Photo Loxias

Plate 51 Thorikos, Doric temple, *c.* 1895, now completely excavated.

Photo DAI Athens (Att 11)

Plate 52 Thorikos, theatre, Temple of Dionysos and ore washery.

Plate 53 Porto Raphti, statue of a Roman emperor of the mid-second century AD.

Plate 54 Brauron, overview of the Sanctuary of Artemis from the east.
Photo Loxias

Plate 55 Brauron, Early Christian basilica.
Photo Loxias

Plate 56 Monastery of Daou Pentelis at Raphina, catholikon.

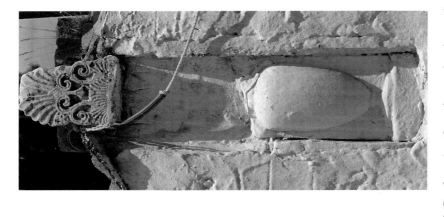

Plate 58 Gerakas, Ay. Georgios, anthemion and grave stele.

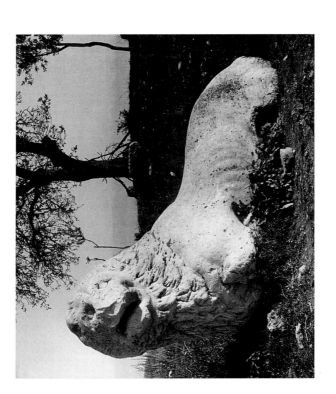

Plate 57 Stavros, the lion of Kantzas, *c.* 1940.

Photo DAI Athens (Att 337)

Plate 59 Marathon – Oinoe, marble courtyard with water works, part of the villa of Herodes Atticus.

Plate 60 Varnava, tower of a farmstead and the church of Ay. Paraskevi.
Photo DAI Athens (Att 302)

Plate 61 Rhamnous, the Sanctuary of Nemesis, the street of tombs and the fortified town.

Photo Loxias

Plate 62 Amphiareion at Oropos: overview from the south.

Photo Loxias

Plate 63 Chalandri, Roman mausoleum, rebuilt as the chapel of Panagia Marmariotissa.

Photo DAI Athens (Att 370)

Plate 64 Kephissia, mausoleum of some of the children of Herodes Atticus.

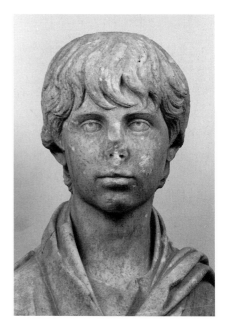

Plate 65 Herodes Atticus, portrait bust from Kephissia (Athens, National Museum).

Plate 66 Polydeukion, foster-child of Herodes Atticus, portrait bust from Kephissia (Athens, National Museum).

Plate 67 Memnon, foster-child of Herodes Atticus, portrait found in a villa of Herodes Atticus in the Peloponnese (Berlin, Altes Museum).

Plate 68 Achilleus, foster-child of Herodes Atticus, portrait of a relief found in a villa of Herodes Atticus in the Peloponnese (Athens, National Museum). Photo DAI Athens (72/442)

Plate 69 Pentelikon, Spilia, marble quarry and chapel.

Plate 70 Phyle: view through the southern gate into the fortress.

Plate 71 Eleusis, frieze of the Lesser Propylaea with the symbols of the cult of Demeter.

Photo DAI Athens (Eleusis 563)

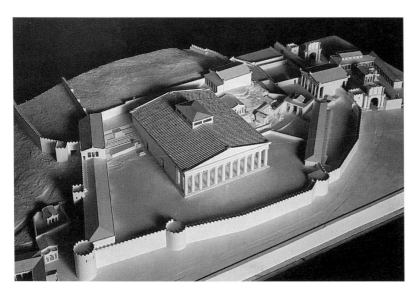

Plate 72 Eleusis, model of the Sanctuary of Demeter, *c.* AD 180.

Photo after postcard

Plate 73 Eleusis, bridge across Kephissos River.

Plate 74 Plakoto: overview of the fortress from the south-east.

Photo Loxias

Plate 75 Thriasian plain, northern part of the Dema wall.

Plate 76 Megara, fountain house of 'Theagenes'.

Plate 77 Megara, Sanctuary of Zeus Aphesios at Marmara, *c.* 1890, now destroyed.

Photo DAI Athens (Megara 1)

Plate 78
Vathichoria, tower
of a Classical
farmstead.

Plate 79
Vathichoria, tower
of a Classical
farmstead, so-called
Pyrgos tou
Germenou.

Plate 80 Porto Germeno, eastern wall of the fortress of Aigosthenai.

Plate 81 Porto Germeno, south-east tower before the earthquake of 1981.

Photo Muthmann

Plate 82 Eleutherai, northern wall of the fortress at the pass across the Kithairon range.

Plate 83 Oinoe, Classical fortress: overview from the west.
Photo Loxias

Plate 84 Monastery of Osios Meletios by Oinoe, catholikon.

Plate 85 Isthmus at Corinth, construction works for the canal in 1890.

Photo DAI Athens (Korinth 14)

Plate 86 Sanctuary of Hera at Perachora: overview from the west.

Plate 87 Classical trireme, reconstruction named 'Olympias' in Piraeus harbour.

Plate 88 Salamis, monastery of Phaneromeni.

Photo DAI Athens (Salamis 9)

Plate 89 Aigina, Kolonna, Sanctuary of Apollon and prehistoric settlement.

Plate 90 Aigina, Temple of Aphaia, *c.* 1900.

Plate 91 Aigina, Mt Oros, festival area of the Sanctuary of Zeus Hellanios from the north-west.

Photo Loxias

Plate 92 Poros, stoa in the Sanctuary of Poseidon on Kalauria.

Photo DAI Athens (Poros 1)

5 The Megarid, the Attic border forts and Perachora

1 Megara

Megara and the land around it, the Megarid, played a special role as a border area between central Greece and the Peloponnese from early on; its key position not only gave the state strength and importance but also meant that it was often fought over, for example in the Classical period, as a buffer state between two leagues. The settlement, which lay on two low hills overlooking a large fertile plain, was already extant in the Bronze Age (Figure **91**), but the city did not become historically important until the Archaic period. As a result of great overpopulation Megara took part in the colonisation of Magna Graecia and the Pontos area and founded, among other sites, Megara Hyblaea in Sicily and Byzantium, later Constantinople. Changing alliances or warlike disagreements with neighbours, such as Athens in the east and first Corinth and then the Peloponnesian alliance in the west, led to considerable loss of power and land (the Peraia fell to Corinth and Salamis was taken by Athens) in the late sixth and fifth centuries BC. In particular the trade embargo by the Delian League in the years around 432 meant that the city was totally isolated. However, in the fourth century BC after the end of the Peloponnesian War Megara blossomed; it is from that time that the saying arose that the Megarians lived as though they would die on the next day, but built as though they would live for ever. Only a few remains are left of what were apparently very beautiful houses at that time. The decline of Megara began during the hostilities between the Diadochs; in 307 BC the city was plundered by Demetrios Poliorketes, after which it played scarcely any further active role in history. In the civil war between Pompey and Caesar the city was on the losing side and had to endure the retaliative measures of Caesar. During the Roman Empire Megara sunk to the level of an unimportant town and in late Antiquity underwent invasions from barbarian hordes. In the following centuries the city became the plaything of the different powers, Catalonian, Venetian, Florentine and Turkish, and attained new importance as the centre of the opposition in the Wars of Independence. Today Megara is a small town, the agrarian centre of the region.

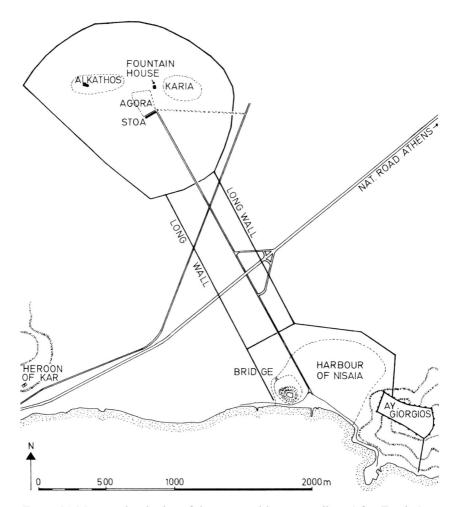

Figure 91 Megara, sketch plan of the town and its surroundings (after Travlos).

Since the modern town covers the area of the ancient settlement, there are only a few traces and archaeological remains belonging to the important Archaic and Classical city of **Megara** preserved (Figure **91**). The ancient city, which was surrounded by walls, lay on two low hills and had, therefore, two acropolises, that of Alkathos in the west and of Karia in the east. Traces of the foundations of an Archaic temple have been found on the top of Alkathos, which was perhaps dedicated to Athena. The small medieval church of Ypapanti containing numerous ancient architectural components and statue bases is located in its neighbourhood. Another temple further down to the east belonged to a sanctuary of Apollo.

Most of the ancient ruins of the town still visible today date to the Classical period. The large **fountain house** is particularly impressive (Figure **92**);

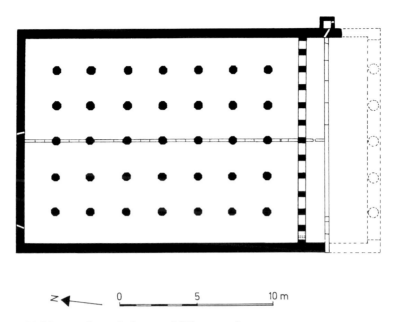

Figure 92 Megara, fountain house of 'Theagenes'.

according to Pausanias it was erected by the Megarian tyrant Theagenes in the
sixth century BC; it stood close to the agora which was framed by colonnades.
The fountain house,[222] which was cleared by German archaeologists in 1898/99
and again in 1957, lies on the main Moraiti Street, at the corner with Krinis.
A large water reservoir is divided into six aisles by five rows of octagonal
columns (Plate 76); slabs have been set into the central row which divide the
length into two halves; the side walls, which are partly set into the surrounding
rock, are composed of well-fitted ashlar blocks, which were once covered with
watertight plaster. The reservoir opened to the south onto a colonnade which
is not preserved; the balustrade slabs which closed it are still extant; beside
them the water flowing out of the overflow holes could be collected in vases
(hydriae) or bailed out. The fountain house was supplied by an aqueduct, which
was partly cut through the underground rock. Contrary to the report of Pausanias
that the fountain house was already extant in the sixth century BC, the preserved
building must date to the fifth century. However, the initiative for a first water
channel may go back to Theagenes; he could perhaps have profited from the
expertise of the famous Megarian engineer, Eupalinos, who constructed a
splendid tunnel to carry a water channel through a mountain on Samos for the
tyrant Polykrates. The fountain house was renovated in the Roman period,
perhaps after the invasion of the Heruli in 267 BC; the interior supports were
shortened by a drum and the roof was repaired.

Remains of houses, which have been excavated in the area of the modern
town, also date to the Classical period; they are not accessible today. They
are noteworthy for their sturdy ashlar walls and, especially, for their sets of

basement rooms, in Antiquity called 'Megara', which are very seldom found in ancient Greek houses; they were probably used here for the storage of grain.

Archaeological Museum: In 2000 a preliminary museum was opened in the nineteenth century town hall (22, Dimarchou G. Menidiati, five minutes' walk to the south-east of the fountain house). There are four rooms on two storeys: downstairs to the right some female statues are exhibited, the missing heads, which once were worked separately (as the arms) and inserted, probably depicted Roman imperial women. Two votive reliefs show heroes as horsemen, another one a reclining hero with a rhyton in his right hand. The mother of the gods, Kybele, is depicted in a shrine sitting on a throne with a tambourine and a lion on her legs. The room to the left of the entrance contains some inscriptions: an honorific decree for two magistrates of Megara, who got gold wreaths by the Orchomenians, a list of names of contributors to the repair of the Apollo temple and some grave stelai. A casualty list of the Peloponnesian War arranged by tribes is most important: since the inscription was found on the ancient agora the small and simple marble slab was (part of ?) a civic monument of Megara (for Athenian monuments of that kind see p. 120; Plates 29–30). Upstairs there is a room with finds from Megarian graves of different periods, and another one with cases with loom weights, terracotta figurines, bronze objects and vases. A fragment of a bowl with a name incised may be the first evidence that, as in Athens, there was in Megara ostracism, the political provision to exile an influential politician for a while to prevent tyranny.

Behind the museum there are some rock-cuttings on the slope of the hill with a small cave. It is presumed that the Demeter sanctuary of Megara was located here.

North of Megara two small Byzantine four-columned cross-in-square domed churches are worth a visit. Ay. Athanasios lies about 2.5 km from the town. Some architectural abnormalities in this church are noteworthy: the entrance has been placed on the central axis with the result that the semi-hexagonal apse does not join the building at a right angle but is diagonal; the door therefore lies in line with the apse. Another irregularity is that the columns on the interior are not equidistant from each other. Where it can be seen, the careless masonry of the Athanasios Church consists of large blocks with courses of bricks added. The church, which is an imitation of a Middle Byzantine church, dates to the end of the Byzantine or the beginning of the Turkish period. The second church, which is about 4 km from Megara, is dedicated to Ay. Nikolaos. The numerous Late Antique or Early Christian spolia in this four-columned cross-domed church are particularly worth looking at (for example, parts of column drums, capitals, the base of a purple-coloured water basin with an inscription). The use of large limestone blocks, especially in the drum, suggests a Late Byzantine date (thirteenth/fourteenth century) for this church.

M egara had two harbours; one gave the city access to the Corinthian Gulf at Pagai, the modern Alepochori (see p. 312); the second was the harbour of **Nisaia** on the Saronic Gulf (Figure **91**), which was connected to Megara from *c.* 460 BC by long walls, just as Athens was with Piraeus. Short parts of these walls have been found deep below the modern ground level south of Megara. The ancient harbour of Nisaia, now silted up, lay between two hills; on the western hill, which was once the small island of Minoa, separated from the mainland, but joined to it by a bridge, the ruins of a medieval fort can be seen from whence there is a good view over Megara with its two acropolises and over the bay of the Saronic Gulf to Salamis; the eastern higher hill with the chapel of Ay. Georgios, which is part of a military zone today, was fortified by means of a simple ancient rubble wall. To the south below this hill lies a small quiet harbour with some fish tavernas.

Not far from Megara, south-west of the town where the old road to Corinth reaches the coast (south of the more recently built National Road), another ancient building[223] worth visiting can be seen above a quarry (one must climb the slope next to the quarry to the east from whence the monument can be reached fairly easily by following the railway line; Figure **91**). It is a large circular building of ashlar masonry, the walls of which were once crowned with a Doric frieze. Next to this building there are remains of walls or rock-cuttings for the foundations of side wings. A grave was found a few metres east cut into the rock, which contained a fine Classical marble sarcophagus closed with a gabled lid; a canal was cut into the protruding rock on the slope above to divert the rain water so that it would not wash into the grave. The interpretation of the, probably Classical, building is controversial; it is probably the **heroon of Kar**, a mythical king of Megara whose name survives in that of the eastern acropolis, Karia, and who is supposed to have been buried on the road to Corinth, as Pausanias records. The marble sarcophagus next to the building cannot be directly connected to the observations of Pausanias, as it belongs to a Late Classical grave, but, together with the figural decoration of the Doric building, it supports its interpretation as a heroon to Kar more than the alternative interpretation that it was a watch tower.

The narrow pass by the sea west of Megara is formed by the so-called **Skironian Rocks**, that is the eastern foothills of Mt Gerania, which are *c.* 500 m high. The myth of Skiron, the road brigand, is supposedly located here; the place is still called Kaki Skala ('evil steps') today. Skiron washed the feet of travellers and while doing so pushed them into the sea, where they were eaten by a huge turtle. Finally the Athenian hero Theseus got rid of the brigand, by giving him the same treatment. Skiron was a monster to the Athenians, but the Megarians revered him as a friendly hero to whom they owed the construction of the cliff road. The old rivalry between Megara and Athens is reflected in this myth. A sanctuary was excavated in **Marmara** above the Skironian Rocks in the last century; it was dedicated to Zeus Aphesios (the Raingiver) according to Pausanias. Apart from some stone blocks and nearby cisterns and terrace walls, there is nothing left from the entire complex today; it consisted of a courtyard with a small temple in antis and a building complex with several dining rooms attached to it; only old photographs from *c.* 1900 remain to give an idea of the sanctuary (Plate 77).

2 Alepochori and Vathichoria in the Megarian hinterland

I f the visitor leaves Megara on the road to the north-west he will reach the road to Alepochori, the ancient harbour of Pagai which lies on the Corinthian Gulf, in an area of rough, almost unspoilt countryside (Figure **93**). Here one can walk along lonely paths through high valleys and round mountain slopes, which often have a marvellous view over the Corinthian Gulf which lies deep below.

Route: from Megara a signposted asphalt road leads to Alepochori (*c.* 15 km). From there one can drive along the coast on narrow roads, which run over a saddle and along the slope at a great height, northwards via Psatha to Porto Germeno (Aigosthenai) or southwards on occasionally poor roads to Perachora. To reach the fine, high plateaux off Vathichoria, which lie east above Psatha, one must turn off the Megara–Alepochori road to Ano Alepochori (signpost) and turn into the eastern entrance to the village on a road with the sign 'Odos Berdas'; 3 km along a crossroads is reached; either one goes on foot straight on over a saddle directly to the plains of Vathichoria (*c.* 1 hour to the ancient round tower) or one drives along the road to the left, which runs some kilometres westwards round Mt Korona, offering a fine view of Psatha and the sea lying *c.* 650 m below, and reaches Vathichoria from the west side. By car it is easier to go from Psatha up the mountain on a new asphalt road to Vathichoria.

A lepochori (Pagai). In contrast to the ancient settlement, the modern fishing and holiday village lies on the sea; Pagai, the old harbour of Megara on the Corinthian Gulf, lay on a small hill a few hundred metres inland. All that is left of the ancient town are the remains of the enclosure wall with its towers. A piece of wall on the east side of the area right next to the modern asphalt road is preserved to quite a height. The almost flat area once occupied by the settlement is covered with fields today; pottery fragments from the fields bear witness to the presence of the ancient town, whose fate was closely bound to that of Megara. However, the harbour still seems to have been important during the Roman period, since there are indications that *c.* 60 BC Pagai even had the status of an independent city. An Archaic sanctuary has recently been found near the sea with thousands of votive terracottas which suggest a cult to Demeter (some of the finds are exhibited in the new museum at Megara). There is no information about the continuation of the settlement during the centuries from post-Antiquity up to the modern age.

The importance of the site in Antiquity was based not only on its harbour, but also on its position at the crossroads of two land routes, that is the road

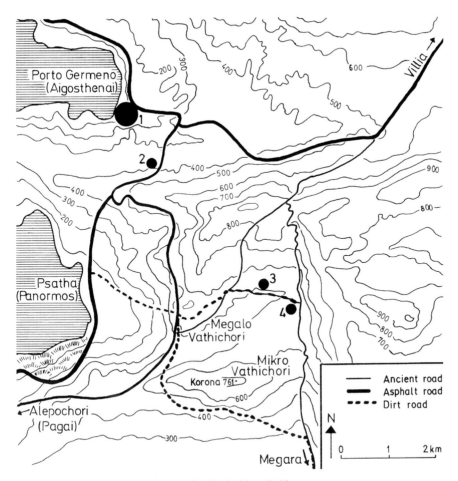

Figure 93 Sketch plan of sites at the Corinthian Gulf.

from Megara north-west over Aigosthenai to west Boeotia and the road from the Peloponnese to the north-east to Thebes. In the last decades the ancient road connections have been more extensively researched. As a result of this roads have been found which have left obvious traces in the country-side.[224]

The plains of **Vathichoria** (Figure **93**) is one such example. In the north below Mt Korona (761 m above sea level) a high plateau is divided in two by a mountain saddle running northwards.[225] The smaller part, to the east (Mikrovathichori) runs towards Megara and opens to the Saronic Gulf; the western part comprises a larger closed area (Megalovathichori) with fertile fields and looks over a flat saddle to the west to the Corinthian Gulf, where the pebble beach of Psatha lies deep below Vathichoria. Numerous terraces on the sides of the gently rising valley as well as the remains of several Classical farms demonstrate that this high plateau was already intensively farmed in

Antiquity. The high-rising monument in Vathichoria dating to this period is a round tower (Figure **93**.3), visible from afar, which was also part of a tower farm, as is shown by a few wall remains belonging to the attached buildings (Plate 78). The tower may also have been used simultaneously as a guard post (Figure **88**). It is still standing about 12 m high with only the uppermost ashlar courses of the superstructure missing; even the drainage of the flat roof is still in place, although the roof itself is not extant. The construction of this round building with its securely dovetailed limestone blocks, which were hewn out of the slope a little to the north, has allowed it to survive all the earthquakes of the last 2,400 years. The tower is used today as a goat pen. South of the modern house, in which the goatherd lives, there is a *c.* 3 m-wide path which runs south-east in the direction of Megara. It is part of an ancient road, lying roughly on the line of the modern asphalt road from Porto Germeno to Psatha, which runs from Aigosthenai over a mountain saddle to the plain of Vathichoria and further on to Megara. In places ancient wheelmarks can be seen. The path passes many field terraces, some ancient grave plots and another tower consisting of a massive rectangular building of ashlar blocks, called Pyrgos tou Germenou, which is located about 15 minutes' walk along the path (Figure **93**.4). Although earthquakes have dislodged some of the upper blocks, the farm tower is still an impressive witness of former life in this area, which is so isolated today (Plate 79). Its construction of carefully coursed ashlar blocks with sharp well-worked edges and the water spout on the former flat roof is impressive. It did not stand alone; there are a few foundations belonging to the attached buildings on its east side and a cistern on its north side. It seems that this tower probably served different purposes; it was both a guard, signalling and watch point on an important crossing between the Megarid and Boeotia and the centre of an agrarian area.

3 The Attic border forts: Aigosthenai, Eleutherai and Oinoe

Attica and the Megarid are cut off from neighbouring Boeotia in the north by high mountain ranges; in Antiquity the mountain ridges could only be crossed via a few passes. Border forts were built at these strategically important points at the end of the fifth and the beginning of the fourth century BC, extending in a long row from the Corinthian Gulf on the west to the Euboean Gulf in the east (Figure **88**); in between lay towers, each in sight of the other, from which news of hostile movements could be passed on by means of beacon fires. Five of the forts can be visited by car from Athens in a comfortable day trip; the tour goes through a changing landscape consisting of mountains, wide high plains and a fine bay with a sand and pebble beach.

Following the route proposed here, it is best to leave Athens on the National Road to Corinth and then turn off west of Eleusis in the direction of Thebes. The road runs across the Thriasian plain over a pass into the Koundoura Valley

(Pateras lies on the west) and from there over a further pass into the plain of Oinoe. In front of the passage between Kithairon and Pastra a road turns off west going past Villia (4 km) to Aigosthenai/Porto Germeno (22 km). Shortly before Porto Germeno an asphalt road turns off left to Psatha (Figure **93**) and from there goes on further to Vathichoria and Alepochori (see pp. 312–13). However, if the Kithairon pass road is followed, then the border fort of Eleutherai, which is best reached from its north side, is about 1 km north of the exit to Villia. A few kilometres south of the pass there is a turn-off to the east in the village of Oinoe (signpost Monastirion Osiou Meletiou) and *c.* 2 km further on along it, but before the turn-off to the monastery, there is a small rural road running south, which goes to the fort of Oinoe (signpost). A few hundred metres further along the asphalt road a road turns off left (3 km) to the monastery of Osios Meletios. The asphalt road climbs up Parnes with many curves and comes out at the village of Panakto in the high plain of Skourta; the fort Panakton is located above the next village of Prasino on a cone-shaped mountain (see p. 268). From Stephani, Eleusis can be reached going southwards via Kokkini; the small fort of Plakoto is then passed on the west edge of the Thriasian plain (see p. 280); alternatively a new asphalt road turns *c.* 1 km north of Stephani eastwards to the border fort of Phyle (see p. 267) and returns to Athens via Ano Liossia.

On the main road from Mandra to Thebes at the small village of **Koundoura**, a wide, isolated valley lies to the west; an asphalt road winds through this mountainous and treeless landscape going past some poorly preserved remains belonging to a Classical settlement and a fort,[226] which is traditionally identified with the site of Ereneia, known from literary sources. The pretty Koimesis Church is located in the village of Palaiochori which lies just west of the main road; it was built in the Turkish period and decorated with wall paintings at the turn of the seventeenth to eighteenth centuries. The whitewashed church belongs to the cross-domed type with a low drum and has a barrel-vaulted narthex added to the side. In the interior the depiction of a stylite (person who lived on top of a column) next to the door stands out among the frescoes. On the hill to the east of the church, ancient wall remains and sherds in the village of Palaiochori bear witness to the presence of an ancient site here, which was settled again in the last century.

Following the main road from Mandra in the direction of Thebes, on the top of the next pass, which has a view over Kithairon and Pateras, an isolated chapel is dedicated to **Ay. Georgios**; it belongs to the village of Oinoe and is a dependency of the monastery of Osios Meletios. It is a cross-in-square domed church with a well proportioned dome, which rests on four arches; the three-sided apse is lit by a double window with two separate arches. There is no fresco decoration, but the walls are simply whitewashed; in some places the careful coursing of the masonry can be seen. The chapel is difficult to date; it could have been built in the twelfth century or in the fifteenth century.

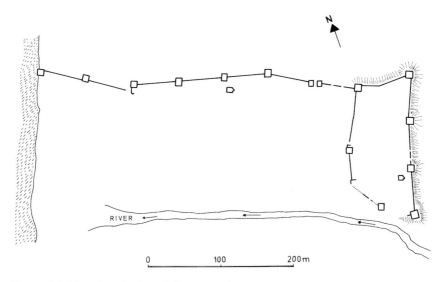

Figure 94 Aigosthenai, plan of fortress and town.

Aigosthenai. Porto Germeno lies in a sheltered bay with some good fish tavernas on the beach (Figure **93**.1) only a few kilometres north of Alepochori and Psatha on the south foothills of the high Mt Kithairon. The pretty bathing bay, which is a quiet village with weekend houses in the autumn, winter and spring months, changes in summer to a busy holiday resort. However, the ancient fourth century BC fort, which is well worth seeing, is rarely visited, although its high-rising walls and towers just above the village dominate the bay (Figure **94**). The narrow east side of the fortification, which was built on a natural rock, is the best preserved (Plate 80); the *c.* 14 m-high south-east tower still stood up to the windows and the edge of its sloping roof until the earthquake of 1981 (Plate 81); today only the upper ashlar blocks are missing. In the twelfth century a Byzantine monastery was built inside the fort; the remains of its cells and chapel are preserved.

A partition wall separates the acropolis from the ancient town, which stretched down to the sea and was also protected by walls. Only the northern city wall with its towers and gates is well preserved and can be followed for its entire length; in contrast the south wall was destroyed by a river course. During Greek excavations carried out in recent decades, and which are still in progress, a Christian basilica dating to the early sixth century was uncovered below the fortification by the north wall; its five-aisled plan can be clearly made out, as also can the few remains of a mosaic floor. A small cross-domed church dedicated to the Panagia was built in its central aisle in the twelfth century; its whitewashed walls can be seen from a distance. Ancient blocks with inscriptions are scattered around or built into the walls of the church.

The ancient history of Aigosthenai is closely connected to that of Megara because of its function as a Megarian border fort. Only once, between 234 and

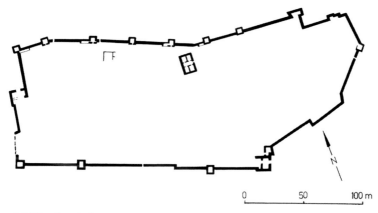

0   50   100 m

Figure 95 Eleutherai, fortress.

197 BC, did this independent town go its own political way, when it joined the Boeotian alliance. Otherwise it acted as a north-west border fort, as an important strongpoint and as a harbour for Megara or Athens. As late as AD 420 a city list names Aigosthenai as an independent town.

Driving from Aigosthenai a few kilometres back in the direction of Villia, an asphalt road soon turns off to the south (right) towards Psatha. A poorly preserved Classical building is located on this road on the right a few hundred metres below the height of the pass; it served as a watch station between the fort, down in the bay, and the area of Psatha (Figure **93**.2), controlling the ancient road which ran from Aigosthenai to the other harbours on the Corinthian Gulf, as well as through Vathichoria to Megara. Remains found by this building suggest it also had an agrarian use. From the top of the pass (*c.* 500 m above sea level) the traveller has a wonderful view over the bay of Porto Germeno with the ancient castle and over the coastal bays of Psatha and Alepochori and further south to Cape Melangavi with the Heraion of Perachora and to the north coast of the Peloponnese.

Eleutherai. Near Oinoe, only a few hundred metres north of the exit to Villia and Porto Germeno, a fourth century BC Classical border fort guards the pass to Thebes (Figure **95**). The identification of this site was disputed until recently, but due to the find of an inscription in Panakton, it is now certain that the site is Eleutherai. The modern name of the site is Gyphtokastro (Gypsy Castle). The fortification wall with seven towers is almost completely preserved on the north side (Plate 82), which is *c.* 300 m long; the stairs to the battlements and the entrance and doors to the towers can be clearly made out in the interior. A narrow postern gate, which strangely never had a lock, gives entry to the fort on the north-west corner. In about the middle of the north wall by the fifth tower the foundations of a building with a central corridor with adjoining rooms are preserved (Plate 82); it is the only building in the interior of the fort, perhaps the headquarters of the garrison; the soldiers stationed here must have been quartered in tents or simple wooden houses.

On the east side of the fort the rock is sheer and the fortification wall has mostly tumbled down below. However, at this point a cistern built below ground can be seen. The entrances to the fort are on the sloping south side and in the west. They consist of small courtyards lying behind the former double doors with more doors at the other end; enemies breaking in could be fought from the walls, both in front of and within this courtyard. On the side of the west door a Greek inscription can be read in favourable raking light, which gives the distance to Plataia.[227] The massive, well coursed ashlar walls of the Classical Greek cities and forts (for example, Sounion, Rhamnous, Phyle, Eleutherai, Aigosthenai) raise questions as to the reasons for the apparently pressing need of safety, which is illustrated by these buildings. The construction of these installations may also have been used to cause fear and arouse admiration. However, in only a very few cases did the elaborate fortifications prevent a town or fort from being captured by the enemy, since most of them were taken by treachery.

To the south below the fort, opposite the exit to Villia the foundations of a temple, some houses and two Early Christian basilicas, which can immediately be seen from the fort, were excavated between 1938 and 1940 by Greek archaeologists. The temple is particularly important for the identification of the site, since Pausanias relates that there was a temple of Dionysos in the plain of Eleutherai in front of the pass to Kithairon, which connects Attica with Boeotia and that the wooden cult image was brought from it to Athens, when the Sanctuary of Dionysos was founded there below the later Theatre of Dionysos. This event took place during the reign of the tyrant Peisistratos, during which the district south of Kithairon passed from Boeotian into Athenian hands. The two three-aisled basilicas indicate that the site was also inhabited in late Antiquity; the fertile plain of Oinoe (= Mazi) provided agrarian support.

Oinoe. A little south of the modern village of Oinoe there are the remains of two walls belonging to a square Classical tower.[228] The slots for joists on the interior and the embrasures of slit windows on different levels demonstrate that it must once have had at least four storeys. This signalling tower must have connected Eleutherai and the neighbouring fort of Oinoe. The Classical fort of Oinoe (Plate 83), which lies east of the modern village of the same name, guarded the wide fertile plain of Mazi; the fort was once also called Myoupolis and is still known by this name today. It lies on a low hill on the north edge of the plain, but only a few remains are preserved; the entire installation was roughly square in plan. A long stretch of ashlar wall made of soft reddish sandstone can be seen on the north side, while on the west façade harder limestone was used. The walls were fortified with towers and at the highest point of the north side a wide door, protected by a tower which is preserved to quite a height, gave entrance to the interior of the fort. Traces of the foundations of the interior buildings and short stretches of the west enclosure wall are still visible; on the south side a few remains of additional buildings are extant, and outside the rectangular fort there were also further remains of settlement, judging from a few traces of foundations.

The fort of Oinoe, together with the forts of Eleutherai, Panakton and Phyle, protected the north side of Attica along the mountain border to Boeotia (Figure **88**).

Velatouri Tower. As has already been mentioned some guard and signalling towers also belonged to the safety system. One of the most strategically important of these towers, the Velatouri Tower,[229] which has a particularly fine and impressive view over the whole Megarid and the Thriasian plain as far as Aigaleo, lies on the peak of the Velatouri (531 m high; Figure **88**) south of the fort of Oinoe, not far distant from the fort of Plakoto (see p. 280).

It is reached from the fort going southwards along a dirt road, which runs across the plain; finally a path (difficult to find) must be followed on foot up the slope to the top of the mountain. The ascent is more difficult on the steep south slope, which is the extension of the Koundoura Valley to the east and which can also be reached from Plakoto turning off before the cement works; however, this route is easier to follow, since the tower is mostly in view.

The round tower is made of large ashlar blocks, which were set up round the peak of the mountain; the blocks were hewn directly from its south side, the working of the slope thus giving rise to a stronger and more secure position. The entrance was not a normal door, but consisted of a shaft which was chiselled in the rock below the east side and led to a stair rising inside the tower. However, today it is closed by a large ashlar block. The view from this tower is particularly impressive: to the north-west the fort of Eleutherai can be seen, to the north that of Oinoe, to the north-east the fort of Panakton sits on its characteristic cone-shaped mountain and to the east is the fort of Phyle; on the south-east lies the Thriasian plain with the Dema wall, which links together Aigaleo and Parnes, and in the south there is a view over the bay of Salamis with its narrow straits at Psyttalia and the mountains of Salamis itself together with the outline of Aigina; finally to the west the mountains of the Megarid and the Koundoura Valley can be seen. This Classical watch tower thus lies in a central position of particular strategic importance for the protection of the border of north-west Attica; the modern traveller can comprehend simultaneously and in an almost unique way the connection between the geographic position of Attica and the Megarid and the protection of their military frontier during the Classical period.

The **Monastery of Osios Meletios** (open: 8–12, 16–sunset). An important Middle Byzantine monastery is located in a fine position on the south slope of the high ridge of Pastra above the plain of Mazi (Oinoe). It is named after its most famous member and reformer. Meletios was born in Cappadocia in 1035; he spent the years between 1053 and 1081 in a monastery near Thebes and then looked for a quieter place to which he could withdraw. He, therefore, chose the monastery of Symboulon lying on the border between Attica and Boeotia; he quickly rose to become the abbot and radically reformed the monastery rules to coincide with his idea of an austere and ascetic life. In so

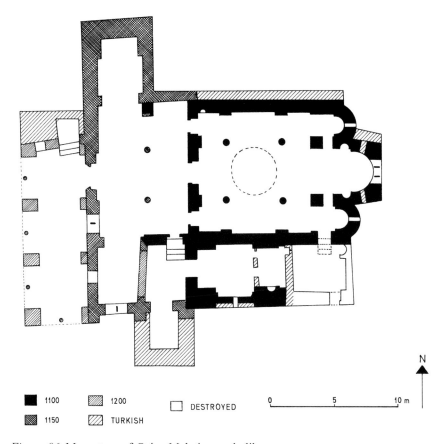

1100   1200   DESTROYED   0   5   10 m

1150   TURKISH

Figure 96 Monastery of Osios Meletios, catholikon.

doing he filled a need of his times and the influx of followers was so great that over twenty additional lodgings had to be found, since only eight to twelve monks had lived there before. The hill on which the monastery was situated was called holy mountain because of its dense settlement at that time. Meletios died in 1105 and was buried in the monastery church. The monastery became known under his name (not to be confused with one of similar name at Mandra near Eleusis) and was of great importance until the seventeenth century. In 1883 it was made a dependency of the Monastery of Phaneromeni on Salamis, whereupon it was neglected and fell into ruin, so that the Metropolitan Bishop of Athens, Chrysostomos, had to have the buildings renovated in 1928 and settle new monks. Since 1950 the buildings house a nunnery.

The site, which is closed on the outside, is entered from the south. The catholikon (Figure **96**), which at first seems a somewhat confusing complex to the visitor, lies in the middle of the courtyard (Plate 84). The central building, which was constructed towards the end of the eleventh century, is a cross-domed church of the four-columned type. Originally it had a narrow narthex, but the west façade of this was torn down as early as the mid-twelfth century. Two columns were erected in its place and the entire vestibule was much widened to the west and on both sides. Thus, an inner double narthex came into being. Although the bones of Meletios were first kept in the crypt under the narthex, they were later put into the north wing. The open outer narthex was first constructed in the post Byzantine period in the form of a stoa with an upper storey over both vestibules. A stair in the tower built onto the side gave entrance to the upper storey; the monastery library was probably stored here. The appearance of the catholikon was further complicated by the addition of a small domed chapel in front of the south side, which is dedicated to the archangels, the taxiarchs. The masonry of the building complex has an unassuming appearance. In the interior of the church the decoration of the lintel, the chancel screen, and the capitals are noteworthy. Although the frescoes of the naos were painted over in the nineteenth century, there are abundant frescoes to be seen in the narthex dating to the transition from the sixteenth to the seventeenth century. The pictorial decoration here follows a typical post-Byzantine scheme; the centre of the vault (the dome in other narthexes) has been kept for the glorification of Christ; on the east wall separate figures appear following their order on the iconostasis (on the right of the central door Christ and John the Baptist, on the left the Virgin and the patron of the church; the four evangelists are on this wall as well). Above the central door appears a bust of Christ with the death of Meletios depicted above that. The remaining themes are arranged horizontally; to the side in the upper zone are the martyrs, below the cornice the glorification of the Virgin, below that separate figures of the saints, martyrs, etc. and finally a decorated frieze.

The catholikon was much damaged in an earthquake in 1981, especially in the inner narthex and outside in the apse. In spite of the supports the danger for this church in its pretty flower-decked courtyard is not over.

Returning to the asphalt road on the edge of the plain of Mazi and following it eastwards, the visitor reaches the high plain of Skourta with the fort of Panakton at Prasino and can continue via Stephani to Phyle (see p. 268).

Although the monuments described in the following sections (4 and 5) already lie outside the Megarid, they are included in this guide, since every modern traveller thinks he has arrived in the Peloponnesian peninsula only after crossing the Isthmus and the Corinth Canal. It must, however, be emphasised that the Isthmus and the countryside lying to the north of it around Perachora, with its famous Sanctuary of Hera, belonged to the political hegemony of Corinth as early as the eighth century BC; both historically and following the modern division of the rural districts one has already left the Megarid a little west of the resort of Kinetta on the Saronic Gulf, after passing the Skironian Rocks.

4   The Isthmus of Corinth and the Diolkos

The ancient Greeks used the term 'isthmus' to describe any narrow strip of land; today the term is mostly used to refer to the six kilometre-wide strip of land connecting central Greece to the Peloponnese. The topography of this place gave rise to the possibility of using fortifications to block access to the Peloponnese; on the other hand attempts have been made since Antiquity to cut a canal through the Isthmus at Corinth and thus shorten by about 100 sea miles the long sea route round Cape Tainaron (called Matapan today), which is also dangerous because of strong winds.

Periander, the tyrant of Corinth at the beginning of the sixth century BC, was the first to have the idea of connecting the Gulf of Corinth to the Saronic Gulf with a canal; but he failed in his purpose; this was also the case with his successors, Demetrios Poliorketes, Caesar and the Roman emperors Caligula, Nero and Hadrian; we know that Nero undertook extensive earth removals with the help of Jewish slaves, traces of which were found when the modern canal was built. Instead of cutting a passage another method of shortening the journey came into use as early as the sixth century BC; a paved road was built across the isthmus on which not only the goods landed from the cargo boats but also small boats themselves could be transported. Wagons with one and a half metre-wide axles, which were probably drawn by animals, were used for this. This towpath, called the **Diolkos**, was often used by entire armies; for example, Thucydides relates that during the Peloponnesian War trireme crews disembarked on one side and, carrying their oars, crossed from one gulf to the other and boarded triremes standing ready on the other side; Philip II of Macedon and Octavian (later the Emperor Augustus) also used the towpath. Some remains of the Diolkos have been excavated by Greek archaeologists; they can be seen on the west end on the south bank right next to the canal.[230] The large limestone blocks of the pavement, in which the wagon wheels have left deep grooves, can be seen for a long stretch, some of them sprayed with water; some of the stones are inscribed with the large Archaic letters of the Corinthian alphabet.

The **canal** through the Isthmus of Corinth, which is one of the best known sights of Greece, was built between 1881 and 1893 by a French and a Greek firm (Plate 85). It is up to 80 m deep, the base is 21 m wide, the water is 8 m deep and at its surface it is 24.5 m wide; the walls consist of limestone and marl. A railway line, a road and now a motorway cross it at a height of *c.* 45 m. In addition there are bridges at both ends since 1988, that is by the eastern harbour of Isthmia and by the western harbour of Poseidonia, which can sink to allow ships to cross. From a business point of view the Corinth Canal has completely lost its importance today, since only ships up to a width of 16.5 m and a depth of 7.3 m can pass through it, on a one-way system. The larger ships are drawn by tugs, but small boats can go through the 5.6 km stretch unassisted. The measurements of ships were often regulated according to the size of the canal; today, in the age of super tankers, only a few ships go through it, mostly cruise ships. They make an impressive picture for the viewer, since they show the true size of the deep cleft.

A few hundred metres south of the old canal bridge next to the National Road the remains of a wide blocking wall are located, which date to the sixth century AD, as the extensive use of spolia (many from the temple of Poseidon at Isthmia) and bricks makes clear. This fortification had many predecessors; a Cyclopean wall was built as early as the late Mycenaean period, at least on the east side of the Isthmus, and before the Persian invasion of 480 BC the Isthmus was also carefully blocked with a wall.

5 Perachora

Afew metres north of the Corinth Canal a road turns off which leads via Loutraki, a favourite bathing and watering place, to the peninsula of Peraia. One can drive to Corinth from Loutraki beach using the bridge at the west end of the canal which sinks into the water. Loutraki itself has numerous hotels, pensions and holiday homes, which offer lodgings for those undergoing the cure of the radioactive sodium chloride springs (beneficial for kidney, gall bladder and rheumatic illnesses). In addition the place is known for its mineral water, which can be bought everywhere in large plastic bottles.

Behind Loutraki the road rises to the north-west and offers a fine view over the gulf to the Peloponnese and to Cape Melangavi with the Heraion of Perachora (Figure **97**). The village of Perachora, which was much damaged in a severe earthquake in 1981, lies 10 km along the road. The road twists from here through olive groves, fields and tracts of woodland and ends at the cape not far from a lighthouse; before this it passes the large Lake Vouliagmeni, which is connected to the sea by means of a modern canal.

The district of Peraia, which is separated from the Megarid by the mountain range of Gerania and which was intensively farmed during the whole of Antiquity, belonged firstly to the hegemony of Megara, until in about the mid-eighth century BC the Corinthians took control of the peninsula and also of the **Sanctuary of Hera**. The buildings of the Heraion,[231] which was to become one of the most important sacred places in Greece from the sixth to the fourth century BC, already lay directly on the sea in a valley which led up from a small bay. A larger plain is separated from this sacred temenos by a ridge running east–west on which the ancient acropolis and the chapel of Ay. Nikolaos are located. This plain was sparsely settled with scattered houses and installations for preserving water for the inhabitants throughout Antiquity; it was bounded from the rest of Peraia by a wall in the east. During Antiquity it was possible for fugitives to seek asylum in a sanctuary; if the priests accepted them as supplicants they were safe from their pursuers and from the law. According to a recent theory the area above the central sanctuary by the temple also belonged to the jurisdiction of the Heraion and thus offered asylum seekers

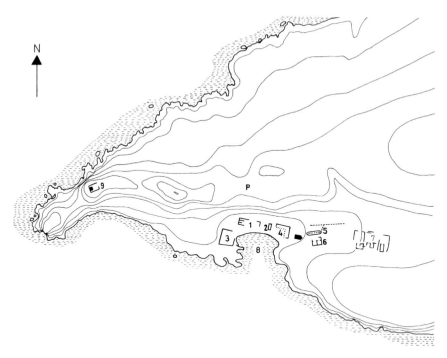

Figure 97 Perachora, Heraion.

1: Temple of Hera; 2: altar; 3: agora; 4: stoa; 5: cistern; 6: dining house; 7: houses; 8: harbour;
9: lighthouse.

shelter and drinking water from underground reservoirs, so that they could live there for an extended period.

The most important of the buildings located here is a Classical **fountain house**; it lies a few metres north of the asphalt road some 400 m from the modern parking area (signpost). The water was collected in three large chambers hewn out of the rock and could be drawn in a vestibule on the west side, which was supported by six Ionic columns. Three draw basins lined with watertight plaster are well preserved; the three chambers can also be clearly recognised, even if today parts of them have fallen in and are filled up. In contrast little is left of the architecture of the fountain house, only a few remains of the limestone columns and the side walls; however, in some places fragments of the stucco, once very fine, can be found, which covered the coarse limestone to give the architecture the appearance of a marble building. A few metres further east the English excavators found a complicated grid of underground passages to which a long stair led down. The galleries cut into the rock were used as cisterns; when they were full the superfluous water ran through a canal into the chambers of the fountain house.

The sacred area (Plate 86) lay east of the lighthouse in a protected bay on the sea (Figure **97**). In spite of the apparently ideal conditions it was still a

dangerous harbour, since there are reefs at the entrance to the bay. The importance of the site lay rather in the great reputation, which the Sanctuary of Hera
Akraia, also called Hera Limenia, enjoyed throughout Greece and in the entire
ancient world. The many votive offerings, which were found during the excavations by British archaeologists, as well as the development of the sanctuary
architecture are evidence of the prosperity which the cult of Hera achieved,
especially from the sixth to the fourth century BC.

In the early eighth century BC there was already a temple in the small bay,
roughly in the area of the later cult building; it was very small having the long
proportions usual at that time and a west wall ending in an apse. In the mid-
seventh century this naos was replaced by a larger rectangular building. At the
same time the area by the temple was terraced and a house was built in the
valley to the east above the bay for use as a dining house. Extensive alterations then took place at the end of the sixth century; the area by the sea was
widened and levelled through the removal of the rock; then a new long temple
was built with a two-columned vestibule, a long cella and a narrow adyton in
the west; its foundations can still be seen clearly today (Figure **97**.1). In front
of the east façade of the temple a strange altar was put up; it consisted of a
low oblong stone construction decorated all round with a metope and triglyph
frieze which lay directly on the ground (a Peloponnesian type); its south side
is missing today since it has fallen into the sea (Figure **97**.2). In the valley
above terraces were also constructed and the dining house was renewed (Figure
97.6). Finally the rock was hewn away south-west of the temple to make an
irregularly cut square, the agora or pompeion, on which the festival processions could assemble during the cult in honour of Hera; it can still be clearly
recognised in its later form (Figure **97**.3).

The Heraion remained in this form until the early fourth century BC, then
the sacred buildings were enlarged. The area in front of the temple was
rearranged, received a supporting wall on the north side and was paved. A
baldachin with Ionic columns was put round the triglyph altar (Figure **97**.2)
and east of this an L-shaped colonnade was put up, slightly off the axis of the
temple and altar so that the rites at the altar could be followed from all parts
of the stoa (Figure **97**.4); this stoa is located directly below the medieval chapel.
At the same time the appearance of the buildings lying in the valley was also
changed; a large outside stair, unfortunately badly preserved, was built on top
of a fill containing the earlier votive offerings; it led up over the different levels
of the area to the dining room (Figure **97**.6). The latter consisted of two, almost
square, rooms with couches in front of the walls and a vestibule; the foundation and the position of the couches can still be seen clearly today. In the area
between this house and the buildings in the bay a large, long oval cistern was
built with a row of supports down the middle, which was fed by a covered
canal (Figure **97**.5); it is one of the best preserved buildings of the Heraion.
A little later in the second half of the fourth century BC, a colonnade was
added to the pompeion south-west of the temple providing a roofed gallery
which made the square appear more impressive (Figure **97**.3). In the following
centuries there was no further extensive building activity in the sanctuary;

occasionally the stucco decoration of the temple and the other buildings was renewed. The Heraion was abandoned as early as the second century BC, probably as a result of the destruction of Corinth by the Roman troops under Mummius (146 BC). The cult of Hera Akraia seems to have been transferred later to the rebuilt Corinth; at any rate Pausanias mentions a temple of Hera Akraia which he saw on his way to the acropolis (Akrocorinth).

The **acropolis** of the Heraion is best climbed from the Classical fountain house, by following a narrow path on the other side of the asphalt road, which twists through the trees from the west. At the foot of the mountain a circular installation was discovered on a small level area a few years ago; its meaning is not yet clear. It consists of a circle of stones 27 m in diameter which once framed a basin lined with watertight plaster. This basin, which was built at the beginning of the fifth century BC, was apparently never roofed; the excavator has suggested it was used for the collection of rainwater. Since there was no channel to supply it, it was either a not very effective cistern or it was a cult place, a sacred pool. This large circular building, which lay above to the east on a small terrace, can be seen clearly from the acropolis. Today the chapel of Ay. Nikolaos stands on this site; the remains of a terrace wall on the north side are ancient. There is a wonderful view from the west peak of the acropolis over the entire sanctuary below in the bay with the cape in the west, as well as over the large plain lying to the north with the fountain house.

6 The islands of the Saronic Gulf: Salamis, Aigina and Poros

1 Salamis

Salamis, which is the largest island in the Saronic Gulf covering an area of 93 km², is visited by only a few tourists. Many visitors are discouraged by its connection with the Attic industrial area of Piraeus-Eleusis manifested in the factories, the harbour installations on the mainland and on the island, and the hulls of old ships in the bay, as well as in the monotonous concrete architecture of the island villages. However, it is still worth a day trip from Athens, for there is charming country and interesting historical monuments on Salamis (Figure **98**).

Route: Salamis can be reached by two ferry connections. The first is from Perama, a western suburb of Piraeus, reached by car by going along the National Road in the direction of Corinth to the first exit behind Daphni (signposted Piraeus); one can also drive along the coast from Piraeus westwards to Perama. A second ferry connection runs from the coast by Megara, from a ferry terminal, also called Perama, to the north side of Salamis near the monastery of Phaneromeni.

Salamis was already settled in the prehistoric period; graves and pottery dating from the Early Helladic to the late Mycenaean periods have been found. In the historical period the island first belonged to the Megarian hegemony. During the time of Solon, Salamis was much fought over by Athens and Megara and was finally attached to Attica by Peisistratos in the second half of the sixth century BC. The island received special status in the Attic state structure; part of the original population was settled in the area of Sounion and given Athenian citizenship, while the island itself was divided between Attic citizens as a cleruchy, that is a piece of land outside Attica obtained by lottery; these citizens continued to remain members of their original home deme. At the same time the main town of the island, of which the original site is uncertain, was probably also settled in the bay of Ambelakia (Figure **98**).

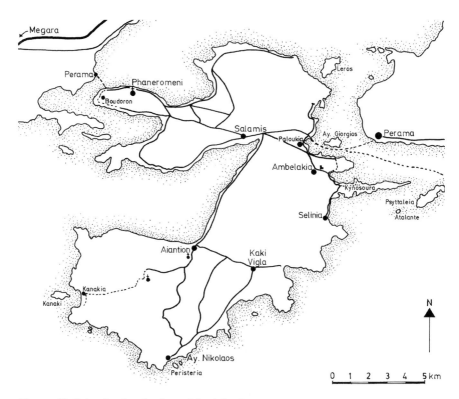

Figure 98 Salamis, sketch plan of the island.

Salamis was famous for the sea battle between the Greeks and the Persians which took place in September 480 BC off the east coast of the island. Ten years after the defeat at Marathon, Xerxes, the Great King of Persia, after careful planning undertook a new attempt to subdue Greece. After the opposition of the Spartans under Leonidas at Thermopylae was overcome by treachery (summer 480), the huge Persian army and navy moved southwards, destroyed Eretria and other sites (e.g. Rhamnous, Sounion) and reached Athens, which was largely abandoned and left to the enemy. Most of the Athenians were evacuated to Salamis and Poros and the men capable of military service served as the crews of the new war fleet; for under the leadership of Themistokles the Greeks had interpreted the Delphic oracle's advice to seek protection in wooden walls as a command to use the newly built wooden trireme fleet to defend Greece. On the day before the battle the Greek triremes lay in the bay of Ambelakia, while the Persians anchored in Phaleron. The Greeks did not want a battle on the open sea. Themistokles must have informed Xerxes by messages about a pretended disagreement among the united Greek rulers and thus enticed the Great King to bring his fleet into the bay between the mainland, the long island of Psyttalia and Salamis. This enabled the Greeks to enter the sea battle under conditions in their favour. They fell on the enemy from both wings with their small, manoeuvrable and swift triremes (Plate 87), thus giving him scarcely any room to manoeuvre his heavy ships, which were far superior in numbers. The battle lasted the whole day; some 200 of the *c.* 600 Persian boats were sunk by the battering rams of the Greek triremes. The remaining enemy ships finally fled to Phaleron and on the next day to the Hellespont. The Greeks were also able to overpower a Persian garrison on Psyttalia towards evening. Xerxes had to watch all this from the throne which, confident of victory, he had installed on the south slope of Aigaleo (between Piraeus and Perama) so he could watch events. A few days later he retired to Asia Minor with his army; only his general Mardonius stayed in Greece until the following year. This last contingent of the Persian army was finally defeated by the Greeks at the Battle of Plataia in 479 BC.

After the Persian Wars only a few historically important events have been recorded for Salamis. During the Peloponnesian War the island was twice a battleground; in 429 BC the Spartans first attacked the Athenian fort of Boudoron on the north-west coast of Salamis in an attempt to capture Piraeus (Figures **88**, **98**). In contrast, two years later the Athenians conquered the Megarian harbour of Nisaia and the fort Minoa from Boudoron (Figure **91**). Finally the Spartan general, Lysander, laid waste the island in 405 BC during the siege of Athens. During the fourth century it remained in Athenian hands. In the Hellenistic period Salamis changed hands several times and was repeatedly the victim of occupation and destruction. The island played no further role in the course of history; only the cult festival of Aianteia continued into the Roman period; it took place in honour of Ajax, the mythical son of the king, who led the Salaminians in the Trojan War and commited suicide in front of Troy.

Very little can be recognised today from the **ancient town** of Salamis. It lay on a hill to the south above the modern harbour of Paloukia in the district of the village Ambelakia (Figure **98**), and is mostly unexcavated. Part of a thick mudbrick wall under a protective roof, which marks the course of the city wall, is clearly recognisable; in addition on the slope of the hill there are some excavated areas containing the foundations of Classical dwelling houses, which have been recently uncovered. Travellers and scholars of the last century still saw traces of walls in the bay of Ambelakia, which reached into the water and belonged to the ancient harbour area. The Sanctuary of Ajax mentioned by Pausanias must have lain near them, while the existence of a Temple of Artemis is known in the town itself from inscriptions. Inscriptions and literary sources also mention an agora, which was framed by stoas, an altar to the twelve gods, a gymnasium, and a cult of Hermes. The theatre in which the epigraphically attested Dionysia took place, is yet to be found.

On the adjoining southern long narrow peninsula of Kynosoura ('dog's tail') a large earth mound with graves and a stone enclosure lies next to a dockyard (signposted as Tymbos from Ambelakia; Figure **98**). It must be the remains of the grave of the Greeks fallen in the Battle of Salamis. The grave mound, called polyandrion, which is as important historically as the monument at Marathon, is unfortunately endangered today through the surrounding industry and by tomb robbery. Nearby a trophy was set up connected to a cult of Zeus, one of two probable victory monuments; according to Plutarch another one was situated on the island of Psyttalia.

The modern harbour of Paloukia shelters the Greek naval headquarters on its north side. Behind (north) and inside this there is a steep rock on the south side of which there is a large terrace wall with polygonal masonry; it probably supported the Sanctuary of Athena Skiras known from literary sources; remains of the temple and the altar are scattered around. There must have been another sanctuary, for Enyalios, a war god, whose identity blends into that of Ares, the god of war.

A wide road runs from Paloukia to the main town of the island, which lies below a steep rock and is called Salamis today, but was once called Koulouri because of the semicircular shape of the surrounding bay. At a main crossroads (Figure **98**) one can exit south in the direction of Aiantion or continue straight along the coast to the small **museum** on the edge of the main town of Salamis, where some Mycenaean finds and some Classical grave reliefs and pottery from Ambelakia are kept. If one turns off at the crossroads just mentioned a charming country road leads via Aiantion to the south and southwest coasts of Salamis. A small church of the **Metamorphosis**, belonging to the cross-domed type and dating to the twelfth/thirteenth century, is located on the south edge of Aiantion between two large cypresses; every year on the fifth of July there is a procession to it. Turning west a few hundred metres further south, one soon passes a cross-domed church dating to the late twelfth century with narthex and side chapel. After about 7 km the road reaches a small pass from which there is a fine view into the bay of Kanakia and to the **Monastery of Ay. Nikolaos**. The monastery was built in the seventeenth century, but fragments of a twelfth century church were used in the construction of the one-aisled catholikon. Decorative slabs from this earlier building have been put next to the entrance; in addition the exterior of the catholikon is decorated with Rhodian plates. A little above the monastery of Ay. Nikolaos lies the church of **Ay. Ioannis**, which dates to the fifteenth century.

The beautiful stretch from Aiantion past Kaki Vigla to the south coast, which runs over a low pass, enables the visitor to forget the industrial area of the island (Figure **98**). Small bays with tiny rocky islands in front of them lie right below the high mountain ridge; the view extends across the Saronic Gulf to Aigina and, on a clear day, to the coast of the Peloponnese. The last bay which can be reached from the coast road, called **Ay. Nikolaos** and lying opposite the islets of Peristeria in which some Athenians have now built their weekend houses, is overlooked by a large **circular Classical building**, which was set up on a hill above the beach and contains numerous graves with stone sarcophagi in its unroofed interior. The enclosure wall, which was only a little higher than it is today, was crowned by a cornice. The circular building is known in folklore as the grave of Ajax. It was thought that the original pre-Athenian settlement of Salamis was located here, since in the nineteenth century numerous ancient wall remains were still visible. Unfortunately, this theory can no longer be tested.

On the mountain slope to the north a large **stalactite cave** has been archaeologically investigated in recent years. It was in use over millennia and also served
in the Classical period as a dwelling. It is thought that the cave can be identified
with the temporary dwelling of Euripides, partly because literary sources say that
the tragedian withdrew to a cave on Salamis and partly because a potsherd was
found here, amongst others, with part of his name, although the sherd dates to
the fourth century BC and the name is wrongly spelt with two 'p's.

The north-west coast of the island can be reached from the main town of
Salamis either along the coast or cross country. The famous convent of
Phaneromeni (Plate 88), which was founded in 1661, is located here near the
Megarian coast (Figure **98**). It is a popular pilgrimage on the church festival
day, 23 August. Ancient blocks built into the walls of the convent show that
Phaneromeni probably stands on the site of an ancient sanctuary (looking from
the church a fine anthemion stele can be seen in the convent courtyard to the
south). The catholikon, a cross-domed church dedicated to the Metamorphosis
(Transfiguration), is decorated on the interior with frescoes by the famous
painter Markos of Argos and his pupils (1735); the same painter also executed
the frescoes in the seventeenth century Panagia tou Katharou in Salamis, which
has an iconostasis worth seeing, and in the Byzantine church of Ay. Ioannis
in Selinia south of Ambelakia.

In the neighbourhood of the convent on the western hill of the peninsula
the Athenians built the Classical fort of **Boudoron** as a defensive position in
the Peloponnesian War. Remains of the enclosure are preserved and also nearby
(*c.* 400 m south of the ferry terminus which crosses to Megara) the ruins of
two ancient towers, which were used to watch the straits; an untrained eye can
see almost nothing in the area today.

2 Aigina

Aigina is the main island in the Saronic Gulf (Figure **99**); as a result of
the good ferry connections it has become a suburb of Athens in recent
years. This island is definitely worth a long day's outing because of its
historically interesting cult monuments and its beautiful landscape; those who
would like more than just a superficial impression should plan to stay at least
one night.

Car ferries and other boats leave several times a day for the island from the
main harbour of Piraeus near the terminus of the metro (*c.* 80 mins to Souvala
on the north coast, 100 mins to the main port); Aigina town can be reached in
35 mins with the Flying Dolphin hydrofoil from the same harbour in Piraeus. Since
the latter is very popular seats should be booked well ahead (in Athens at the
Minoan Lines agency near the ancient stadium or in Piraeus directly on the
harbour, in Aigina immediately on arrival).

Figure 99 Aigina, sketch plan of the island.

Thanks to its central position in the Saronic Gulf, Aigina[232] had a key position as a cargo unloading place and as a trading centre from early on. The island was already settled at the end of the fourth millennium BC and *c.* 2000 BC a fortified harbour was built on the west coast.

According to myth Aiakos, the son of Zeus and the nymph Aigina, ruled here; his sons Telamon and Peleus are known as participants in the voyage of the Argonauts and the hunt of the Kalydonian boar; his grandsons Achilles and Ajax are two of the most famous leaders in the Trojan War.

In the early historical period Aigina rose to become to a leading maritime power; in the eighth century BC the island was a member of the Amphictyonic League of Kalauria (see p. 350) on equal terms with the other members, and by the mid-seventh century BC the Aiginetan silver coin was used as a proto-type in the world of the Greek city-states. In the following centuries the island developed into a major naval power. At the same time it was well known for its bronze alloy and its pottery production. The expansion of Aiginetan trade in the sixth century BC is illustrated by finds from the entire Mediterranean, from Naucratis in the Nile Delta across to Spain. At that time the sculpture workshops on the island were also at their acme.[233] After the victorious sea battle against the Persians at Salamis Aigina finally enjoyed immense respect, since the contingent of Aiginetan ships with their skilled crews had played a decisive role in the Greek success at the battle. However, soon after, a development began which led to the downfall of the flourishing island state. Athens had grown to be an important trade rival by the late sixth century, and now, after building a fleet and setting up a maritime alliance (the Delian League), it was no longer willing to put up with its neighbouring rival. When, as a result of this, the Aiginetans aligned themselves politically with Sparta it came to open warfare, which Athens won. In 456 BC Aigina had to give up its fleet, enter the Delian League and pay a high tribute every year to the treasury of the league. The power of Aigina was finally broken when Perikles compelled the population of the island to leave in 431 BC and settled it with Athenian citizens as colonists (cleruchs). Sparta enabled the few survivors to return after 404 BC, but Aigina was no longer in a position to practise independent politics. In the following centuries the island fell under the leadership of Sparta, Thebes, Macedonia and the Achaean League; from 211 to 133 BC it belonged to the Pergamene empire and enjoyed a time of peace and prosperity. Then the Roman Empire took over. In late Antiquity, Aigina was once again used as a place of retreat from invading barbarian hordes. By the fourth century AD there was a Christian community.

In the centuries after Antiquity the island became a pirates' lair. In changing hands (Catalan, Venetian and Turkish) from 1204 onwards Aigina offered an important place of refuge for Greek rebels and from 1826 to 1828 it was the seat of the first free government under Kapodistrias; for a time King Otto I planned to make his permanent residence here.

The island, which covers *c.* 85 km², is almost completely mountainous (Figure **99**). The highest peak is Oros ('Mountain') at 532 m above sea level. In the north-west, in particular, the land opens out into fertile plains, in which pistachio nuts (which are known throughout Greece as 'Aiginetan' and served with ouzo), almonds and figs are harvested. The main town of the island lies here and most of the island's holiday life, which is an important further source of income for the local population, takes place here. In contrast the south is more isolated and less accessible.

The most important sites worth seeing comprise the Kolonna excavations in the main town, the Aphaia sanctuary above Ay. Marina, the Zeus Hellanios sanctuary on Oros and the medieval town of Palaiochora with its many churches. On a day trip to Aigina it is best to visit the Temple of Apollo on the hill of Kolonna first and then to drive to the Aphaia temple; on the return journey Palaiochora can be visited and finally, if there is still time, the Oros sanctuary in the afternoon. However, this last site can be included in a one-day trip only if the visitor has their own transport (taxi, hired car or scooter).

Aigina Town and the Sanctuary on Kolonna (Figures **100**, **101**). The sites worth visiting in the area of the modern town of Aigina mostly date to the nineteenth and twentieth centuries. On the harbour mole the shining whitewashed double-domed church of Ay. Nikolaos greets arrivals; in the background some Neoclassical façades with cafés in front of them border the harbour side. In the town itself the house of Admiral Kanaris (north-west of the harbour) is worth looking at and the former orphanage (on the south

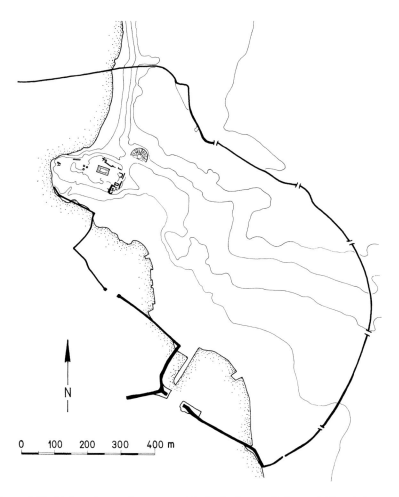

Figure 100 Aigina, the ancient town with its harbours, Kolonna hill and the supposed position of the theatre.

edge), in which a prison was later installed and then an animal shelter; it will shortly be turned into a museum; the cathedral, dating from the War of Independence, is in the centre of the town with the first high school of the free Greek state next to it; the latter was recently used as the island museum and is now going to become a public library. A few metres to the north there is a massive defensive dwelling tower, the Markellos Tower, in which Kapodistrias temporarily had his seat of government.

   Although the coastal stretches lay abandoned in the Middle Ages, the foundations of two basilicas show that the area had an Early Christian settlement; one basilica lay on the site of the modern Panagia Church, the other (Vardia) in the north of the town (straight northwards from the large Church of Ay. Nikolaos). The foundations of an early synagogue have also been found (near the police station); the mosaic floor of this building has been removed to the Kolonna excavation site immediately on the right behind the entrance.

The ancient town lay on a hill north-west of the modern harbour (Figure **100**). The naval harbour lay below this hill, which is called Kolonna after the one remaining upright column of the Temple of Apollo; remnants of moles in the water belong to this harbour; the modern port was used in Antiquity as a commercial harbour, and north of the Kolonna peninsula there was a third harbour with a large mole. The excavations on the hill of Kolonna (Figure **101**), which were carried out by German and Austrian archaeologists at the beginning of the twentieth century and then again in recent decades, have uncovered finds dating from *c.* 2500 BC to the Late Byzantine period. The site is dominated by the massive foundations of the main temple, which was dedicated to Apollo (Figure **101**.1; Plate 89). Since the temple was used as a 'quarry' for centuries – the moles were built of these stones in the nineteenth century – there is not much left to see of its architecture; only one column from the late sixth century BC Doric peripteros has been left standing to guide sailors; it belongs to the back porch of the temple (opisthodomos), which was surrounded by a colonnade forming a rectangle of 6 by 11 columns. Cult on this site can be traced back to the seventh century BC. A second, easily recognisable monument belonging to the ancient town is the wall to the north of the temple, which is preserved to quite a height (Plate 89); a long portion of the fortification wall of fine ashlar blocks can be seen between two towers (Figure **100**.6); the blocks were used as spolia in this late Roman wall; before this they had decorated an impressive dining room belonging to the officials of the Apollo cult who were sent to Delphi; the names of the dignitaries and inscriptions for the manumission of slaves were cut on the walls of this building. To the south below the foundations of the temple lie the remains of walls dating to the early period of the settlement of Aigina; the prehistoric fortifications, which were extended in several building phases, can still be clearly seen (Figure **101** hatched). Houses, which have been partly excavated, lie inside and outside these fortification walls (west and east of the Apollo Temple, which has been excavated down into these early levels as were the foundations of the altar made of ashlar blocks at the east side). In addition, Early Byzantine house architecture was found in the upper levels in this area. A few metres to the south-east, by the ascent from the museum to the temple, fine house walls are still standing, which, although they are built in an unusual way of contrasting light poros stone and dark volcanic blocks, were nevertheless covered with plaster in Antiquity and so were not visible. These are followed by the foundations of the former propylon to the sanctuary, in which the wheel marks of the wagons can be seen (Figure **101**.4). Two smaller shrines were situated to the west of the Apollo Temple; next to them are the foundations of a circular building made of spolia, which is known as the heroon of Phokos, one of the sons of Aiakos. A Hellenistic cult building, again constructed of spolia, was located on the west edge of the peninsula, partly fallen into the sea. It is attributed to the Pergamene king Attalos II, who was a benefactor of Athens and Aigina.

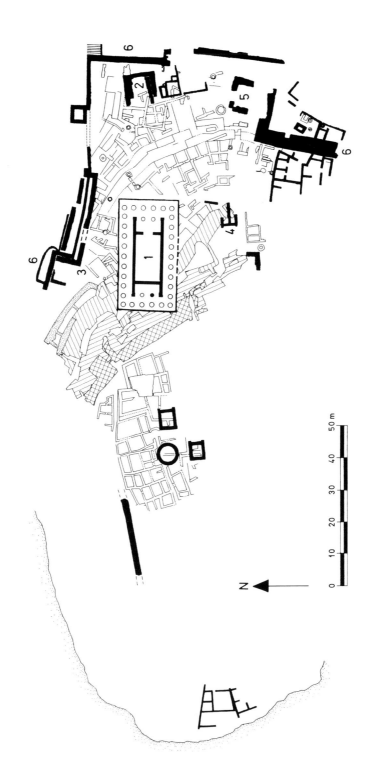

Figure 101 Aigina, Kolonna hill (hatched and white: remains of the prehistoric settlement; black: historical monuments).

1: Temple of Apollo; 2: altar of the Sanctuary of Apollo; 3: temenos wall; 4: propylon; 5: foundations of a treasury (?); 6: Late Antique fortification wall built with spolia.

The modern museum contains some sculptural fragments from the Apollo temple (main room) and the Aphaia temple (room on the right) and other Greek sculptures, including some fine Classical grave reliefs, a Roman portrait and pottery from all the island, as well as the model of a prehistoric house with an upper floor. Many grave reliefs are displayed in the courtyard under a protective roof, most of which come from the islands of the Cyclades and were brought here during the early period of the modern Greek state. (The museum will soon be reorganised.)

North-east of the hill of Kolonna lay the theatre mentioned by Pausanias in his guide; he compared it to that in the town of Epidauros (not that in the Sanctuary of Asklepios), which was found a few years ago; so it can be supposed that the Aiginetan theatre was of marble too (and indeed this is indicated by rounded seats, which could still be seen in the last century), and of small proportions (Figure **100**). The stadium, also known from literary sources but not yet found, must be located next to the theatre.

The cemeteries of the town have been found in the south as well as in the north-east. Although chambers cut into the sandstone with sarcophagi dating to the sixth and fifth centuries BC have been excavated opposite the former orphanage on the road to Phaneromeni, the graves with elaborate architectural decoration on the other side of the town mostly date to the Hellenistic period; they were reached by a stairway, had doors, plastered walls with wall paintings, painted inscriptions and, often, pillars supporting the roof.

The monastery of Phaneromeni lies just behind the exit from the town to the south-east on the road to Ay. Marina called Phaneromeni. On the site of a three-aisled basilica, of which the apses are still clearly recognisable, a large church was begun in the thirteenth century, which, however, remained unfinished. In the nineteenth century the bishop of Aigina lived in a nearby house. Two underground chapels can be reached from the garden of this house and a small cave, in which an icon of the Virgin is supposed to have been found during the construction of the church in the thirteenth century. The house and the estates around it belong today to the monastery of Chrysoleontissa, which lies further inland (see p. 340).

The Omorphi Ekklesia and Palaiochora. On the drive to the Aphaia Temple or to Ay. Marina one turns off left two kilometres from the centre of the town of Aigina by a sign 'Ay. Asomatoi' and turns shortly afterwards again left to reach the Omorphi Ekklesia, the 'Beautiful Church'. The small church, which is dedicated to Ay. Theodoros, was built in 1282 according to a dedicatory inscription (to the left of the door). The interior of the one-aisled barrel-vaulted church is decorated with fine frescoes showing episodes from the life of Christ. The masonry is partly composed of limestone blocks from an ancient building with medieval ship graffiti.

On the road between Aigina and Ay. Marina the modern monastery of Ay. Nektarios lies about six kilometres from the port. Turning off here northwards from the road and going past the monastery a small church (Stavros) is reached on the right of a gently rising road; from here the hill of Palaiochora can be comfortably visited.

The monastery of **Ay. Nektarios**, formerly Ay. Triada, was founded at the beginning of this century. It was used by the archbishop Nektarios as a place of retreat before his death in 1920. In 1961 Nektarios was canonised and the monastery, which in the meantime had become a very popular pilgrimage with many modern buildings, was named after him. The huge church is still under construction.

There is a good view to the north-east from the monastery over the rocky hill of Palaiochora, the medieval capital of Aigina (Figure **102**). After an attack by Saracen pirates in AD 896 the inhabitants of the old town fled to the mainland or withdrew into the interior of the island. On a site, which is thought to be the Oia mentioned by Herodotos, the new settlement of Palaiochora grew. However, even that location so far from the coast did not protect the site from repeated occupation and destruction (1537 by the Turks, 1665 by the Venetians). Palaiochora continued to be inhabited until 1800, after which the population slowly returned again to the coast below. In 1830 it was finally abandoned. Only a few ruins, foundations and heaps of stone are left from the houses of that period; however, over 30 churches on the hillside recall the centuries in which Palaiochora was a flourishing site. During his visit to the churches the visitor should take time to appreciate the atmosphere, which somewhat recalls that of Mistra in the Peloponnese.

The churches, some of which are still cared for today, and even restored, date both to the Byzantine and the post-Byzantine period and were built in their own local style. They are generally small one-aisled buildings with a barrel-vault and a high iconostasis. Where the slope did not permit the regular orientation of the whole church, the altar area at least was orientated to the east, so that in some churches there is a strange asymmetry where the bema and iconostasis have been added to the long side wall. The churches are decorated with frescoes and some have artistically worked stone floors. Throughout the area of Palaiochora there are ancient and Early Christian architectural fragments, which are partly built into the churches and partly decorate the courtyards.

A tour (marked with a red arrow) begins on the road with the small church of Stavros (Figure **102**.1) and runs round the whole hill. The churches are signposted by name. Only a few examples are described here following the route of the tour (Figure **102**.1–13).

The path goes up steps to the church of Ay. Georgios Katholikos (Figure **102**.2), which dates to the fourteenth century. The building was originally dedicated to the Greek Orthodox faith, but it was rededicated under Catalan rule and was a temporary shelter for the skull of Ay. Georgios, which was taken to Venice in 1462. The Episkopi Church, which was dedicated to Ay. Dionysios of Zante, is located further up the slope (Figure **102**.3). Dionysios was bishop of Aigina from 1576 to 1589; he used to distribute holy bread from the steps next to the church entrance. The chapel in which he lived lies opposite the church. For a while the Episkopi Church, which has a main and a side aisle as well as a dome, was the main church of Palaiochora. Going now northwards, past the church of Ay.

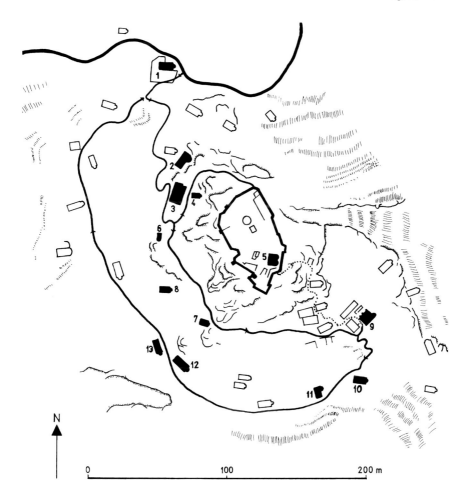

Figure 102 Aigina, Palaiochora.

1: Stavros; 2: Ay. Georgios Katholikos; 3: Ay. Dionysios of Zante (Episkopi); 4: Ay. Nikolaos;
5: Ay. Georgios and Ay. Demetrios; 6: Ay. Anna; 7: Ay. Theodoroi; 8: church of the Taxiarchs;
9: Ay. Kyriaki-Zoodochos Pigi; 10: Ay. Ioannis Theologos; 11: Ay. Nikolaos; 12: Ay. Demetrios;
13: Koimesis tis Theotokou.

Nikolaos (which has a carefully worked door frame; Figure **102**.4) a steep path
leads to the top of the hill, from which there is a wonderful view around the
island. The Venetians built a fort here in 1654 with battlements, cisterns and
dwelling houses. Apart from fallen walls, only the double church of Ay. Georgios
(for Catholic mass) and Ay. Demetrios (for Orthodox service) is preserved (Figure
102.5). The descent to the south-east is rather steep, but gives a fine view over
the colourful roof shingles of Ay. Kyriaki (Figure **102**.9). However, it is easier to
return to Episkopi (Figure **102**.3) and follow the path southwards from there. It
goes past the small church of Ay. Anna (Figure **102**.6), which is partly cut into

the rock and contains numerous spolia; there is a cistern below the apse. From Ay. Theodoroi (Figure **102**.7) the superstructure of the church of the Taxiarchs (Figure **102**.8) can be seen diagonally below; this is an interesting cross-domed church dating to 1293 with fourteenth century frescoes. The court-yard decorated with many ancient spolia in front of the monastery church of Ay. Kyriaki-Zoodochos Pigi (Figure **102**.9), which was the centre of Palaiochora from the seventeenth century to 1830, is particularly full of atmosphere. The double church contains well preserved frescoes. Ay. Ioannis Theologos with a belfry and a dome (Figure **102**.10), immediately recognisable from its light blue colour, is located below. The pretty church dates to the early fourteenth century. From here the path initially goes westwards round the hill back to the exit; churches to the right of the path include Ay. Nikolaos with a side apse (Figure **102**.11) and Ay. Demetrios (seventeenth century; Figure **102**.12) and to the left of the path the Koimesis tis Theotokou (seventeenth century) with particularly fine frescoes (Figure **102**.13). Outside the round tour described here, the chapel of Ay. Charalambos is located below the road to the Nektarios Monastery some 200 m to the west. Its lintel consists of a High Classical marble stele with the boundary inscription of an Athena sanctuary written in fine letters (similar boundary inscriptions have been found in other places on the island; they are in the museum); the steps in front of the door are made of further ancient stones.

The oldest church of the neighbourhood, Ay. Nikolaos Mavrika, stands on the south side of the Aigina–Ay. Marina road opposite the hill of Palaiochora and thus east of the Nektarios Monastery. This fine church, which is dedicated to the patron saint of seafarers, was built in the thirteenth century. The building belongs to the cross-in-square domed type. The frescoes on the interior date to 1330 according to an inscription; a further inscription mentions 1522. Some graffiti of ships on the wall plaster are also noteworthy.

Opposite the monastery of Ay. Nektarios a very narrow road leads south-wards to the **monastery of Chrysoleontissa**, which is reached via a small pass. It was founded in an isolated position on a small fertile plain in 1600 and enlarged at the beginning of the nineteenth century. Its exterior gives a fortress-like impression with its tower and high walls behind which there is a court-yard full of flowers. The artistically carved iconostasis in the church and an early icon of the Virgin are worth seeing. Even today, when there is a drought on this very dry island, a procession takes place to pray for rain in which this icon of the Virgin is carried.

Following a path on foot from the monastery in a southerly direction up the mountain a second higher-lying plain is reached called **Bourdechti**, which is bordered on its north side by a post-antique retaining wall. The ruins of a tower, of which the polygonal masonry in the lower courses dates to the late sixth century BC, stand on its north-east side next to a chapel. The tower, to which neighbouring buildings, two cisterns and terrace walls of huge blocks on the south side of Bourdechti belong, was used in Antiquity as the centre of a farm.

From Bourdechti one can continue across a saddle lying to the south and then reach Lazarides in the east and Oros in the south (see p. 345).

The **Sanctuary of Aphaia**. The Sanctuary of Aphaia,[234] one of the finest situated and best preserved ancient temples in Greece, is located on the north-east side of the island of Aigina about 12 km from the main town (Figure **103**). The ruins of the Late Archaic temple are located on a *c*. 200 m high mountain saddle amongst pine trees (Plate 90); the site offers a wonderful view across the sea of the bay of Athens; to the south the tourist village of Ay. Marina can be seen below and the east coast of the island.

There was initially an open air sanctuary here dedicated to the nymph Aphaia, a Cretan goddess of vegetation; pottery and figurines date the cult back to around 1400 BC. Later, probably in the Late Archaic period, Aphaia shared the cult in the sanctuary with Athena, perhaps as part of an attempt at a political rapprochement with the neighbouring rival, Athens. The rock surface, which was originally constricted, was continually widened from the early years of the cult. First a small terrace was made, which was surrounded by a wall *c*. 700 BC; this enclosure contained a cistern, an altar in the centre and a building with several rooms, a so-called priest's house, on the south edge. In the seventh century an entrance building was added in the temenos wall next to this house and perhaps a first shrine was already set up. The simple sanctuary was decorated with monuments *c*. 570 BC (Figure **103**: grey); the remains of the enclosure wall of the terrace can be seen north of the temple; the terrace was widened extensively on the south and west by means of immense filling operations, while the altar, of which parts are visible in the excavation belowthe later one, was obviously enlarged and a first Doric stone temple was built (it lies beneath the later building). It had four columns on the façade; behind the vestibule with an interior Doric frieze, lay a long cella. During the German excavations so many architectural components were found in the earth fill that the building could be extensively restored; the fresh, strong colours which are preserved on the building components were a particular surprise for the architects and archaeologists (a model of the temple and a partial reconstruction of the façade is displayed in a study collection in the Aphaia sanctuary, which is accessible every hour on the hour for 15 minutes). North-east of the temple next to the cistern a votive offering was set up which dominated the whole sanctuary; it consisted of an Archaic marble sphinx on a tall Ionic column, which guarded the site; it is similar to the sphinx of the Naxians in the Sanctuary of Apollo at Delphi or a similar sculpture in the Apollo Temple on the Aiginetian hill of Kolonna.

In the penultimate decade of the sixth century BC a fire destroyed the temple and so the Aiginetians decided to build a new one and make impressive alterations to the whole site (Figure **103**: black). Although the temple and the altar remained on the original site, yet the temple was now given, *c*. 500 BC, a regular rectangular plan. New terraces were laid to support this large temple, especially on the north-west side, and the entire oblong area was surrounded

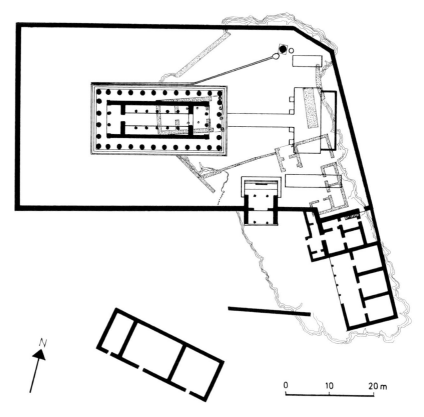

Figure 103 Aigina, Sanctuary of Aphaia (grey: *c.* 570 BC; black: *c.* 480 BC).

with a high temenos wall. A large propylon, with the roof supported on the exterior and interior by two octagonal columns, protected the entrance to the area in front of the temple. Outside the temenos to the east of the entrance a large new house was constructed for pilgrims and the administration; there was a bathroom with three bathtubs and a draw basin in a small annex. On the now uniform level of the terrace inside the enclosure wall the temple, a wide ramp and the long sacrificial altar made an impressive complex. Two long bases for group sculptures stood on each side of the altar. In the north next to the old cistern, which was fed by a channel collecting rainwater from the temple roof, the imposing Archaic sphinx column still rose above all. A cave at the north-east edge of the plateau served as a sanctuary of Pan.

The remains of the buildings put up then can be visited today (Figure **103**: black). They were probably used only up to 431 BC, when the Aiginetans were driven out by the Athenians and had to leave the island. After English travellers visited the ruins as early as 1675, the temple was rediscovered in 1811 by two English architects and a Bavarian architect (Cockerell, Foster and Haller von Hallerstein); the pedimental and other sculptures from the sanctuary were purchased by Ludwig I of Bavaria and sent to Rome, where they were restored by B. Thorvaldsen, before they were installed in the newly built Glyptothek in Munich.

The temple was built of limestone (poros), like all the buildings of the Aphaia sanctuary, and had the outer surface covered with a fine, partly painted, layer of plaster. It is an outstanding example of Late Archaic Doric architecture (Plate 90). The substructure of the temple, set on an artificial platform, consists of three steps. The peristasis of 6 to 12 columns is on the highest step; it is a building of strikingly squat proportions for its time. The Doric capitals support the architrave which carried a frieze of triglyphs and (undecorated ?) metopes, all lost today. Above this the east and west pediments of the roof were decorated with many statues made of fine Parian marble (see below with Figure **104**). The corners above the pediments were decorated by marble sphinxes, the apex of each tympanon was crowned with an acroterion of volutes and palmettes framed by two female figures. The roof area itself was covered with clay tiles with the exception of the outer row of tiles which was of marble, i.e. the entire roof edge (sima) was made of marble slabs, which ended on the long sides in painted palmettes.

The cella of the temple had a vestibule two interaxial spaces deep and an opisthodomos one and a half interaxial spaces deep; both were closed to unauthorised persons by grilles, which were put between the antae and the columns, and both were connected by doors to the cella (that of the opisthodomos was opened later).

The interior of the temple had a red plaster floor and was divided into three aisles by two two-storeyed rows of columns. The restoration of parts of this interior division contributes to the impressive appearance of the Aphaia Temple; it is easy to imagine the entire superstructure, except that the inner room was very dark and not flooded with bright light as it is today. On the axis of the northern row of inner columns next to the door of the opisthodomos, the old small cult image of Aphaia, made of wood, was fixed on a limestone base; the base is still in place; the central aisle was dominated by an over life-size bronze statue of Athena, who was probably also worshipped in the sanctuary since the Late Archaic period.

Athena also appears as the central figure in the pediments (Figure **104**), which are on show today in the Munich Glyptothek, apart from a few fragments (see pp. 115 and 337). In the east pediment she takes part in a battle with a lunging gesture, but she dominates the west pediment by standing erect. On both sides of the goddess a battle takes place; the theme is disputed by scholars, but it probably depicts two battles at Troy in which the Aiginetans took part; on the east the first mythical battle with Telamon and Herakles; on the west the second campaign against Troy with Ajax and Achilles. A comparison of the two pedimental groups makes it immediately obvious that they are differently conceived and that the figures are variously depicted in their interpretation of the fate of mankind, although the actual body structure and the style of sculpture of the two pediments differs only a little, if at all. This is because the statue groups were fashioned at the time of transition from Archaic

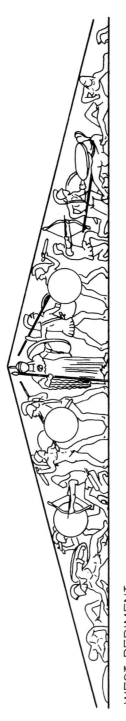

WEST PEDIMENT

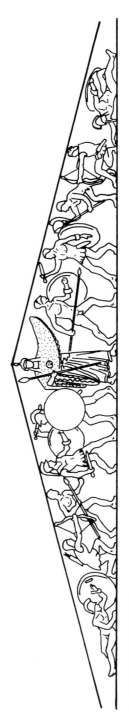

EAST PEDIMENT

Figure 104 Pediment sculptures of the Temple of Aphaia.

to Early Classical art (*c.* 480 BC). On the west pediment there are only warriors fighting duels, but on the eastern one widely spread compositions appear, with fighting pairs which cross over the entire width of the pediment (for example, the opponent of a so-called Herakles (perhaps recognisable from his lionskin helmet), who is shooting with his bow on the right, is 'Laomedon', who is lying far away in the left corner of the gable). A comparison of the anatomy of the figures shows that the statues of the east gable are more relaxed and less frontally arranged and thus more obviously affected by the battle than those of the west pediment; in the east pediment the statues react to the solemn events more aptly, while in the west even the warriors pierced by spears appear cheerful and untroubled (particularly apparent in the fallen men lying in the corners).

As well as these two figural groups there were probably two more statue groups, which were displayed in the area in front of the temple in two small stoas. Their style and size is close to that of the west pedimental figures, so it was thought that these figures were first designed for the east pediment, but that, towards the end of the construction, because of the stylistic development of that time a new more modern group was made; however, they may have been separately planned and displayed as dedicatory offerings. The fragments from the area in front of the temple (most of them in Munich) belong to a group of fighting warriors, perhaps Greeks against Amazons, and perhaps to the rape of the nymph Aigina by Zeus, an important scene for the cult history of the sanctuary, since the Aiginetan ruling house of the Aiakids sprang from this union.

The Sanctuary of Zeus Hellanios on Oros. The highest mountain on Aigina, Oros (Figure **99**), was a particularly sacred place from early on. The Sanctuary of Zeus Hellanios was located here; he later became Panhellenios ('of all the Greeks'), as on special days in the year his festival, which was similar to that of Zeus in Olympia, brought peace throughout the country. All the city-states sent participants to the festival days and they were allowed free passage even in times of war. An idea of the importance of the sanctuary can be obtained by reading the odes of the poet Pindar, who lived on the island for a time as a friend of the Aiginetan ruling house and composed odes in honour of their victors in the games of the great Greek festivals. A further indication that this cult of Zeus was the most important on Aigina is that Aiginetan sailors founded a sanctuary of Zeus Hellanios in their trading colony in the city of Naucratis on the Nile Delta.

Route: leave Aigina town going to the south-east in the direction of Phaneromeni, Nektarios, Ay. Marina, turn right by the former prison and then turn left after a school. The asphalt road runs through fields with almond and pistachio trees and finally winds up a mountain slope eastwards in the direction of Lazarides. After a few kilometres a small chapel is passed on the left of the road and then again on the left the branch road to Lazarides; a little later a dirt road turns off right; after 250 m park the car and continue on foot along a stony field path which goes up to a church visible on the left (south) and a long terrace wall with a stepped ramp. If the dirt road is followed westwards along the slope of Oros up the mountain, the peak of Oros can easily be reached from the saddle in the west in about 20 minutes. From the terrace installations on the north slope there is a path – marked with red – leading up to the top in about 40 minutes.

A myth dating to the early history of Aigina is connected with the Sanctuary of Zeus Hellanios. During a lengthy period of drought the farmers are said to have come to King Aiakos pleading for help; he then begged Zeus for rain from the peak of Oros. When his prayer was heard the Aiginetans set up an altar on Oros, which became the origin of the sanctuary, and worshipped Zeus as the Cloud Gatherer. Even today clouds gathering above Oros are interpreted by the population of Aigina as a certain sign of an imminent rainstorm and on the site of the ancient altar, to which a small temple also belonged, they pray for rain in the chapel of Prophitis Elias.

On the mountain, traces of a prehistoric settlement have been found on ancient terraced slopes surrounding the hilltop. During the ascent remains of the former fortification walls can be seen standing quite high with small groups of rooms built of rubble in their interior (another settlement of this kind lies south-east of the nearby village of Lazarides). Today the peak of Oros is crowned by the chapel of Prophitis Elias; on its north side there is a foundation of large rectangular blocks which belonged to the ancient sanctuary on this site; further ashlar blocks are built into the walls of the chapel. There is a wonderful view round the Saronic Gulf from the chapel, which makes the ascent worthwhile. On the south-west and west sides the Peloponnesos coast with Methana and Poros in front frames the panorama; on the south-west tip of Aigina the small fishing village of Perdika with its simple tavernas is visible; in front of the coast lies the tiny islet of Moni, north-west of it the island of Angistri; to the north the flatter areas of the island can be seen and the coast of Salamis and the Megarid; on the other side of the church on a clear day the view extends to the bay of Athens, to the south of which the long ridge of Hymettos rises up; and in particularly clear weather even Cape Sounion can be seen, in the gap between the Attic mainland and Patroklos island.

The ruins of a large installation on a terrace are located on the north slope below the peak of Oros (Plate 91); it was connected by a path to the small temple and the altar of Zeus on the peak (Figure **105**). As a result of the recent excavations the impressive architecture of the area with its high retaining walls and wide stepped ascent on the north side can be dated to *c.* 500 BC; an annex with a three-aisled colonnade dates to the years of Pergamene rule (211–133 BC). The high point of the site is shown not only by the impressive architecture but also by an Archaic dedicatory offering support in columnar form with an inscription (recently displayed at the top of the stepped ascent); further documents, such as a sacrificial plate with an inscription dating to the sixth century BC and a bronze hydria from *c.* 460 BC with a dedication from two brothers to Zeus Hellanios, are stored in the museum.

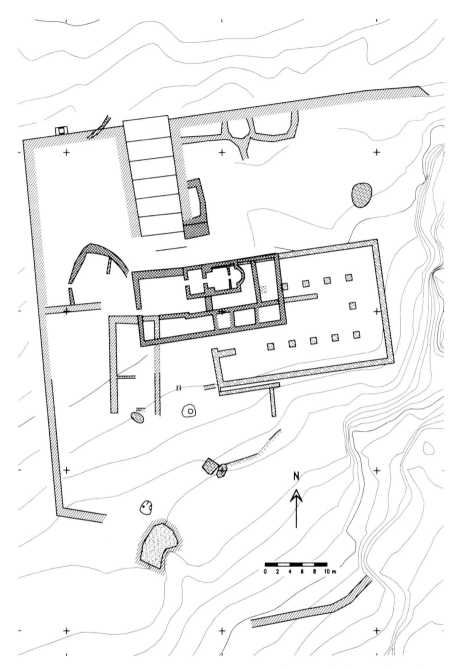

Figure 105 Aigina, festival area of the Sanctuary of Zeus Hellanios on the north slope of Mt Oros.

The terraced installation consists of a high wall on the north side (the western third is much robbed out, since it was made of ashlar blocks suitable for reuse in later buildings), in the centre of which a gently rising stepped ramp leads up to a plateau (Plate 91). The sides of the ascent are made of carefully bonded rectangular blocks; the other parts of the terrace wall are of irregular construction. In the south-east the area of the sanctuary is bounded by an impressive rocky outcrop, from which the building material of the walls and foundations comes. In contrast, excavations have shown that the upper architecture of the Doric building was of Aiginetan poros stone, which had been brought up from the coast. This very impressive installation must be interpreted as a festival area for the community rites and feasts of the pilgrims, who had taken part in the sacrificial acts on the peak beforehand; many animal bones, some with traces of cutting and burning, support this idea.

A Byzantine monastery with a church of the Taxiarchs has been constructed above the centre of the installation using ancient spolia; wall remains of the cells can still be seen. The cross-domed church with a long narthex was built of countless blocks from the sanctuary; its north side runs exactly along the length of an ancient wall which belonged to the Hellenistic stoa; only the narthex of the church was built on later, at which point an ancient base for a bronze statue was incorporated into its masonry.

South of the courtyard of the Byzantine monastery there is first a small cistern then, about 100 m further up, a large cistern cut into the rock; the bronze hydria already mentioned with a dedicatory inscription to Zeus Hellanios cut on the lip was found in it. The cisterns, in Antiquity covered with thin rooftiles, gathered water for the pilgrims. Today goatherds draw the cistern water for their animals; they drink from some hollowed stone blocks which function as troughs.

The terrace architecture of Zeus Hellanios near the foot of the north slope of Oros belongs to a type particularly popular in the Late Archaic period (there are similar sanctuary constructions particularly in the Cycladic islands) and which came back into fashion in the Hellenistic period (the Asklepieion on Kos, the Athena Lindia sanctuary on Rhodes, etc.); pilgrims were meant to be impressed by the spacious buildings spread over a mountain slope and the construction of massive terrace walls. On Aigina this concept is carried out on a relatively small scale, but the sanctuary together with the high-rising Oros and its altar on the peak will not have failed to make an impression.

3 Poros

The small island of Poros, lying only a few metres in front of the east coast of the Peloponnese (Figure **106**), is a favourite Athenian resort; its combination of fine sandy beaches and forested mountains makes Poros particularly charming. In addition the ruins of a famous sanctuary to Poseidon can be visited. The island is easily and quickly reached from Piraeus

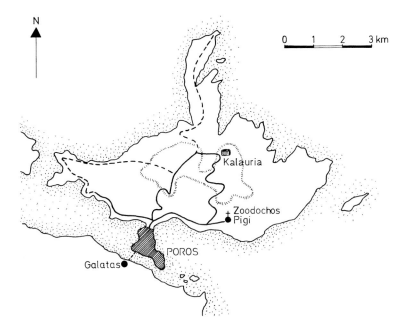

Figure 106 Poros/Kalauria, sketch plan of the island.

and is worth a day trip or, combined with a visit to Aigina, a stay of several days on the islands of the Saronic Gulf.

The car ferries which go to Aigina and Poros are located in the harbour of Piraeus near the terminus of the metro; early in the morning at 8am there is also an express passenger boat, which makes a quick stop in Aigina and then continues on to Methana and Poros. Those who wish to get as much as possible out of a day trip to the island should take the hydrofoil to Poros, which, unlike the one to Aigina, starts from Zea Marina.

The island of Poros consists of two parts which are connected today by a swampy isthmus, but which were separated from each other in Antiquity; in the south was the small island **Sphairia**, on which the town of Poros is located today, and in the north the large island of Kalauria with the Sanctuary of Poseidon in the centre (Figure **106**). The Poros peninsula (the name means 'ford') was connected to the Peloponnese until late Antiquity; then the land sank giving rise to the present canal, which is *c.* 250 m wide and only 4m deep, over which small private boats cross to Galatas opposite. The town of Poros was founded by Albanians in the seventeenth century on the slope of a low mountain; with its Neoclassical houses it has a scenic appearance, which is emphasised by its position on the straits with the mountains of the Peloponnese and the peninsula of Methana in the background.

A naval academy is located in a bay to the north-west of the town; it was founded as early as the time of King Otto I and is, therefore, housed in Neoclassical buildings. On the south side of the town a small museum is situated on a small square in a beautifully restored building dating from the nineteenth century; it was opened in 1998 to show finds from the area (prehistoric pottery, Classical, Hellenistic and Roman sculpture).

Crossing the isthmus to the north one enters the **island of Kalauria** which is dominated by three mountains rising to 390 m. It was already settled in the Mycenaean period, but did not achieve eminence until the Archaic and Classical periods when the Sanctuary of Poseidon offered the right of asylum.[235] The cult of the god of the sea extends back to the Geometric period. In the eighth century the centre of the Kalaurian League, to which numerous harbour towns of the Saronic Gulf, as well as Athens and Boeotian Orchomenos, belonged, was located here; this league of city-states with its religious centre in Kalauria seems to have flourished again in the third century BC. After the vain opposition of Athens to the Macedonian rulers in 322 BC, the famous politician and orator, Demosthenes, fled here and committed suicide, before the Macedonians could catch him. Kalauria was mostly politically dependent on Troizen, which lies on the Peloponnesian mainland opposite the island. Not until the time of the War of Independence against the Turks did Poros again play a historically relevant role; in 1828 a conference took place here between the English, French and Russian protective powers to deliberate over the formation of the modern state of Greece. Two years later the naval academy was founded; it became the theatre of a conflict between President Kapodistrias and Admiral Miaoulis of Hydra on 13 August 1831 when part of the Greek fleet including the flag-ship 'Hellas' was destroyed in Poros harbour, since Miaoulis did not wish to hand it over to the Russians, as the government had ordered.

Poros is very good for walking, but a car, taxi or scooter can also be used to get around; a particularly good way to get to know the island is a tour with a rented bicycle. On the south-east coast of Kalauria the **monastery of Panagia Zoodochos Pigi** ('Mary of the spring of life'; Figure **106**) lies above a pretty bay with numerous tavernas 4 km along a good road which follows the coast. It was built in the eighteenth century amidst trees near a spring. There is an older carved iconostasis dating to the sixteenth century in the catholikon, which comes from Caesarea in modern Turkey. During the War of Independence two Greek admirals were buried here; their graves can be seen in the monastery courtyard.

The **Poseidon Temple of Kalauria**, which is situated in a saddle between two mountain peaks, is reached by a very winding road which runs through wooded countryside. In the fenced excavation area,[236] which lies to the right of the road, only a few traces of the temple can be seen today, since the ancient buildings were robbed for many centuries to provide building material until excavations began in 1894; in the last few years new excavations by Swedish archaeologists have been taking place. The plateau with its pine and olive trees, is called Palatia ('palace') in memory of the former importance of the site.

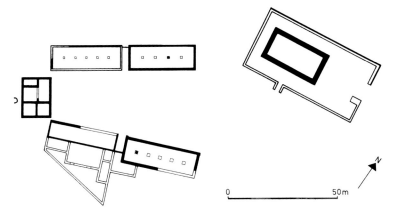

Figure 107 Sanctuary of Poseidon on Kalauria.

Outside the fenced excavation area opposite the entrance a somewhat square building was found; its function is unclear; perhaps it was a lodging house. Entering the excavated area (Figure **107**) on the left by the entrance there is a 48 m-long stoa which had slightly protruding wings on its ends and was probably built in the third century BC. It leads to a propylon in front of which a semicircular curved base (exedra) is set up. Next to it a passage with two columns on the exterior and interior led into the sanctuary area. This consisted of a square which widened and opened towards the temple and was framed by four colonnades; the stoas were not all constructed at the same time, but were put up one after the other between 420 and 320 BC. The side and back wall foundations of their architecture can still be seen, partly built of finely cut blue-green blocks, together with the bases and some column drums belonging to the central and front rows of columns (Plate 92). The temple lying on the east of this square was separated from the rest of the temenos by its own enclosure wall of irregular blocks; two doors inside this temenos wall, comprising a large propylon on the axis of the altar and temple on the east side and a smaller adjacent entrance in the south, allowed entrance to the temenos. The temple was built *c.* 520 BC as a Doric peripteros with six to twelve columns. Today practically nothing remains of its foundations; they are almost completely robbed out; however, the temenos wall with the two entrances is still clearly recognisable in the excavated area. North-east of the temple the plateau falls steeply to the sea; there is a fine view here of the north coast of Poros/Kalauria with some deep bays and over the Saronic Gulf to the mountainous peninsula of Methana and to Aigina.

A visit to the island of Poros, which belongs today to the district of Attica and was also connected to Athens in Antiquity for a time, offers the opportunity to make a side trip to the Peloponnese, where the **Sanctuary of Hippolytos** can be visited and the ruins of the ancient city of **Troizen**, which are situated in an area of lemon groves. In spring in blossom time, when the fruit is also hanging on the trees, this district is filled with a strong scent, which, together with the image of the white flowers and yellow lemons shining among the deep green leaves, will remain as an unforgettable memory. On a hill above the northern entrance to the bay of Poros several **Mycenaean tholos tombs**, which have been carefully investigated in recent years, can be visited. A round trip over the steep peninsula of **Methana** is worthwhile but time consuming; it offers numerous interesting ruins and wonderful views of the landscape.

Appendices

1 The geography of Attica

Travellers to Greece will notice the strongly articulated landscape; high mountain ranges separate the different provinces from each other and give rise to areas suitable for small settlements. In spite of the good road connections today the mountains still form an obvious barrier. A second geographical aspect, which marks the landscape of Greece, is the close unity of land and sea. Almost every Greek province has several outlets to the Mediterranean; long stretches of land are closely connected to the sea by deep inlets. The geological structure of the country thus meant that in the past contact between the different areas of settlement took place more often by sea than by land. It is apparent, at least during Antiquity, that the structure of the landscape contributed essentially to the political formation of Greece, even though occasionally a city-state would consciously cross the natural borders in order to annex a neighbouring settlement area.

The dry, barren landscape of Attica seems to the traveller to be divided by mountain ranges and not to be particularly uniform. To the north Parnes, Pastra and Kithairon form a natural barrier with Boeotia. In addition Parnes and parts of Pentelikon cut off from the Oropia, which was much fought over by Boeotia and Attica in Antiquity, from the Attic heartland. South of Parnes the plain of Athens, called Pedion, and the Thriasian plain around Eleusis both open to the Saronic Gulf. These plains are separated from each other by the range of Aigaleo. In the north-east the settlement area of Athens is bounded by Pentelikon, beyond which the bay of Marathon, which was divided in Antiquity into four districts (Tetrapolis), lies to the east. Hymettos extends to the east of Athens, cutting off the city from the plain of the Mesogeia. The mountains of Merenda, Paneion, the Attic Olympus and the hilly country of the Laurion unfold south of this once-fertile plain.

The Megarid has a particular position. Today it is part of Attica, but during its long history it was at one point independent and an enemy of Athens, at another a member of other alliances, and at another also allied with Attica by treaty. The district, which is called after its main town of Megara, extends west of the Pateras range making up a narrow mountainous strip between the Saronic and Corinthian Gulfs. In the late eighth century BC, when Corinth took the western corner of the Megarid with the Sanctuary of Hera at Perachora, and again in the sixth century BC, when the Athenians plundered Salamis, the area of the city-state of Megara was considerably reduced. However, the city played an important role in Greek history, although shifting alliances, especially in the Classical period; even before this it had contributed greatly to the founding of colonies.

The present appearance of Attica is partly determined by the great aridity which dominates this area, but it has also suffered heavily from the havoc which civilisation has wreaked on it in recent decades. During World War II 45,000 hectares of forest in the Athens-Megara district were destroyed by reckless exploitation. The post-war years brought further extensive casualties. Even now many hectares of forest are burnt every year, mostly through negligence, and the careful reforestation process can barely keep up. Moreover, the almost unimaginably speedy expansion of Athens has taken its toll of nature: 150 years ago Pheidiou St, just beyond Omonia Square (Figure 2), was outside the town, but today not only is the plain of Athens completely covered with houses, but building is now pushing itself up the mountains and along the coasts in an almost unbroken chain down to Sounion. The countryside around Athens is completely built over by small houses, which often remain for years as unfinished concrete frameworks; large parts of the countryside also lie fallow, since building speculation promises a high profit. Only in a few areas in the Mesogeia, which is now being built over by a new airport, or the district around Marathon and Rhamnous, or in the Thriasian plain, a glimpse of olive groves, vineyards and cornfields enables the visitor to realise that Attica once possessed stretches of fertile land; these have been almost entirely destroyed in the last four decades.

2 The modern structure: administration and economy

The modern administrative districts, called nomoí, reflect on the whole the ancient landscape and its city-states (poleis); the modern boundaries diverge from those of Antiquity only in details; the ancient boundaries are not known for sure in every case and did not necessarily remain the same over long periods; for example, the Peraia, the small settlement area by the Sanctuary of Hera at Perachora bounded by mountains and the sea, originally belonged to the Megarid, but it was taken by Corinth in the late eighth century BC and even today it is not part of the district of Attica. The districts (nomoí) are subdivided into eparchies (countries, for example the Megarid) and these are further divided into demoi (municipalities; here the ancient term of 'demos' has been kept) with a mayor (demarchos) at the head; on a lower administrative level there are the koinotita (country community) and the oikismos (hamlet) with a representative. Each nomós has a main town; Athens is not only the capital of the whole country (the Democracy of Greece), but also the centre of Attica which is divided into several nomoí.

Greece has an average density of population of *c.* 65 inhabitants per square kilometre. The abandonment of the land together with the explosion of population in some city centres has given rise to huge differences in the density of settlement; in Athens there are *c.* 6,000 and in Piraeus over 8,000 people living in a square kilometre. Naturally, immense social changes have occurred as a result. The Greek is a person who is tightly bound to his place of birth or his original family village; for this reason even today the Greeks travel regularly 'to their village' to vote in elections and for the summer holidays.

The large industrial complexes are located in the countryside around the cities of Athens and Piraeus; the bay of Eleusis has been disfigured by the petroleum industry; small industrial areas in the Attic countryside are increasing continuously, such as marble quarries (Hymettos and Pentelikon supply the marble and limestone) or branches of central European pharmaceutical firms. The Mesogeia east of Hymettos is a centre for wine and olive cultivation, but this will quickly change when the new airport opens. The hilly country of the Laurion produces ores and marble, but these, however, are now no longer in demand. Since early on trade has been one of the most important economic bases of Greece, and the export of *c.* 90 per cent of raw minerals, citrus fruit, olives and olive oil, fish, tobacco, cotton and wine makes up the economic resources of the land; shipbuilding, the production of cement and the textile industry complete this branch of the economy; the tourist industry must also be reckoned as one of the most important assets. Animal husbandry, too, should be mentioned; it has mostly shrunk to sheep and goats, which are intensively farmed, but cover only internal needs. Most recently cows and chickens are kept in batteries. However, in summary it is clear that, without the support of the European Union, Greece could only exist on the lowest level in comparison with a developed country.

3 The flora

In spite of regional variations the Mediterranean climate is generally characterised by mild, damp winters and hot, dry summers. The plants which are adapted to this climate have their growing and blooming period in the rainy season from October to April. During the hot summer months most plants go through a rest period. Herbs and the parts of tuberous and bulbous plants which are above ground die off. In contrast the evergreen sclerophyllous plants are able to survive the lack of water during the dry period through the special adaptation of their small, leathery, often needle-shaped, leaves. Other plants survive by means of extended underground storage organs such as root stocks.

In the Mediterranean area the original vegetation consisted of forests. Today the area has become almost entirely barren as a result of complete deforestation, burning and overgrazing; unprotected earth is eroded by storms and rain and new build-ups of humus, which arise from the undisturbed growth of plants, do not exist. In Attica, too, all the transitional phases of this development can be seen.

Remains of the forests have been preserved especially in the northern and eastern areas of Euboia, in the high areas of Parnes, Pateras and, much reduced since 1998, Pentelikon. The Aleppo pine is the dominant tree, but oaks, especially the kermes oak, are present. Plane trees and silver poplars grow in damp districts and in the neighbourhood of springs. In addition there are cypress trees, carob trees and mulberry bushes, etc. Acacia and eucalyptus trees, originally imported from Australia, have now become completely at home in Greece. Trees grown agriculturally, which are nevertheless also found wild, include the fig, almond, pistachio (especially on Aigina), olive and pomegranate.

The maquis is a thicket of tall shrubs 1 to 2 m high. It consists of myrtle, laurel, arbutus, broom and juniper, as well as mastic, bean trefoil, tree medick and the unassuming oleander, which blooms everywhere from May until September.

The garrigue or phrygana consists of low dwarf bushes, mostly under 50 cm high, which often have thorns and thus avoid being eaten by animals. However, if erosion continues, then only the smallest and most unassuming plants will be able to survive on the rock. In contrast, bulbous and tuberous plants flourish and short-lived herbaceous growths. Typical garrigue plants comprise the ilex ilex, red currant, types of spurge (including the thorn bush) and the many kinds of thistles. Thyme, rosemary and sage are used as cooking herbs. The buds of the caper bush, which blooms in June, are pickled in brine as capers. To these flora can be added all the short-lived herbs, the bulbous and the tuberous plants, which produce a colourful sea of blooms during the rainy period.

The flower calendar, curtailed here to a few examples, begins in September/October with the appearance of the pink cyclamen and the yellow sternbergia after the first rains. In November different crocus and colchicum types follow and wild narcissi can be seen. In December and January the pink anemones bloom, in February hyacinths, scillas and numerous types of clover; there are also leek flowers and asphodel. In March and April the red poppies dominate the floral scene; yellow and purple irises and a small green-brown iris, called hermodactylos, can be found, as well as goat's beard, reseda, viper's bugloss, daisies and small marigolds. Dyer's bugloss (henna) is obvious from its bright blue colour. The frail Greek lloydia are typical of Greece, as also the fritillaries (fritillaria graeca), which look like small tulips and have a fine netting design in rust red and yellow-green on the interior of their petals. In May campanula, snapdragons, scabious and the ubiquitous gladioli come into flower. The grasses include aegilops, wild oats, dog's tail grass, goldentop grass and quaking grass. The violet petalled sea lavender and the yellow Mediterranean immortelles are particularly suited to the dry climate. In May and June purple mallow, yellow mullein and acanthus flowers can be seen everywhere; the leaves of the latter played a role as the prototype for the tendril ornament and capital decorations of ancient architecture. The thistles (for example the golden carline thistle, the blue globe thistle, the red cotton thistle and the lady's thistle) also bloom in

May and June. Two plants which dominate the plant community of the Mediterranean lands, including Greece, originally came from America: the agave with blooms several metres high and the prickly pear with small yellow flowers and juicy fruit.

Caper bushes, wild larkspur, black caraway and aniseed are among the few July flowers; on the whole the countryside is already brown and dry and from now onwards a slight lapse of attention can start a fire with devastating consequences.

A last observation concerns the wild orchids which can still be found in large numbers in Greece, although they, too, are in great danger and therefore in need of special protection, as a result of the rapid changes of environment and misuse by man (pulling off the blooms and collecting the bulbs). Only those types which are the commonest of the many Attic types are mentioned. The flowering period of the orchid is February to May. The mastorchis (barlia robertiana) appears first, followed by man-orchis (aceras anthropophorum) and the wild orchis and ophrys (orchis italica, quadripunctata, papilonacea, pauciflora, provencialis, dactylorhiza romana, ophrys lutea, tenthredinifera, aesculapii, fusca, attica, ferrum-equinum, mammosa and oestrifera). Serapias flowers relatively late. With some luck the sword-leaved and the white helleborine (cephalanthera longifolia and damasonium) can be found in wooded areas.

4 The fauna

The number of wild mammals is small in comparison to the endless variety of insects, spiders and reptiles which inhabit Greece; although hares, rabbits, hedgehogs and small rodents are common, the fox, for example, is seldom seen in Attica. In contrast huge numbers of bats, which are also mammals, are a daily feature of the twilight and night hours.

The range of native birds is large. As well as sparrows, robins, chaffinches and treecreepers there are partridges, pheasants, the hoopoe, the nightingale and many others. Different types of gulls and herons live on the water. Swifts and swallows leave the country only during the winter months. The presence of the raptors must also be mentioned; the small types, especially falcons and sparrow-hawks, can be seen everywhere. In contrast the owl family is declining. In the past, the little owl nested on the rocks of the Acropolis; its Latin name, Athena noctua, is a reminder that it was the emblem of Athens in Antiquity and decorated the reverse side of the coinage (Figure **67**).

The reptiles are well represented by the tortoise family, of which the most prominent member, the Greek land tortoise, is ubiquitous. During breeding time in spring the males fight ponderous battles with loud gasps and try to overturn each other. The lizards, which are very common in Greece, are particularly well adapted to the warm climate. The large emerald lizard with its bright green coat of scales is striking. A particularly useful house-guest is the wall gecko; the fine grooved suction pads on its toes allow it to hunt insects and vermin upside-down on the ceiling. The snakes include many harmless ones, but there are also poisonous vipers. Although snakes are very shy animals, the visitor should wear long trousers and strong shoes on overland hikes as protection against them and should also remember that in the early morning hours they cannot escape as quickly as in great heat; for the body temperature of these animals with variable temperature is dependent on the surroundings. It cannot be said with certainty which of the reptile types was worshipped in Antiquity as the symbol of the healing god Asklepios: there is, however, agreement that it must have been a snake capable of climbing, such as, for example, the so-called Aesculapian snake (Elaphe longissimus), which can reach a length of two metres and has a brown topside.

The amphibian family is represented chiefly by frogs and toads, which are found in ponds, marshes and also ancient cisterns (the Laurion).

Only a few examples from the well-represented insect family can be mentioned here. Butterflies, for example, include the large swallowtail with black and white-yellow striped wings, which has now become rare in central Europe, the burnet moth with red dots on pale blue wings or the small tortoise-shell, the red admiral, the swallowtail, etc., which are also local to central Europe. In spring one can see long wandering chains of caterpillars, which cause considerable damage; their spun nests hang in the pine trees, often in great numbers; they are the caterpillars of the inconspicuous pine lappet moth. In the neighbourhood of brooks and rivers there are different types of dragonflies; large hornets, wasps, bumblebees and bees hum everywhere, and small beehives are put out on many mountain slopes. The sawing chirp of the cicadas depends on the activity of the insects and the temperature of their surroundings, so that, in particular, the hottest hours of midday from July onwards are filled with their almost alarming noise. Among the crickets living in Greece the mole cricket is particularly impressive. The glowing colours of the shieldbug are decorative. Also worth mentioning are the gold-green glittering rose beetle, the stag beetle, the rhinoceros beetle and the immense number of small ladybirds. The dung beetle, which lays its eggs in carefully made balls of dung, was venerated in ancient Egypt as a sacred beetle because of its propagative peculiarities. The widespread occurrence of the anopheles fly was a grave problem for Greece as late as the twentieth century, for malaria carried by it was one of the commonest causes of death. After World War II a field campaign lasting five years was carried out on the breeding places of this fly with the support of England and America, so that there is no longer any risk of infection today.

Among the spiders, Argiope bruennicli merits particular attention not only for its striking black and yellow markings but also for its very fine wheel-shaped web. The malmignatte, black with red spots, is a poisonous spider; its bite is not life threatening for humans, but can give severe pain and eventually an allergic reaction. The same is true of the sting of the light scorpion, which sits happily under stones, and of the bite of the centipede, a long, light arthropod, which will even fight a scorpion.

The many types of sea creatures must not be forgotten. Countless traces of them can be found on the beaches, such as, for example, the shells of many water snails and shells like the murex, which in ancient times produced the costly purple dye, the limpet and the cockle, the file shell, tellins, mussels and razor mussels. Sea urchins attach themselves to the rocks in front of the coast and are sometimes washed onto land, as also starfish and the white cuttle of the octopus. Small hermit crabs with their snail houses can be watched underwater between the rocks; Moray eels are supposed to live singly in underwater caves on the east coast of Attica. Crabs, shrimps, lobsters and also octopus are part of the coveted catch of a fisherman; in addition there are many perch-type fish (barbel, grey mullet, etc.) near the coast. However, the Greek coasts have long since become less rich in fish than they used to be; the catching of fish with trawling nets, with dynamite, fishing for sport and the pollution of the seas (Athens has only one sewage purification plant – on Psyttalia – the smaller towns still do not own one at all) have nullified the healthy regeneration of stocks. It is particularly thrilling on a sea voyage, for example to the Cyclades, to see dolphins, which occasionally come close to the ferry boats and ships and accompany them for a while with their high jumps.

5 Some basic concepts of ancient architecture

Greek architecture is divided into three orders, Doric, Ionic and Corinthian (apart from local peculiarities). The Doric order is prevalent on the Greek mainland; it is, however, enriched with elements from the Ionic order as a result of mainland connections to Greek Asia Minor, where that order evolved. The Corinthian Order is a late form, which first appeared on the exterior of buildings in the thirties of the fourth century BC (see p. 97). Independent of the orders of architecture, temples (and treasuries) have different ground plans, which can be divided into types. A special vocabulary has developed for the most important building components, partly based on the handbook of the Roman architect Vitruvius. The most important terms are illustrated and explained below.

Glossary

abacus	the uppermost member of the capital (Doric: plain; Ionic/Corinthian: moulded)
amphiprostylos	temple with a portico of columns in the front and the rear, see Figure **110**
anathyrosis	a polished band at the two vertical edges and across the top of the sides of wall blocks in order to secure a close contact of the joints
anta	pilaster of slight projection at the end of the lateral wall of the cella
architrave	lintel carried from the columns, the lowest part of the entablature, see Figures **108**, **109**
bead-and-reel	pattern of a small moulding of rounded, convex section

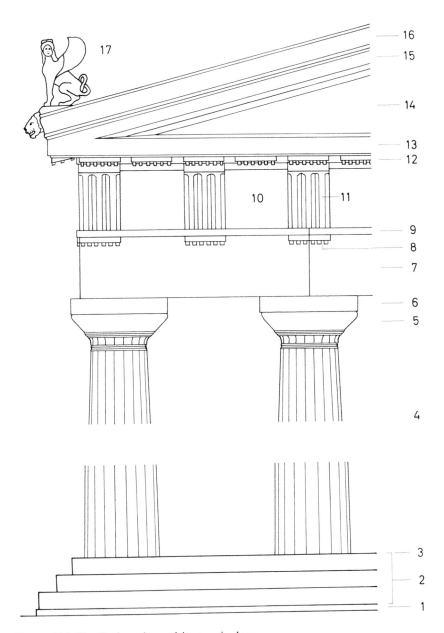

Figure 108 The Doric order and its terminology.

1: euthynteria; 2: steps; 3: stylobate; 4: column shaft with flutes; 5: echinus; 6: abacus;
5 + 6: capital; 7: architrave (epistyle); 8: regula with guttae; 9: taenia; 10: metope; 11: triglyph;
10 + 11: frieze; 12: mutule with guttae; 13: horizontal cornice (geison); 14: pediment (tympanon);
15: slanting (raking) cornice (geison); 16: sima; 17: acroterion.

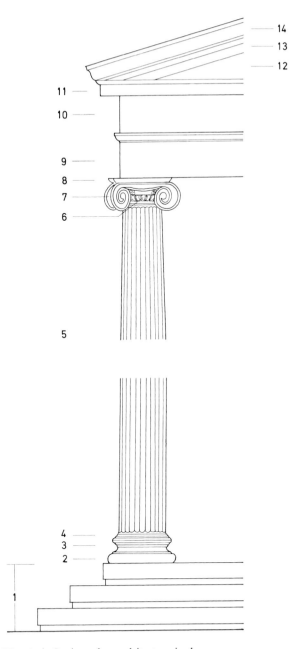

Figure 109 The Attic-Ionic order and its terminology.

1: steps; 2: torus; 3: trochilus; 4: torus; 2–4: column base; 5: column shaft with flutes; 6: echinus; 7: volute with canalis; 8: abacus; 6–8: capital; 9: architrave (epistyle), 10: frieze; 11: horizontal cornice (geison); 12: pediment (tympanon); 13: slanting (raking) cornice (geison); 14: sima.

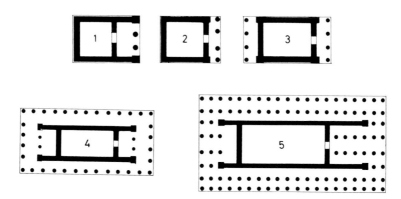

Figure 110 Types of Greek temple.

1: temple in antis; 2: prostyle; 3: amphiprostyle; 4: peripteros; 5: dipteros.

capital	the uppermost member of a column
cornice	upper member of the entablature (Greek: geison), see Figures **108**, **109**
curvature	the stylobate of a temple is curving slightly upwards in the middle, it is not a level platform; this sometimes continues up to the roof
cyma	a wave moulding of double curvature
dipteros	temple with a double row of columns round the cella, see Figure **110**
echinus	circular convex moulding of a Doric capital supporting the abacus
egg-and-dart	pattern of the ionic ovolo profile
entasis	a slight convex curve on the column
epistyle	Greek: architrave, see Figure **109**
flute	vertical channels of shafts of columns
frieze	middle member of the entablature; Doric: metopes + triglyphs, see Figure **108**; Ionic/Corinthian: horizontal band, sometimes enriched with relief sculpture
geison	see cornice; see Figures **108**, **109**
guilloche	a continuous plaited pattern of interwoven fillets
metope	sunk panels between the triglyphs (sometimes with reliefs), see Figure **108**
monopteros	round columnar building without cella
opisthodomos	the recessed porch in the rear of a Greek temple, see Figure **111**
orthostats	the lower courses of the temple wall, higher than the other blocks
pediment	triangular termination of a ridge roof, including the tympanon and the angled cornice above, sometimes with sculptural decoration

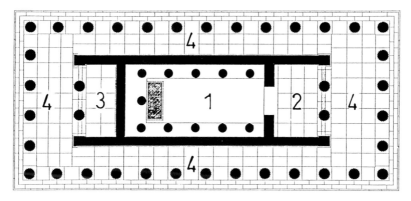

Figure 111 Components of a peripteros (Hephaisteion).
1: cella with base of cult image and arrangement of columns; 2: pronaos; 3: opisthodomos;
4: colonnade (peristasis).

peripteros	temple with one row of columns surrounding the cella, see Figures **110**; **111**
peristasis	colonnade (Doric, Ionic or Corinthian columns) around the cella of a temple
polygonal	carefully fitted masonry of stones which are hewn into polygons with an accurate adjustment to the neighbours
poros stone	a beige or brown lime- or sandstone, soft and coarse
pronaos	the porch in front of the cella, see Figure **111**
prostylos	temple with a portico of columns in front, see Figure **110**
pteron	wing or flank colonnade of a temple, see Figure **111**
sima	roof gutters
spolia	reused material from demolished or ruined buildings
stylobate	upper step of a temple, the platform for the columns
triglyph	projecting member separating the metopes, emphasised with two vertical channels and at each end a chamfer, see Figure **108**

6   Observations on Byzantine church building in Greece

(a) The Early Christian period (306–527)

When Constantine the Great ascended the throne of the Roman Empire in AD 306, life changed dramatically for the Christians, who had been oppressed up until then. The Edict of Tolerance (311) and the victory at the Milvan Bridge (312) were followed by the Edict of Equality of Christians (313). In AD 330 Constantinople (formerly Byzantium) became the capital of the Roman Empire and the cultural traditions of the east gained much more influence. In AD 395 the final division of the Roman empire into a western and an eastern part took place.

Christianity became the state religion as early as 380. Whereas in the first centuries after Christ, Christian services had been secret and had mostly taken place in private rooms, the Christian community could now worship openly. Heathen temples were rededicated and used as Christian churches, in some cases with alterations to the buildings. This rededication was demonstrated by carving a cross on heathen architectural components, reliefs, altars, etc. Christian saints replaced ancient gods and heroes, often having similar names and attributes to their heathen predecessors.

Examples of Early Christian churches in ancient buildings are numerous in Athens; the Parthenon, the Erechtheion on the Acropolis, the Hephaisteion (Figure 22), the Asklepieion, the Ilissos Temple (Figure 34), as well as the Library of Hadrian, were all turned into Christian churches.

At the same time in the fourth century AD the first purely Christian build-ings were put up; they followed the architectural plan of the basilica. During their construction the foundations and the stone material of ancient temples and secular buildings were often reused. The basilica remained the dominant church type into the sixth century. Remains of Early Christian basilicas are to be seen, for example, in Brauron (Figure 72), Elympos (Plate 43) or Glyphada (Figures 50; 51.1).

The Early Christian basilica (Figure 112) is a long building orientated to the east. The interior is usually divided into three, or occasionally five or more, long aisles. The central nave (Figure 112.1), which rose above the side aisles (Figure 112.3), can carry an additional gallery. The church was lit by rows of windows put on both sides of the upper area of the central nave (clerestory). The nave ended in an apse (Figure 112.2), which had a bench for the priests running round it (synthronon). In front of the apse was the altar. The entire, slightly raised altar area, or sanctuary, was divided from the rest of the church by a chancel screen (templon). At the side of the area for the congregation (naos) there was a pulpit made of two desks (ambo) for readings from the gospels and the epistles. A three-arched arcade supported by columns (trivelon) decorated the passage from the naos to the vestibule (narthex, Figure 112.4). There was often a colonnaded courtyard (atrium) in front of the narthex. Mosaics were also used in the interior decoration of the basilica, or alterna-tively the floor could be paved with marble slabs. Altar, chancel screen, synthronon and ambo were usually also made of marble, less often of lime-stone.

The basilica, with its roots in Antiquity, remained the standard church building in the west for more than 1,000 years, being repeatedly copied on the same unchanging plan. In the east, however, the era of the Early Christian basilica ended in the sixth century, even though isolated basilical forms continued to appear and even underwent a certain renaissance in the Middle Byzantine period.

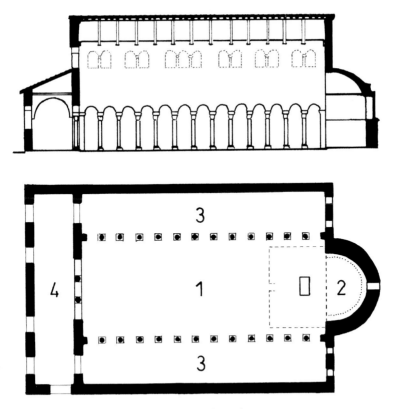

Figure 112 Early Christian basilica, plan and section.

1: central nave; 2: apse with synthronon; 3: aisles; 4: narthex; 1 + 3: naos.

(b) The Early Byzantine period (527–843)

In 527 Justinian ascended the throne of the eastern Roman Empire. With the closure of the last schools of philosophy and the Academy of Plato in Athens (529) the transition from Antiquity to the Christian world was complete. This period also gave rise to a new orientation for the architecture of the eastern Roman Empire. While the west stayed true to the concept of the basilica for church buildings, new forms, which derived from the public buildings of late Antiquity (graves, garden buildings, baths), evolved in the east. This new arrangement of space, emphasised by a central dome, was a decisive basic assumption for church buildings of the following centuries. 'Byzantine architecture began with Justinian' (Krautheimer).

After the death of Justinian the empire collapsed. Byzantium had to battle against attacks from Slavs, Bulgars and Arabs and lost a large amount of its imperial territory. Severe economic crises shook the empire. Iconoclasm, which led to a bitter battle over the use of figural depictions in church art, divided both clergy and worshippers into two parties (726–768; 813–843); the iconoclasts wanted only crosses and symbols to be used in the church; however, in 843 the controversy was finally decided in favour of the iconodules, who wanted representational decoration.

In Attica the period between the seventh and ninth centuries was a dark age. Old buildings dating to the Early Christian or Early Byzantine period were destroyed or fell down and were not rebuilt. In other districts, however, church building continued, but the plan of the late Justinian church or that of the years immediately afterwards was imitated repeatedly. Besides the domed basilica, in some cases with protruding short side aisles, the cross-domed church, which was based on the Greek cross with four arms of equal length, developed. This church type is full of symbolism; plan and arrangement of all the architectural elements are closely bound to the final establishment of the Byzantine liturgy, which developed between the late sixth and early eighth centuries.

(c) The Middle Byzantine period (843–1204)

Iconoclasm ended in 843, and in 867 the rise of the Macedonian dynasty began with Basil I. During the following period – the Golden Years – the Byzantine Empire reached a zenith. Scholarship and art were strongly supported, and valuable historical and literary documents dating to this period were produced. This development continued under the leadership of the Dukas dynasty (1059–1081) and the Comnenes (1081–1185).

In spite of repeated wars with Bulgars and Arabs as well as internal power struggles the position of the Byzantine Empire became stronger. Byzantium played an important intermediary role between the West, the Slavic Balkans and the Islamic empire as a result of its position at the central junction of the trade routes. In 961 Crete was freed from the Arabs, in 1014 and 1018 Basil II defeated the Bulgars and celebrated this victory with a triumphal procession to the Acropolis of Athens.

The influence of the Byzantine church also grew continuously. At the end of the ninth century two missionaries from Salonica, the brothers Cyril and Methodius, received an order to convert the Slavs and so developed a special alphabet to translate the Bible into the Slavic tongue. In 1054 the final break between the Roman and the Byzantine church took place. With the conquest of Constantinople in 1204 by the Crusaders of the Fourth Crusade this prosperous period came to an abrupt end.

Set against this innovative background renewed building activity took place in the ninth century. A highly developed building style evolved for ecclesiastical building. Whereas the most important works of the early Middle Byzantine period are located in Boeotia (Skripou, Osios Loukas), the main works of the Middle Byzantine 'Classic' period (end of the eleventh century to beginning of the twelfth century) are found in Attica (i.e. Daphni, Figure **44**). Next to shortened cross-domed churches there are simple barrel-vaulted churches and basilical buildings, which underwent a certain revival. However, the architectural concept of the cross-in-square domed church was characteristic of church building of that period. The plan is that of the Greek cross, which is inscribed

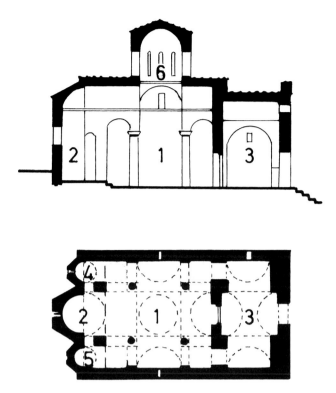

Figure 113 Plan and section of a Middle Byzantine cross-in-square domed church (Asteri).

1: naos with four columns and four squinches; 2: bema; 3: narthex; 4: diakonikon; 5: protheson (or prothesis); 6: drum and dome.

in a square. The four barrel-vaults cross each other on the main axis and appear as saddle roofs on the exterior. The central area was bounded by four columns, of which there are variants with four pillars or pillars in antis, with two pillars and two columns or with four columns. Spherical triangles (pendentives) above the supports or arches built across the corners of the square (squinches) effected the connection to the circle or polygon of the drum. There were four corner niches or side chapels on the diagonals; the two eastern side chapels and the eastern cross arm ended in apses (Figure **113**). The altar, which was separated from the naos by a chancel screen (templon, often called iconostasis), was located in front of the central, largest apse. The northern side chapel was used for the preparation of the sacrament (prothesis), the southern housed the liturgical equipment and vestments (diakonikon). A narthex is often added on in front of this central building with sometimes an additional narthex in the form of a stoa.

It is unclear whether the spacious eight-columned building found in the west developed from the cross-in-square domed church with four columns or was merely a widening of the octagonal central building found in the east, which

Figure 114 Window of the apse of a Middle Byzantine church.

then had an all-covering dome put over it. Although the building plan has its roots in the Byzantine tradition, elements of other lands appear to be integrated into its construction (Armenian, Islamic). The severe division of the four-columned type is relieved through arches and niches whose supports form a square. Above them squinches lead to an octagon, which is again connected by pendentives to the dome. This system allows the whole area of the proth-esis, bema and diakonikon to be covered by a wide vault.

Greece went entirely its own way in the building technique and decoration of its churches, not always following the taste of the capital. While the large eight-columned building was preferred in Byzantium and also in Salonica, in the rest of Greece the four-columned type is more popular; the drum was round on the exterior or, as is typical of Athenian churches, octagonal in appearance; zigzag friezes frame the windows and divide the walls horizontally; from the early eleventh century onwards the contours of the window were further empha-sised by arcades supported on columns; from *c.* 1080 several narrow windows were generally embraced by a common single arch (Figure **114**); from *c.* 1150 windows, as well as arches and drums, were framed with stone. A style of

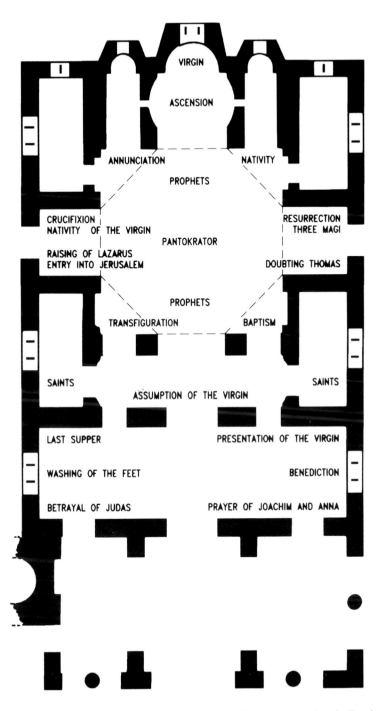

Figure 115 Decorative system (frescoes/mosaics) of a Byzantine church (Daphni).

masonry came into being, the so-called cloisonné masonry, with a unique composition, which was emphasised by structure and colour. In the tenth century the cloisonné masonry was made of irregular blocks, which were framed by horizontal and vertical courses of bricks; bricks were also used loosely to fill out the spaces between the stones. From the beginning of the eleventh century onwards the masonry technique was fully developed and was very carefully constructed. The house stones were replaced by worked ashlar blocks, which were laid in regular courses, horizontally in one or two rows. In the eleventh century vertical courses of bricks were used as further decorative elements, which displayed pseudo-Kufic characters (Figure **57**). Over time whole friezes of such brick decoration developed, which were later also used to adorn clay slabs. Towards the end of the eleventh century this decorative form disappeared. From *c.* 1080 the base of the exterior walls was often made of cross-shaped courses of blocks.

In the tenth century a fixed decorative programme was initiated for the interior decoration of the church, which was either carried out in elaborate and expensive mosaics or in painted frescoes (Figure **115**). In the dome, Christ as pantocrator can be seen, or, alternatively, the preparation of the throne for the Supreme Judge, with the prophets between the windows of the drum. The pendentives carried pictures of the evangelists or the main events in the life of Christ, such as the Annunciation, Nativity, Baptism and Presentation in the temple or the Resurrection, which is depicted in the Orthodox faith as the Descent of Christ into Limbo and the raising of Adam and Eve. The Virgin can be seen in the main apse. The vaults of the cross arms and the upper wall zones carried scenes from the life of Christ, from the events after his death or from the life of the Virgin. The supporters of the church, saints and Christian Fathers, are portrayed on the lower wall areas. To the right and left of the entrance from the naos to the bema Christ, the Virgin, John the Baptist and the patron saint of the church are displayed. Painted inscriptions describe the personages depicted and the scenes; these inscriptions were necessary for the picture to fit into the standard programme of ecclesiastical decoration. Three-dimensional depictions are forbidden in the Byzantine church.

(d) The Late Byzantine period (1204–1460)

In 1204 the Frankish crusaders conquered Greece and divided it into baronies. Athens became a Frankish dukedom under the house of de la Roche.

In 1261 the Palaiologue emperors established themselves in the Peloponnese; their Byzantine empire existed, with a short interval under the Cantacuzene dynasty (1348–1382), until the conquest of Greece by the Turks. Attica and Athens were exposed to attacks from the Catalans (1311), the Florentines (1387) and the Venetians. In the fifteenth century Islam advanced; Constantinople was conquered in 1453 by the Turks, Athens fell in 1456. With the conquest of Mistra, the seat of the Palaeologues, the Byzantine period ended in 1460, even though Euboia remained under Venetian rule for ten more years.

Influences in church architecture and art during this period came from the Peloponnese. The cross-domed type of church continued to dominate, but alongside it there was a late development of the basilica in which the transept was widened and raised above the other aisles, thus emphasising the cruciform shape of the roof; this type was especially common on Euboia from 1250. The body of the cross-domed church was now given narrower and higher proportions. The dome was made smaller, with the drum of comparable height. The masonry was careless, the decoration was poor and proliferated rapidly. Stamped bricks with wave, hook or pointed ornament came into use. Mosaic decoration on interiors was almost non-existent. The composition of the frescoes took on retrospective tendencies; this style of painting, which came from Constantinople in the fourteenth century, was popular on Crete in the fourteenth and fifteenth centuries and developed there into the Cretan School, which was followed in Greece until the seventeenth century.

From the thirteenth century onwards icon painting developed into a high art. The origin of the icon probably lay in the time of iconoclasm, when this portable image offered a possibility of escape to the supporters of figural representations. There were also strict rules (and still are) for icon painting, for the themes and how they are portrayed as well as the disposition of the icon in the church. Each icon has its appointed place.

(e) The post-Byzantine (Turkish) period (1460–1830)

During the Turkish occupation the Christians were allowed to practise their religion freely; however, they had to pay a high tax and marriage with Muslim or conversion to the Muslim faith was strictly forbidden. The sultan chose the Patriarch in Constantinople, who thus in his turn became a secular dignitary of the Ottoman empire and head of the Greek Christian Church. This procedure led to bitter strife amongst the clergy. It was largely up to the Turkish governor of the time to decide whether the Christians should be severely repressed. In many cases the Church became the focus of Greek opposition to the conqueror, as the preserver of the Christian Byzantine tradition.

From the beginning of the seventeenth century there was much building activity in Attica. Monasteries were repaired and enlarged and many churches were built. Besides simple church halls there were cross-domed churches with relatively low domes; the masonry was of rubble or coarse blocks; the interior of the church appeared dark, since it was only lit by a few narrow windows. The bema was often bounded by a simple walled iconostasis. The Cretan School of church painting was replaced in the seventeenth century by the Peloponnesian School; the depictions show traits of folk art.

7   List of the most important monuments in chronological order

Prehistoric periods

Museum of Cycladic and Ancient Art (Goulandris Museum); National Archaeo-
logical Museum, Rooms 4–6. Peninsula of Ay. Kosmas; Perati; Kato Vraona;
Raphina, Askitario; Athens, Acropolis; Menidi; Kiapha Thiti; Thorikos; Koropi,
Kastro tou Christou; Marathon. Aigina: Kolonna, Lazarides, Oros.

Geometric and Archaic periods

Architecture
Athens, Acropolis: Old Parthenon; Old Athena Temple; Old Propylaea. Agora:
   South East Fountain House. Acropolis, South Slope: Temple of Dionysos;
   Fountain House. Attica: Vari, Lathouriza; Vari, Cemetery; Anavyssos,
   Cemetery; Eleusis, Telesterion. Diolkos (by Loutraki); Perachora, Sanctuary
   of Hera. Aigina, Kolonna, Aphaia, Oros.

Sculpture and vases
Athens: Acropolis Museum, Rooms 1–6; National Archaeological Museum,
   Rooms 7–13; Kerameikos Museum; Piraeus, Archaeological Museum;
   Aigina, Kolonna Museum.
Vases: Athens: National Archaeological Museum, Room 7 and Vase Collection
   (Upper Floor); Agora Museum; Kerameikos Museum; Museum Kanello-
   poulos. Museums of Brauron, Marathon, Eleusis.

Classical period

Architecture
Temples: Athens, Acropolis: Erechtheion; Temple of Athena Nike; Parthenon;
   Propylaea. Acropolis, South Slope: New Temple of Dionysos; Asklepieion.
   Hephaisteion; Temple of Apollo Delphinios. Attica: Vouliagmeni, Cape
   Zoster: Temple of Apollo; Sounion, Sanctuaries of Athena and Poseidon;
   Brauron, Sanctuary of Artemis; Koropi, Prophitis Ilias; Stavros/Pallene:
   Temple of Athena (= Temple of Ares, Agora); Rhamnous, Temple of
   Nemesis; Amphiareion by Oropos, Daphni, Sanctuary of Aphrodite; Eleusis,
   Sanctuary of Demeter and Kore. Perachora, Sanctuary of Hera. Poros/
   Kalauria: Sanctuary of Poseidon.
Theatres: Athens, Theatre of Dionysos; Piraeus, Trachones; Thorikos;
   Dionysos/Ikarion; Rhamnous.
Other state buildings: Athens, Acropolis, South Slope: Odeion of Pericles;
   Agora: Civic buildings for the administration of the city-state: Stoas; Pnyx;
   Kerameikos, Pompeion; Stadium. Piraeus: Shipsheds; Skeuotheke. Megara:
   Fountain House. Perachora: Fountain House.

City and fortification walls: Athens, Kerameikos, Olympieion, Klavthmonos Square. Piraeus. Vari, Lathouriza; Sounion; Thorikos; Rhamnous; Eleusis; Dekeleia/Tatoi; Phyle; Panakton; Oinoe; Eleutherai; Aigosthenai.

Choregic monuments: Athens, Acropolis, South Slope, Sanctuary of Dionysos (above, west and east); Street of Tripods. Dionysos/Ikarion; Amphiareion by Oropos (Museum).

Dwelling houses: Athens, Acropolis, South Slope; Agora, South-west Area; Hill of the Nymphs and Mousaion Hill (Rock-cut Athens). Voula, Kalambokas, Pigadakia; Thorikos.

Grave monuments: Athens, Kerameikos. Piraeus, Archaeological Museum; Tomb of 'Themistokles'. Voula, Pigadakia; Vari; Sounion Area: Agriliza, Charaka; Thorikos; Stavros (lion of Kantzas); Marathon, Grave Mounds; Rhamnous, Street of Tombs. Megara, Mausoleum of Kar.

Workshops, Farmsteads, Country houses with towers: Athens, Agora, South-west Area; Kerameikos; Laureotike; Thorikos. Vari; Vouliagmeni; Sounion Area: Agriliza, Charaka, Legraina; Thoriko; Limiko (by Markopoulo); Varnava; Vathichoria.

Caves (sanctuaries of Pan, Nymphs, etc.): Athens, Acropolis, North Slope; Vari; Daphni; Phyle; Marathon – Oinoe.

Sculpture

Athens: Acropolis Museum; National Archaeological Museum, Rooms 14–28; Agora Museum. Museums of Piraeus, Brauron, Marathon, Eleusis. Aigina, Kolonna Museum. Poros, Museum. Megara, Museum.

Hellenistic period

Architecture

Temples and public buildings: Athens: Olympieion. Acropolis, South Slope: Stoa of Eumenes; Agora: Stoa of Attalos; Middle Stoa; South Stoa; Tower of the Winds; Colonnaded Street. Eleusis, Lesser Propylaea. Amphiareion by Oropos: Theatre.

Fortifications: Athens, Hill of the Muses. Piraeus, Mounychia Hill. Voula, Kastraki; Sounion; Koroni; Plakoto; Palaiokastro; Kastri (Pentelikon).

Sculpture

Athens, National Archaeological Museum, Rooms 28–31; Agora Museum; Piraeus, Museum.

Roman imperial period

Architecture

Temples: Athens, Acropolis, Temple of Roma and Augustus; Agora (Temple of Ares; South-east and South-west Temples (transported from other Attic sites); Olympieion; Temple of Kronos and Rhea by the Ilissos; Temple of

Tyche on Ardettos Hill. Eleusis: Greater Propylaea; Porch of the Telesterion; Temples of Artemis and Sabina; Marathon: Sanctuary of the Egyptian Gods; Rhamnous, restoration of the Temple of Nemesis.

Public buildings: Athens: Agora, Odeion of Agrippa, Nymphaion, Library of Pantainos; Odeion and Stadium of Herodes Atticus; Hadrian's Library, Arch, Aqueduct. Eleusis, Courtyard with Arches and Nymphaion.

Dwelling houses: Acropolis, South Slope; Hill of the Areopagos, West Slope; Agora, South Area.

Mausoleums: Kerameikos; by the Stadium; Chalandri; Kephissia; Aspropyrgos.

Sculpture

Athens: National Archaeological Museum, Rooms 31A–33; Agora Museum; Kanellopoulos Museum. Porto Raphti, statue on island; Museums of Brauron, Marathon, Eleusis, Megara, Aigina, Poros.

Ancient quarries

Marble: Pentelikon; Hymettos; Agriliza; Rhamnous. Limestone: Piraeus, Akte and Mounychia; Brauron, west of; Aigina, Northern Coast.

Early Christian and Early Byzantine period

Basilicas and other churches: Conversion of the Parthenon, Erechtheion, Hephaisteion; Library of Hadrian; Hill of the Areopagos, Church of Dionysios Areopagites; Kaisariani, Church of the Taxiarchs; Glyphada; Kiapha Thiti; Elympos; Brauron; Pikermi; Aigosthenai.

Art: Athens, Byzantine Museum.

Middle Byzantine period

Churches and monasteries: Athens, Ay. Apostoloi (Agora); Plaka: Ay. Ioannis Theologos, Ay. Nikolaos Rangavas, Ay. Aikaterina, Soteira tou Kottaki, Metamorphosis Soteiros; Little Metropolis; Kapnikarea; Ay. Theodoroi; Lykodimou; Ay. Asomatoi; Moni Petraki; Ay. Panton; Omorphi Ekklesia (Kalogreza); Monasteries on Mt. Hymettos: Kaisariani, Asteri, Kareas, Ay. Ioannis Theologos, Ay. Ioannis Kynigos. Attica: Ay. Demetrios; Ay. Nikolaos, Panagia Varaba (by Markopoulo); Daphni; Osios Meletios. Aigina, Ay. Theodoroi; Palaiochora: Ay. Nikolaos, Ay. Stephanos, Ay. Ioannis Theologos, Ay. Nikolaos Mavrika.

Art: Athens, Byzantine Museum; Kanellopoulos Museum; Benaki Museum.

Turkish period

Athens: Roman Agora, Fetiye Moschee; Koran Seminary (Medresse); Monastiraki Square, Moschee.

Neoclassical period

Athens: Makrygianni Museum (Weiler's Hospital); Old Palace (Parliament); Zappeion; Old Parliament; Iliou Melathron (house of H. Schliemann); Academy; University; National Library; German Archaeological Institute; Odeion; National Archaeological Museum; houses in Plaka; villas in Kephissia; Aigina, houses at the harbour.

Grave monuments: First Cemetery of Athens.

Index of sites and monuments

Bibliography

The bibliography listed below is confined to the most important titles relevant to this guide and particularly to the most recent. They are meant to facilitate the beginning of academic research on specific topics and to provide the information for the specialist reader on which the descriptions in the guide are based.

The abbreviations are in accordance with the Archaeological Bibliography ('Archäologische Bibliographie') edited by the German Archaeological Institute (DAI) at Berlin.

1　General bibliography (see below n. 2 ff. the special bibliography for the respective sites):

Lexika: S. Lauffer (ed.), *Griechenland. Lexikon der historischen Stätten*. Von den Anfängen bis zur Gegenwart (München 1989). D. Leekley, R. Noyes, *Archaeological Excavations in Southern Greece* (Park Ridge 1976) 1–29 (Attica). D. Leekley, *Archaeological Excavations on Greek Islands* (Park Ridge 1976) for Aigina, Salamis und Poros. D. Müller, *Topographischer Bildkommentar zu den Historien Herodots*. Griechenland (Tübingen 1987). R. Stillwell (ed.), *The Princeton Encyclopedia of Classical Sites* (Princeton 1979). J. Travlos, *Pictorial Dictionary of Ancient Athens* (London 1971). J. Travlos, *Bildlexikon zur Topographie des antiken Attika* (Tübingen 1988).

Greek architecture: W.B. Dinsmoor, *The Architecture of Ancient Greece* (New York 1975). G. Gruben, *Die Tempel der Griechen* (München 1986). H. Knell, *Perikleische Baukunst* (Darmstadt 1979).

Byzantine architecture: Αρχείον των βυζαντινών μνημείων της Ελλάδος (ed.) A.K. Orlandos. 1, 1935–12, 1973 (reprint 1999). R. Krautheimer, *Early Christian and Byzantine Architecture* (Penguin Books 1965). Ch. Bouras, A. Kaloyeropoulou, R. Andreadi, *The Churches of Attica* (Athens 1970). P. Hetherington, *Byzantine and Medieval Greece* (London 1991).

Early travellers: E. Dodwell, *Views in Greece* (1821). A. Kokkou, Ημέριμνα για τις αρχαιότητες στην Ελλάδα και τα πρώτα μουσεία (Athens 1977). A. Papanikolaou-Christensen, *Athens 1818–1853*; *Views of Athens by Danish Artists* (Athens 1985); R. Stoneman, *Land of Lost Gods. The Search for Classical Greece* (University of Oklahoma Press, Norman & London 1987).

Modern Athens and the historical monuments: A. Papageorgiou-Venetas, Athens. *The Ancient Heritage and the Historic Cityscape in a Modern Metropolis* (Athens 1994).

2 M. Παντελίδου Γκόφα. *Η Νεολιθική Αττική* (Athens 1998). The most recent overview: J.M. Hurwitt, *The Athenian Acropolis* (Cambridge 1999).

3 S.E. Iakovides, *Ἡ μυκηναϊκὴ Ἀκρόπολις τῶν Ἀθηνῶν* (Athens 1962); id., *Late Helladic Citadels on Mainland Greece* (Monumenta graeca et romana, 4. Leiden 1983); P.A. Mountjoy, *Mycenaean Athens* (Jonsered 1995).

4 J.C. Wright, The Mycenaean Entrance System at the West End of the Akropolis of Athens. *Hesperia* 63, 1994, 323–60.

5 W.H. Plommer, The Archaic Acropolis. Some Problems. *JHS* 80, 1960, 127–59; W.H. Schuchhardt, Archaische Bauten auf der Akropolis von Athen. *AA* 1963, 797–824; E. Kluwe, Peisistratos und die Akropolis von Athen. *WissZJena* 14, 1965, No.1, 9–15; R.R. Holloway, The Archaic Acropolis and the Parthenon Frieze. *ArtB* 48, 1966, 223–6; F. Preisshofen, Zur Topographie der Akropolis. *AA* 1977, 74–84; S. Bancroft, *Problems Concerning the Archaic Acropolis at Athens*. Diss. Princeton University 1979 (Ann Arbor 1981); G. Nenci, Il 'Pelargico' (Thuc. II, 17, 1–3; Parke-Wormell, Delphic Oracle, II n.1) e la zona di rispetto nelle città greche arcaiche. *Aparchaí. Nuove ricerche e studi sulla Magna Grecia e la Sicilia antica in onore di P.E. Arias* (Pisa 1982) 35–43. See n. 35 and 48.

6 F. Glaser, Ein Vergleich des Brunnenhauses in Aulis mit der Darstellung im Olivenbaumgiebel. *ÖJh* 51, 1976–77, *Beibl.* 1–10; B. Kiilerich, The Olive-Tree Pediment and the Daughters of Kekrops. *ActaAArtHist* 7, 1989, 1–21.

7 L. Schneider, *Zur sozialen Bedeutung der archaischen Korenstatuen*. Hamburger Beiträge zur Archäologie. Beih. 2 (Hamburg 1975); F.W. Hamdorf, Zur Weihung des Chairedemos auf der Akropolis von Athen. Στήλη. *Τόμος εις μνήμην Ν. Κοντολέοντος* (Athens 1980) 231–5; M. Vickers, Early Greek Coinage. A Reassessment. *NumChron* 145, 1985, 1–44; R. Tölle-Kastenbein, Die Athener Akropolis-Koren. Ort, Anlässe und Zeiten ihrer Aufstellung. *AW 23*, 1992, 133–48; I. Τριάντη, *Το Μουσείο Ακροπόλεως* (Athens 1998) 21–225.

8 G.C.R. Schmalz, Athens, Augustus, and the Settlement of 21 BC. *GrRomByzSt* 37, 1996, 381–98; P. Baldassarri, *ΣΕΒΑΣΤΩΙ ΣΩΤΗΡΙ. Edilizia monumentale ad Atene durante il Saeculum Augustum* (Roma 1998).

9 J. Tobin, Herodes *Attikos and the City of Athens. Patronage and Conflict under the Antonines* (Amsterdam 1997).

10 A. Frantz, Herculius in Athens. Pagan or Christian? *Akten des VII. Internationalen Kongresses für Christliche Archäologie* (Città del Vaticano 1969) 527–30; A. Frantz, A Public Building of Late Antiquity in Athens (IG II² 5205). *Hesperia* 48, 1979, 194–203; A. Frantz, *Late Antiquity: A.D. 267–700. The Athenian Agora XXIV* (Princeton 1988); P. Castrén, Post-Herulian Athens. *Greek and Latin Studies in Memory of C. Fabricius* (Göteborg 1990); I. Baldini Lippolis, La monumentalizzazione tardoantica di Atene. *Ostraka* 4,1 (1995) 169–90.

11 General descriptions: F. Brommer, *Die Akropolis von Athen* (Darmstadt 1985); U. Muss, C. Schubert, *Die Akropolis von Athen* (Graz 1988); L. Schneider, C. Höcker, *Die Akropolis von Athen. Antikes Heiligtum und modernes Reiseziel* (Köln 1990); R.F. Rhodes, *Architecture and Meaning on the Athenian Acropolis* (Cambridge 1995); M. Μπρούσκαρη, *Τα μνημεία της Ακρόπολης* (Athens 1996); J.M. Hurwitt, *The Athenian Acropolis* (Cambridge 1999).

12   IG II² 3055; W.B. Dinsmoor, *AJA* 14, 1910, 459 ff.

13   E.V. Hansen, *The Attalids of Pergamon* (Oxford 1971) 105; 310 n.73; 457; H.J. Schalles, *Untersuchungen zur Kulturpolitik der pergamenischen Herrscher im 3. Jahrhundert v.Chr.* IstForsch 36 (1985) 125 n. 724a.

14   P. Baldassarri (n. 8) 247 ff. pl. LVIII.

15   B. Wesenberg, Die Propyläen der Akropolis in Athen. *U.R. Schriftenreihe der Universität Regensburg* 15, 1988, 9–30; J. de Waele, Mnesikles' Propylaia on the Athenian Akropolis. *Daidalikon. Studies in Memory of R.V. Schoder* (Wauconda 1989) 397–414; R.A. Tomlinson, The Sequence of Construction of Mnesikles' Propylaia. BSA 85, 1990, 405–13; J. de Waele, *The Propylaia of the Akropolis in Athens. The Project of Mnesikles* (Publications of the Netherlands Institute at Athens, 1. Amsterdam 1990); T. Tanoulas, M. Ioannidou, A. Moraitou, *Study for the Restoration of the Propylaia* (Greek with Engl. summary; Athens 1994); I. Mylonas Shear, The Western Approach to the Athenian Akropolis. *JHS 119*, 1999, 86–127.

16   P. Hellström, The Asymmetry of the Pinacotheca once more. *OpAth 11*, 1975, 87–92; W.B. Dinsmoor Jr, The Asymmetry of the Pinakotheke for the Last Time? *Studies in Athenian Architecture, Sculpture and Topography, presented to H.A. Thompson* (Princeton 1982) 18–33; id., Preliminary Planning of the Propylaia by Mnesicles. *Le dessin d'architecture dans les sociétés antiques* (o.O. 1985) 135–47; W. Hoepfner, Propyläen und Nike-Tempel. *Kult und Kultbauten auf der Akropolis.* Intern. Symposion Berlin 7.–9.7.1995 (Berlin 1997) 160–77.

17   G. Gruben, Weitgespannte Marmordecken in der griechischen Architektur. *Architectura* 15, 1985, 105–16.

18   Th.E. Kalpaxis, *Hemiteles. Akzidentelle Unfertigkeit und 'Bossen-Stil' in der griechischen Baukunst* (Mainz 1986) 127–33.

19   W.B. Dinsmoor Jr, *The Propylaia to the Athenian Akropolis, 1. The Predecessors* (Princeton 1980); J.C. Wright, Appendix: The Archaic Cistern and the North-western Corner of the Akropolis. *Hesperia* 63, 1994, 349–60; H. Eiteljorg, *The Entrance to the Athenian Acropolis before Mnesicles* (Dubuque 1995).

20   T. Tanoulas, The Propylaea of the Acropolis at Athens since the Seventeenth Century. Their Decay and Restoration. *JdI* 102, 1987, 413–83; Τ. Τανούλα, *Τα προπύλαια της αθηναϊκής Ακρόπολης κατά τον Μεσαίωνα* (Athens 1998).

21   Φ. Μαλλούχου – Tufano, *Η αναστήλωση των αρχαίων μνημείων στη νεώτερη Ελλάδα* (Athens 1998) 13 ff.

22   I.M. Shear, Kallikrates. *Hesperia* 32, 1963, 337–88; J.A. Bundgaard, Le sujet de IG I² 24. *Mélanges helléniques offerts à G. Daux* (Paris 1974) 43–9; B. Wesenberg, Zur Baugeschichte des Niketempels. *JdI* 96, 1981, 28–54; H.B. Mattingly, The Athena Nike Temple Reconsidered. *AJA* 86, 1982, 381–5; I.S. Mark, *The Sanctuary of Athena Nike in Athens. Architectural Stages and Chronology.* Hesperia Suppl. XXVI (Princeton 1993); D. Giraud, *Study for the Restoration of the Temple of Athena Nike* (Greek with Engl. summary; Athens 1994); I.S. Mark, Levels Taken on the Nike Bastion. *Hesperia* 64, 1995, 331–9; B. Wesenberg, *Gnomon* 70, 1998, 235–40.

23   M. Korres, Ein Beitrag zur Kenntnis der attisch-ionischen Architektur. *Säule und Gebälk. Bauforscherkolloquium Berlin 16.–18.6.1994* (1996) 103–33 'Tempel D 1–5'.

24   G. Despinis, Τὰ γλυπτὰ τῶν ἀετωμάτων τοῦ ναοῦ τῆς Ἀθηνᾶς Νίκης. *ADelt* 29, 1974, 2–24; E. Simon, La decorazione architettonica del tempietto di Atena Nike sull'Acropoli di Atene. *Museum Patavinum* 3, 1986, 271–88; E. Simon, Τα γλυπτά του ναού και του θωρακείου της Αθηνάς Νίκης. *Archaiognosia* 4, 1985–86, 11–27; W. Ehrhardt, Der Torso Wien I 328 und der Westgiebel des Athena-Nike-Tempels auf der Akropolis in Athen. *Beiträge zur Ikonographie und Hermeneutik. Festschrift für N. Himmelmann* (Mainz 1989) 119–27; M. Brouskari, Aus dem Giebelschmuck des Athena-Nike-Tempels. *Beiträge zur Ikonographie und Hermeneutik. Festschrift für N. Himmelmann* (Mainz 1989) 115–18. A. Linfert, Vier klassische Akrotere. Drei Akrotere des Nike-Tempels. Ein Akroter des Ilissos-Tempels. *AA* 1968, 427–34; P.N. Boulter, The Akroteria of the Nike Temple. *Hesperia* 38, 1969, 133–40.

25   E.B. Harrison, Notes on the Nike Temple Frieze. *AJA* 74, 1970, 317–23; E.B. Harrison, A New Fragment from the North Frieze of the Nike Temple. *AJA* 76, 1972, 195–7; E.B. Harrison, The South Frieze of the Nike Temple and the Marathon Painting in the Painted Stoa. *AJA* 76, 1972, 353–78; E.G. Pemberton, The East and West Friezes of the Temple of Athena Nike. *AJA* 76, 1972, 303–10; F. Felten, *Griechische tektonische Friese archaischer und klassischer Zeit* (Schriften aus dem Athenaion der Klassischen Archäologie Salzburg, 4. Waldsassen 1984) 18 ff.; F. Brommer, Zwei klassische Reliefbruchstücke. *JbBerlMus* 27, 1985, 5–13; F. Brommer, Zwei klassische Reliefbruchstücke. Πρακτικά του IB' Διεθνούς συνεδρίου κλασικής αρχαιολογίας III (Athen 1988) 28–32; E.B. Harrison, The Glories of the Athenians. *The Interpretation of Architectural Sculpture in Greece and Rome* (ed. D. Buitron-Oliver; Hanover and London 1997) 109–25.

26   O. Palagia, A New Relief of the Graces and the Charites of Socrates. *Opes Atticae. Miscellanea philologica et historica R. Bogaert et H. Van Looy oblata* (ed.) M. Geerard (The Hague 1990) 347–56.

27   M. Brouskari, Die Nike 7304 des Akropolismuseums und ihre Bedeutung im Zusammenhang mit späteren historischen Abenteuern der Nikebalustrade. *Festschrift für J. Inan* (Istanbul 1989) 153–60; T. Hölscher, Ritual und Bildsprache: Zur Deutung der Reliefs an der Brüstung um das Heiligtum der Athena Nike in Athen. *AM* 112, 1997, 143–66; M.S. Brouskari, Το Θωράκιο του ναού της Αθηνάς Νίκης. *AEphem* 137, 1998 (Athens 1999) 1–268 (with bibliography).

28   E. Kluwe, Studien zur grossen ehernen Athena des Phidias. *Die Krise der griechischen Polis* (Berlin 1969) 21–8; E. Mathiopoulos, *Zur Typologie der Göttin Athena*. Diss. Bonn (1968); A. Linfert, Athenen des Phidias. *AM* 97, 1982, 66–71.

29   Baldassarri (n. 8) 237 ff.

30   G.P. Stevens, *Hesperia* 5, 1936, 442, 494 fig. 44.

31   G.P. Stevens, *Hesperia* 15, 1946, 7 fig. 9; Μπρούσκαρη (n. 11) 237.

32   J.J. Dobbins, The Sanctuary of Artemis Brauronia on the Athenian Akropolis. *Hesperia* 48, 1979, 325–41; S. Angiolillo, Pisistrato e Artemide Brauronia. *PP* 38, 1983, 351–4.

33   G. Despinis, Neues zu einem alten Fund. *AM* 109, 1994, 173–89; id., Zum Athener Brauronion. *Kult und Kultbauten auf der Akropolis. Intern. Symposion Berlin 7.–9.7.1995* (Berlin 1997) 209–17.

34   L. La Follette, The Chalkotheke on the Athenian Akropolis. *Hesperia* 55, 1986, 75–87.

35   M. Korres, Die Athena-Tempel auf der Akropolis. *Kult und Kultbauten auf der Akropolis. Intern. Symposion Berlin 7.–9.7.1995* (1997) 218–43.

36   B. Wesenberg, Kunst und Lohn am Erechtheion. *AA* 1985, 55–65.

37   K. Jeppesen, Further Inquiries on the Location of the Erechtheion and its Relationship to the Temple of the Polias, 1. Prostomiaion and Prostomion. *AJA* 87, 1983, 325–33; E.M. Stern, Das Haus des Erechtheus. *Boreas* 9, 1986, 51–64; K. Jeppesen, Once again. Where was the Erechtheion? – Πρακτικά του IB᾽ Διεθνούς συνεδρίου κλασικής αρχαιολογίας IV (Athens 1988) 77–80; C. Pinatel, Raoul-Rochette et un énigmatique moulage de l'Erechthéion. Πρακτικά του IB᾽ Διεθνούς συνεδρίου κλασικής αρχαιολογίας IV (Athens 1988) 166–71.

38   M. Korres (n. 35) 243 n. 99; Μπρούσκαρη (n. 11) 172 fig. 118.

39   H. Lauter, *Die Koren des Erechtheion* (Antike Plastik 16. Berlin 1976); M. Vickers, Persepolis, Vitruvius and the Erechtheum Caryatids. The Iconography of Medism and Servitude. *RA* 1985, 3–28; A. Leibundgut, Künstlerische Form und konservative Tendenzen nach Perikles. Ein Stilpluralismus im 5. Jh.v.Chr.? *10. TrWPr* (1991) 1–68.

40   A. Scholl, ΧΟΗΦΟΡΟΙ: Zur Deutung der Korenhalle des Erechtheion. *JdI* 110, 1995, 179–212; id., *Die Korenhalle des Erechtheion auf der Akropolis. Frauen für den Staat* (1998).

41   M. Korres, An Early Attic Ionic Capital and the Kekropion on the Athenian Acropolis. *Greek Offerings. Essays on Greek Art in honour of John Boardman* (ed. O. Palagia; Oxford 1997) 95–107.

42   See n. 38.

43   U. Schädler, Ionisches und Attisches am sogenannten Erechtheion in Athen. *AA* 1990, 361–78.

44   E.M. Stern, Glass and gold in classical Greek architecture. Πρακτικά του IB᾽ Διεθνούς συνεδρίου κλασικής αρχαιολογίας III (Athens 1988) 304–8.

45   P.N. Boulter, The Frieze of the Erechtheion. *Antike Plastik* 10 (Berlin 1970) 7–28; F. Felten, *Griechische tektonische Friese archaischer und klassischer Zeit* (Schriften aus dem Athenaion der Klassischen Archäologie Salzburg, 4. Waldsassen 1984) 110 ff.; M. Brouskari, Ζωόδια λαίνεα. Nouvelles figures de la frise de l'Erechtheion. *Kanon. Festschrift E. Berger zum 60. Geburtstag* (Basel 1988) 60–8; K. Glowacki, A New Fragment of the Erechtheion Frieze. *Hesperia* 64, 1995, 325–31.

46   H.J. Kienast, Der Wiederaufbau des Erechtheion. *Architectura* 13, 1983, 89–104; A. Papanikolaou, Τα σχιστοειδούς μορφής ανοίγματα στο Ερέχθειο. *ADelt* 33, 1978 [1984], Nr.1, 191–7; K. Zampas, Αναδιάταξη των λίθων στο νότιο τοίχο του Ερεχθείου. *ADelt* 33, 1978 [1984], Nr.1, 168–90.

47   See n. 35.

48   M. Korres, Wilhelm Dörpfelds Forschungen zum Vorparthenon und Parthenon. *AM* 108, 1993, 59–78; *BCH* 118, 1994, 698 fig. 1.

49   M. Korres, *Study for the Restoration of the Parthenon 4. The West Wall of the Parthenon and Other Monuments* (Greek with an Engl. summary; Athens 1994) 19–29; 12–122 pl. 1.

50   M. Korres, The Architecture of the Parthenon. *The Parthenon and its Impact in Modern Times*. (ed.) P. Tournikiotis (Athens 1994) 54–97.

51   L. Schneider, C. Höcker, *Die Akropolis von Athen. Antikes Heiligtum und modernes Reiseziel* (Köln 1990) 121–86.

52   M. Korres, *BCH* 112, 1988, 612–14 fig. 3; id. (see n. 35) 227–9 fig. 2–3.

53   A.K. Orlandos, Ἡ ἀρχιτεκτονικὴ τοῦ παρθενῶνος I–III (Athens 1977); E. Berger, Das Basler Parthenon-Modell. Bemerkungen zur Architektur des Tempels. *AntK* 23, 1980, 66–100; M. Korres (see n. 50).

54   F. Brommer, *Die Skulpturen der Parthenon-Giebel* (Mainz 1963); E. Berger, Parthenon-Studien I. *AntK* 19, 1976, 122–42; II. *AntK* 20, 1977, 124–41; O. Palagia, *The Pediments of the Parthenon* (Monumenta graeca et romana 7. Leiden 1993); O. Palagia, First among Equals: Athena in the East Pediment of the Parthenon. *The Interpretation of Architectural Sculpture in Greece and Rome* (ed. D. Buitron-Oliver; Hanover and London 1997) 28–49.

55   F. Brommer, *Die Metopen des Parthenon. Katalog und Untersuchung* (Mainz 1967); E. Berger, *Der Parthenon in Basel*. Dokumentation zu den Metopen (Studien der Skulpturhalle Basel 2. Mainz 1986); A. Mantis, Beiträge zur Wiederherstellung der mittleren Südmetopen des Parthenon. *Beiträge zur Ikonographie und Hermeneutik. Festschrift für N. Himmelmann* (Mainz 1989) 109–14; A. Mantis, Parthenon Central South Metopes: New Evidence. *The Interpretation of Architectural Sculpture in Greece and Rome* (ed. D. Buitron-Oliver; Hanover and London 1997) 67–81.

56   F. Brommer, *Der Parthenonfries* (Mainz 1977); I. Jenkins, *The Parthenon Frieze* (London 1994); B. Wesenberg, Panathenäische Peplosdedikation und Arrhephorie. Zur Thematik des Parthenonfrieses. *JdI* 110, 1995, 149–78; J.B. Connelly, Parthenon and Parthenoi: A Mythological Interpretation of the Parthenon Frieze. *AJA* 100, 1996, 53–80; E. Berger, M. Gisler-Huwiler, *Der Parthenon in Basel. Dokumentation zum Fries* (Studien der Skulpturhalle Basel 3. Mainz 1996).

57   N. Leipen, *Athena Parthenos. A Reconstruction* (Toronto 1971); U. Muss, C. Triebel-Schubert, Zu B. Fehr, Zur religionspolitischen Funktion der Athena Parthenos im Rahmen des delisch-attischen Seebundes 1–3. *Hephaistos* 4, 1982, 171–6; B.S. Ridgway, Parthenon and Parthenos. *Papers in Honour of J. Inan* (Istanbul 1989) 295–305; J.M. Hurwitt, Beautiful Evil: Pandora and the Athena Parthenos. *AJA* 99, 1995, 171–86; G. Nick, *Die Athena Parthenos – ein griechisches Kultbild*. B. Schmaltz, Die Parthenos des Phidias, zwischen Kult und Repräsentanz. *Kult und Kultbauten auf der Akropolis. Intern. Symposion Berlin 7.–9.7.1995* (1997) 22–4, 25–30.

58   M. Korres, F. Mallouchou-Tufano, P. Tournikiotis, D. van Zanten, *The Parthenon and its Impact in Modern Times* (ed.) P. Tournikiotis (Athens 1994) 136–309.

59   M. Korres, *BCH* 110, 1986, 674 fig. 8.

60   K.K. Carroll, *The Parthenon Inscription* (Greek, Roman and Byzantine monographs, 9. Durham, North Carolina 1982).

61   Ch. Bouras, Restoration Work on the Parthenon and Changing Attitudes towards the Conservation of Monuments. *The Parthenon and its Impact in Modern Times* (ed.) P. Tournikiotis (Athens 1994) 310–39.

62   W. Binder, *Der Roma-Augustus Monopteros auf der Akropolis in Athen und sein typologischer Ort* (Stuttgart 1969); P. Baldassarri, Augusto soter: ipotesi sul monopteros dell' Acropoli ateniense. *Ostraka* 4,1, 1995, 69–84; id. (see. n. 8) 45–63; Μ.Σ. Μπρούσκαρη, *Τα Μνημεία της Ακρόπολης* (Athens 1996) 159–62.

63 Μπρούσκαρη (see n. 62) 163–6.

64 Μπρούσκαρη (see n. 62) 167–8.

65 L. Beschi, Contributi di topografia ateniese. *ASAtene* 45–6, 1967–68, 511–536: O. Dally, Kulte und Kultbilder der Aphrodite in Attika im späteren 5. Jh.v.Chr. *JdI* 112, 1997, 13–15.

66 I. Τριάντη, Το Μουσείο Ακροπόλεως (Athens 1998).

67 J. Tobin, *Herodes Attikos and the City of Athens* (Amsterdam 1997) 185–94; M. Galli, *AntW* 29, 1998, 519–28.

68 M. Korres, Vorfertigung und Ferntransport eines athenischen Grossbaus und Proportionierung von Säulen in der hellenistischen Architektur. *Bauplanung und Bautheorie der Antike* (Berlin 1984) 201–07.

69 L. Beschi, Il monumento di Telemachos, fondatore dell'Asklepieion ateniese. *ASAtene* 45–6, 1967–68, 381–436; R.A. Tomlinson, Two Buildings in Sanctuaries of Asklepios. *JHS* 89, 1969, 106–17; T.E. Gregory, The Christian Asklepieion in Athens. *AnnByzConf* 9, 1983, 39–40; S.B. Aleshire, *The Athenian Asklepieion. The People, their Dedications, and the Inventory* (Amsterdam 1989).

70 Th.G. Papathanasopoulos, Το ιερό και īο Θέαīρο īου Διονῡσου (Athens 1993); P.G. Kalligas, *Η εριοχή του ιερού και του θεάτρου του Διονύσου στην Αθήνα. The Archaeology of Athens and Attica under the Democracy* (ed.) Coulson, W.D.E. (Oxford 1994) 25–30.

71 G. Despinis, *ASAtene* 1999, forthcoming.

72 H.R. Goette, Griechische Theaterbauten der Klassik – Forschungsstand und Fragestellungen, in: E. Pöhlmann, *Studien zur Bühnendichtung und zum Theaterbau der Antike*. Studien zur klassischen Philologie 93, (ed.) M.v. Albrecht (Frankfurt 1995) 9–48.

73 M.C. Sturgeon, The Reliefs on the Theater of Dionysos in Athens. *AJA* 81, 1977, 31–53; A. Frantz, The Date of the Phaidros Bema in the Theater of Dionysos. *Studies in Athenian Architecture, Sculpture and Topography, presented to H.A. Thompson* (Princeton 1982) 34–9; Α. Δεσποίνη, Παρατηρήσεις στα ανάγλυφα του Βήματος του Φαίδρου. *Πρακτικά του ΙΒ' Διεθνούς συνεδρίου κλασικής αρχαιολογίας III* (Athens 1988) 70–3.

74 K. Fittschen, Zur Rekonstruktion griechischer Dichterstatuen I. Die Statue des Menander. *AM* 106, 1991, 243–79.

75 H.R. Goette, Mausoleum oder choregisches Monument. Festschr. G. Traversari (forthcoming); see n. 78.

76 R.F. Townsend, A Newly Discovered Capital from the Thrasyllos Monument. *AJA* 89, 1985, 676–80; P. Amandry, Monuments chorégiques d'Athènes. *BCH* 121, 1997, 459–63.

77 P. Amandry, Monuments chorégiques d'Athènes. *BCH* 121, 1997, 446–59.

78 A. Choremi, K.N. Kazamiakis, Η οδός των Τριπόδων και τα χορηγικά μνημεία στην αρχαία Αθήνα. *The Archaeology of Athens and Attica under the Democracy* (ed.) Coulson, W.D.E. (Oxford 1994) 31–44; C. Schnurr, Zur Topographie der Theaterstätten und der Tripodenstraße in Athen. *ZPE* 105, 1995, 139–53; see n. 75.

79 M. Korres, *ADelt* 35, 1980 (1988) B1, 14–18.

80 A.L.K. Robkin, The Odeion of Perikles. The Date of Its Construction and the Periklean Building Program. *AncWorld* 2, 1979, 3–12; id., The Tent of Xerxes

and the Odeion of Themistokles. Some Speculations. *AncWorld* 3, 1980, 45–6; B. Schmaltz, Perikles, die Musik und die Meerzwiebel. *AM* 110, 1995, 247–52.

81   G.S. Dontas, The True Aglaurion. *Hesperia* 52, 1983, 48–63; N. Robertson, The City Center of Archaic Athens. *Hesperia* 67, 1998, 283–302; D. Harris–Cline, Archaic Athens and the Topography of the Kylon Affair. *BSA* 94, 1999, 309–20 (with bibliography).

82   T.L. Shear, Ἰσονόμους τ᾽ Ἀθήνας ἐποιήσατεν: The Agora and the Democracy. The Archaeology of Athens and Attica under the Democracy (ed.) W.D.E. Coulson (Oxford 1994) 225–48; Chr. Schnurr, Die Alte Agora Athens. *ZPE* 105, 1995, 131–5; S. Miller, Architecture as Evidence for the Identity of the Early Polis. M.H. Hansen (ed.), *Sources for the Ancient Greek City-State* (Copenhagen 1995) 201–44; N. Robertson, The City Center of Archaic Athens. *Hesperia* 67, 1998, 283–302.

83   O. Broneer, Notes on three Athenian Cult Places. *AEphem* 1960, 54–67; O. Dally, Kulte und Kultbilder der Aphrodite in Attika im späteren 5. Jh.v.Chr. *JdI* 112, 1997, 1–20.

84   P.J. Riis, A Colossal Athenian Pan. *ActaArch* 45, 1974, 124–33.

85   K. Clinton, Apollo, Pan, and Zeus, Avengers of Vultures. *AJPh* 94, 1973, 282–8.

86   H. Lauter-Bufé, H. Lauter, Wohnhäuser und Stadtviertel des klassischen Athen. *AM* 86, 1971, 109–24; J.W. Graham, Houses of Classical Athens. *Phoenix* 28, 1974, 45–54; H. Lauter, Zum Straßenbild in Alt-Athen. *AW* 13, 1982, no.4, 44–52.

87   See n. 23.

88   U. Kron, Demos, Pnyx und Nymphenhügel. Zu Demos-Darstellungen und zum ältesten Kultort des Demos in Athen. *AM* 94, 1979, 49–75.

89   B. Forsén, G. Stanton (ed.), *The Pnyx in the History of Athens* (1995).

90   M.H. Hansen, The Construction of Pnyx II and the Introduction of Assembly Pay. *ClMediaev* 37, 1986, 89–98 (= id., The Athenian Ecclesia 2 [Copenhagen 1989] 143–53).

91   S.I. Rotroff, J. Camp, The Date of the Third Period of the Pnyx. *Hesperia* 65, 1996, 231–61.

92   D.E.E. Kleiner, *The Monument of Philopappos in Athens* (*Archaeologica* 30. Roma 1983); H.R. Goette, Zwei Relieffragmente in Athen. *AA* 1991, 389–98.

93   U. Knigge, *The Athenian Kerameikos. History – Monuments – Excavations* (Athens 1991); *AM* 114, 1999 (forthcoming); preliminary reports of the new excavations by J. Stroszeck, *AA* 1999, 147–72.

94   A. Parlama, *Η πόλη κάτω από την πόλη. Exhibition Goulandris-Museum Febr. 2000 – Dec. 2001* (Athens 2000).

95   J.M. Camp, *The Athenian Agora. Excavations in the Heart of Classical Athens* (London 1986); *The Athenian Agora. A Guide to the Excavation and Museum*[4] (Athens 1990).

96   J.K. Papadopoulos, The Origial Kerameikos of Athens and the Siting of the Classical Agora. *GrRomByzSt* 37, 1996, 107–28 (with a date even after 480 BC); see n. 81–2.

97   J. Dörig, *La frise est de l' Héphaisteion* (Mainz 1985); E.B. Harrison, Alkamenes' Sculptures for the Hephaisteion, 1. The Cult Statues. *AJA* 81, 1977, 137–78; 2. The Base. *AJA* 81, 1977, 265–87; 3. Iconography and Style. *AJA* 81, 1977,

411–26; K. Reber, Das Hephaisteion in Athen – ein Monument für die Demokratie. *JdI* 113, 1998, 31–48.

98   T.L. Shear, Ἰσονόμους τ' Ἀθήνας ἐποιήσατεν: *The Agora and the Democracy. The Archaeology of Athens and Attica under the Democracy* (ed.) W.D.E. Coulson (Oxford 1994) 225–48.

99   T.L. Shear Jr, The Monument of the Eponymous Heroes in the Athenian Agora. *Hesperia* 39, 1970, 145–222; U. Kron, *Die zehn attischen Phylenheroen*. AM Beih. 5 (Berlin 1976); E.B. Harrison, The Iconography of the Eponymous Heroes on the Parthenon and in the Agora. Greek Numismatics and Archaeology. *Essays in Honor of M. Thompson* (Wetteren 1979) 71–85; C.C. Mattusch, The Eponymous Heroes: The Idea of Sculptural Groups. *The Archaeology of Athens and Attica under the Democracy* (ed.) W.D.E. Coulson (Oxford 1994) 73–81; Cl. Vatin, La base des Héros Eponymes à Athènes au temps de Pausanias. *Ostraka* 4, 1, 1995, 33–41.

100   H. Knell, Der jüngere Tempel des Apollon Patroos auf der Athener Agora. *JdI* 109, 1994, 217–37.

101   O. Palagia, No Demokrateia. *The Archaeology of Athens and Attica under the Democracy* (ed.) W.D.E. Coulson (Oxford 1994) 113–22; T.L. Shear, id. 225–48.

102   M. Osanna, Il culto di Hermes Agoraios ad Atene. *Ostraka* 1, 1992, 215–22. Aphrodite Ourania: O. Dally, Kulte und Kultbilder der Aphrodite in Attika im späteren 5. Jh.v.Chr. *JdI* 112, 1997, 1–20.

103   M. Vickers, The Oenoe Painting in the Stoa Poikile, and Herodotus' Account of Marathon. *BSA* 80, 1985, 99–113.

104   S. Angiolillo, Hestia, l'edificio F e l'altare dei 12 dei ad Atene. *Ostraka* 1, 1992, 171–6; L.M. Gadbery, The Sanctuary of the Twelve Gods in the Athenian Agora. A Revised View. *Hesperia* 61, 1992, 447–89.

105   M. Korres, Από τον Σταυρό στην Αγορά. *Horos* 10–12, 1992–98, 83–104.

106   H.R. Goette, Athena Pallenis und ihre Beziehungen zur Akropolis von Athen. *Kult und Kultbauten auf der Akropolis. Intern. Symposion Berlin 7.–9.7.1995* (1997) 116–31; id., *Horos* 10–12, 1992–98, 105–18.

107   Th. Schäfer, *Spolia et signa. Baupolitik und Reichskultur nach dem Parthererfolg des Augustus*. Nachrichten der Göttinger Akademie der Wissenschaften 1998, 2, 46–123.

108   J.M. Camp, The Philosophical Schools of Roman Athens. *The Greek Renaissance in the Roman Empire* (London 1989) 50–5; P. Baldassarri, *ΣΕΒΑΣΤΩΙ ΣΩΤΗΡΙ. Edilizia monumentale ad Atene durante il Saeculum Augustum* (Roma 1998) 115–41.

109   R.F. Townsend, *The East Side of the Agora. The Remains beneath the Stoa of Attalos. The Athenian Agora XXVII* (Princeton 1995). Perhaps in Classical times there was the Heliaia in the northern part of the later stoa; the courtyard building at the southwest corner of the agora then should be interpreted as the Aiakeion: R. Stroud, *ZPE* 103, 1994, 1–9; M. Munn, *The School of History* (Berkely, Los Angeles, London 2000) 264–72 fig. 8.

110   M. Hoff, The Early History of the Roman Agora at Athens. *The Greek Renaissance in the Roman Empire* (London 1989) 1–8; P. Baldassarri, *ΣΕΒΑΣΤΩΙ ΣΩΤΗΡΙ. Edilizia monumentale ad Atene durante il Saeculum Augustum* (Roma 1998) 99–113.

111   J.v. Freeden, *Οἰκία Κυρρήστου. Studien zum sogenannten Turm der Winde in Athen* (Archaeologica 29. Roma 1983); W. Heinz, R.C.A. Rottländer, W. Neumaier, Untersuchungen am Turm der Winde in Athen. *ÖJh* 59, 1989, 55–92; S. Berti, Gli orologi pubblici nel mondo antico. Il caso di Atene e di Roma. *Archeologia e astronomia* (Roma 1991) 83–87; H.J. Kienast, Untersuchungen am Turm der Winde. *AA* 1993, 271–5.

112   M.C. Hoff, The So-called Agoranomion and the Imperial Cult in Julio-Claudian Athens. *AA* 1994, 93–117; M. Korres, *The Parthenon and its Impact in Modern Times* (ed.) P. Tournikiotis (Athens 1994) 144 n. 38, fig. 8.

113   W. Martini, Zur Benennung der sog. Hadriansbibliotek in Athen. *Lebendige Altertumswissenschaft. Festgabe zur Vollendung des 70. Lebensjahres von H. Vetters* (Wien 1985) 189–91; D. Willers, *Hadrians panhellenisches Programm. Archäologische Beiträge zur Neugestaltung Athens durch Hadrian* (*AntK*, Beiheft 16. Basel 1990) 14–21.

114   A. Spetsieri–Choremi, Library of Hadrian at Athens, recent Finds. *Ostraka* 4,1, 1995, 137–47.

115   I. Travlos, Τὸ τετράκογχο οἰκοδόμημα τῆς βιβλιοθήκης τοῦ ʼΑδριανοὺ. Φιλία ἔπη εἰς Γ.Ε. Μυλωνάν (Athens 1986–89) I 343–7; I. Baldini Lippolis, La monumentalizzazzione tardoantica di Atene. *Ostraka* 4,1, 1995, 169–190.

116   T. Karagiorga-Stathakopoulou, Δημόσια έργα και ανασκαφές στην Αθήνα τα τελευταία πέντε χρόνια. *Horos* 6, 1988, 87–108.

117   I. Travlos, Πολεοδομικὴ ἐξελίξις τῶν ʼΑθηνῶν (1960; repr. Athens 1993).

118   S. Miller, Old Discoveries from Old Athens. *Hesperia* 39, 1970, 223–31; P. Amandry, Trépieds d'Athènes, 1. Dionysies. *BCH* 100, 1976, 15–93; H. Bauer, Lysikratesdenkmal, Baubestand und Rekonstruktion. *AM* 92, 1977, 197–227; J.R. McCredie, The 'Lantern of Demosthenes' and Lysikrates, Son of Lysitheides, of Kikynna. *Studies presented to S. Dow* (Durham 1984) 181–3; M. Korres, *ADelt* 36, 1981 (1988) B1, 5–7; T. Kossatz, A. Kossatz-Deissmann, *Kotinos. Festschr. E. Simon* (1992) 469–78; W. Ehrhardt, *AntPl* 22, 1993, 7–67; P. Amandry, Monuments chorégiques d'Athènes. *BCH* 121, 1997, 463–87.

119   E. Lippolis, Tra il ginnasio di Tolemeo ed il Serapeion. La ricostruzione topographica di un quartiere monumentale di Atene. *Ostraka* 4,1, 1995, 43–67.

120   A. Adams, The arch of Hadrian at Athens. *The Greek Renaissance in the Roman Empire* (London 1989) 10–16; D. Willers, *Hadrians panhellenisches Programm. Archäologische Beiträge zur Neugestaltung Athens durch Hadrian* (AntK, Beiheft 16. Basel 1990) 68–92.

121   Willers op. cit. 54–67, 93–103; C. Antonetti, V. Marotta, *Ostraka* 4,1, 1995, 149–67.

122   Willers op.cit. 26–53; R. Tölle–Kastenbein. *Das Olympieion in Athen* (Köln 1994) with the critic of H.J. Kienast, *Gnomon*, 71, 1999, 247–50.

123   Results of a research by M. Korres: *ANΘEMION. Eνημερωτικό Δελτίο της Eνώσεως Φίλων Ακροπόλεως* 50, January 1999, 27–9.

124   Not yet found are the temple of Apollo Pythios and – on the other side of the river – the sanctuary of Herakles Kynosarges: M.F. Billot, Le Cynosarges, Antiochos et les tanneurs. Questions de topographie. *BCH* 116, 1992, 119–56; M.F. Arnush, The Career of Peisistratos Son of Hippias. *Hesperia* 64, 1995, 135–62.

125   M.M. Miles, The Date of the Temple on the Ilissos River. *Hesperia* 49, 1980, 309–25; H. Büsing, Zur Bauplanung ionisch-attischer Säulenfronten. *AM* 100, 1985, 159–205; M. Korres, Ein Beitrag zur Kenntnis der attisch-ionischen Architektur. *Säule und Gebälk. Bauforscherkolloquium Berlin 16.–18.6.1994* (1996) 103–33.

126   A. Krug, Der Fries des Tempels am Ilissos. *Antike Plastik XVIII* (Berlin 1979) 7–21; W.A.P. Childs, In Defense of an Early Date for the Frieze of the Temple on the Ilissos. *AM* 100, 1985, 207–51; M. Krumme, Das Heiligtum der 'Athena beim Palladion' in Athen. *AA* 1993, 213–27; K.-V. v. Eickstedt, Bemerkungen zur Ikonographie des Frieses vom Ilissos–Tempel. *The Archaeology of Athens and Attica under the Democracy* (ed.) W.D.E. Coulson (Oxford 1994) 105–111.

127   J. Tobin, *Herodes Attikos and the City of Athens. Patronage and Conflict under the Antonines* (Amsterdam 1997) 162–85.

128   D. Photopoulos, A. Delivorrias, *Η Ελλάδα του Μουσείου Μπενάκη* (Athens 1997).

129   Chr. Doumas, *The N.P. Goulandris Collection of Early Cycladic Art* (Athens 1968); id., *Cycladic Art. Ancient Sculpture and Pottery from the N.P. Goulandris Collection* (London 1983); L. Marangou, *Αρχαία Ελληνική Τέχν. Συλλογή Ν.Π. Γουλανδρή* (Athens 1985).

130   C.E. Ritchie Jr, The Lyceum, the Garden of Theophrastos, and the Garden of the Muses. *A Topographical Re-evaluation. Φιλία έπη εις Γ.Ε. Μυλωνάν* (Athens 1986–89) III 250–60.

131   See n. 23.

132   H. Lauter, *Der Kultplatz auf dem Turkovuni. Attische Forschungen I.* (12. Beih. *AM* 1985).

133   P.D. Stavropoullos, Ἀνασκαπηαὶ ἀρχαίας Ἀκαδημείας. *Prakt* 1960–1963; D.G. Kyle, *Athletics in Ancient Athens* (Mnemosyne, suppl. 95. Leiden 1987); P. Balatsos, Inscriptions from the Academy. *ZPE* 86, 1991, 145–54.

134   S. Benton, Echelos' Hippodrome. *BSA* 67, 1972, 13–19; E. Kirsten, Ur-Athen und die Heimat des Sophokles. *WSt* 86, 1973, 5–26.

135   K.-V. v. Eickstedt, *Beiträge zur Topographie des antiken Piräus* (Athens 1991); W. Hoepfner, E.-L. Schwandtner, *Haus und Stadt im klassischen Griechenland* I² (München 1994) 22–50; G. Steinhauer, *Τα μνημεία και το Αρχαιολογικό Μουσείο του Πειραιά* (1998).

136   O. Dally, Kulte und Kultbilder der Aphrodite in Attika im späteren 5. Jh.v.Chr. *JdI* 112, 1997, 1–20.

137   K.-W. Weeber, *Smog über Attika* (Zürich-München 1990).

138   M.K. Langdon, A Sanctuary of Zeus on Mount Hymettos. *Hesperia* Suppl. 16 (1976); H. Lohmann, *Atene* (Köln 1993) 234 n. 1589–93.

139   J. Ober, Rock-Cut Inscriptions from Mt. Hymettos. *Hesperia* 50, 1981, 68–73 Nr. 1; H.R. Goette, Investigation of the greyish-blue Marble of Pentelikon and Hymettus. *Actes de la IVéme Conférence Internationale, ASMOSIA IV* (Bordeaux 9–13 October 1995; 1999).

140   J. Ober, *Hesperia* 50, 1981, 68 ff.; M. Langdon, Hymettiana I. *Hesperia* 54, 1985, 257–60; id., *Hesperia* 68, 1999, 481–508; see G. Stanton, *BSA* 91, 1996, 361–62.

141   M.K. Langdon, Hymettiana I. *Hesperia* 54, 1985, 260–63.

142   Chr. J. Korres, Sphettia Odos – Part of the Road to Kephali and Sounion. *Proceedings of a Conference on Ancient Roads in Greece, Athens 23 November 1998* (forthcoming).

143   M.K. Langdon, Hymettiana IV: Ancient Routes through Hymettos. *Proceedings of a Conference on Ancient Roads in Greece, Athens 23 November 1998* (forthcoming).

144   H.R. Goette, *Griechische Theaterbauten der Klassik* – Forschungsstand und Fragestellungen, in: E. Pöhlmann, *Studien zur Bühnendichtung und zum Theaterbau der Antike*. Studien zur klassischen Philologie 93, ed. M.v. Albrecht (Frankfurt 1995) 16–17.

145   A. Orlandos, *PAA* 5, 1930, 258 ff.; E. Giannopoulou-Konsolaki, *Γλυφάδα. Ιστορικό παρελθόν και μνημεία* (1990) 155 ff.

146   H. Lauter, *Attische Landgemeinden in klassischer Zeit* (Attische Forschungen 4). MarbWPr 1991 (1993); I. Andreou, Ο δήμος των Αιξωνίδων Αλών. *The Archaeology of Athens and Attica under the Democracy* (ed.) W.D.E. Coulson (1994) 191–209; M. Matthaiou, *Horos* 10–12, 1992–98, 133–69; H.R. Goette, G. Schörner, *Die Pangrotte von Vari* (Mainz; forthcoming) Chapter I.

147   H. Lauter, *AA* 1980, 242 ff.; G.R. Stanton, *BSA* 79, 1984, 298 ff.; M.K. Langdon, *Chiron* 18, 1988, 43 ff.; H.R. Goette, *Klio* 76, 1994, 120 ff.; G. Stanton, *BSA* 91, 1996, 353–64.

148   H. Lauter, *Lathuresa. Beiträge zur Architektur und Siedlungsgeschichte in spät-geometrischer Zeit* (Attische Forschungen II. 1985) 64 ff. fig. 9.

149   Lauter op. cit. (n. 148).

150   H. Lauter–Bufe, *AM* 94, 1979, 161 ff.

151   M.K. Langdon, *Chiron* 18, 1988, 43 ff.

152   Lauter op.cit. (n. 148). A. Mazarakis Ainian, *Ε' επιστημονική συνάντηση νοτιοανατολικής Αττικής 5.–9. 12. 1991* (1994) 231 ff.; id., *Klados. Essays in Honour of J.N. Coldstream*. Bulletin of the Institute of Classical Studies Univ. of London. Suppl. 63 (1995) 143 ff.

153   Goette, Schörner (see n. 146).

154   J.E. Jones, A.J. Graham, L.H. Sackett, *BSA* 68, 1973, 355 ff.

155   J. Travlos, *Bildlexikon zur Topographie des antiken Attika* (1988) 468 fig. 601–2.

156   K. Kourouniotis, *ADelt* 11, 1927/8, 9 ff.

157   H. Lauter, H. Lauter-Bufe, *Festschr. W. Böser. Karlsruher gewissenschaftliche Schriften* (1986) 285 ff.

158   D. Hagel, H. Lauter (Hrsg.), Kiapha Thiti. Ergebnisse der Ausgrabung. *MarbWPr* 1989 (1990).

159   H.R. Goette, *AM* 110, 1995, 235–46.

160   G. Stanton, *BSA* 91, 1996, 358–9; Goette, op.cit. (n. 159).

161   M. K. Langdon, *Festschr. E. Vanderpool. Hesperia* Suppl. 19, 1982, 90–1; H. Lohmann, *Atene* (1993) 160 n. 1205.

162   H. Lohmann, *Atene* (1993) 60–74.

163   H. Lauter, Ein ländliches Heiligtum hellenistischer Zeit in Trapuria (Attika). *AA* 1980, 242–55.

164   H. Lohmann, *Atene* (1993) 142–4, 248–51.

165   H. Lohmann, *Atene* (1993) passim; esp. 196–218.

166   H. Lohmann, *Atene* (1993) 86–98; esp. 86 n. 675; 95–6; 164–6.

167   H. Lohmann, *Atene* (1993) 88–94.

168   H.R. Goette, Ὁαξιόλογος δῆμος Σούνιον. Landeskundliche Studien in Südost-Attika. *Internationale Archäologie* 59 (Rahden 2000).

169   H. Mussche, *BCH* 88, 1964, 423 ff.; H. Lauter, *MWPr* 1988, 11 ff.

170   A. Corso, *BSA* 92, 1997, 383 ff.; Goette (see n. 168).

171   H.R. Goette, *AM* 110, 1995, 171–4; H.R. Goette, Städtische Siedlungen in Attika. Stadt und Umland. *DiskAB* 7 (Berlin 1999) 160–7.

172   E. Kakavogiannis, *ADelt* 32, 1977 A (1982) 205 n. 94; 206 n. 103; J.E. Jones, *GaR* 29, 1982, 169 ff.; M. Salliora–Oikonomakou, *ADelt* 34, 1979 A (1986) 161 ff.; id., *ADelt* 34, 1979 B (1987) 89; Travlos, Attika 405–6 fig. 536–42; Goette (see n. 168).

173   J.H. Young, *Hesperia* 10, 1941, 163 ff.; C. Conophagos, *Le Laurion antique* (1980) 287 ff. fig. 11.9–11.11; Κ.Γ. Τσαῖμου, *Αρχαιογνωσία των μεταλλών* (1993) 150 fig. 59.

174   C. Conophagos, *Le Laurion antique* (1980); Goette (n. 168).

175   J.H. Young, *Hesperia* 25, 1956, 122 ff. no. 1; S. Thielemans, MIGRA 9 (1994) 136–7 n.55 ff.; Goette (n. 168).

176   J.H. Young, *Hesperia* 25, 1956, 124 ff. no. 2; M.K. Langdon, V.L. Watrous, *Hesperia* 46, 1977, 162 ff.; M. Waelkens, *MIGRA 5. Studies in South Attica I* (1982) 149 ff.; H.R. Goette, *Klio* 76, 1994, 133–4 Nr. 5; Goette (n. 168).

177   H.R. Goette, *AM* 106, 1991, 201 ff.; D. Vanhove, *MIGRA* 9 (1994) 40 ff.; Goette (n. 168).

178   J.E. Jones, *ArchRep* 1984/5, 106 ff.; id., *BSA* 89, 1994, 307 ff.; Goette (n. 168).

179   H.F. Mussche, *Thorikos. Eine Führung durch die Ausgrabungen* (Gent/Nürnberg 1978); H.R. Goette, Städtische Siedlungen in Attika. *Stadt und Umland. DiskAB* 7 (Berlin 1999) 160–7.

180   V. Petrakos, *To Ἔργον 1996*, 19–23; id., *To Ἔργον 1997*, 23–4.

181   H.R. Goette, Griechische Theaterbauten der Klassik – Forschungsstand und Fragestellungen, in: E. Pöhlmann, *Studien zur Bühnendichtung und zum Theaterbau der Antike*. Studien zur klassischen Philologie 93 (ed.) M.v. Albrecht (Frankfurt 1995) 12–13.

182   H.F. Mussche, *BCH* 85, 1961, 176–205.

183   St.G. Miller, *Hesperia* 41, 1972, 192–7; C.C.C. Vermeule, *Hesperia* 45, 1976, 67–76.

184   H. Lauter-Bufe, *MarbWPr* 1988, 67–102.

185   J. Mylonopoulos, F. Bubenheimer, *AA* 1996, 7–23; S. Grebe, Jüngere oder ältere Mädchen. Zu Aristophanes, Lysistrate 641–7. *MusHelv* 56, 1999, 194–203.

186   M.K. Langdon, *Studies in Attic Epigraphy, History, and Topography presented to E. Vanderpool. Hesperia Suppl.* 19 (1982) 97–8.

187   H. Knell, Der Tempel der Artemis Tauropolos in Lutsa. *AA* 1983, 39–43; M.B. Hollinshead, Against Iphigeneia's Adyton in three Mainland Temples. *AJA* 89, 1985, 419–40.

188   D. Theocharis, *AEphem* 1953/4, III 59–76; M. Pantelidou Gopha, Η νεολιθική Αττική (1997) fig. 91.

189   E. Mastrokostas, *AAA* 5, 1972, 298–324; E. Karakasi, *AW* 28,6, 1997, 509–17.

190   A. Kaloyeropoulou, *BCH* 93, 1969, 56–71.

191   H. Lauter, *MarbWPr* 1991, 97–101.

192   U. Knigge, Zum Löwen von Kantzas. *AM* 91, 1976, 167–73; X. Arapogianni, Ανασκαφή στην Κάντζα Αττικής. *Πρακτικά Β' επιστημονικής συνάντησης ΝΑ. Αττικής* (Kalyvia Attikis 25–8 Okt. 1985; 1986) 255–61; H.R. Goette, A. Zimmermann, *Der Wandel archäologischer Denkmäler in historischen und zeitgenössischen Photographien. Exhib. Zürich 1995/6* (Zürich 1995) 77–9.

193   H.R. Goette, Athena Pallenis und ihre Beziehungen zur Akropolis von Athen. *Kult und Kultbauten auf der Akropolis. Intern. Symposion Berlin 7.–9.7.1995* (1997) 116–31; id., *Horos* 10–12, 1992–98, 105–18.

194   M. Korres, *Horos* 10–12, 1992–98, 83–104.

195   B. Petrakos, *Marathon. Archaeological Guide* (1996); Th. Weber, *Marathon. Schlachtfeld und Sommerfrische.* Sondernummer AW (Mainz, forthcoming).

196   J. Tobin, *Herodes Attikos and the City of Athens. Patronage and Conflict under the Antonines* (Amsterdam 1997) 241–83.

197   W. Wrede, *Attische Mauern* (1933) 56–57 pl. 68, 82.

198   V. Petrakos, *Rhamnous* (1991); excavation reports of V. Petrakos in *Prakt* and Ergon, newest plans in *Prakt* 1991 (1994) 1 ff. fig. 1 and in *Ergon* 1996, 13 ff.; H.R. Goette, Städtische Siedlungen in Attika. *Stadt und Umland. DiskAB 7* (Berlin 1999) 160–7; B.Ch. Petrakos, Ὁ δῆμος τοῦ Ῥαμνοῦντος I–II (Athens 2000).

199   J. Bergemann, *Demos und Thanatos* (München 1997), esp. 1–34, 198–201 N 1–8.

200   A. Mazarakis Ainian, *Ergon* 1998, 24 ff.

201   B. Ch. Petrakos, Οἱ ἐπιγραφὲς τοῦ Ὠρωποῦ (Athens 1997) 641–7 (bibliography) pl. A and Z; M. Pologiorgi, *ADelt* 43, 1988 (1995) 114–37.

202   H.R. Goette, Beobachtungen im Theater des Amphiareion von Oropos. *AM* 110, 1995, 253–60.

203   J.R. McCredie, *Fortified Military Camps in Attica. Hesperia Suppl.* 11 (1966) 52–6.

204   A. Tschira, Eine römische Grabkammer in Kephissia. *AA* 1948/9, 83–97.

205   J. Tobin, *Herodes Attikos and the City of Athens. Patronage and Conflict under the Antonines* (Amsterdam 1997) 211–39.

206   M. Korres, *From Pentelicon to the Parthenon* (Athens 1995), esp. 62–127 with bibliography.

207   W.R. Biers, Th.D. Boyd, Ikarion in Attica: 1888–1981. *Hesperia* 51, 1982, 1–18; for the theatre see. n. 72.

208   I. Romano, The Archaic Statue of Dionysos from Ikarion. *Hesperia* 51, 1982, 398–409.

209   E. Voutiras, A Dedication of the Hebdomaistai to the Pythian Apollo. *AJA* 86, 1982, 229–33.

210   J. Ober, *Fortress Attica: Defense of the Athenian Land Frontier, 404–322 BC.* (Leiden 1985); M.H. Munn, *The Defense of Attica. The Dema Wall and the Boiotian War of 378–375 BC.* (Berkeley, Los Angeles, Oxford 1993).

211   M. Munn, The First Excavations at Panakton on the Attic-Boiotian Frontier. *Boeotia Antiqua VI* (ed. by J. Fossey; Amsterdam 1996) 47–58.

212   J.R. McCredie, *Fortified Military Camps in Attica. Hesperia Suppl.* 11 (1966) 56–58.

213   McCredie op. cit.

214   H.W. Parke, *Festivals of the Athenians* (London 1977) 55–72; K. Preka-Alexandri, *Eleusis* (Athens 1991); K. Clinton, *Myth and Cult. The Iconography of the Eleusinian Mysteries* (Stockholm 1992).

215   J. Travlos, *Bildlexikon zur Topographie des antiken Attika* (Tübingen 1988) 91–169; A. Jördens, IG II^2 1682 und die Baugeschichte des eleusinischen Telesterion im 4. Jh. v.Chr. *Klio* 81, 1999, 359–91.

216   Δ. Ζιρώ, *Τα μεγάλα προπύλαια της Ελευσίνας* (Athens 1991).

217   D. Willers, *Hadrians panhellenisches Programm. Archäologische Beiträge zur Neugestaltung Athens durch Hadrian* (AntK Beiheft 16. Basel 1990) 84–92; id., Der Vorplatz des Heiligtums von Eleusis – Ueberlegungen zur Neugestaltung im 2. Jahrhundert n. Chr., in: *Retrospektive: Konzepte von Vergangenheit in der griechisch-römischen Antike* (ed.) M. Flashar, H.-J. Gehrke, E. Heinrich (München 1996) 179–225.

218   J.R. McCredie, *Fortified Military Camps in Attica. Hesperia Suppl.* 11 (1966) 72–5.

219   J.E. Jones, L.H. Sackett, C.W.J. Eliot, *BSA* 52, 1957, 152–89; see n. 210.

220   J.E. Jones, L.H. Sackett, A.J. Graham, *BSA* 57, 1962, 76–114.

221   M.K. Langdon, A Cyclopean Bridge and Rutted Road in the Thriasian Plain. *Studi micenei ed egeo–anatolici* 34, 1994, 51–60.

222   G. Gruben, Das Quellhaus von Megara. *ADelt* 19, 1964,1, 37–41.

223   J. Travlos, *Bildlexikon zur Topographie des antiken Attika* (Tübingen 1988) 259, 278–9.

224   H. Lohmann, Ancient Roads in Attica and the Megaris. *Proceedings of a Conference on Ancient Roads in Greece*, Athens November 23, 1998 (forthcoming).

225   J. Ober, *AJA* 91, 1987, 569 ff; H. Lohmann, Agriculture and Country Life in Classical Attica, in: *Agriculture in Ancient Greece. Proceedings of the seventh Intern. Symposium at the Swedish Institute at Athens*, 16–17 May, 1990 (ed.) B. Wells (Stockholm 1992) 29–57.

226   H. Lohmann, *MWPr* 1988, 34–66.

227   L. Beschi, La fortezza ellenica di Gyphtokastro. *Atti VIII. Congresso Scientifico del Istituto Internazionale dei Castelli* (Athens 1968) 127–45.

228   J. Ober, Early Artillery Towers. *AJA* 91, 1987, 569–604.

229   M.H. Munn, *The Defense of Attica. The Dema Wall and the Boiotian War of 378–375 BC.* (Berkeley, Los Angeles, Oxford 1993) 94; H. Lohmann, *Pyrgos* (forthcoming).

230   N.M. Verdelis, Der Diolkos am Isthmus von Korinth. *AM* 71, 1956, 51–9.

231   U. Sinn, *AM* 105, 1990, 53 ff.

232   G. Welter, *Aigina* (Berlin 1938; Greek: Athens 1962); J.P. Harland, *Prehistoric Aigina. A History of the Island in the Bronze Age* (Rome 1966); N. Faraklas, *Αρχαία Αίγινα, Η ανθρώπινη κατοίκηση* (Athens 1980); H. Walter, *Ägina. Die archäologische Geschichte einer griechischen Insel* (München 1993).

233   E. Walter, *Karydi, Die äginetische Bildhauerschule. Alt–Ägina* II 2 (Mainz 1987).

234   A. Furtwängler, *Aegina. Das Heiligtum der Aphaia*. Text. Tafeln (München 1906); E.-L. Schwandner, *Der ältere Porostempel der Aphaia auf Aegina* (Berlin 1985); H. Bankel, *Der spätarchaische Tempel der Aphaia auf Aegina* (Berlin 1993).

235   R.W.M. Schumacher, Three related sanctuaries of Poseidon: Geraistos, Kalaureia and Tainaron. *Greek Sanctuaries. New Approaches* (ed.) N. Marinatos, R. Hägg (London – New York 1993) 62–87.

236   G. Welter, *Troizen und Kalauria* (Berlin 1941) 43–50.